THE PROPHET'S CHILDREN

HM

HISTORICAL MEMORIES

Published

A World Remembered: 1925–1950
Bernard Smith

The Prophet's Children
Travels on the American Left
Tim Wohlforth

Forthcoming

Notebooks for the Grandchildren
Mikhail Baitalsky
Translated by Marilyn Vogt-Downey

THE PROPHET'S CHILDREN

Travels on the American Left

Tim Wohlforth

HUMANITIES PRESS
NEW JERSEY

First published 1994 by Humanities Press International, Inc.
Atlantic Highlands, New Jersey 07716.

Library of Congress Cataloging-in-Publications Data

Wohlforth, Tim.
The prophet's children : travels on the American left / Tim Wohlforth.
p. cm.
Includes bibliographical references and index.
ISBN 0-391-03819-2. — ISBN 0-391-03802-8 (pbk.)
1. Wohlforth Tim. 2. Socialists—United States—Biography. 3. Socialism—United States—History—20th century. 4. Socialism and youth—United States—History—20th century. 5. Socialism —History—20th century. I. Title.
HX84.W63A3 1993
335′.0092—dc20 93-26388
[B] CIP

A catalog record for this book is available from the British Library.

Printed in the United States of America

PRINTED WITH SOY INK

In Memoriam

I dedicate this book to the following people who have died since I began my political journey in 1953. They chose the difficult road of socialist politics for at least part of their lives. They were all exceptional human beings. Each touched my life in some fashion. They all deserve to be remembered. If my book serves no other purpose than to save them from oblivion, it will have been well worth the effort.

George Breitman (1916–1986)
James P. Cannon (1890–1974)
Ann Chertov (Chester) (1905–1983)
Bob Chertov (Chester) (1912–1975)
Pearl Chertov (1921–1992)
Farrell Dobbs (1907–1983)
Anne Draper (1917–1973)
Hal Draper (1915–1990)
Carl Feingold (1929–1993)
Arthur Felberbaum (1935–1979)
Art Fox (1920–1975)
Dick Fraser (1913–1988)
Cecil Frank Glass (John Liang, Li Fu-jen) (1901–1988)
Fred Halstead (1927–1988)
Joe Hansen (1911–1979)
Mike Harrington (1928–1989)
Gerry Healy (1913–1989)
Rose Karsner (1889–1968)
Tom Kerry (1899–1982)
Sherry Magnan (Patrick O'Daniel) (1904–1961)
George Novack (William F. Warde) (1905–1992)
Art Preis (1911–1964)
George Rawick (1930–1990)
Evelyn Reed (1905–1979)
Max Shachtman (1904–1972)
Bob Shaw (1917–1980)
Carl Skoglund (1884–1960)
Arne Swabeck (1890–1986)
Murry Weiss (1915–1990)
George Weissman (1916–1985)
Steve Zeluck (1918–1985)

Contents

Acknowledgments

This project would not have been possible without the encouragement, help, and input from a number of people who understood the importance of the story I was seeking to tell. The support of scholars who have written about various aspects of the left experience in the United States has been particularly valuable. These include Paul LeBlanc, Nelson Lichtenstein, Alan Wald, Sam Farber, and Paul Buhle. Richard Bucci put in many hours helping me prepare the manuscript for submission to publishers.

Special mention must be made of my close friends and intellectual companions in Great Britain who shared with me some of the best and worst experiences chronicled in this book, particularly Adam Westoby, Mark Jenkins, and Robin Blick. Here at home Daniel Anker and Jack Gerson played a similar role, encouraging me to continue with the project and acting as sounding boards for the ideas contained within it.

My wife, Joyce, who is perhaps blessed by *not* sharing with me the experiences chronicled in this book, has nevertheless been most supportive. She has never ceased to be amazed at the rather colorful language used by some political rivals in the past to describe her husband!

Explanation of Special Terms

Because some words used in *The Prophet's Children* will be entirely unfamiliar to many readers, and a good many more apparently familiar words are used here in narrow and highly specialized ways, an introductory lexicographical essay might be helpful. For further explication of peculiar terminology, see the "Annotated Abbreviations" on pp. xiii–xviii.

The vocabulary of what is known as the *workers movement* is in some cases over a hundred years old, and many words in this vocabulary have an American origin. A nationwide socialist organization, whatever its proper name may be, is also known as the *party*, and it may have an affiliated youth movement, often known as the *youth*. The individual chapters of the party are its *locals* or *branches*, terms borrowed from the American trade union movement. The person in charge of the day-to-day operation of the branch is the *organizer*. A *contact* is a potential party recruit, and may be considered part of the party *periphery*, sympathizers and contacts politically close to, or in the *orbit* of the party. The party may try to increase the size of its periphery by intersecting an entire *layer*, that is, attracting to it a whole group of people who have a common political background and experience. It is likely that a layer will be found within a certain *milieu*, a difficult word which could mean any of several political arenas in which the party may be active or play a leading role, such as the college campuses or the trade unions. But it is also common on the U.S. Left to speak of the Communist Party's milieu, which itself is a large network of political people from many different arenas, whose political activity may occasionally be coincident with that of the CP.

Many of the remaining special terms in this book have come to the U.S. in one way or another from Europe. Immediately prior to World War I, the *Second International*, founded by among others Friederich Engels himself, was the single worldwide Marxist umbrella organization. It commanded the allegiance of millions of workers, who were organized into the *social democracies* or *socialist* parties: the large, working class parties in the United States, Germany, Austria, which in many cases still exist today.

The Third, or "Communist" International (*Comintern*) was founded in 1919, after the Russian Revolution of October 1917. The Comintern created new *Communist* parties by encouraging the left wing factions of the social democracies which had opposed the war to split away. The American affiliate was formed from the dissident Left Wing of the American Socialist Party and was eventually called the Communist Party USA (CP). The CP brought to the United States many organizational forms from the Russian movement. The names for these forms have varied throughout the years with the political climate in the U.S. The small leading body of the party can be either the *Politburo*, *Political Bureau*, or the more American *Political Committee*. Likewise, the larger leading body of the party is sometimes the *Central Committee*, or sometimes the more American *National Committee*.

Annotated Abbreviations

ACLU	American Civil Liberties Union
AJS	Alliance des Jeunes pour le Socialisme (post-1968 name of FER, OCI youth organization)
ALP	American Labor Party (CP-aligned party initially formed to endorse La Guardia's New York mayoral campaign)
ATUA	All Trade Union Alliance (trade union arm of the SLL in the late 1960s and early 1970s)
AWP	American Workers Party (radical labor party led by A. J. Muste and James Burnham, merged with official Trotskyists in 1934)
AYD	American Youth for Democracy (1950s CP youth group)
AYS	American Youth for Socialism (1950s SWP youth group)
BLP	British Labour Party
CAMD	Committee to Aid the Monroe Defendants
CCF	Cooperative Commonwealth Federation (Canadian social democratic organization, precursor of the NDP)
CCNY	City College of New York
CIPA	Committee for Independent Political Action (mid-1960s grouping of New Leftists, including Clark Kissinger and Lyndon LaRouche, which was oriented toward electoral politics)
CLA	Communist League of America (official U.S. Trotskyists, 1928–34)
Comintern	Communist (Third) International (international revolutionary party founded by Lenin and Trotsky in 1919, abolished by Stalin in 1943)

CORE	Congress of Racial Equality
CORQI	Le Comité d'Organisation pour la Reconstruction de la Quatrième Internationale (OCI's international grouping after it left the IC in 1971)
CP	Communist Party
DSA	Democratic Socialists of America (DSOC after it merged with NAM)
DSOC	Democratic Socialist Organizing Committee (1972 left-split from the SP, led by Michael Harrington)
ERAP	Economic Research and Action Project (antipoverty project of SDS usually associated with Tom Hayden, founded in 1963)
FER	Fédération des Étudiants Révolutionnaires (OCI youth organization, banned in 1968, reborn as AJS)
FI	Fourth International, World Party of Socialist Revolution (Trotskyist party intended as successor to Comintern, founded in 1938)
FLN	Front pour Libération National (Algerian independence movement, led by Ben Bella, victorious in 1960)
IC, ICFI	International Committee of the Fourth International (Cannon/Healy/Lambert wing of the FI, opposing entrism, formed in 1953)
ILA	International Longshoremen's Association (East Coast dockworkers' union)
ILGWU	International Ladies' Garment Workers Union
ILWU	International Longshore and Warehousemen's Union (West Coast dockworkers' union)
IMG	International Marxist Group (British supporters of Ernest Mandel, formed in the early 1970s)
IS	International Secretariat of the Fourth International (Pablo/Mandel wing of the FI, favoring entrism, 1952–63)
IS	International Socialists (name adopted by ISC in 1969)
ISC	Independent Socialist Clubs (dissident left-wing Shachtmanites led by Hal Draper)
ISL	Independent Socialist League (Max Shachtman's party, 1949–58)
ISP	Independent Socialist Party (an alliance of Trotskyists

	and former Stalinists which ran Corliss Lamont for Senate in New York in 1958)
ITU	International Typographical Union
LID	League for Industrial Democracy (affiliate of American SP; became moribund in the 1950s, except for its youth arm, SDS)
LO	Lutte Ouvrière (post-1968 name of VO)
LPYS	Labour Party Young Socialists (YS minority which became official BLP youth group in 1965, when majority supported SLL)
LYL	Labor Youth League (official youth group of the CP in the 1950s)
MNA	Mouvement Nationaliste Algérien (Algerian independence movement, led by Messali Hadj, suppressed by the FLN)
M2M	May Second Movement (early antiwar student organization, led by PL)
NAC	National Action Committee (executive body of the YSL, equivalent of a PC)
NAM	New American Movement (dissident Communists and New Leftists led by Dorothy Healy, merged with DSOC)
NC	National Committee (large leadership body of the SWP, equivalent of a central committee)
NDP	New Democratic Party (large social democratic party in Canada, roughly equivalent to the British Labour Party)
NEC	National Executive Committee (executive body of the YSL, equivalent of an NC)
NLF	National Liberation Front of Vietnam
NO	National Office (national headquarters of the SWP, in New York)
NPAC	National Peace Action Coalition (large anti–Vietnam War organization initiated by the SWP)
OCI	Organisation Communiste Internationaliste (name of Lambert/IC wing of PCI from 1965)
PC	Political Committee (small leadership body of the SWP, equivalent of a Politburo)
PCI	Parti Communiste Internationaliste (originally the party of Molinier/Frank wing of French Trotskyism founded

	in 1936; split into Frank/IS and Lambert/IC wings in 1952)
PEP	Political Education Project (reformist wing of SDS associated with Steve Max)
PL	Progressive Labor (left split from the CP in 1960 led by Milt Rosen and Bill Epton; gained control of a wing of SDS; in the summer of 1965 it became "Progressive Labor Party," sometimes called PLP)
POR	Partido Obrero Revolutionario (Bolivian Trotskyists led by Guillermo Lora, joined IC in 1969)
RDR	Rassemblement Democratique Révolutionnaire (1948 split from French Trotskyism led by David Rousset and supported by Jean-Paul Sartre and Albert Camus)
RMC	Revolutionary Marxist Committee (1970s split from the RSL; joined the SWP)
ROTC	Reserve Officers Training Corps
RSL	Revolutionary Socialist League (1970s left split from the International Socialists)
RYM	Revolutionary Youth Movement (anti-PL faction in SDS; in 1969 split into RYM-I [Weatherman], and RYM-II [Maoists])
SDF	Social Democratic Federation (right-wing split from SP in 1934, reunited with SP in 1960s)
SDS	Students for a Democratic Society (American mass radical student organization, originally the youth arm of LID, known as SLID in the 1950s; spawned a German namesake in the Federal Republic of Germany in the late 1960s) (see also RYM)
SDUSA	Social Democrats, USA (name of main body of American social democrats after 1972)
SED	Students for Economic Democracy (youth group of the CED)
SLID	Student League for Industrial Democracy (orginizational precursor to SDS, youth arm of LID)
SLL	Socialist Labour League (anti-Pabloite Trotskyist party founded by Gerald Healy in 1959, renamed WRP in 1973)
SMC	Student Mobilization Committee (student arm of NPAC, dominated by the YSA)

SNCC	Student Non-Violent Coordinating Committee
SP	Socialist Party (home of the official Trotskyists, 1936–38, and the Shachtmanites after 1958; tiny minority retained name after 1972, when splits formed DSOC and SDUSA)
SP-SDF	Socialist Party–Social Democratic Federation (immediate precursor of SDUSA)
SSEU	Social Services Employees Union (New York–based welfare workers' union)
SWP	Socialist Workers Party (official Trotskyist party in the U.S. from 1938)
SWP	Socialist Workers Party (Shachtmanite-style group in Britain, led by Tony Cliff)
SYL	Socialist Youth League (Shachtman's youth group before 1953)
TUALP	Trade Union Alliance for a Labor Party (WL union group)
UAW	United Auto Workers
UNAM	L'Universidad Nacional de Mexíco (National University of Mexico; largest and oldest in the Western Hemisphere, the site of much student unrest in 1968)
US	United Slaves (L.A.-based black nationalist organization led by Ron Karenga which participated in FBI COINTELPRO against the Black Panthers)
USec	United Secretariat of the Fourth International (FI leadership body produced by defection of Cannon and SWP from the IC to the IS in 1963)
USWA	United Steel Workers of America
VO	Voix Ouvrière ("workerist" or strongly industrially oriented tendency of French Trotskyism, with roots back to the 1930s; banned in 1968, reborn as Lutte Ouvrière)
WL	Workers League (party founded by Tim Wohlforth, North American section of the ICFI)
WP	Workers Party (official Trotskyist party, 1934–36)
WP	Workers Party (Max Shachtman's party, 1940–49)
WRP	Workers Revolutionary Party (name adopted by the SLL in 1973)
YPA	Young Progressives of America (CP-oriented 1950s youth group)

YPSL	Young People's Socialist League (youth group of the SP)
YPSL-Fourth	YPSL (Fourth Internationalist) (youth group expelled from SP in 1938, affiliated with SWP, 1938–40)
YS	Young Socialists (1950s youth group of the BLP, became SLL youth group when BLP expelled majority in 1965)
YS	Young Socialists, *Young Socialist* (respectively, youth group of the Workers League, founded in 1973, and the group's newspaper)
YSA	Young Socialist Alliance (youth group of the SWP, from 1959)
YSL	Young Socialist League (Shachtman's youth group from 1953–58)

1

The Early Years

THE STORY OF TROTSKYISM

The Trotskyists represent a small movement whose influence has extended way beyond the confines of their immediate membership and periphery. I believe that the history of the American Left is incomplete—in fact, not fully understandable—without consideration of the Trotskyist movement. The Left has not had the influence within the United States that it has had in other nations. Yet a history of the United States that does not include the contribution of the Left to the political life of the nation as a whole would be one-sided and inadequate.

Our story begins with the Russian Revolution. The victory of communism in Russia had a profound impact on the socialist Left in the United States, particularly on its immigrant worker members. The Socialist Party (SP) split, the majority leaving to form the Communist Party. The new Communist movement had little impact on the country until the 1930s. During the depression the Communists grew into a significant political force, and their influence extended into the labor movement, into the black movement, among intellectuals, and even into government. The Socialists, however, remained a relatively minor force, overshadowed by their Moscow-oriented offspring.

Millions of Americans had their dreams of progress shattered by the depression and at the same time witnessed the growth of fascism in Europe. Tens of thousands of intellectuals, writers, artists, trade unionists, and black activists thought they had found in communism a real alternative to the failures of capitalism and the spread of fascism. The Soviet Union seemed to them to be a new society in the process of being created. Most of these Communists and their supporters did not see any conflict between their new Communist dream and the democratic values they had been brought up with. Many liberals, while not becoming Communists, believed that the Soviet Union led the anti-Fascist camp and was, in some ill-defined way, "progressive." These liberals assisted the Communists in their political aims.

Trotskyism developed in this political atmosphere as the critic from within, the conscience of the revolutionary movement. The Trotskyists shared with the Communists the belief that the Communist ideal was consistent with, was actually the fulfillment of, the democratic ideals of the American nation. However, they insisted that Soviet reality represented a *betrayal* of the original Communist idea. Very few today, even on the Left, would dispute this latter notion. However, in the 1930s the Trotskyists were the pariahs of the Left, while their continued faith in pure communism isolated them from many non-Communists.

Trotskyist ideals were translated into militant trade union practice, which found a following here and there in the labor movement. Most important was the leadership role Trotskyists played in the International Brotherhood of Teamsters (Teamsters Union) in the Minneapolis area. However, the major impact of Trotskyism was ideological. A significant group of writers, who became known as the New York Intellectuals, rejected Stalinist reality as a betrayal of the socialist dream.[1] These included James Burnham, Max Eastman, Sidney Hook, Irving Kristol, Irving Howe, Dwight MacDonald, Norman Podhoretz, James T. Farrell, Harvey Swados, Philip Rahv, Mary McCarthy, Lionel Trilling, and Edmund Wilson. Not all of these people became adherents of Trotskyism, but they were all part of an anti-Stalinist leftism ideologically dominated by Trotskyism.

This gave the American Left a special quality that persisted right through the 1960s. The Left remained predominantly Communist, and the main opposition to official communism came from within—from Trotskyism. Of course a non-Communist socialist movement continued to exist and at one point in the 1930s had tens of thousands of members. Yet, significantly, when the Trotskyists entered the Socialist Party in the late 1930s they immediately won over the majority of its youth. The Socialist Party emerged from World War II barely intact. When the SP sought to renew its depleted ranks with young recruits, these young people overwhelmingly defected to the Trotskyists.

The reason for this was, I believe, ideological. The Russian Revolution had won over the American Left. Those who rejected the American present dreamed Communist dreams. Those who looked deeper into contemporary Communist reality and rejected that reality as well continued to dream Communist dreams as Trotskyists.

This was the state of the Left when I entered it in 1953. The group I joined, the Young Socialist League (YSL), had just been formed by a fusion of the former youth group of the Socialist Party, the Young People's

Socialist League (YPSL), which was led by Mike Harrington, and the old Trotskyist Max Shachtman's Socialist Youth League. What little life remained on the Left in those dark days of McCarthyism was dominated by the shell of the once powerful Communist Party, and by the tiny Trotskyist rump groups. Even the pacifist circles—later to play an important role in the anti–Vietnam War movement—were ideologically heavily influenced by Trotskyism. The Reverend A. J. Muste, for example, was a former Trotskyist leader.

The student radicalization of the 1960s was very much shaped by this past. A new Left emerged made up largely of the children of those who had been part of the Communist Party and its periphery. While rejecting the old leftist parties, this new generation did not come to grips in a conscious way with the predominant Communist ideology of American radicalism. Therefore, during the great implosion when Students for a Democratic Society (SDS) self-destructed, its constituents returned to communism in a Maoist guise. Nowhere else in the Western world did Maoism grow as it did in the United States.

During the same period the Trotskyists experienced the greatest growth in their history. This permitted the Trotskyists to gain a leading position in the anti–Vietnam War movement and to shape its direction. The antiwar movement, in turn, had its impact on the course of the Vietnam War and therefore on American history.

This is not the whole story of the influence of Trotskyism on the course of American politics. Its influence extended to the *political right* as well as shaping the rebirth of *social democracy* in the United States. In 1940 the Trotskyists split into two groups: The majority, headed by James P. Cannon, continued to adhere to an orthodox position; but a minority, headed by Max Shachtman, took the view that the Soviet Union represented a new class society. Most of the New York Intellectuals supported the Shachtman viewpoint. In the postwar period of prosperity, cold war, and witch-hunting, many of these intellectuals shifted to the right politically. They carried with them into their new political alignment Shachtman's view of the Soviet Union. This group, including figures such as Irving Kristol (Kristol's son William was Dan Quayle's chief of staff in 1992), Norman Podhoretz, and Jeane Kirkpatrick, made a major contribution to the theoretical outlook of neoconservatism.

In 1958 Max Shachtman took his followers into the Socialist Party. Their ideological sophistication and organizational ability led to their almost immediate dominance within the Socialist Party. When that party later split, *both* wings of this social democratic movement in the United States—Democratic Socialists of America (DSA) and Social Democrats USA—were led by former Shachtmanites. Michael Harrington, America's leading socialist until his death in 1989, was politically and ideologically formed by his experience as part of the Shachtmanite movement.

The story of these Trotskyist rebels has been almost totally neglected by historians of the Left, which has resulted in a distortion of the history of the American Left. This inadequacy needs to be overcome through a serious, objective, and critical history of the Trotskyist component of the American Left. Such a history will reveal the theoretical strengths of the Trotskyist critique, which have permitted it to influence diverse political trends from neoconservatism through social democracy to the ultra Left. At the same time an examination of Trotskyist ideas can help us extract the kernel of valid thought from Trotskyism's encrusted Leninist shell, which has condemned Trotskyists to splits, impotence, and regrettably, at times to mimicking in practice the very Stalinism Trotskyism rejects.

It is my belief that it would be beneficial if the American Left broke fully and for good with its Russian roots. The result would be a movement capable of influencing broader layers of the American public and in this fashion would positively contribute to America's future. I continue to believe in the socialist ideal, which I see as the fulfillment of the American democratic dream. Those of us who share this vision cannot accomplish its realization through a denial of what has been the reality of the leftist experience in the United States.

I do not pretend to tell the whole story of the Trotskyist experience. My story is a personal as well as a political voyage. It is the story of people bound together by an all-pervasive ideology. These are, however, ordinary human beings, at times petty and selfish and at other times brave and selfless, who seek to act out in practice their ideals. The conflict between idea and actual practice is an important part of the political experience. My political travels over three decades have brought me into intimate contact with the major trends and personalities within American Trotskyism as well as throughout the world. Therefore, while I do not tell the complete story, I am able to present a portrait of a movement that has many strands with somewhat conflicting ideas and yet possesses a distinct identity when contrasted with the rest of the Left and with political life in general in the United States.

Early Images

I was brought up in a political atmosphere that shaped my future outlook on the world and yet that was quite distinct from the kind of party politics that would dominate my mature years. My parents were part of an intellectual milieu influenced by the American Communist Party. These intellectuals had an attitude toward America and the world rather than a specific doctrine or thought-out analysis. I was brought up to believe that the labor movement represented a progressive movement for change in the country, to favor racial and social equality, to love FDR, to support the war effort, and to believe in peace when the war was over. My parents' attitude toward the Soviet Union was friendly and supportive, though certainly not thought-out.

I was brought up feeling that intelligent people were concerned about political matters and were committed to the downtrodden. Socialism was rarely mentioned and Marxism was mentioned not at all. It was a political milieu but not a party milieu. Comments on world affairs drifted seamlessly into discussions of gardening, into humor (usually my father), into gossip. I noticed as I grew older, and as we all passed from the period of hope immediately after the war into the cold war and prosperity, a global shift in these discussions. Politics became less central, less intense, and the personal dominated. My parents even made friends with conservatives. The milieu aged, it adjusted to the new realities of the postwar world, and it enjoyed the prosperity that came to those whose brilliance and talents had developed in a more exciting, hopeful, creative period. The adjustment was not an easy one, and many of my parents' friends as well as my parents were to be victimized in the new climate. Politics never completely went away, and commitment, while bent and softened, was never totally given up.

My parents were writers and political people. My mother, Mildred, was a career woman in a period when there were few of them. She was the first woman editor of the *Wisconsin Literary Magazine* at the University of Wisconsin, where she actively opposed the sorority system. She wrote her first novel, *Fig Leaves*, soon after getting out of college. Prior to working on a newspaper, she wrote another novel, *Headlines*, about the real people whose tragic lives become the subject of newspaper articles. She went to work for William Randolph Hearst's *New York Journal* as a sob sister. She covered various murder trials and then went to Germany, where she interviewed the head of the Gestapo, Hermann Göring. When she returned to the United States she tried to create public interest in the growing danger of fascism. She wrote one of the first *New Yorker* profiles, on Paul Robeson, the black singer and actor. In later years she worked on magazine publicity for the Planned Parenthood Federation.

My mother is a very independent woman with a strong will and personality. She loves to tell the story of her interview with Göring. Göring had one of those huge offices where you seem to walk for miles to get to his desk. As she approached Göring's desk she noticed lying next to the desk a pet lioness whose purpose it clearly was to strike fear in all who met Göring. My mother, figuring it must be tame if it was there, simply went up to the animal and petted it like a cat. This made Göring furious.

My father, Robert, was also a writer. He had been brought up by a very strict German father who had a rather low opinion of him. After spending an unsuccessful year at Princeton, my father attended West Point, from which he succeeded in graduating. He claims that all he ever learned there was how to dance and how to carve meat. He also was a newspaper reporter, which was how he met my mother. He wrote an antiwar novel about his West Point experience, *Tin Soldiers*. Then he became an investigator for liberal congressional committees. He first worked for the Nye Committee, which was investigating the munitions industry. Its thesis was that munitions makers encourage war, since war is good for their business. Then he worked for the La Follette Committee on Labor and Education. This committee was primarily concerned with illegal employer efforts to use violence to prevent labor from organizing. For example, my father went to Harlan County, Kentucky, to investigate antilabor violence there.[2] Later he worked as an investigator for the Anti-Trust Division of the Department of Justice, appointed to the position by Franklin Delano Roosevelt.

We lived in Ridgefield, Connecticut, but we were not really part of the town. My parents had a wide circle of friends who lived in nearby Redding, Wilton, and Westport: writers, painters, union leaders, intellectuals. It was a cultured and, especially in my earliest memories, intensely political group. I remember George Seldes, Ruth McKenney, Norman Rockwell, Jack Lawrenson, Robert Fawcett, Harold Rome, Henry Wallace, and Paul Robeson, but there were many others. Wherever my parents went my brother and I tagged along. Usually there were no other children at these soirées, so we sat with the grown-ups and listened.

I have dim memories of politics of the war years. I was eight years old when the war started. At some point in the middle of the war a movie came into town that I wanted to see: *The Chetniks*. My parents would not let me go, explaining that the movie glorified Fascists and that we supported Tito's Partisans.

Our town was largely Republican and conservative, and I felt very much an outcast within it. There were no more than eighteen registered Democrats in the town. I still remember one boy, Eugene Lavatore, as the only other person in my class who supported Roosevelt. This led to a friendship between us.

One day my teacher in public school wrote on the board that the Soviet Union was a dictatorship. I raised my hand to say with impeccable logic that the Soviet Union was our ally in a war against German fascism and for democracy. Therefore it could not be a dictatorship. I also remember her telling us that the Soviet Union was a dictatorship because the babies were wrapped in swaddling clothes. I asked her how the Germans wrapped their babies.

The war had little impact on us. We had a huge scrap pile in the center of the town. Some of the old-estate owners who had remained in the town dismantled their beautiful wrought iron fences and gates and threw them on the pile. I remember walking along a dirt road and spotting a small iron bar. I picked it up to carry home to put on the pile. Along the way, being a bit of a klutz, I tripped and broke my front tooth. It stayed chipped for the next thirty years or so as my "war injury." We had the ration stamps and points and our car had "A" and "B" labels on it, which meant we got extra gas, as it was used for commuting.

There was another aspect of my early life that may have contributed to my personality and, in an indirect way, to my political outlook. I was adopted by my parents at the age of two and a half. I always knew I had been adopted, yet I do not recall ever being told. I never asked my mother about it. In recent years I have wondered why I never did. So many adopted children are obsessed with finding their original parents, yet I did not want to look. I suspect I just didn't want to rock the boat. I was accepted where I was and didn't want to threaten the arrangement.

Many years later, when I was already middle-aged, my mother volunteered the scant information I now possess on my earliest life. I was born on May 15, 1933, in Bridgeport, Connecticut, in the midst of the depression. My name, when I was born, was James Sutton. My biological mother was the youngest of six children; her mother died shortly after her birth. My mother's father was a seaman who was in no position to raise the children. All the children but my biological mother were placed with relatives. It seemed no one wanted the youngest—and a girl to boot. She therefore became a ward of the state and was brought up in institutions. When I was born she was still a ward of the state, probably no more than eighteen years old. She did not want to get married to my father, who was also very young. She nursed me for a month but was persuaded to place me in a foster home.

It seems I had a really wonderful foster mother—she was, if anything, overindulgent, giving me just about anything I wanted. This lovely person fed me a diet that consisted almost exclusively of bacon, hot dogs, and cake! She had adopted the last two foster children she had taken care of and wanted to adopt me. The problem was that her husband worked in a gas station and simply did not make enough money to adopt a third child.

In the meantime my life was complicated by my biological mother, who also loved me and wanted to be with me. However, she was a very mixed-up person and disciplined me too harshly. When she didn't think I was walking soon enough, she spanked me. The state authorities—I, like my biological mother, was their ward—instructed my foster mother not to let me out of her sight when I was with my biological mother. But my biological mother would plead, and occasionally my foster mother relented; off I would go, only to return in quite a state.

Such was my life until I was two years and four months old. At this point my present parents entered the scene and adopted me. They already had two sons: Eric, who was just thirteen months older than I, and Jim, who was seven or eight years older, the child of my new mother's first marriage. The adoption was carried out in the rather clumsy, hurtful way it was done in those days. My new parents turned up with brother Eric. Eric and I were given toys to play with while the adoption official, the foster mother, and my new mother and father watched. Then the foster mother and official disappeared and I was left alone with three strangers. I cried and would not let my mother-to-be touch me. I had a fear of all women but my foster mother. My father-to-be finally was able to comfort me, but I refused to go to the bathroom for a day for good measure. I finally came around once hot dogs, bacon, and cake were produced. My parents changed my first name from Jim to Tim to distinguish me from their oldest son, Jim. So James Sutton became Timothy Wohlforth.

Having three mothers in a two-and-a-half-year period helped to shape my personality in a fashion I have only recently been able to understand. Most important, it has given me a sense of being an outsider, of being implanted somewhere rather than growing up naturally, of being a permanent guest within my family and within society. This self-image did not in itself make me a radical, an outsider in grown-up society. The political atmosphere of my adopted household had a much greater effect in shaping my future values. Even the little town of Ridgefield, Connecticut, had a perverse impact on this political outlook. Yet I believe my earliest life gave a bite, a depth, to my future radical perspective.

The role of political outsider, once I took it up, was a natural pose for me. The radical, like the immigrant, is an outsider in his relations with the broader society yet finds acceptance within his own close, warm, and intense community. As a result of their being isolated from the mainstream, fellow outsiders create a sense of community far more intense than that experienced by members of the larger community. It was only as a radical that I finally felt that I belonged. I was no longer a guest; I was really part of my new family.

We lived in the small New England town of Ridgefield, Connecticut. My father was one of its few citizens who commuted the fifty-five miles to New York City to work. Ridgefield in those days existed as if it were a thousand miles from New York City. Most of its three thousand inhabitants were first- and second-generation Italian-Americans. Around the turn of the century the town was dominated by a few great estates of wealthy families who liked its New England simplicity and relative closeness to New York

City. These wealthy families brought in Italian masons and gardeners to work for them. They brought over relatives, and relatives brought other relatives. The Italians stayed, and the wealthy gave up their estates for more modern and efficient facilities elsewhere.

I remember always feeling very much out-of-place in that town. In my class in school I felt quite alone. There were fifteen or sixteen Italians, three or four Irish, and me. I was not Italian, I was not Catholic, and I was not poor. Most of the Italian kids lived within walking distance of school in big old houses holding extended families with eight or nine brothers and sisters and all sorts of older relatives who did not speak English. The kids cursed a blue streak in Italian. Their mothers were always shouting and hanging out laundry in the backyards. It was no doubt a limited and even difficult life, but to me it was warmth, community, acceptance.

This feeling of being apart particularly struck me at lunchtime. My mother always packed me a healthy concoction—she was into whole grain breads, cod liver oil, and vitamins way before their time—that really was not very appealing. The Italian kids would head off the school grounds toward the Italian section of town, down the hill past the Italian American Hall where old men were playing bocce ball, across the railroad tracks to a little Italian grocery store. There they would plunk on the counter one red point—it was wartime and you needed ration stamps or little tokens for meat—and some change and in return received a huge piece of Italian bread stuffed with salami, provolone cheese, and mustard, which they would down with a bottle of decadent orange pop.

My family had two cars. One was a relatively new Mercury convertible—prewar, as they made no cars during the war—and the other, actually bought by my eldest brother for twenty-five dollars, was a 1930 Model A Ford. My brother Eric and I reacted to those cars differently. My brother liked being picked up from school in the more prestigious Mercury, while I preferred the Model A, as I wanted so much to be like my poorer classmates.

BOARDING SCHOOL

In the eighth grade I went away to school, as my parents felt Ridgefield Public School was pretty bad. Rarely did more than half a dozen of the graduating class go on to college and of those most went to Danbury State Teacher's College. My parents chose Oakwood School, a Quaker institution in Poughkeepsie, New York. There were around two hundred students, boys and girls, at the school. It consisted of a series of simple white clapboard buildings along a ridge just off Route 9, which followed the Hudson River. A large IBM typewriter factory was situated across Route 9 from us. Actually the school was a very good choice, attracting an intelligent middle-class student body but lacking the preppy pretenses of so many other boarding schools.

The Quaker philosophy appealed to me very much. I even considered becoming a Quaker. My only problem was that I did not believe in God, and since I was an honest soul, this was a stumbling block. I considered myself a pacifist and was very antiwar. This was the time when the cold war was developing in earnest and the witch-hunts were just beginning. I remember finding a book in the school library called *A Handbook of Isms*. I read brief descriptions of every variety of socialism and anarchism and decided that I was a philosophical anarchist. I am not quite sure now what I meant by this other than one who feels a general antipathy to all forms of coercion and holds that people should be able to relate to each other on the basis of morality and honesty. This definition fitted well with the Quaker pacifist outlook. But it did not seem to affect my keen interest in politics or mean that I should abstain from politics or elections.

I remember intense discussions that went on for hours. Most of us were not Quakers or even religious. Our zeal was partly a matter of our age—we were beginning to think out our own thoughts and felt proud and possessive about them. Partly we were a product of the times—the postwar glow of hope had not yet faded into cold warriorism and material gain. Partly our debates reflected the kind of children who came to a Quaker school. We debated God's existence, the good and the bad, pacifism, the injustice of racism and of poverty, philosophical materialism. No subject was too big for us, and lack of experience or knowledge was no deterrence to a strong opinion on a matter.

Every Sunday we all went to the Quaker meeting and sat in total silence for one hour waiting for the "spirit" to move someone to say something. Sometimes it was pretty phony: A teacher would rise and say that the spirit moved him to suggest that we all sing the hymn on page 234 of our hymnals. Sometimes there would be a moving experience. Yet the quiet itself was pleasant. I never did go for religion, but I decided then and there that the Quakers were the best.

I attended Oakwood for three years, the eighth, tenth, and eleventh grades. The eighth grade was my philosophical year, when I thought through all the basic questions facing humankind. Tenth grade was my political year at Oakwood. It was the 1948 election year with a new party, the Progressive Party, which backed Henry Wallace against Harry Truman of the Democratic Party and Thomas Dewey of the Republican Party. I remember listening to the Progressive Party Convention on the radio during the summer while I was working at a summer theater in Ridgefield.

It sounded so exciting, so different from the old parties, especially with all the folk songs and music. Wallace seemed to be the last hope to stop the world's drive toward war, as well as to realize the hopes of the people, which the war had stirred up. We wanted advances for the workers, civil rights for the blacks, and no more war. We were convinced the Progressive Party would get at least five million votes. We underestimated the impact of Red-baiting combined with the populist appeal of Truman's last weeks of campaigning.

I campaigned hard for Wallace at Oakwood, as did my brother Eric. Oakwood held a straw vote, and Harry Truman received eighteen votes with the rest of the votes divided evenly between Dewey and Wallace. Oakwood was not typical of American society in 1948. The day after the election Eric got up in the dining hall of the school to announce that he was resigning from the Young Progressives of America and no longer supported Wallace. I guess Wallace's defeat—he received barely one million votes—was too much for Eric. I remember at the time resenting his action. It seemed to me a kind of opportunism. Wallace's poor showing at the polls did not mean that his ideas were incorrect.

For some reason, and I doubt that it was politics, my brother and I drifted apart in those years. We attended the same school but had different friends and rarely talked with each other. He developed his life in one direction, which led ultimately to a very successful career as a lawyer in Anchorage, Alaska, and I followed a very divergent political path. Whatever the reasons, we both lost something in our adult lives, the companionship we had when we were very young.

I became interested enough in Quaker activity to spend a summer at a Quaker work camp in the Ozark Mountains of Missouri. We stayed at a mission of the Evangelical and Reform church, a predominantly German moderate Protestant denomination near the little town of Timber, Missouri, population ten. We had no phone or electricity. The boys in the group slept on the second story of a goat barn. Our aim was to help the poor subsistence farmers in the area learn to raise cash crops so that they could rise above the poverty level. However, the surrounding population did not seem to be very highly motivated.

Even this isolated area was not untouched in those days by politics. One of the more prosperous farmers, active in support of the mission's work, was a member of the Socialist Party and had been since the 1930s. A retired worker from St. Louis who lived nearby was an open member of the Communist Party. Most of my fellow work campers were Jewish and from New York City. Several had been brought up in what is known as the "progressive" milieu, and it was at this Quaker camp that I first learned radical songs from the *People's Song Book*, such as "Midnight Special,"

"This Land Is Our Land," "Take This Hammer," and "The Banks Are Made of Marble."

By pure chance it was here, in the backward mountains of Missouri, that I first heard about Trotsky. An elderly man passed through and gave us a little talk about the sharecropper struggles that took place in the cotton-growing panhandle area of southeastern Missouri during World War II. Evicted from their land by the owners, the strikers had camped out in tents on the thin strip of federal land that lies along all federal highways. The owners and their supporters denounced these poor blacks as Communists seeking to overthrow the government. In answer the black tenant farmer leader "confessed" that he was receiving his instructions directly from Leon Trotsky, that he was planning an armed insurrection, and that he was planning to establish a Missouri soviet. The "confession" was so outlandish, especially once the locals learned that Trotsky was dead, that it exposed the ludicrous character of such Red-baiting.

Years later I discovered that the Trotskyists, at the urging of C. L. R. James (James R. Johnson) and Ernest McKinney, had, along with others, actively aided the sharecroppers. When I joined the Shachtman group in 1955–1956, their paper *Labor Action*, which had at the time only a minuscule circulation among radical intellectuals, was still subscribed to by some of these black farmers.[3]

I spent my senior year at Buxton School in Williamstown, Massachusetts. Buxton was one of six progressive boarding schools sprinkled throughout the pretty countryside of New England. The oldest and most famous was Putney School in Putney, Vermont. These schools were devoted, in one fashion or another, to the progressive educational tenets of John Dewey and other reformers. The schools were coeducational, democratically run, encouraged creativity, and sought to combine work with education. Our school was housed in a beautiful old mansion on a hillside outside of Williamstown. An old barn had been converted into the boys' dormitory. I loved my room because it had a big split raw-wood door with old iron hinges. There were less than forty of us in the school.

The school was owned and run by Mrs. Sangster, a gentile lady of very good family and considerable private wealth, which she made available to the school. She was a lady of very high ideals, devoted to progressive causes and to the arts and with "enthusiasms" that changed from time to time. Each summer she went to a different, interesting part of the earth, learned about it, and brought back with her, as some people bring souvenirs, students for her school.

Each Sunday we, the seniors, attended a literary tea in Mrs. Sangster's office, which also served as her living room. We were served real tea with a silver service and fine china cups. We would write little poems and things, and read and discuss them. One Sunday I came in with a modest piece of free verse. It told the story of one of my parents' parties, where brilliant people gathered yet talked of petty matters: gardens, food, gossip. It was a bitter little poem reflecting, in part, the pretenses of the overly serious teenager. It also reflected a change that was slowly taking place in the 1950s in the outlook and life of a whole generation. The activism, sharp social concerns, sometimes even creativity, of the thirties generation of progressives and liberals was passing. A generation was losing its vitality. I would see the same general phenomenon expressed in the more radical circles I was going to enter.

Mrs. Sangster also collected another kind of student for her school, the problem children of the wealthy. I was not aware of this the first blissful weeks of natural beauty and culture. Then one day I entered my room and sat down on the bed only to find a huge lump in the mattress. I lifted the mattress and discovered a shiny black German Luger pistol! One of the students turned up shortly and said he had had to stash it there because one of the teachers was coming by. I soon discovered that there was a small group of students who were getting handguns from somewhere and were going out in the woods for practice. I began to feel very uneasy, but a sense of loyalty to students over teachers made me keep my mouth shut.

We held our elections for a kind of student council to supervise the boys' dormitory. This group of troubled kids with guns won all the positions. There were only two of us who didn't fit in with this new regime. I was one, and the other was an extremely talented boy who was a fine sculptor. His mannerisms were a bit effeminate, which did not go over well with our democratically elected leadership. One evening I walked down the hall on the second floor of the dorm and found one of the gang slowly sharpening a large machete in front of this fellow's door, just, I was told, to keep the fellow in line.

One snowy evening one of the members of the gang, who had been a friend of mine, invited me to go outside with him for a drink. This seemed harmless enough, though, of course, illegal. We left the dormitory and walked into a bitterly cold Massachusetts night. The moon lit our way, brightly reflected off the snow, which covered everything on the hill. I shivered.

We had traveled only fifty yards when Chuck, who led the group, stopped. Handsome, blond-haired Chuck was the most popular boy in the school, the lead in our play, senior class president, and Mrs. Sangster's favorite. They were all standing around me in a circle. Chuck started to hit me. Soon they all joined in and I fell down on the snow. My glasses came off and my nose started bleeding. I offered no resistance and I pleaded with them to stop. I would agree to anything. I felt small and weak, lying there, and they seemed so strong and powerful hovering over me. They started to kick me. I could not make out what they were saying, why they were attacking me. I was overcome with my own weakness. I hurt everywhere, but the sensation that seized me totally was fear, terrible, uncontrollable fear.

Chuck was speaking directly to me; his face was red, his voice filled with hatred: "We don't like the way you clean your room. From now on you are to obey the council. Don't go near Carol!"

I understood the first part of what Chuck said, but the reference to his girlfriend left me dumbfounded. I couldn't believe it. It made no sense at all. Chuck was jealous of me? I viewed his girlfriend as someone totally out of my class.

This was a crisis in my life. My self-image was partially shattered. I should not have given in. I should have lived up to all those heroic images a boy has in his head. I took the matter incredibly seriously. Still I did not go to the administration. Even in this little progressive community, one just didn't "rat." I lived out the rest of the semester there with fear and terrible self-doubt, along with the moments of cultural development.

As I look back now upon this incident, which remains so vivid in my memory, I realize that it presaged events that brought my long political career to a dramatic end. Buxton School was Mrs. Sangster's attempt to live a dream by creating an ideal educational environment that would transform the most difficult products of society at large into ideal citizens. Yet, at least during that brief period I participated in her dream, evil had secretly transformed utopia into a nightmare. So it would come to pass in the socialist movement.

Oberlin College

I went to Oberlin College in the town of Oberlin near Cleveland, Ohio. The school is more famous for its music conservatory than for its liberal arts school, yet it had a very fine general academic program. There also was a very good theological seminary and a certain Christian presence in the place. It had a fine history. In the period prior to the Civil War a debate broke out at a theological seminary in Cincinnati about Christianity and slavery. It raged nonstop for weeks until the dissidents, who felt that slavery was un-Christian, broke away and came to Oberlin. Oberlin College was a link in the Underground Railroad for escaped slaves heading for Lake Erie and Canada. It also was one of America's first coeducational colleges.

Oberlin was a favorite college for children of missionaries. In the very center of the campus, on Tappan Square, an arch had been erected to commemorate the death of missionaries who had died during the Boxer Rebellion in China. It was our free-speech area and we would have little rallies there. When the political storms of the sixties hit Oberlin, many years after I had left the place, the students erected a counterarch to commemorate the deaths of the Chinese who died in the rebellion. One day I checked a book out of the library on Marxism and found that the last person to check it out had been Anna Louise Strong in the 1930s. Anna Louise Strong, the daughter of a missionary, was brought up in China. Later she became a strong supporter of the Chinese Revolution and a friend of Mao Tse-tung.

Most of the two thousand or so members of the student body were the children of missionaries, ministers, and hardware-store owners from small towns in the Middle West. A minority came from the New York area, were predominantly Jewish, secular, intellectually inclined. These were my people.

About one-third of the town was black. Some of the oldest black families traced their ancestry back to freed slaves. Some worked for the college, while others worked in the smokestack industries in nearby Lorain and Elyria. Their world was quite separate from our college life.

Some of us crossed the invisible line that divided the communities. Just outside the city limits was a black roadhouse, the Cosmo Club. We knew this was the place's name, but there was no sign. There regular beer was served as well as the greatest ribs, baked in a brick oven. On the walls were signs that were ignored: No Bumps or Grinds. The music was rhythm and blues and sometimes jazz. The owner's son liked to play modern jazz, and sometimes white jazz buffs from the conservatory would come up and play by the hour with him while couples danced. Our little group of friends were the only white people who went there outside of the jazz musicians. We were always welcomed; there was no tension.

After a while the place was closed for some reason or other—no doubt in part because it was black. It then reopened as a private club. This simply meant that it could stay open all night and you brought what you wanted to drink. I remember going to the Cosmo Club one night after a very boring college dance—girls in chiffon full-length dresses with stays, everyone uptight, the event over by eleven and all to bed by twelve. We rode our bicycles into a different world. Lights were blazing and the parking lot was full. It was midnight and the party had just begun. I noticed a commotion by the door but paid no attention. Then I realized that on one side of the entry path stood a man with a shotgun. On the other side was a woman—his wife or girlfriend?—with another man. I had just walked between gun and intended target. Inside a blues musician was playing the guitar hypnotically while couples bumped and ground. I believe the fellow played one blues number nonstop for at least an hour! Pints of bootleg whiskey were on sale under the table, as was a homemade wine that was very sweet and tasted just like Manishevitz kosher wine.

We were considered the silent generation, and certainly most lacked the idealism and activism of the immediate postwar student generation. We had our Beats and a few of us became political dissidents. Yet on the whole, as a generation we were much like the current student generation. What we did not know was that we were a transitional generation—between the postwar progressives and the sixties antiwar and civil rights activists.

At Oberlin we had separate men's and women's dormitories, but we had coed dining in the women's dormitories. Two of the dormitories had been turned into co-ops and were administered by the students. My second year at Oberlin was spent at the Pyle Inn Co-op. We shared in the work, decided the kind of food we would eat, and at the end of the year we got a rebate of whatever we were able to save over the established charges for all eating facilities. We held a house meeting once a week on Sunday afternoon, and it was this body that made basic decisions. Pyle Inn was my first taste of direct democracy.

Pyle Inn was about as political a place as one found at Oberlin in the fall of 1952. An election campaign was underway, and certainly Adlai Stevenson had the full support of Pyle Inn's members. A number of us got hold of cars and went to nearby Elyria to greet Stevenson at a whistle stop train appearance. He knew Oberlin students were in the crowd and devoted his whole short talk to us. This made me feel a bit uncomfortable, as most of us could not vote and I felt it more important that he speak to the ordinary citizens of Elyria. With his wit and intellect, Stevenson was a candidate students took to heart. However, a majority of the people in the country were not students and chose Eisenhower. Some of us were going to make the trip to Cleveland to see Vincent Hallinan, the Progressive Party's presidential candidate. We didn't really support the fellow, but a curiosity as well as a rebelliousness in relation to the pervading witch-hunt atmosphere attracted us to him. But the car ride fell through and we missed the experience.

It was at Pyle Inn in the fall of 1952 that I met my first wife, Martha Curti. Her main interest was in music, and she was attending the conservatory. I was attracted to her by her spirit, her vivacity. While I knew little about music and she was not much into politics, we were able to talk about almost anything and spent much time doing just that. My relationship with Martha was very intense. We spent as much time as possible together, and I did my best to transform the relationship into a permanent, stable life together. I had such a deep need for the security of a relationship that I was determined that we get married as soon as possible. We were very young and terribly inexperienced. Nevertheless we got married at the end of my sophomore year.

The witch-hunt was now at its height, and Joe McCarthy was in full stride. This was having a big personal impact on my family, which I could sense whenever I was home from school. My father, as a federal employee, had been under a security investigation ever since such investigations had been instituted by the Truman administration. He had never been a member of or even peripherally involved with the Communist Party. He had not been a big signer in a period when many liberals were signing this or that statement or petition on the Spanish Civil War, the need for peace, or what have you. Yet he had a circle of friends that included the intellectual periphery of the Communist Party. I could sense the fear and insecurity the investigation created in my parents. I remember being in the backseat of the car while my parents discussed whether to visit an old friend who they knew was a Communist. I could sense that they were sickened that they had to discuss such a question. It certainly was upsetting to me. It violated my strong sense of fairness and belief in civil liberties and democracy.

A little later, after Eisenhower took over the presidency, my father lost his government position. The regulations were changed and merely his past association with known Communists was sufficient cause for dismissal. Luckily there were people in this country who did not accept this approach. A publishing firm whose Republican owners believed in civil liberties hired him as treasurer. This actually ended up being a career advancement.

Enter the Socialists

I became a socialist in 1953, right at the height of McCarthyism and at the lowest ebb that the American socialist movement had ever experienced. I was a sophomore at Oberlin College in Oberlin, Ohio. I was won to socialism by the Shachtmanites, a group that made up in intellectual vitality for what they clearly lacked in members. The Shachtmanites were the dissidents of the dissidents, the uncompromising defenders of democracy in a world dominated by totalitarianism and during a period when the Left itself was by no means untouched by totalitarian thought and practice.

The socialists came to Oberlin that fall. Their arrival was quite an event, not totally unlike the landing of a flying saucer, and many turned out to hear them out of curiosity alone. We were graced with two socialists—Scott Arden and Bogdan Denitch—from the newly formed Young Socialist League.[4] Neither I nor anyone else at Oberlin College had ever heard of the group. The group's membership was over one hundred, which in the dark days of McCarthyism made it the largest socialist youth organization in the United States. In fact I believe it was the *only* socialist youth organization outside of the Communist Party's Labor Youth League (LYL), which was down to two campus branches and was almost defunct. The organization was, as I would later learn, vaguely in the Trotskyist tradition, heavily influenced by veteran Trotskyist leader Max Shachtman. This gave Denitch and Arden a rather attractive political coloration: very militant and critical of American society and foreign policy yet committed to democracy and just as critical of the Soviet Union as they were of the United States.

These socialists, for all their small numbers and sectarian background, made a very big splash. Some two hundred students turned out to hear them at the First Congregational Church. I can still remember the main outlines of their speeches. They said that the world was divided into two imperialist camps, one headed by Russia and the other by the United States. They opposed the two camps with the creation of a "third camp" made up of the colonial countries and the workers of all countries. America's foreign policy, they maintained, was antidemocratic, propped up dictatorships around the world, and opposed social progress everywhere. It therefore offered no real alternative to Soviet imperialism. The American economy had pulled out of the depression only through rearmament and World War II. It avoided a threatened postwar slump through rearmament during the cold war. We now lived under a permanent war economy. If we wished peace and disarmament, it would have to be on the basis of a socialist society. Denitch and Arden were socialists but they were not Communists. Socialism in their view was the logical extension, the full development of democracy.

The speakers were challenged from the floor by two professors from the college who had worked for the government under the Truman administration. They defended the basic outlines of American foreign policy as necessary to combat the dangers of communism while challenging the thesis that the American economy was dependent on war industries for its prosperity. Denitch and Arden immediately challenged the two professors to a debate. The two professors could hardly refuse in front of an audience of two hundred students, and the debate was set for the same place the following evening.

The debate the next evening went over the same basic points. The professors were in trouble from the beginning as having been advisers to the previous government; they were forced to defend almost all actions of that government in the mounting cold war. At the same time they were liberals, not cynical politicians, and they continuously tripped over their liberal convictions as they followed a line of realpolitik. Arden and Denitch were skilled debaters with years of experience in the socialist movement. They knew absolutely nothing about economics, and their theory of the permanent war economy was, I would learn many years later, a one-sided explanation of the postwar boom. Yet these limitations did not hamper them and—at least as I remember the event—they creamed the professors. Nothing pleases a student more than to see his professors have their heads handed to them; the audience was with the socialists.

Bogden Denitch painted a colorful and somewhat exaggerated picture of the YSL. He gave a most astounding interview to the college newspaper. He stated that the YSL's membership was "under 30,000" and went into great detail about a "training school" the YSL ran to turn out machinists to invade industry and form socialist cells to challenge the conservative union bureaucracy. The newspaper painted the organization as if it were a big Red plot. I found out the truth a couple of years later when I turned up in New York City and needed a job. Two older comrades, Herman Benson (Ben Hall)[5] and Julius Jacobson (Julius Falk),[6] had a small machine shop. If you pleaded with them enough they would give you a fifteen-minute lesson in running an automatic screw machine. Their instruction was rather inadequate; luckily I never had to work in industry.

About a dozen of us met with Arden and Denitch and decided to organize our own socialist club on campus, which we called the Eugene V. Debs Club, naming it after the famous early leader of American socialism.[7] It was not formally affiliated with the YSL but it reflected the YSL's political outlook, and in time, three or four of us joined the YSL. The club was quite broad and included some students whose politics were closer to the Communist Party than to our stridently anti-Communist radical socialism. One thing we all had in common was a deep hostility to McCarthyism. The struggle against McCarthyism became a struggle for the survival of the club itself.

We applied to the college to be accepted as a regular club with access to college facilities. The administration requested that we give them a complete list of our members. We refused to do so, explaining that such membership lists were being turned over by college administrations across the country to witch-hunting committees and to prospective employers. The request, therefore, was an infringement on our First Amendment rights. I remember distributing over a thousand copies of a statement on the matter to the student body and receiving overwhelming support. The college was finally forced to back down on the issue.

Then we decided to show the film *Salt of the Earth* as a club activity. The film was made by the International Union of Mine, Mill, and Smelter Workers, which had been expelled from the CIO for being Communist-dominated, and projectionists had refused to show it in New York City. It was actually a very fine film about a strike by copper miners in New Mexico that united Anglo and Chicano workers, males and females. The administration again sought to stop us. The liberal sociology professor, who was our club sponsor, threatened to resign, which would have meant we would lose the legal status of the club. A club meeting was packed with fearful anti-Communist liberals, and we lost that battle.

We sponsored a meeting for Dirk Struik, a mathematician who edited the pro-Communist academic journal *Science and Society*. (Struik had been indicted under a Massachusetts criminal anarchy statute in 1951. MIT had suspended him with full pay, making his case an important academic freedom issue in that period.)[8] He was a gentle, gray-haired, scholarly looking man whose very energetic wife had organized his tour. He spoke for us on the history of science and technology. I remember it as a brilliant lecture attended by several totally unpolitical science majors who loved it. It was classical historical materialism at its best.

We, of course, sponsored several speakers reflecting the more anti-Communist (we always used the word Stalinist) political viewpoint of the YSL. Of these, two stand out: B. J. Widick and Max Shachtman himself. Widick was working at the time in an auto plant in Detroit. He had written a very good book on the United Auto Workers (UAW)[9] and followed this union for *Labor Action*, the paper of Shachtman's group, the Independent Socialist League (ISL). Widick's topic was "The Intellectuals and the Labor Movement." Just before the meeting a student came up to me to explain that his father, a professor from Akron, had urged him to come to the meeting. This fellow's father had heard Widick speak in the middle of the sit-down strike in the 1930s that organized the rubber industry. Widick had given a fiery speech; he visualized sit-downs spreading through American industry, an insurrection being carried out, and a Soviet America constructed on the basis of these plant occupations.

You can imagine the student's shock when he heard Widick, now a veteran of more than twenty years of a bureaucratized union movement, speaking during the low point in the history of American socialism. Widick's lecture was devoted to discouraging intellectuals from seeking jobs within the trade union apparatus. "The bureaucrats will corrupt you. They do not want ideas, or social progress. They just want to preserve their own political machines." Widick, a very honest man, spoke the truth. But he did not make many recruits for our struggling Eugene V. Debs Club.

One day Max Shachtman showed up in a beat-up old Chevy driven by his wife, Yetta. He was on a national tour of what was left of his organization. Oberlin was the high point of the tour. I was immediately struck by Shachtman's appearance—the fierce anti-Communist socialist looked to me exactly like Nikita Khrushchev! He was a very Russian-looking fellow with a large balding head. He was a product of the Russian Jewish New

York City working class and spoke in its traditions. He was exceedingly long-winded and could go on and on about any topic. But he was always interesting and extremely witty. His technique was to go into a lengthy Jewish or Russian folk parable in the middle of the speech and then use the parable to illustrate a point in contemporary politics. About sixty people turned out to hear him, which was a damn good crowd in those days, and he gave them an hour-and-a-half nonstop entertaining performance.

I had embraced socialism quickly, with little resistance, and had thrown my energies fully into spreading socialist ideas through the Eugene V. Debs Club. I had already developed on my own a very radical and critical assessment of American life prior to meeting the socialists. I was pro-labor, deeply sympathetic to the underdog in American society, disturbed by the undemocratic and warlike character of American foreign policy, and shaken by the effects of McCarthyism on the principles of fair play and freedom I believed in. While I had been brought up in an atmosphere of sympathy toward the Soviet Union, I, like many liberals, had become increasingly critical of the USSR's conduct, especially in relation to East Europe.

The socialism of the YSL fitted in very easily with my radical but liberal outlook because the YSL posed its socialism as a logical extension of liberal democratic values. We saw socialism as the extension of democracy into the economic sphere so that industries would be controlled by those who worked in them. This would not only increase the democratic control of the ordinary person but would take away the very unfair advantage large economic holdings give to wealthy individuals to undermine the democratic process. At the same time, socialism seemed to us to be a fairer society with incomes more equally distributed. Thus I changed easily from a democratic liberal into a democratic socialist. It was much later that I would have to try to square this democratic vision with the theoretical complexities of vanguards, democratic centralism, and the dictatorship of the proletariat.

Not only did socialism seem to us to be a *better* system but the idea gained a *necessity*, particularly from a critique of American foreign policy. We saw the United States acting throughout the world in support of reactionary leaders: Chiang Kai-shek in Taiwan, Franco in Spain, and a series of petty tyrants in Latin America. At the same time, the United States had built up a huge nuclear arsenal and seemed uninterested in seriously negotiating its reduction. This U.S. practice provided sufficient evidence to convince us that it was acting as an *imperialist* power. We then applied the Marxist theory of imperialism and the state to the United States, which proved to us, and our periphery, that the United States *had* to act as it did as long as it remained capitalist. Worldwide economic interest required it. This meant that both world peace and progress toward democracy and development in the colonial world required opposition to capitalism in the United States. This very same thinking process, which in the 1950s affected only a few, would influence hundreds of thousands of students in the next decade.

I must mention the appeal of Marxism itself. It represented a wonderful combination of idealism, of belief in a utopian vision of a better way for human beings to live, with an intellectually rigorous and useful method for understanding history. Historical materialism had a marvelous quality of placing you in history and presenting that history in such a manner that its overall development made sense. History became more than a series of facts, personalities, and events. Marx had done for human history what Darwin had accomplished with his theory of the evolution of species. I still remember the genuine intellectual excitement of reading a book like Marx's *Eighteenth Brumaire of Napoleon Bonaparte*.

I had a very nice economics professor, a Professor Bell, who, while a critic of Marxism, believed that there were too many "Marxists" in the world who never read Marx. He set up a reading tutorial for me in Marxism, and I could see he really enjoyed our discussions and occasional arguments. He may not have been a Marxist, but Marxism challenged him, sharpening his own thinking. I remain very much indebted to him, as well as to Denitch and Arden for introducing me to socialism itself. My life certainly has not be an easy one, and I suffered from some rather extreme occurrences during my later party years. Yet my life, my mind, have been enriched by them.

Notes

1. See the outstanding study of this period, Alan Wald, *The New York Intellectuals* (Chapel Hill: University of North Carolina Press, 1987).
2. Jerold S. Auerbach, *Labor and Liberty: The La Follette Committee and the New Deal* (Indianapolis and New York: Irvington Pubs., 1966), pp. 82ff.
3. Paul Buhle, *C. L. R. James: The Artist as Revolutionary* (London: Verso, 1988), pp. 82–83.
4. The group was formed in 1953 out of a fusion of the Young People's Socialist League (YPSL), led by Mike Harrington, which had split from the Socialist Party, and the Socialist Youth League (SYL), the youth organization of the Independent Socialist League (ISL), headed by Max Shachtman. Arden was from the SYL and Denitch from the YPSL.
5. Herman Benson wrote on labor matters in the ISL's *Labor Action* and has been active in more recent years promoting democracy in the trade unions, editing for a time a newsletter devoted to that purpose. Unless otherwise noted, I will use a person's actual name followed by the pseudonym in parentheses.
6. Julius Jacobson was founder and editor in later years of the theoretical magazine *New Politics*.

7. Eugene V. Debs had been a trade union leader who went to jail for leading a nationwide rail strike. He was a founder of the Socialist Party and its presidential candidate several times. He headed the party in the period just prior to World War I, when socialism was receiving its strongest support in the United States.
8. David Caute, *The Great Fear* (New York: Simon and Schuster, 1978), p. 411. The indictment was dismissed by the Supreme Court in 1956.
9. Irving Howe and B. J. Widick, *The UAW and Walter Reuther* (New York: Random House, 1949).

2

Life with Shachtman

POSITIVELY 14TH STREET

In June 1955 my wife Martha and I hooked up the house trailer we were living in to our old but reasonably powerful Chrysler and headed for New York City, the *center*, as we had been told so often, of political life in America. We traveled down the Pennsylvania Turnpike to the New Jersey Turnpike and headed straight into New York City. We got off the expressway at almost the last exit before the Lincoln Tunnel, pulled into a gas station, and asked the attendant if he knew of a trailer park. He directed us to Moonachie, New Jersey, a flat stretch of marshy land that filled the space between the Secaucus pig farms and the oil refineries near Newark. The environmental contrast with Ohio could not have been greater. That was okay. We were young. It was all still an adventure.

My first act after parking our trailer was, of course, to go to the "headquarters." The third floor at 114 West 14th Street in lower Manhattan was the nerve center of Max Shachtman's political empire and housed both the adult group, the Independent Socialist League, and its youth group, the Young Socialist League. The building was not easy to find. I walked past it twice before I spied it sandwiched between a pawnshop and a cut-rate variety store just west of 6th Avenue. I later discovered that the office was usually identified by Smith's Bar on the corner, which in those days still served a sickeningly salty free lunch. For fifty-five cents, however, a really nice, thick roast beef on a roll was available. By coincidence, when I later shifted my allegiance to Shachtman's rival, the Socialist Workers Party (SWP), its headquarters was also across from a Smith's Bar.

I walked up dark, dusty stairs past the second-story loft devoted to some obscure and not very prosperous aspect of the garment trade. (In two-and-a-half years of going up and down those stairs almost daily, I never saw a single human being enter this loft. Business on the third floor was a bit better—but not by much.) I found myself in a small hall that could seat sixty or so people, and that clearly had not been painted since the Shachtman group moved into the place after its birth in 1940. As you moved toward the back you went past a room stuffed with old volumes of the party publication *Labor Action* and an antiquated hand-operated Addressograph machine. Next came a couple of cubbyhole offices for the "national staff" of the ISL and YSL. Somewhere in the midst of all this must have been a bathroom.

The place had a depressing atmosphere that struck me that first day in 1955 and that returns to me even now as I think back. At Oberlin, politics had been lively—despite the pressures of McCarthyism, we always had an audience—so it was easy to maintain optimism. Here the very documents that had excited us out in Ohio's cornfields lay around covered with dust. You could not remove the musty odor from your nostrils. Those walls, were they originally gray or green, or perhaps blue? Or were they the color all lofts in New York City become, regardless of what is first put on the surfaces? The street below teemed with people—shopping, going to work, going home. That life, however, did not make it up the two flights to the headquarters.

The feeling of being part of a past totally disconnected from present-day life in America could not be avoided on the third floor of 114 West 14th Street. We tried tenaciously to touch our own times in some fashion. Our suffering was not self-inflicted; our times simply had no room for us. Most of us who sat around in that dusty hall in 1955 would, in the next ten years, become a part of a meaningful Left in America. Yet in 1955, that future was not yet in evidence.

One of the back cubbyholes contained Gordon Haskell, who did all the little things that maintain an organization. He did them well and efficiently in the little time he had available; the party had no funds to pay him for full-time work. I remember Gordon as a dapper man with a little mustache, bright but not particularly original in his thinking.[1] Gordon shared his cubbyhole with Hal Draper, the editor of *Labor Action*. Hal didn't need much space, as he also had a small office for editing at the print shop. Hal Draper was quite different from Gordon. He had a very forceful personality, was continuously developing new ideas, and had an impressive capacity for conducting serious research and study. He could also write fast and well. In all my experience on the left, as well as in the commercial world of editorial writing, Hal is the only person I have ever known who could single-handedly put out a weekly paper. For some issues he accomplished this by writing most of the paper himself. Hal struck me at the time as a bit aloof. I never really got to know him as a person and I knew of no one, other than his wife, who was close to him. Years later, friends of mine who had collaborated with him for years claimed he was abrasive and difficult to work with. All I can say is that he was never that way with me back then. Perhaps the vagaries of faction life wore on him in later years as, in different ways, it wore on all of us.

Hal Draper had been a leader of the Trotskyist youth in the 1930s, the Young People's Socialist League—Fourth Internationalist (YPSL Fourth). His brother Theodore supported the positions of the Communist Party (CP) in this period. In 1940, when the Communist Party supported the Soviet Union's pact with Hitler, Theodore Draper broke with the CP along with James Wechsler, who would later become editor of the *New York Post*. Theodore became a somewhat embittered anti-Communist, what we called a "cold war liberal." He has nevertheless remained fascinated by the Marxist movement, as evidenced by his preoccupation with the history of the Communist Party and the Cuban Revolution.[2] Hal eventually turned to a writing career, producing some very fine scholarly material on Marxism.[3]

Most socialist newspapers are written by intellectuals "for workers." The result is usually a product that bores the former without enticing the latter. *Labor Action* did not fit this mold. It was written by and for intellectuals, including intellectually inclined workers. The result was a paper not always "correct" in the Marxist sense—rarely correct as I now look back at it—but always interesting. I discovered this at Oberlin, where I distributed my little bundle of fifty papers each week to a growing group of regular readers.

Labor Action supporters were devoted to the task of finding the "third camp"[4] somewhere in an increasingly bipolarized world. This was no simple task in 1955; it required ingenuity, imagination, and a dose of self-deception. The *Labor Action* staff's problem with finding this third camp was most sharply evidenced by the situation in Vietnam. The Communists controlled the North, and the Diem regime in the South was rapidly falling under American control. *Labor Action*, in good conscience, could embrace neither the North nor the South. Then Hal discovered two religious-military sects, the Cao Dai and the Hao Hao.[5] These two formations were definitely battling the Communists and the Catholic-oriented Diem regime. The only problem was that these groups were battling *for* their own semifeudal fiefdoms!

My arrival in New York City did not go unnoticed by the Federal Bureau of Investigation. My political activity at Oberlin College had been closely watched by the Cleveland office of the FBI, which had made me the subject of a Communist Index Card. The Cleveland file was forwarded to the New York office, which opened its own investigation.

I must say, as I read these FBI reports today, I am rather proud of my activities of over thirty-five years ago. On April 24, 1956, an FBI agent observed me, along with a modest group of twelve other participants, picketing the Consulate of the Dominican Republic and handing out a leaflet entitled "Down with Trujillo!" On April 27 I was observed in front of the French Consulate, protesting French colonialism in Algeria. I ended a rather busy month of picketing by attending the Communist Party's May Day rally at Union Square. There I handed out a leaflet criticizing the Treasury Department's action in seizing the office of the Daily Worker *while at the same time criticizing the lack of democracy in the Soviet Union. Later that year, on November 3, I joined thirty-five persons to picket the Russian delegation in the United Nations to protest Russian suppression of the working class in Hungary.*

The FBI placed agents regulary in front of our dismal little office and photographed people, including me, going in and out the door. I must assume that they rented a loft across the street and used a telephoto lens.

Soon I made the New York office's Security Index (SI) list. The Internal Security Act (MacCarran Act) passed in 1950 included a provision (actually proposed by the liberal Democrats Hubert Humphrey and Paul Douglas) for the mass detention of "subversives" should the president declare a national emergency. Radicals would be placed in facilities similar to those for Japanese Americans in World War II. This law legalized a detention program established by the FBI in 1948. The Security Index was set up in order to provide a ready basis for locating potential detainees. The FBI needed to have a photograph, a handwriting specimen, a home address, and a work address for everyone on this list. This information had to be checked at least once a year.

In the mid-fifties, when my name was added to this list, there were almost thirteen thousand people on the list![6]

I, along with my wife, Martha, accepted the task of putting out the mailing for the Friday-night forum. We sent our leaflets to fifty or so people, and each week fifteen or twenty would assemble in that dreary hall to hear one of our people lecture on some topic of the day. The problem was that the attendees were almost all members; we were the convinced talking to the convinced. At one of our very first forums a young fellow came up to us and introduced himself: "I'm Mike Shute. I am *the* contact." We lost that "contact" six months later when he became a member.[7]

The Saturday-night social—held perhaps once a month—was a little better. I can remember my first one. It was held in the same hall, the ambiance only slightly improved by dimmer lighting. A person sat at the door taking the small admission charge, and beer was being served in a corner. The hall was barely filled with clusters of people talking excitedly about various political points or just catching up on gossip. The crowd had more older members, who had learned through the years to avoid the dull forums and turn up at parties instead to keep in touch with old friends.

Then Hal Draper walked in with his wife, Anne, who was wearing, as she did indoors and out and on all occasions, a hat. Anne was the opposite of Hal—vivacious, open, warm. For years Anne had represented a group of workers who made women's hats. These workers, predominantly immigrant males, adored their female and very radical union representative. I heard that when she turned up years later among the striking Columbia students (who responded to her as warmly as did the hatters), she wore a steel-reinforced hat in case of problems with billy clubs.

Hal and Anne went over to the record player and put on a Jewish folk tune, and soon the entire place was dancing Israeli circle dances. I clumsily joined in. I had traveled a long distance from Ohio. I suspect that same night, in a similar hall in the Brighton Beach section of Brooklyn, the much-hated Communists were dancing the same dances. Radicalism in New York City in those days was very Jewish.

I rarely saw Max Shachtman. He came infrequently to the hall, keeping to himself and a small coterie of acolytes. One night I was privileged to go with him to a meeting of the Workmen's Circle. In the pre–World War I days of Debsian socialism many immigrant workers joined the Socialist Party and formed their own foreign-language federations. These, in turn, created fraternal orders that supplied insurance and death benefits to the immigrants. Most of these groups had split, in reaction to the split between the Communist Party and the Socialist Party. The Workmen's Circle had remained with the socialists and was composed primarily of Jewish garment workers. The meeting was held in one of the small rooms at the Central Plaza Hotel on the Lower East Side, and the topic of discussion this night was our favorite—the Russian question. To make matters more interesting, this branch of the Workmen's Circle was dominated by former members of the Jewish Bund. The bund had a long history and deep roots among Yiddish-speaking Polish workers. In 1903 it had supported the

Mensheviks against Lenin's Bolsheviks. It had leaned to the left within Menshevism and in the 1930s was not without members who were sympathetic to the USSR. At the beginning of World War II, two leaders of the bund went to the USSR and were never heard from again. They were presumed killed by Stalin.

Max Shachtman started the evening with a none-too-short exposition of his theory of the USSR as a new class society having nothing to do with socialism. Then the bund speaker got up. He turned to the small audience of fifteen-or-so people in the steamy room and declared, "Comrades, if you do not mind I will speak in my native tongue. This way I can express my thoughts more precisely." He then began an oration in Yiddish punctuated by the grandest gestures and facial expressions, as if he were speaking to a mass audience numbering in the thousands. I could not understand a word, and to this day I do not know what the theory of the bund was or is on the Russian question. But I will never forget that speech. The man was clearly a great orator, and he had learned to speak in the only way great speaking can be learned—in a mass movement in a period before television. No doubt before the war he had spoken to thousands in the Warsaw ghetto. Most of his former audience had since perished in Hitler's gas chambers, his leaders had died at the hands of Stalin, and he now lived the life of exile and isolation, linked to a past that could not be revived or relived. This night he had to be content with fifteen old comrades and one goy.

I was not the only goy in the Shachtmanite movement. There was also Mike Harrington. Mike used to complain about the tendency of the Jewish radicals to unconsciously hide their ethnicity. Comrades chose what we called "party names," or pen names for writing in *Labor Action*. Max Dumbrow became Max Martin, George Rawick was transformed into George Rawlings, and Albert Glotzer became Al Gates. Even our one Italian, Sam Bottone, used the name Sam Taylor. Mike decided to write some articles as Eli Fishman!

Mike Harrington was a handsome Irish fellow whose brown hair even then was salted with gray. He had a ready smile, a winning personality, and could effortlessly do almost anything requiring the assembling of words. He spoke well and wrote well. Sometimes he would get an idea, find an unused old typewriter at 114, sit down and knock out a fifteen-page theoretical article for the discussion bulletin in an evening. To save comrades trouble he would type it directly on a mimeograph stencil. I would not say Mike was the deepest thinker I ever met, but there could have been no better choice for the National Chairman of the YSL. Even in those days he was beginning to write outside the narrow confines of our small movement, mainly for the *Village Voice*, as he started on the road that would lead him to write *The Other America*.[8] He chose the right topic at the right moment and, luckily, caught the eye of President Kennedy. President Johnson actually hired Mike for a while as an adviser. In this fashion Mike made his contribution to the reform movement of the 1960s. Of course we did not see this in Harrington in 1955. I do believe, though, that Mike saw that potential in himself.

Mike Harrington had come to radical politics through the Catholic church. He had been a member of the *Catholic Worker* organization headed by Dorothy Day. This very unusual group combined an "alms to the poor" kind of rehabilitation work in the Bowery with a socialist/anarchist vision projected through their paper (which they sold for one penny if you had it). Dorothy Day was a tough lady who stood up to both the witch-hunters and the Catholic hierarchy while never swerving from her Catholic faith. Mike later joined the youth group of the Socialist Party, the Young People's Socialist League, then led one of the many splits of YPSL from its parent and fused his little group with Shachtman's children.

The Way We Thought

While at college I had evolved politically from liberalism toward revolutionary socialism of the Marxist variety. In New York City my studies of Marxism intensified. I used to walk along 14th Street to Union Square and then down University Place to the University Place Book Store. It was one of those wonderfully cluttered used-book stores that once flourished in the area. The place was managed by Joe Carter, a former Trotskyist who had played an important role in the evolution of the Shachtman political tendency.[9] There I would search out rare editions of Trotsky's works and other Marxist classics. In those days most of Trotsky's writings were not in print. I spent twenty dollars, half a week's wages, for a rather mangled edition of Trotsky's *History of the Russian Revolution*.

What I did not realize was that Max Shachtman and those closest to him in the ISL and YSL were traveling in exactly the opposite direction. Starting with a revolutionary socialist outlook as followers of Lenin and Trotsky, these people were moving toward liberalism. Perhaps this is what made the YSL so effective in appealing to liberals like myself. The difficulty was that I and others like me among the youth did not wish to travel back to where we had come from. It was precisely these opposite trajectories that led to the faction fight and split that soon would develop in the YSL.

In order to make these developments understandable, I will need to explain a bit about the way we thought in those days. What is this Trotskyism that had such an impact upon me, my comrades, and many others the world over?[10]

Trotskyism is, to begin with, a form of communism, of what many call today Marxism-Leninism. Trotsky, as a leader of the Russian Revolution, endorsed that revolution as a model for all future revolutions and Leninism as the series of beliefs and practices that would make possible such revolutions. This meant that the correct ideology was critical to a victorious revolution. Part of the task of a socialist was to develop and defend this ideology against "revisionist" and "reformist" deviations. Such deviations represented, to one degree or another, compromises and adaptations to the capitalist system that blocked the revolutionary overthrow of that system. We could see very clearly that the major parties of the Second International (the large social democratic parties of Europe) had betrayed the working class of the world by supporting their respective governments in World War I. It was, to us, a mockery of internationalism that the German socialists mobilized workers to fight against the Russians while the Russian Mensheviks (the competing group to the right of the Bolsheviks) mobilized workers to fight against the Germans. It also seemed very clear to us that the Mensheviks' policy of participating in and supporting a coalition government with the capitalists after the February Revolution would never have led to socialism.

The reader may very well wonder how relevant such thoughts were in 1955 and 1956 in a very conservative country going through a boom period, a country in which socialism barely survived in the form of miniscule groups. We believed that the inner workings of the laws of capitalist development would, in time, transform the politically inert working class into an active force seeking radical social transformation. At such a point the key would then be a *party* that had the correct *program*. This meant that our task, even in times of great isolation, was to construct the embryo of such a party and defend its revolutionary program so that it would be preserved for future use. Of course we realized that even in periods of isolation we needed to function, to publish our propaganda, and even, occasionally, to initiate a minor action. Such actions, however, were to be consistent with our overall revolutionary aims. We were people whose political specificity had relevance only to a distant past and a distant possible future. No wonder we were torn between a tendency to retreat into sectarian irrelevance and a tendency to relate to the present by adapting to it and thus losing our revolutionary objectives.

We Trotskyists viewed ourselves as *true* Communists, the defenders of a golden age of democratic workers' rule in the Soviet Union under Lenin and Trotsky between 1917 and 1923. It is not important whether our image of that period was accurate; what mattered was that we believed in that image and sought its reproduction in contemporary and future revolutionary events.[11] Socialism for us was not simply a matter of steel-production statistics but of a living, vital, communal democracy of the masses, an egalitarian society of great creative energy.

In the Trotskyist view, Stalin usurped power in the Soviet Union and established a bureaucratic rule that crushed the earlier Soviet democracy. At the same time, Stalin reversed the revolutionary line of the Comintern to fit the conservative needs of the bureaucracy; this in turn led to the defeat of the working class in revolutionary situations in various countries. Trotskyists saw themselves as the inheritors of the Leninist tradition and viewed the official Communists as betrayers and usurpers. We conducted a continuous critique of Communist policy within and outside of Russia.

We were the leftist critics of the official Communists. We held that under Stalin the worldwide Communist movement had gone over to the reformist views of Menshevism and reformism. We certainly could make a pretty good case on the basis of Communist policy since 1934.[12] The Communists had supported Roosevelt during the 1930s and scuttled efforts of the labor movement to form its own party. During World War II the Communists had supported a no-strike pledge, even suggesting that it be extended into the postwar period, and refused to fight segregation in the army. This brought them into conflict with black leaders like A. Philip Randolph as well as with militant workers.

We Shachtmanites looked back upon the history of our American Trotskyist movement with a certain pride. Max Shachtman had been one of its founders in 1928, along with James P. Cannon.[13] Certainly when contrasted to Trotsky's failures in Europe, the experiences of the American group, which became known as the Socialist Workers Party, were marked by a degree of prosperity in the late 1930s. The group had quite a few working-class members and was not without influence in the trade union movement. It was particularly proud of its leadership of the Teamsters' strike in Minneapolis in 1934.[14]

Shachtman's Independent Socialist League evolved mainly out of the intellectual strata within the SWP. Trotskyism's blend of Communist orthodoxy and utopian vision, and its credible explanation of Stalin's perversions of that vision, expressed particularly in the Moscow Trials, had an appeal for a significant minority of intellectuals. Its supporters included James Burnham, who was a professor of philosophy at NYU; Sidney Hook; Max Eastman; George Novack; the writers James T. Farrell and Saul Bellow; Philip Rahv and William Phillips, the editors of *Partisan Review*; their friend Dwight MacDonald; the poets John Wheelwright and Sherry Mangan; and *Fortune* editor Herbert Solow.[15] Young intellectuals like Irving Howe, Irving Kristol, and Hal Draper were being recruited from the student milieu.

Max Shachtman broke with Trotsky in 1940 over the nature of the Soviet

Union.[16] Trotsky, while a harsh critic of the Soviet bureaucracy, still insisted that the Soviet Union had to be considered a "workers' state," and, as such, the Left should defend it against imperialism. Shachtman refused to defend the USSR after it occupied half of Poland and went to war with Finland in 1940. Shortly after his break with Trotsky, Shachtman developed his own theory, bureaucratic collectivism, which held that the USSR was a new class society.[17]

When I stumbled upon the ISL in 1953, it had been passing through difficult times, politically evolving parallel to the far larger liberal intellectual public. Immediately after the split with Trotsky, James Burnham denounced Marxism, left the party, and began work on his book *The Managerial Revolution*. In the postwar period Burnham joined William Buckley on the staff of the conservative journal *National Review*. In 1941, Dwight MacDonald left and, three years later, began publishing the maverick semianarchist journal *Politics*.[18] In 1952 Irving Howe left to publish *Dissent* magazine, which promoted a socialist vision quite similar to Shachtman's but with a nonparty and somewhat more right-wing slant. *Partisan Review* and the intellectuals around that publication moved even further to the right. Individuals such as Irving Kristol became "neoconservatives," bringing to that political position some elements of thinking that went back to the original Shachtman tendency.[19]

So we were not just Trotskyists; we were *Shachtmanites*. We were the dissidents among the dissidents. How much more obscure could you get? We were very proud of our special theory of the Soviet countries as "new class societies" and were able to expound on the matter at great length. We viewed the mainstream Trotskyists in James P. Cannon's SWP as "Stalinoids"; they viewed us as "Stalinophobic." Both groups were still very much hypnotized by the Russian Revolution and were still debating its consequences for "the world revolution."

Politics, Politics, Politics

The movement I was part of between 1955 and 1957 was definitely one in transition from a radical Communist past toward a predominantly social democratic future.[20] Yet few outside of perhaps a core of personal friends around Shachtman were aware of where we were going politically. Certainly I was not. Many of us still studied Trotsky's works and borrowed arguments from Lenin. Others were clearly embarrassed by such utterances. Stalinism was the main (some seemed to suggest only) enemy, and democracy was the battle cry. Imperceptibly, radical Communists were becoming social democrats. Their outlook fitted well the dominant mood of the times: The American public and American intellectuals were being mobilized to serve in the cold war against the Evil Empire. What the Shachtmanites did not realize is that their very adaptation to the 1950s is what hindered them from taking advantage of the new radicalization of the 1960s.

I was a member of the Young Socialist League's "leading committee," the National Action Committee (NAC). We met each week for two or more hours (usually more), and it was our task to decide national policy between meetings of the National Executive Committee (NEC) or national conventions. We carried out this awesome task by discussing all matters freely and at great length. The committee members included Mike Harrington and Little Max (Max Dumbrow/Martin). Sam Bottone (Taylor) was in that period as close to Little Max as the latter was to Shachtman. Max and Sam were members of the ISL's "leading committee," so they were of like minds by the time they made it to our meeting. Bogdan Denitch was a member for part of the time I was on the NAC.

Sy Landy was our leftist. While adhering quite rigidly to a Shachtmanite view of the world, he favored a more radical tactical course in this country. Sy was the consummate New York radical. He ate and breathed politics, speaking authoritatively and endlessly on any matter (usually out of the side of his mouth in a conspiratorial manner no matter how mundane the topic). He loved to debate, talk, maneuver, combine, bloc, split. Sy, like almost all the other YSL leaders, was really too old for a youth movement. He was in his middle twenties then, but he looked considerably older due to glasses and thinning hair. It does not surprise me that today Sy has his own miniscule group.[21] Certainly his experience in the 1950s trained him for it.

George Rawick (Rawlings)[22] was my favorite because we could never be sure what would come out of his mouth. I have found most radicals, to the contrary, to be deadeningly predictable. On a typical evening we would all be discussing our tactical line with Sy being the most militant and I, soon also of the Left, joining him or being a bit more extreme. Max was the voice of calm reason, always an advocate of the careful, cautious tactic. George would get flustered and his face would glow a bright red, not unlike the face of Gerry Healy,[23] a man I would meet a decade later. George would start coming down hard on the side of the Left. Then came the vote, and he would line up with Max, Mike, and Sam. Afterward he would go up to Max, saying, "Sorry, I got carried away. I know I shouldn't read Trotsky before I come into one of these meetings!" In his own way George represented much of the YSL's membership: Their hearts were with "The Revolution," but their practical side led them to a very conservative line of action. Perhaps they initially felt that little more could be done in those severe times, but soon their actions led to permanent changes in theory and in heart.

THE HUNGARIAN REVOLUTION

The Twentieth Congress of the Russian Communist Party was held in February 1956. Khrushchev's secret speech leaked to the world press and in this manner made its way into Eastern Europe. For many years Trotskyists had been hounded by Communists for saying what the highest leader of the Soviet Union was now asserting was true. Khrushchev did not reveal all of Stalin's crimes, but he admitted enough to deliver a shattering blow to the thinking of many Communists in the West and to encourage powerful movements in East Europe.

In June the explosion of workers at Poznan in Poland encouraged a broad reform movement to gain control of the Polish United Workers Party. Some students and intellectuals raised ideas very close to Trotskyism, and workers' councils were formed in the factories. Events in Poland in turn encouraged a movement of intellectuals in Hungary called the Petofi Circle, which soon led to a nationwide movement involving the workers. In October workers' councils were formed and a reformist group around Nagy took over the Communist Party. The Hungarian Revolution had begun! On November 4, virtually on the eve of the anniversary of the Russian Revolution, Soviet tanks rolled across the border into Hungary to crush the revolution. Nevertheless, a heroic general strike of workers in the Csepel district held out for two more months.[24]

We followed these events daily, hourly. This was a real revolution in our times and was based on a political program that we felt was very close to ours. Workers' councils were formed as they were during the great Russian Revolution. Workers formed soviets once again, but this time they were against the "Soviet" Union. How well we knew the Russian Revolution: February, the April Theses, the June days, the July days, Kerensky, Kornilov, Lenin, Martov, Dan, even Sukhanov. But now we had our own. We devoured the *New York Times*, clipping it into little pieces and filling file folders. We were particularly fascinated by the reports of Communists from the West such as British *Daily Worker* correspondent Peter Fryer, who would become a Trotskyist.[25] We admired the old Communist militant Pal Maleter, who had fought in the Spanish Civil War and who was now the head of the Budapest workers' council. He still wore a red star on his cap and a pistol in his belt. One small-town workers' council met in the old party headquarters with Lenin's picture still on the wall.

We romanticized the events and we did do a bit of embroidering, but I believe our reaction was basically correct. The Hungarian Revolution represented an end of an epoch when Stalinism was upheld by millions of people as the realization in practice of socialism and democracy. Stalinism did not go away after 1956; but it survived more on realpolitik and brute strength than through an ideological grip on the minds of advanced followers in most nations. Because of what happened in 1956, the student movement in the 1960s was remarkably free of Stalinist influence. And, what was so important for us, Trotskyism finally got a chance.

It is difficult now to realize the degree to which the Trotskyist movement had been made into the pariah on the Left. Communist Party members simply did not speak to Trotskyists. For the most part they sincerely believed we were Fascist agents. We were driven from meetings and organizations controlled by Communists. In 1956, all that decisively changed. To me it was summed up in a mass meeting called in New York City by the Communist Party to attempt to explain to the membership the meaning of the events in East Europe. A small band of Socialist Workers Party members turned up with a leaflet bearing the headline "Trotskyism Vindicated!" This was none too subtle, and later the tactical approach became more sophisticated. But after the imprisonment and death of so many Trotskyists and Communists and the murder of Trotsky himself, the SWP had earned the right to one leaflet originating in the adrenal gland and aimed at the political jugular.

The Hungarian Revolution was a rich time in another way for me. It challenged the theoretical worldview I had learned from Shachtman. Superficially it might seem that these new crimes of Stalinism would simply reinforce Shachtman's grim view of the Soviet Union and similar countries. Such a view (which was how most Shachtmanites interpreted these events) missed the main significance of the Hungarian Revolution: the fragile, temporary character of these new societies. According to Shachtman, Stalinism represented a new class society that had the capability of replacing socialism as the next step beyond capitalism in the grand march of history. It was this side of Shachtman's thought that was linked with Hannah Arendt's nightmares of atomized individuals living under totalitarian regimes and Burnham's managerial revolution. "Soviet totalitarianism" was Shachtman's rationale for his political shift in the direction of the Western capitalist camp.

It became very clear to me during 1956 and 1957 that Stalinist societies, whatever label we wished to apply to them, were highly unstable, temporary phenomena. This gave me hope that our socialist dream had some possibility of realization as a better way of living than under either capitalism or Stalinism. It also led me toward the orthodox Trotskyist theory of Stalinism, which Shachtman had rejected in 1940. What particularly appealed to me in Trotsky's thinking was his concept of Stalinist society as being a terribly degenerated kind of *transitional* society situated between capitalism and socialism.

It is fascinating to look back at 1956 with today's knowledge. The revolutions of that period were crushed by Soviet tanks in Hungary and slowly strangled in Poland, yet these measures achieved only temporary stabilization. Of course, I do not claim we predicted the dramatic changes of the 1980s. We had a kind of tunnel vision that could only project into the future the narrow image we had of the Russian Revolution. We were dreamers, utopians, and so young! We expected that the workers' councils and village committees organized as defense organs in Hungary and Poland could form the basis for the kind of communitarian government sketched in Marx's writings and in Lenin's *State and Revolution*.

We dismissed lightly a capitalist alternative in East Europe, in part because fear of capitalist restoration was used by Communist Party hardliners like Herbert Aptheker to justify Soviet repression and in part because of our belief in the workers' commitment to socialist property forms. Today we face the reality that over forty years of forced "socialism" has turned the majority of the people, including many workers, in a procapitalist direction.

The Hungarian Revolution destroyed the political equilibrium for all groups on the Left in the United States. Its effect upon the Communist Party and its periphery was, of course, catastrophic. Literally tens of thousands of people left the Communist movement. The Hungarian events functioned as a traumatic catalyst, bringing to a head a process that had been proceeding slowly for a decade. A combination of disappointment with the failure of socialism in postwar America, a prosperity that lifted many radical Jewish workers into the comfortable middle class, and a malaise created by the undemocratic features of both the Soviet Union and internal party life had loosened the grip of communism on many who maintained a formal loyalty. This is why the desertions were so extensive when they came and also why so few former Communists had the energy to continue in leftist politics once they left the party.

The postwar world was an even greater disappointment for Shachtman's followers than it was for the Communists. At least the Communists could gain encouragement from the triumphs of their sister parties in East Europe and in China. Shachtman viewed these collective developments as an unmitigated disaster, as the spread of a rival imperialist power. The Shachtman group was also affected by a devastating combination of personal prosperity and the lack of opportunities of any sort for leftists in and out of the labor movement. The Shachtman group had become, especially for the few older cadres left, a combination of a holding operation for ideas still deeply believed in and a social club for comrades who had spent over two stormy decades together.

The Hungarian Revolution created the conditions for ending the holding operation. While most Communists abandoned their movement, the Shachtmanites liquidated theirs. Many members had given up the *idea* of an independent movement a long time earlier. Now it was time to get rid of the organizational shell that remained.

My First Faction Fight

It was in September 1956 that the YSL leadership, following the lead of the ISL, proposed a merger with the Socialist Party.[26] The Socialist Party itself had recently gone through a unification with its old minority, the Social Democratic Federation, which had split to the right in the 1930s. The joint party was now known as the SP-SDF. It had a membership of less than a thousand, and most members were older and entirely inactive. It had an extremely anti-Communist program that, except for the part that formally professed socialism, was indistinguishable from the Democratic Party's.

The leadership of the YSL based its unity proposal on several different grounds. First, it sought through unification to break out of the narrow, ingrown, sectlike existence of the ISL/YSL. This was, without a doubt, the most appealing side of the proposal. The organization had sufficient life to realize that its day-to-day existence had become deadly dull. Further, the idea fitted the mood on the left in 1956. With the Communist Party profoundly shattered by the crisis of international Stalinism, *regroupment* was on everyone's lips. The proposal for unity with the SP-SDF represented one pole of regroupment. Second, the liquidation was justified by a general theory of the development of the American working class. The YSL leadership believed that the workers would slowly pass through the stage of liberalism before becoming social democrats, and only after a prolonged period would they adopt the more "revolutionary" ideas that the ISL/YSL was supposed to hold. The SP was therefore seen as a necessary "opening to the right" for revolutionaries, and it was projected that any radicalization in the United States would lead to the massive growth of the SP. This particular argument was meant to appeal—and it generally did—to the more radical element within the group. Third, for Shachtman and his lieutenants, the unity proposal had a deeper political significance: It expressed their desire to finally abandon what remained of a Communist tradition in favor of a social democratic one. They kept quiet about this aspect of things, however, until after unification was achieved.

We on the left opposed the unification primarily because it seemed to us to mean going over to the political positions of what we called State

Department socialism. Yet we did not wish to be sectarians, and therefore we countered the majority's unity scheme with an appealing one of our own. We, too, felt the need to go beyond the sect existence of the YSL. However, we looked in the direction of the ferment within the Communist Party and its periphery for the material with which to build a regrouped militant independent youth movement. We believed that the State Department politics of the SP would be a major roadblock preventing that organization from seriously reaching the dissidents breaking away from the Communist Party. While we were soon to find that we were too optimistic about what could be won out of the CP ferment, the Socialist Party path of our right-wing competitors within the YSL proved to be even more sterile. The student radicalization of the 1960s swept past both the SP and the Communist Party, finding new and more militant political channels. We gathered the forces of the Left Wing Caucus around this simple perspective of regroupment to the left.

This was my first faction fight and has a place in my memory like my first love. It was fresh, spirited, optimistic, brash, at times excessive, and a little clumsy. We started with thirteen people and ended with thirty or so, but we produced more written material in a few months than many mass parties do in years. We filled a thick monthly faction publication, the *Left Wing Bulletin*, as well as a good part of the frequently published YSL discussion bulletin. I was the organizer of the faction and its representative on the NAC. In the last weeks of the struggle I worked full time on the project, writing every day to each of our small groups of supporters in different parts of the country.

Shane Mage was our best theoretician. Shane was a young intellectual, the son of a Manhattan dentist. He always had a smile on his face, something close to a smirk. It suggested that Shane, removed from what was around him, felt superior to his contemporaries. This made the man a bit difficult to take. The problem was he *was* superior to most of his contemporaries. Of course that made him even more unbearable! But it also made it worthwhile putting up with him.

The third major leader of our little faction was James Robertson. Jim was tall, skinny, and slightly stoop-shouldered. He wore little round silver wire-rimmed glasses and a navy blue wool seaman's hat. Jim had lived for many years in Berkeley, California, attending the university there for at least a decade. When I met him he had run out of excuses for keeping his student status, yet he still camped out on the campus. He lived in an old house on Dwight Way, a few blocks from the university.

In the midst of the formation of our faction, within days of the collapse of the Hungarian Revolution, my first son, Carl, was born. Of course we named him after Karl Marx but thought it best to Anglicize the spelling. I do remember that despite the deep factional tensions that existed in the New York branch of the YSL, all the comrades chipped in and sent us twenty-five dollars and a nice card. By that time we had abandoned our trailer and the swamps of New Jersey and lived in a very small, dark apartment in the back of the ground floor of a tenement on 21st Street, just off 2nd Avenue. Today it is a rather desirable neighborhood and even then, except for our building, it was pretty nice.

The SWP played an important role in the political development of our tendency. My own thinking was leading me closer to SWP views.[27] I felt a need to talk with SWPers, to test my new thoughts in discussions. At one event Murry Weiss of the SWP Political Committee approached me. "I have been corresponding for some time now with a colleague of yours, Shane Mage, on certain theoretical matters related to the colonial revolution and his state capitalist theory. Perhaps you would like to see the correspondence and discuss it with me?" I thought this a most friendly approach and responded by pouring out my innermost political thoughts. This was not tactically wise, I suppose, but I desperately needed someone to talk to about the theories that were possessing me at that time.

Murry Weiss was an exceptional man. He was a large man with a big face, wire-rimmed glasses, and receding hair. Murry had a sparkle in his eyes, which gave him a boyish look. He always wore a crumpled suit and an open white shirt. He was a completely self-taught Jewish intellectual from a working-class background. He had left school in the eighth grade, and what he knew, he learned in the movement. And he knew a lot. Many, many years later Murry left the SWP and was forced to find a way to earn a living. He had a knack for communicating with people, understanding people. So he decided to become a psychologist. He passed his high-school equivalency test and then went on to college to get the degrees he needed—when he was almost sixty years old!

In a very short while I was collaborating with the SWP through Murry Weiss. Murry would come over to my little apartment almost every day and we would discuss tactics. I found that I was in very close agreement with the SWP, particularly on the next stage of developing a youth movement. We agreed that we needed to turn our movement toward the crisis within the Communist Party and its milieu and patiently seek to recruit some of these people into our new youth movement. Even if such recruitment was not possible, our efforts could only strengthen the position of what we viewed as our revolutionary forces and weaken Stalinism. The SWP did not have a youth movement and had, in fact, drawn rather negative conclusions about young people from the loss of virtually all of them to Shachtman in 1940. The opportunity to make up for this by winning over a few of Shachtman's youth seventeen years later was just too tempting for the SWP leadership to ignore. So, with some reservations, Murry was given a pretty free hand to work with us.

I have a very murky memory of what must have been the 1957 convention of the SWP. It was held in Werdermann's Hall, an old decaying building at 160 3rd Avenue. It was left over from an earlier period in New York City when the neighborhood had a German population. Even in 1957 it had become populated by derelicts and the lowest level of prostitutes. It was a secret affair without any indication outside the hall of what was going on. I did not attend any session, but I was taken to a back room of the convention hall to say hello to Jim Cannon.[28]

Cannon used the occasion to give me a not overly friendly lecture on the critical importance of the Russian question. In his opinion the then-current right-wing course of Shachtmanites was rooted in Shachtman's deviations from Trotsky. While I agreed with Cannon on the substance of the matter—that the Soviet Union remained a workers' state—my fellow factionalists had different positions on the old theoretical dispute. However, I found when listening to Cannon that the best tactic was to keep my mouth shut (never easy for me to do, especially in those days!).

Even though I was at Werdermann's Hall for no more than one hour, I was photographed entering and leaving the building. The FBI had set up an elaborate photo surveillance of the hall, taking pictures with telephoto lenses from three different locations. It must have been a boon to the local landlords, who had plenty of empty lofts for rent. They took fifty-two rolls of film. After the New York office identified most of the persons entering the hall, they made sheets of all the unidentified photos. These were then circulated to every FBI office in cities where an SWP branch existed. The aim was to eventually identify all participants. This suggests that the FBI had agents watching each individual SWP branch as well as, in all probability, informants in each branch.

As if this treatment were not sufficient, a movie camera was also used. Five reels of film were taken as a backup measure.

Back in Shachtmanland, the discussion within the YSL proceeded in a poisoned atmosphere. We felt the tension the moment we entered the hall on 14th Street; voices were lowered and we were dealt with in a most formal way. We were the pariahs; we were shunned. To the YSL leadership we were simply "Cannonites" and were dismissed as such. This characterization had its impact on an oppositional layer within Shachtmanism that actually was quite close to us on tactical matters. This group included Hal Draper, Gordon Haskell, and Sy Landy. To one or another degree, they opposed unification with the SP and accused Shachtman, to use Draper's words, of "a systematic adaptation to social democracy."[29] But their traditional hostilities toward the SWP were so great that they refused to work with us and, in the end, went with Shachtman into the SP. I suppose we could have reached some kind of agreement with these people if we had hidden our SWP sympathies. But we were young and brash and particularly bad at hiding anything from anybody. Perhaps more important, we were convinced that the SWP was a more useful ally in creating the kind of militant youth movement that the opportunities of the period required.

In March 1957, in the middle of our faction fight, an event occurred that revealed with extreme sharpness the conflicting orientations of left and right in the YSL. The Reverend A. J. Muste, who briefly passed through the Trotskyist movement in the 1930s,[30] invited all tendencies on the left to attend a meeting to organize a forum for the purpose of encouraging a regroupment discussion.[31] Muste was then a prominent pacifist with impeccable credentials on the left; no one was better suited for the effort. All factions initially responded favorably. Norman Thomas, under pressure from the right wing of his group, almost immediately withdrew from the project, fearing such a close association with Communists, even Communists in crisis. Max Shachtman immediately followed in Thomas's footsteps, claiming that unless the forum came out for democracy everywhere, it would not be respectable "in the eyes of the working class." Of course it was precisely this matter of democracy everywhere that would be the main subject of discussion. The Communist Party was divided over the forum with a dissident, doubting wing, grouped around *Daily Worker* editor John Gates, favoring participation. Old-time Communist leader William Z. Foster bitterly opposed participating in the forum because of the presence of Trotskyists. The Gates wing prevailed, and Albert Blumberg was sent to represent the party. David McReynolds, a left-wing member of the SP, participated as an individual, as did I. The SWP was represented by Farrell Dobbs, and various small groups and unaffiliated leftists such as Dave Dellinger also participated.

On 13 May the *New York Times* announced the formation of the American Forum for Socialist Education. Then on May 15 a witch-hunt was launched against the forum. It began with an editorial in the *Times* noting that "this new organization provides a formal means of cooperation, even if only for purposes of discussion, of prominent Communists and non-Communists who do have claims to stand in the main traditions of genuinely American radicalism." The *Daily News* was less subtle with an editorial entitled "Look into this Mob." The Senate Internal Security Committee did just that, subpoenaing four forum members. The SP got into the act by attacking the forum for using the name "socialism" and launched a campaign against McReynolds, which forced him to resign from the forum.

All this hullabaloo was created because some non-Communists wanted to talk to some Communists in order to encourage the latter to break from Stalinism. Thinking back on these events today, I am amazed at how deeply embedded McCarthyism still was in American life in 1957, and how stupid and blind even some purported leftists were in the face of it. The *New York Times* and its less sedate friends seemed determined to assist the Kremlin in keeping its ideological control over the American Communist Party and much of the Left. I felt then that the role of the SP and Shachtman represented a disgusting capitulation to the American government and what we Marxists called the ruling class. Perhaps I felt this a little more strongly and personally than some of my YSL colleagues because I remembered my father losing his government job because of a witch-hunting loyalty investigation.

The American Forum survived the attacks and went on to organize a mass meeting of over one thousand people, quite a crowd for those days. It was the first meeting that had official representatives of the Communist Party and the Socialist Workers Party on the same platform. I was also there and on the platform representing officially the Left Wing Caucus of the YSL. I even spoke for a few minutes; this time to an audience a bit larger than my usual fifteen or twenty listeners. It seemed to us then that Shachtman had chosen an inglorious way to end his career as head of an independent tendency on the left. For us it was the glorious beginning of what we hoped would be a new, regrouped, and growing revolutionary youth movement.

My participation in the American Forum received prominent treatment in my FBI files. J. Edgar Hoover had concluded that the forum was actually initiated by the Communist Party as an attempt to form a "broad organization" to subvert the nation. The agent present at the mass meeting referred to above dutifully reported:

"MUSTE asked any employees of the FBI present to take the message contained in his next remarks to Mr. HOOVER: He charged that Mr. HOOVER was prostituting his office when on one hand he

claimed that the files of the FBI were super secret, while on the other hand on his own initiative, HOOVER made public statements smearing certain people, including MUSTE and ELEANOR ROOSEVELT, as allegedly Communists."

The agent went on to report on my short remarks:

"WOHLFORTH stated that the youth throughout the nation is being attracted to the radical movement and he feels that the AFSE will aid considerably in the eventual unification of the youth in the radical movement."

In the middle of this faction fight I became involved in a rather bizarre civil liberties case, a minor skirmish in the continuing battle against the witch-hunt atmosphere. I received notice in the mail that I had been rejected by Selective Service because I was a security risk. Strange as it may seem for those who fought the draft in the next decade, I and the YSL felt it was important that I fight my rejection. Of course, I did not really wish to go into the army and was not even too worried that that would happen. I was then about to become a new father, a condition that pretty much assured my being legitimately ineligible for service. The point was to challenge the security-risk accusation and to aid the ISL, which at that time had a suit going against the government for its inclusion on the infamous Attorney General's List of Subversive Organizations. A civil liberties attorney agreed to handle the case.

The first stage of the case was an interview with Military Intelligence. I headed across town to a building on Irving Place and met two plainclothes soldiers who conducted the interview. The next step in the process was my "trial" at Fort Jay on Governor's Island at the tip of Manhattan. It was a pleasant ferry trip to this idyllic little island, which seemed to have more golf courses than parade grounds. I was accompanied by my lawyer and Mike Harrington, who was to testify about the YSL.

The whole thing was very weird because I was appearing before three army colonels who were to judge me and who were advised by an army lawyer. But I was a civilian, so the legality of these proceedings was extremely unclear. I came in with a pack of letters from prominent friends of my parents, who stated what a loyal and idealistic fellow I was. My lawyer raised many kinds of objections, all of which were overruled on the advice of the army lawyer, and the strange trial came to an end.

I believe this exercise helped convince the army that they had to find a better way of handling "subversives," since the old way would probably not stand up to a legal test. They found me "innocent" and therefore draftable. Luckily my victory did not lead to my being drafted because my son Carl promptly arrived. Shortly thereafter the army abandoned this kind of screening system, finding it safer to draft radicals and then hold them at Fort Dix. About this same time, the ISL won its suit and got its name off the Attorney General's List of Subversive Organizations. The ISL was, after all and without a doubt, the most moderate and anti-Communist of the groups so listed. The list itself would not last long thereafter. The witch-hunting mechanisms were beginning to be dismantled.

The investigation by Army Intelligence in preparation for this "trial" led to a large volume of communications between Army Intelligence and the FBI. My FBI file was forwarded to the army, and the army's file of almost three hundred pages was placed in my FBI file.

It was in this period that a shift took place in my FBI files. The heading changed from "Subject: Young Socialist League, Internal Security—ISL" to "Subject: Socialist Workers Party, IS-SWP." The watch continued.

The YSL held a national convention in late June devoted exclusively to our faction fight. The convention took place in the old hall at 114 West 14th Street. It was open to the "public," which did not flock to the event. We had no problem of overcrowding even though all the New York membership attended as well as delegates from out of town. Sitting in the back of the hall in the visitors' section was Murry Weiss of the SWP. Max Shachtman sat down beside him and together they watched "their youth" fighting it out. It was a kind of Lilliputian repeat of the 1940 debate. As Murry reported to me the next day, at one point he turned to Max and said, "Well you have gone and done it Max. You have really crossed the Rubicon this time." Shachtman chuckled and answered, "I have crossed the Rubicon so many times in the pages of the *Militant* that I have gotten seasick!"

The convention was an anticlimax; we had discussed the issues so thoroughly for more than a year that there was little new to add. Although the YSL/ISL leadership was determined to expel us, it couldn't because it had not quite made up its mind how to do it. So the convention ended without accomplishing anything more than a formal endorsement of the majority's line.

The 1957 Young Socialist League Convention did not go unnoticed by the FBI. A photographic surveillance was carried out and eight rolls of film taken. Each photo was sent to agents around the country for identification. At that time the Independent Socialist League was in the process of being removed from the Attorney General's List; the YSL was never placed on that list.

The expulsion came on Labor Day of 1957. I remember we were scattered at that moment; I was with wife and child at my father-in-law's farm in New Hampshire. We received notification by mail, and when we all got back to New York City we dashed off our answer to the expulsion. The grounds was our participation in a joint regroupment forum series with the SWP youth and independents during that summer. The expulsion was even more anticlimactic than the convention. We and the SWP youth were already well along in preparing the first issue of our paper and if we hadn't been expelled when we were, it would have been most embarrassing. The expulsion was very much like a divorce arranged after each party was already living with different partners.

AND SO IT CAME TO PASS

Shachtman's entry into the Socialist Party did not proceeded smoothly due to resistance on the part of the SP leadership. In the meantime, to use Hal Draper's words, the Shachtmanites' politics had to be "bent, fitted, filed, rubbed, carved, trimmed or cold-storaged so as to ingratiate us as good dogs with the SP right wing."[32] The merger was finally agreed to in the fall of 1958.[33] Once inside, the Shachtman group's superior theoretical and political training brought them immediately into the leadership of their new host party. Simultaneously, the group traveled so far to the right politically that it shifted rightward the position of the Socialist Party. This was expressed most sharply in the Socialist Party's subsequent abandonment of any independent political strategy and its support of the Democratic Party.[34]

In time divisions developed among the Shachtmanites inside their new home. One group associated with Hal Draper broke away to form the Independent Socialists (IS), a group that later played a role in the Peace and Freedom Party and the Teamsters Union. The IS (which has since gone through a number of splits) represented a return, in a New Left atmosphere, to the more radical roots of the Shachtman group.[35] The rest of the Shachtmanites, divided amongst themselves, later caused a split in the Socialist Party over which factions within the Democratic Party and the AFL-CIO they should support. A group of virulent anti-Communists around Shachtman supported Albert Shanker of the American Federation of Teachers and the mainstream and conservative Democrats such as Senator Henry Jackson of Washington. They called their group the Social Democrats USA. Another younger group around Mike Harrington supported the McGovern wing of the Democratic Party and the more liberal union leaders like Victor Gotbaum. Harrington formed the Democratic Socialist Organizing Committee (DSOC), which then merged with the New-Left New American Movement (NAM) to form the Democratic Socialists of America.[36]

How do I now assess the Shachtman episode in the life of the American Left? As I thing back over my experiences with the Shachtmanites, I find I hold two quite contradictory assessments. There was something wonderfully *maverick* about them. They dared to look at the leaders of the Russian Revolution critically. They accepted a theoretical heritage and yet questioned it. This gave the group a life that I found sorely missing in my later travels among the more "orthodox" Trotskyists. The Shachtmanites were right in their insistence on seeing socialism as an extension of democracy. This linkage is still far too weak in leftist circles today. And they didn't do too bad a job of practicing what they preached in their internal life, as I found out in the course of my travels within other trends of Trotskyism.

But there was a side of Shachtmanism that I was most happy to abandon after 1956. The Shachtmanites were so embittered by anti-Communism that they failed to see human progress when that progress took an impure form. Their worldview was consistent with George Orwell's *1984*, Hannah Arendt's *Origins of Totalitarianism*, or James Burnham's *Managerial Revolution*. "The World According to Shachtman" was a world swiftly falling under the iron heel of totalitarian, bureaucratic slaveholders. The only force resisting this historic sweep of the "Stalinist Hordes" was the embattled and, of course, far-from-perfect Western democracies. Shachtman was the original theorist of the Evil Empire.

It is difficult now to recapture the atmosphere within the ISL/YSL at that time, but that *was* the way Max and his friends really thought. We left-wing Shachtmanites were even more pessimistic about the prospects for socialism, for we saw no hope in the West. Sometimes I wonder why we bothered with politics at all. I suppose each of us, underneath, had a martyr complex. We envisioned ourselves alone in the world, wandering in a forest repeating the words of a novel we had committed to memory.

Great revolutions did sweep the postwar world, and humanity is better off for them. But it is possible to recognize the great changes in China, in Cuba, in Vietnam, without at the same time accepting these societies as they are, without abandoning that vital linkage between socialism and democracy to which Shachtman and his friends made such a positive contribution.

Notes

1. Gordon became an important staff person in the New York chapter of the American Civil Liberties Union. This certainly fitted well with his organizational skills and his sincere dedication to democracy. Later he became active in the Democratic Socialists of America.
2. *The Roots of American Communism* (New York: The Viking Press, 1957); *American Communism and Soviet Russia* (New York: The Viking Press, 1960); *Castro's Revolution: Myths and Realities* (New York: The Viking Press, 1962); *Castroism: Theory and Practice* (New York: The Viking Press, 1965).
3. *Karl Marx's Theory of Revolution,* volume 1: *State and Bureaucracy* (New York: Monthly Review Press, 1977); volume 2: *The Politics of Social Classes* (New York: Monthly Review Press, 1978); volume 3: *The "Dictatorship of the Proletariat"* (New York: Monthly Review Press, 1986).
4. Since the Shachtmanites, at least in theory, rejected support of any sort for either the American camp, which they considered capitalist and imperialist, or the Russian camp, which they considered bureaucratic collectivist and equally imperialist, they sought a "third camp" they could support. This camp was seen as made up of the working class of all nations and the colonial revolution. It was rare indeed in this period to find these forces expressing themselves independently of the American-Russian confrontation.
5. For more information on these groups, see Eric R. Wolf, *Peasant Wars of the Twentieth Century* (New York: Harper & Row, 1969), pp. 193ff.
6. Frank Donner, *The Age of Surveillance* (New York: Vintage Books, 1981), pp. 162ff. Material in italics is based on my FBI files furnished under a Freedom of Information Act request. So far I have received material from a file of 8,049 pages. Over 90 percent of the material furnished to me is blacked out.
7. Mike Shute remained active in Shachtmanite politics, in the left of YPSL, and then in the early days of the Independent Socialists, dropping out in the late 1960s.
8. (New York, 1962).
9. In 1937, Carter had written an article, along with James Burnham, questioning Trotsky's theory of the Soviet Union.
10. Robert J. Alexander has produced an exhaustive (also exhausting!) and generally quite accurate account of world Trotskyism encompassing some 1,125 pages of small type: *International Trotskyism 1929–1985* (Durham, NC: Duke University Press, 1991).
11. For my views now, see "The Two Souls of Leninism," *Against the Current* 4/5 (Detroit, September/October 1986), pp. 43–47. See also Sam Farber, *Before Stalinism* (London: Verso, 1990), as well as my comment on that book in *Against the Current* 36, 38 (Detroit, January/February 1992, and May/June 1992).
12. Between 1929 and 1934 Stalin imposed a super-radical policy on his interna-

tional followers. This was rather bewildering to the Trotskyists, who were forced to make some telling moderate criticisms of Communist strategy, particularly in urging a united front with the Social Democrats in Germany against Hitler. But on the whole Trotskyists have been left critics of Stalinism.

13. James P. Cannon, *The History of American Trotskyism* (New York: Pioneer Publishers, 1944), pp. 1–59. Theodore Draper, *American Communism and Soviet Russia* (New York: The Viking Press, 1960), pp. 357–76.
14. Farrell Dobbs, *Teamster Power; Teamster Rebellion; Teamster Politics; Teamster Bureaucracy* (New York: Monad Press, 1972, 1974, 1975, 1977).
15. Alan Wald has written some very worthwhile material on this layer. *James T. Farrell, The Revolutionary Socialist Years* (New York: New York University Press, 1978); *The Revolutionary Imagination: The Poetry and Politics of John Wheelwright and Sherry Mangan* (Chapel Hill, NC: University of North Carolina Press, 1983); *The New York Intellectuals* (Chapel Hill, NC: University of North Carolina Press, 1987).
16. For Trotsky's side of the dispute see *In Defense of Marxism* (New York: Pioneer Publishers, 1942). For Shachtman's views see Leon Trotsky, *The New Course* and Max Shachtman, *The Struggle for the New Course* (published together, New York: New International Publishing Company, 1943). I wrote on the matter twice: *What Makes Shachtman Run?* (New York: privately published, 1957), pp. 6–8, and *The Struggle for Marxism in the United States* (New York: Labor Publications, 1971), pp. 48ff.
17. The term was coined by Bruno Rizzi, an obscure Italian dissident follower of Trotsky's. See Adam Westoby's fascinating introduction to the first English edition of Rizzi's work: *The Bureaucratization of the World* (New York: Tavistock Publications, 1985).
18. Robert Cummings, "Dwight MacDonald in the 1940s," *New Politics* (New York, Summer 1986).
19. One element in particular was a vision of a worldwide struggle for democracy as well as their theoretical view of the Soviet countries. See Sidney Blumenthal, *The Rise of the Counter-Establishment* (New York, 1986).
20. I should explain what the term "social democrat" meant to us then. Social democrats were the right-wing socialists who accepted capitalism in practice, seeking to reform it rather than overthrow it. We were all schooled to the Great Betrayal of the Second International in 1914–1917, when its constituent parties lined up in support of their respective capitalist ruling classes in World War I. It was not difficult to draw parallels to socialist organizations in the United States in the 1950s who found what we considered American imperialism to be the lesser evil.
21. The League for a Revolutionary Party.
22. George Rawick taught for many years at Washington University in St. Louis. In later years he became very interested in the ideas of the black revolutionary and former Trotskyist C. L. R. James. Rawick died in July 1990.
23. Gerry Healy was a leading British Trotskyist.
24. For instance, see Melvin J. Lasky, ed., *The Hungarian Revolution: A White Book* (New York: Frederick A. Praeger, 1957), and Andy Anderson, *Hungary 56* (Bromley, England: Solidarity, 1964).
25. Peter Fryer, *Hungarian Tragedy* (London: New Park Publications, 1956, reissued in 1986).
26. See Shane Mage, "Lessons of the Recent NEC Meeting, Part 1," in *Which*

Road for Socialist Youth? (Berkeley: Young Socialist Alliance, 1959).

27. I had come over to the views of the SWP on the nature of the Soviet Union. My two main collaborators in the minority held different views. Shane Mage viewed the USSR as a state capitalist country; James Robertson remained an orthodox Shachtmanite.
28. James P. Cannon, the founder of American Trotskyism, was at the time the National Chairman of the SWP. He was living on the West Coast, leaving, by and large, the active running of the group to Farrell Dobbs, who was National Secretary.
29. Eric Thomas Chester, *Socialists and the Ballot Box* (New York: Praeger Publishers, 1985), p. 124.
30. Muste led a group called the American Workers Party, whose members had led the Toledo Autolite strike in 1934. The group fused with the Trotskyists in 1934. In 1936 Muste supported a group that opposed the entry of the Trotskyists into the Socialist Party and left the Trotskyists with that group. In the 1950s Muste was a prominent pacifist affiliated with the Fellowship of Reconciliation. During the Vietnam War he played a very important role in building united demonstrations against the war.
31. Tim Wohlforth, "The Strange Case of the American Forum," in *Which Road*, pp. 24ff.
32. Ibid., p. 34.
33. Chester, *Socialists and the Ballot Box*, p. 125.
34. This was opposed by a group around David McReynolds, which later broke away to form its own Socialist Party.
35. It produced, in addition to the IS, the International Socialist Organization (ISO); the Revolutionary Socialist League (RSL); Revolutionary Marxist Committee (RMC), which joined the SWP; Workers Power (fused with an ex-SWP group, Socialist Unity, and the IS to form Solidarity); League for a Revolutionary Party (Sy Landy); and a remnant of the Independent Socialist Clubs around Hal Draper.
36. Mike Harrington died in the fall of 1989, after battling cancer for several years. His last book, which expresses his political outlook at the time of his death, is *Socialism Past and Future* (New York: Little, Brown, 1989).

3

The Birth of the Young Socialist Alliance

REGROUPING THE YOUTH

We started on our new political life with a great deal of enthusiasm. Gone was the gloom of my days in the YSL in 1955 and 1956. We could sense the beginnings of a change in the political climate in the country. Certainly there was ferment and opportunity enough within the Left. We were determined to make every effort to create out of this ferment a strong beginning for a new socialist youth movement. We were at that moment in the center of it all and had no serious rivals. Our former comrades in the YSL were hamstrung, oriented as they were to unification with the Socialist Party (which had not yet decided to let them in). The Communist Party youth simply did not exist as an organized body. It would take several years for the Communist Party to reassemble a youth organization.

We were also involved in another level of regroupment—the fusion of our left-wing Shachtmanite group with our friends in the Trotskyist mainstream. This was not a simple process, and I guess, in a way, we never really succeeded at it. To begin with, when we started our collaboration, the Socialist Workers Party had no youth organization. James P. Cannon and the rest of the leadership had erroneously concluded from their split in 1940 with Shachtman, who had taken most of the youth, that a youth organization was a dangerous thing to have around, as it could develop "petty bourgeois" deviations. Only workers were to be trusted. Faced with our existence, the new possibilities among youth in the Communist Party's orbit, the lack of opportunities on an adult level, and an aging cadre, the party leadership decided to create a youth group.

In New York in the spring of 1957 the SWP organized a group called the American Youth for Socialism (AYS), made up of somewhat elderly "youth" and one or two children of party members. Its main purpose was to collaborate with our left-wing faction within the YSL. It was headed by Bert Wainer (Deck), a competent fellow who looked older than his actual mid-thirties. (In those days being a "youth" was a party assignment not necessarily dependent on how old the assignee was.) Helping Wainer out was James Lambrecht, who was not only still in his twenties but had a young look and temperament. Also in the group was Nora Roberts, daughter of *Militant* editor Dan Roberts. Nora was a high-school student and probably not more than fifteen at the time. We were soon joined by Sherry Finer, who was the youngest of three daughters of Farrell Dobbs, National Secretary of the SWP. In fact, considering the lack of youth work on the part of the SWP for so many years, party children made up no small proportion of the new youth groups around the country.

Our faction of the YSL met in common with the AYS comrades over the summer of 1957. Together we organized a rather successful public forum series that led, as already noted, to our expulsion from the YSL. That fall we transformed the AYS/ex-YSL grouping into the New York Young Socialist Alliance (YSA).

Our first common project after the forum series was a monthly newspaper, the *Young Socialist*. I was its first editor. Ours was the only radical youth publication in the country at the time, and it made an impact. It was the center around which we would organize our distinctive youth organization. But this was no easy task. First we had to somehow become a part of the ferment taking place around the Communist Party.

The FBI paid very close attention to our new organization: "For the information of the Bureau and interested offices the NYO is currently preparing a report on captioned organization, incorporating all pertinent information previously received and handled under the caption 'Young Socialist Forum; IS-SWP.' This action is being taken inasmuch as information is available disclosing a fusion of the American Youth for Socialism, the left-wing caucus of the YSL, and other groups into the formation of the Young Socialist Forum (YSF) and subsequently a clear transition of the YSF to the Young Socialist Alliance, a duly constituted organization."

That fall we saw our first opening. An important group of youth from the Communist Party milieu began to come around and join us in the YSA.

Their leader was Steve Max, who brought with him into the YSA about a dozen young people, largely high-school students. Steve was the son of Alan Max, the foreign editor of the *Daily Worker* and the coleader, with John Gates, of the liberal wing of the Communist Party. Steve was well aware that he was dealing with Trotskyists, and it took a tremendous amount of discussion—here Jim Lambrecht in particular played a critical role—to convince him and his friends to join us. Steve, like his father, had many questions about the Soviet invasion of Hungary and about democracy within the USSR. He also was critical of the Communist Party's internal rigidity. Yet, in most other respects, he maintained views quite close to the party. Most important was his support for *realignment*—the strategy of working in the Democratic Party to coalesce labor, liberal, and minority forces into an eventual new "progressive" party.

The YSA was a wonderful, diverse, throbbing, political mess. We picnicked with guitars and the *People's Song Book* on Orchard Beach in the Bronx, held chaotic branch meetings, barely collected dues, and shared a common vision of a very large national youth movement. Our comrades in other cities were attempting—generally not as successfully—to do what we were doing in New York. Independent campus clubs of former Communist Party youth members sprouted, and we tried to bring them in too. We called this calliope of forces the "IBM clubs," which stood for "independent," "broad," and "militant." As youth groups go, we were certainly independent and broad, but no one had a very clear idea of what "militant" meant.

One independent soul in our milieu, Martin Wilner, deserves special mention. Marty first showed up at one of our summer forums in 1957 and immediately expressed interest in socialism and our project. He was a bit older than most of our new people, but we could not be choosy. Soon Marty was very active in our movement. He had no strong political views but was interested in all classes on socialism. He pitched in and became our first treasurer. The problem was that he did not like to collect dues, which is not a good attribute in a treasurer. Marty made up for it by giving generously of his own resources. When we had a party Marty graciously supplied all the booze, telling us that his father owned a bar. Above all, he had a great sense of humor and added much to the life of our little group.

He even wrote a short article for the *Young Socialist* subtitled "I Cover Regroupment."[1] It was a humorous piece about selling papers at a meeting and how he tried to straighten out a confused cop about all the factions that showed up.

> "How can you tell them apart?" asked the people's protector.
> "Oh, that takes years," I replied proudly.
> "Could you maybe give me a five-minute capsule version?" said he

I laughed condescendingly.

"By the way," said the officer, "who are you?"

I am ashamed to admit that I was tempted to give him a silver bullet or reply, "Some folks know me as the Blue Beetle," but I fought off these impulses and said:

"Oh, just a casual observer of the American scene"—and faded into the night.

Marty Wilner, I learned some years later, was an FBI agent. This is not just conjecture on my part, since the fellow "came in from the cold," as the expression goes. Wilner was the key government witness in an effort to add the DuBois Clubs to the Attorney General's List of Subversive Organizations.

The high point of our youth regroupment work was a national youth conference we held in Chicago on February 1 and 2, 1958. There were 150 young people in attendance representing groups in some sixteen cities and about a dozen campuses. We claimed that the conference represented about five hundred youth, which was probably an exaggeration. But it was not a bad turnout for a group that had split from the YSL with about thirty people.

At the same time, the conference also reflected serious weaknesses in our regroupment efforts. The Communist Party exerted great pressure to prevent people under their influence from attending. I remember that originally the daughter of Gil Green, the jailed Communist Party leader, was scheduled to speak on his behalf, but she withdrew at the last minute. The conference did not lack a broad focus, but it was incapable of acting in a politically coherent way. It passed only resolutions about civil liberties and made no mention of the Hungarian Revolution and democracy in the USSR. I spoke for the *Young Socialist*, which had a reasonably clear position on Soviet democracy, but we did not feel the time was right to get an endorsement from the conference for the paper or to take any other serious step in the direction of consolidating a national youth movement.

The Chicago FBI office was in charge of watching our conference: "enclosed ten photos of individuals who were to have attended the Midwest Conference for Youth in Chicago on 2/1–2/58.

"These photos were exhibited to the indicated informants who have furnished reliable information in the past. Identifications made by these informants, and their comments, if any, are set forth with the location of the original information in Chicago Office files."

Our troubles had only begun. The CP had been covertly waging a Trotsky-baiting campaign against us for some time. This had its effect on Steve Max and his supporters within the New York YSA. This group began to differentiate itself from the SWP/Ex-YSL grouping, and we could sense the beginnings of factionalism. Their mood also reflected a consolidation of political thinking in the Gates wing of Communists and former Communists. The Gatesites had said about all they intended to say critical of the Soviet Union and were determined to uphold the realignment politics they shared with the Fosterites.[2] They were not moving any closer to Trotskyism.

For a while the political struggle took on an almost guerrilla character. We added representatives of the Max group to the editorial board of the *Young Socialist* to the point where they had almost half of the members. We were so anxious to win over the Maxites that we were conciliatory with them on editorial policy. About the only way an anti-Stalinist line got into the *Young Socialist* was through little boxes I would drop in just before the paper went to press.

Matters finally came to a head at a special meeting of the editorial board called to discuss the board's composition. Representing our faction were Bert Deck, Jim Lambrecht, Shane Mage, and I. We met beforehand with Tom Kerry, National Organization Secretary of the SWP. I stressed that a confrontation was unavoidable and that the *Young Socialist* had to remain essentially under Trotskyist control. Tom settled the matter in a very direct, if not too subtle fashion, no doubt learned in years of trade union work: "The paper is our possession and we are not about to give it away." Steve Max lost the vote and walked out of the organization.[3]

Our regroupment work did not end with the departure of Max, as we were able to discover a more receptive political arena. The initiative this time came from the SWP. They had discovered some interested supporters of the weekly the *National Guardian*, which was published by former members of the American Labor Party and the Progressive Party. In 1952, the Progressive Party ran the San Francisco labor lawyer Vincent Hallinan for president of the United States. The Communist Party, already moving to reintegrate its members into the Democratic Party, gave only lukewarm support to this campaign. The *Guardian* group's political disaffection with the CP began as a result, a process sped up by the events of the Hungarian Revolution, particularly the murder of Imre Nagy. We were able to organize a new party, the Independent Socialist Party, which ran Corliss Lamont for United States senator and John T. McManus of the *Guardian* for governor of New York State in the November 1958 elections. Lamont was a millionaire with a "progressive" political orientation and an interest in civil liberties and philosophy. He helped finance the campaign.

On October 10, 1957, the YSA held an election rally in support of the new party attended by 190 people, according to the FBI's count. I was the first speaker: "WOHLFORTH stressed the importance of the various socialist elements making a solid vote against the capitalist candidates in the forthcoming elections. He stated that this would be the first step towards the eventual formation of a labor party."

Lamont got 45,000 votes, a fair number considering the conservatism and McCarthyite atmosphere of the time. The young people attracted to the campaign were more interested in Trotskyism than was the Steve Max crowd. I believe their commitment to independent socialist political action brought them closer to us than were those former Communists who sought integration into American liberalism and the Democratic Party.

I did my best to implement party policy. This led me to take a leave of absence as editor of the *Young Socialist* and to work on the *National Guardian* staff for two months. I carried out technical tasks and wrote a column each week made up of little tidbits of information. We held weekly staff discussions on editorial content and policy, which I was free to participate in. Even though I had many political differences with the *Guardian* staff, I didn't raise them too often. I recognized that it was their paper, and I didn't want to be disruptive. I must say, they were a pleasant group of people to work with. I had a lot of respect for Jim Aronson, the editor, who for years had maintained political differences with the Communist Party. While I was there he wrote a very strong editorial condemning the Soviets for executing Imre Nagy, the dissident Hungarian Communist.

The staff was mainly composed of professional journalists who had worked on the big dailies or wire services and who had taken huge wage cuts to work for a paper they believed in. There was one fellow—he wrote occasionally on labor issues and edited and marked up all copy—who looked like a character right out of the old play and movie *Front Page*. I sat next to him and noticed that every now and then he opened a desk drawer, took out a flask, and poured himself a shot of whiskey. He was an excellent copy editor and never appeared in the slightest way drunk. I remember I was paid $75 a week, which for me was a raise over the $43.75 I received to put out the *Young Socialist*. All *Guardian* staffers got the same pay. In the 1960s, that generation left the paper and their younger replacements played an important role in what was to become the Maoist New Communist Movement.

"A telephone call by a Special Agent of the FBI on May 28, 1958, to the offices of the 'National Guardian,' Weekly Guardian Associates, 197 East Fourth Street, New York City, ascertained that subject was employed by the above publication at that time."

The regroupment process was not a total failure, but it certainly did not come out as we first thought it would. We won hardly any new recruits directly from the Communist Party. I do not believe this was because of any big mistakes we made; it reflected more the unhealthy nature of the American Communist Party. In England, hundreds of Communist Party intellectuals, including some of considerable stature, joined various Trotskyist groups or started independent journals like *New Left Review*. This process formed the intellectual framework for the new radicalism of the 1960s. The result was that the British New Left in the 1960s took on more of a Trotskyist coloration than the American New Left. They also had and still have an important impact on the left wing of the British Labour Party. The American Communist Party largely lacked an intellectual Marxist layer. To a far greater extent than in England, the crisis of Stalinism here simply produced the desertion of thousands from leftist politics of any fashion.

I believe this crisis also affected the evolution of the young radicals of the 1960s. These young leftists had little or no direct connection with the Communist Party crisis of the 1950s. Many of these New Lefters came from the homes of former Communist Party members but had no particular loyalty to the Communist Party. Their intellectual inspiration came primarily from the British New Left journals or from émigré professors such as Herbert Marcuse. Only a minority of these New Lefters were attracted to Trotskyism; a much larger group experimented with Maoist versions of Stalinism in the early 1970s.

On the Road for Socialism

During the spring of 1958, without abandoning our regroupment work, we began to pay attention to the American campuses. We had learned very well in the YSL that the vitality of any youth organization depended on its base among college and high-school students. Our first step was direct, aggressive propaganda. We distributed or sold our paper on campuses, and we held street meetings in front of schools, expounding our socialist views.

These actions immediately brought us into conflict with various regulations and police practices established in the McCarthy period. The result was a series of free-speech fights that helped to unravel McCarthyism as well as to establish the reputation of the *Young Socialist.*

At the Boulder campus of the University of Colorado, the authorities banned the *Young Socialist.* We challenged the ban at a Board of Regents meeting, and, with the support of the Colorado branch of the American Civil Liberties Union and the campus student newspaper, we won our case. In Detroit, comrades distributed the *Young Socialist* at the Ann Arbor campus of the University of Michigan. Photographers showed up from the "red squad" of the Detroit police department, and they were promptly surrounded by irate students supporting our right to free speech without harassment. The *Michigan Daily* wrote an editorial supporting us, entitled "Let a Thousand Socialists Bloom." In New York City our comrades held a street-corner meeting in front of the Bronx High School of Science and were arrested by the police. We returned to the scene armed with documents from the ACLU. Dick DeHaan,[4] a maverick independent member of the YSA who loved a civil liberties fight, got up on our little soapbox and began speaking: "We are here to test and enforce the Constitutional guarantees of freedom of speech and assembly." He was dragged off to the police station. After some *New York Post* articles and further complaints to the police department by the American Civil Liberties Union and the Emergency Civil Liberties Committee, we returned. This time Jim Lambrecht addressed a crowd of three hundred high-school students while Jim Robertson, who was in town from the West Coast, held the American flag. About twenty cops watched but did not intervene. We had won our civil liberties. Jim never forgave me for publicizing the fact that he was holding the American flag.[5]

I went on a nationwide tour of forty-five college campuses in the fall of 1958. It was the biggest campus tour I would ever make, and it proved to be a huge success, establishing the Young Socialist Alliance as the most important socialist youth group in the country. More than that, it made a contribution to establishing the right of socialists to be heard on campuses and in so doing blazed a trail for the next stage of 1960s student radicals.

"A pretext telephone call to subject's last reported residence by a Special Agent of the Federal Bureau of Investigation (FBI) on

October 30, 1958, ascertained from an individual, who identified herself as subject's wife, that subject resided at 118 West 90th Street, New York City, but that he was 'on tour' and would return to this address in early December, 1958."

The tour started on the West Coast. I flew into Los Angeles and was met at the airport by Carl Feingold, the SWP branch organizer, and by Jack Jersawitz (Arnold), who was my Los Angeles organizer. Jack was quite a character. Originally a New Yorker, Jack was a bit overweight and had a heavy beard. Jack had spirit, he had loyalty, and he was creative when it came to things mechanical and electrical. I discovered the latter characteristic when we entered party headquarters, which was on the second floor of a commercial building in one of the many nondescript Los Angeles neighborhoods. The minute we opened the door an auto started honking, but the sound wasn't coming from the street. It seemed to be coming from the roof, a strange place, even in Los Angeles, to hear car noises. Jack dashed in ahead of us looking for the switch to turn off what turned out to be a homemade alarm system. Jack deeply believed in security and had recently devoted his energies to safeguarding the headquarters.

Jack took me upstairs to inspect his latest invention, which he viewed proudly as key to my whole Los Angeles–area tour. It was a portable collapsible soapbox. I need to explain briefly the history of the soapbox technology in order for the reader to grasp the magnitude of Jack's breakthrough. Originally a soapbox was a wooden box used to deliver unwrapped bars of laundry soap to small stores in early twentieth-century America. The combination of the advent of supermarkets and new cardboard packaging had led to the demise of the wooden soapbox, while the need for a portable speaking platform for socialists persisted. As an interim solution we used boxes designed to deliver milk cartons, which were, many times, carelessly left stacked outside closed stores. Jack's invention was a radical leap in design comparable, in its own field, to the portable personal computer. His soapbox was a light four-sided frame held together by hinges. A special platform was placed on top when the frame was unfolded. His contraption was higher and larger than the traditional soapbox while being completely portable. Thus it could fit easily into the back seat of a car or could be picked up and carried should it become best to speedily conclude an oration and run for it. Of course, my tour might have gone even better if

Jack had spent more time arranging indoor meetings than designing the best technology for unscheduled outdoor meetings.

The first stop on my tour was the University of Southern California (USC). Jack and I threw his invention in the back of his old car, and we rumbled down the freeway. Exactly why he decided to start out our socialist soapboxing at one of California's most expensive and conservative institutions, I do not know. I learned later that key members of the Watergate gang, John Erlichman and H. R. Haldeman, were attending USC at that time, heading up the Young Americans for Freedom campus branch. I was dressed most conservatively—as was my style in those days—with a gray suit, white shirt, narrow tie, and close-cropped hair. My idea was to defy the wild image people then had of radicals. The meeting went uneventfully, drawing a small crowd with which I was able to have a good back-and-forth discussion. We made the front page of the *Daily Trojan* the next day, which no doubt must have encouraged Erlichman and Haldeman to increase their vigilance against the Left. Our next stop was Los Angeles City College, a two-year school with a more proletarian student body. We attracted around 250 students, and the discussion went on for some two-and-a-half hours. It was a bit of a strain, with traditional heckling, but an exhilarating experience nonetheless.

The next day Jack had actually gotten me a *room* at UCLA so that I addressed, under more comfortable conditions, 150 students on "Marxism: Science or Religion?" All in all the Los Angeles tour was successful. Carl Feingold, the Los Angeles party organizer who had met me at the plane with Jack, was very supportive of our youth work. This was very helpful, as Carl had the ear of the old party founder, the still influential Jim Cannon. Carl led a branch of ninety party members, many of them quite old—people who had come to the West Coast as a kind of political and personal retirement.

The next stop on my tour was the San Francisco Bay Area. There my old YSL buddy Jim Robertson was in charge. The Bay Area comrades, somehow or other, had wangled an invitation for me to speak at the University of Santa Clara, a Jesuit institution. I didn't just speak there; I was sponsored by the university itself through a student forum committee. The topic they chose from my tour brochure was "Marxism: Science or Religion?" We all piled into the one vehicle available to our comrades, an old Chevy with bald tires and stuffing coming out of the seats. Two flat tires later we made it down Route 101 to the sumptuous Santa Clara campus. We were greeted by a small delegation of students—all males in those days—in suits and ties and exceedingly polite and solicitous.

They took us on a tour of the campus, which to me, an Easterner, was downright exotic (today it is in the center of Silicon Valley, surrounded on all sides by high-tech facilities). We started out in the gardens and were shown a century plant celebrating its hundredth year of life with a beautiful bloom. Then on we went to look at the old Spanish mission. I began to feel I was being softened up a bit so that the power of tradition and perhaps even God himself could be brought to bear on my errant Marxist soul. I walked into the hushed, dimly lit interior of the mission and went toward the altar to get a better look. Then I tripped on a cobblestone and fell prostrate right in front of the altar. Jim Robertson began laughing hysterically and our Jesuit guides passed knowing glances among themselves.

Next came the formal dinner of the forum group. The fellow next to me, making light mealtime conversation, asked me if I believed in God. I answered no; he gulped, moved his chair a little bit away, and asked me if I believed in heaven and hell. I answered a very meek no, again hoping others at the table were not listening in on us. Then he moved on to his real point, saying with a trembling voice, "If I did not believe in hell I do not think I could control myself!" I did not inquire as to what wild misadventures he had been dreaming about.

I spoke to a crowd of over three hundred students, and the speech went very well. I was impressed by several of the Jesuit fathers who had been active in California agricultural workers' struggles and who spoke from a strongly moralistic Christian socialist outlook. I was informed that I was the first Marxist and atheist to speak at the college since its founding one hundred years earlier. We didn't win over any recruits that night but I, for one, will never forget the evening.

After visiting the Bay Area I headed up the coast to Portland, Oregon. We had no branch in Portland at the time, so I had to make my own way to the Reed College campus, where my meeting was sponsored by the FOCUS Club. This club, which had been started ten years earlier as a branch of the Young Progressives, was still led by students from "progressive" families. Politically the group was close in outlook to the Wisconsin Socialist Club, New Lefters certainly willing to listen to my views. The club was headed by a very attractive young lady from Mill Valley, in fashionable Marin County, who was writing a senior thesis on Bertolt Brecht. We attracted an audience of one hundred on a campus of six hundred students, which was not too bad.

Vancouver was interesting. It was my first experience with what is known in the Trotskyist movement as *deep entry*. The idea goes something like this: The mass of workers in a particular country have decided to support and participate in a reformist socialist party. We Trotskyists, standing outside their chosen party, have been unable to persuade them to join our small group. Why not, Trotsky proposed in the 1930s, join them if they would not join us, removing an organizational barrier to our political influence over these workers? Sometimes Trotskyists joined mass reformist parties while maintaining outside them a public press and some independent activity. This was considered a *shallow entry*. When Trotskyists completely abandoned any independent activity, integrating themselves fully in a mass party and hoping for a political differentiation to occur within that party over the long run, then the entry was *deep*.

My tour in Vancouver was sponsored by the Whitney group, which practiced an entry so deep I seem to be the only one who has ever heard of them. They were, I must say, a very sweet bunch of people. The object of their entry was the Cooperative Commonwealth Federation (CCF), a Canadian social democratic group that, a few years later and with the support of the Canadian labor movement, emerged as the New Democratic Party (NDP). At the time the CCF controlled the provincial government in Saskatchewan and had considerable influence throughout western Canada.

I stayed in the modest home of the Whitneys, who represented a good one-third of the group. I was struck by the amount of CCF literature around the place, especially raffle tickets. Mass social democratic parties appear to have a lot of raffles. The Whitneys arranged for me to address the Stanley Park Club of the CCF, and the thirty-or-so middle-aged members warmly greeted my presentation. Clearly the CCF was in great need of new young blood. I suspect today the Whitneys, if they are still alive (they were middle-aged then, as I am now), are attending meetings of the Stanley Park Club of the NDP and selling raffle tickets at the old-age center. They, like many practitioners of deep entry during a conservative period who take a circuitous road to socialism, became so absorbed with the trip that they lost interest in what was supposed to lie at the end of the road. Were they so wrong? Have we sect-builders of the 1970s done more or less than they for humanity?

After visiting Vancouver, I pushed on into the Midwest. My first stop was the Twin Cities. I knew the working-class history of Minneapolis very well. It was in Minneapolis in 1934 that we Trotskyists led a Teamsters' strike—a mass militant strike quite unlike labor struggles today. We had our own kitchen, a ladies' auxiliary, mass picket lines, and a "flying" squad armed with baseball bats to defend the union from attack. At the "Battle of Deputies Run" the union men had routed armed deputies and won the strike.[6] But that was 1934. The Twin Cities SWP branch in 1958 was made up of old working-class comrades, dispirited, living on memories, and doing precious little. But could it be otherwise? Yesterday's revolutionaries are rarely able to make a successful transition into a new period.

What passed for a "youth" group in Minneapolis reflected this situation of dormancy. The party youth group was headed by Tom Leonard, a nice enough fellow who believed that workers should say as little as possible but under all circumstances vote correctly in branch meetings. Since he considered himself a worker, he so acted. Yet, either from party loyalty or possible unverbalized personal conviction, Tom did his best to get some youth activity started in the area. He did not get much help from his fellow "youth," children of old party members whose names read like an honor roll of the Minneapolis labor movement of two decades earlier. These young people, who struck me as being older in some ways than their parents, did not really believe "youth work" was quite the proper thing for "real Bolsheviks" to do. The proper thing, it seemed, was to pay party dues while getting a degree at the university. The children of radical workers were entering the middle class just as were the millions who were raised in white diapers.

Detroit was a different story. Here was an area where the SWP had actually organized a youth group prior to the YSL's recruitment. They had started a club at Wayne State University and published a quite presentable mimeographed magazine. This work was led by Bob Himmel and Evelyn Sell. Evelyn Sell had been a supporter of the little group in the party led by Art Fox.[7] She had a talent for writing and helped a lot with the *Young Socialist*. Bob Himmel, a clean-cut fellow, was a top-notch organizer, speaker, and all-around political person. The Detroit party branch was headed by Ed Shaw, another strong, silent, worker type. Ed and his wife, Rita, gave me a dinner of corn bread and chicken wings; it was actually quite good.

Cleveland was the high point of the Midwestern segment of my tour. I stayed at the very comfortable home of the branch organizer, Jean Tussey (Simon), a heavyset middle-aged woman who had been a member of the printer's union, the International Typographical Union (ITU), for many years.

I arrived in Cleveland just a few days before the November 1958 elections. There was only one issue in Ohio that year: an attempt by business interests to pass a state "right-to-work"[8] proposition. The issue deeply affected the unions in this heavily industrialized and unionized state. As a result the trade unions went all out to mobilize their members against the proposal. The rank and file came out to campaign and the result was something to see. I went on a tour of Cleveland early election-day morning. There were union people giving out literature at just about every polling place. Union-organized taxi services ferried the elderly and sick to and from the polls. People greeted each other as "brother" and "sister." It was one of those rare times when you see American labor acting politically, independently, and in concert, with real rank-and-file participation. To me it showed the potential that a labor party could have in the United States. The right-to-work measure was roundly defeated in Ohio and four other states that year. It gave me hope.

I know now that the campaign in Cleveland was not the beginning of a new labor radicalization in the United States; it was a defensive reaction of a prosperous and institutionalized union movement, which was far stronger then than it is today. The next stage of radicalization in the country would occur largely outside the labor movement, in the poor black neighborhoods, north and south, as well as on the expanding university campuses. The "classical" 1930s model of radicalization was not to be repeated any more than the "classical" October Revolution model was to be repeated. I, and the others in our movement in that period, were classicists.

I summed up the campus situation quite soberly:

> One can notice the beginnings of political awakening on campus. Attendance at socialist meetings is larger than a year or two ago. The number of young people who are seriously considering a radical solution to the world's problems is on the increase. . . .
>
> The American student is by and large docile, apathetic and isolated from his fellow men. However, small but important currents of opposition can be noted. It is in these pockets of opposition, of life and critical thought, that the future of the American student can be seen.[9]

When I look back at our campus work in 1958, I am struck by the change it did represent from the depths of radical despair in the early 1950s. McCarthyism was losing its grip on the American mind, and small beginnings were being made among a new generation of students. The open advocacy of socialist ideas itself represented a blow to the witch-hunt and contributed to the next period of American radicalization. Our small group helped this process.

On Kisses and Sit-Ins

In the fall of 1958 the civil rights struggle in the South began to heat up. Young people took the lead in the struggle, beginning a process that would reshape the consciousness and militancy of the black struggle in America. A group of more militant black leaders, including Martin Luther King, Jr., and A. Philip Randolph, sponsored a youth march on Washington for October 25, 1958. Some ten thousand youth participated, most organized by the black churches. The New York YSA sent three carloads, and others joined us from Philadelphia and Baltimore. We got a warm response to our leaflets and the *Young Socialist*.

On April 18, 1959, the NAACP organized a follow-up youth march that attracted twenty-six thousand young people and trade unionists. We mobilized our people from as far away as Chicago and sold 450 papers. The demonstrators were not, by and large, middle-class college students but young people from the neighborhoods and the churches and the children of trade unionists, all mobilized primarily from the South. There were new stirrings in the country. The black militancy of the 1960s was in preparation.

The YSA was able to make its own contribution to the civil rights struggle that went beyond the *Young Socialist*. One day a young comrade of ours, Nora Roberts, noticed a small article in the *New York Times* reporting that two young black boys in Monroe, North Carolina, had been sent to a reformatory for kissing a white girl. Nora thought that there was a story here for our paper and that perhaps we could do something about the situation. So we raised some money and Nora went off to Monroe.

There she met Robert F. Williams, who was president of the local chapter of the NAACP. She discovered that two boys, Hanover Thompson, aged nine, and Fuzzy Simpson, eight, had played a game on the way home from school with a white girl of the same age, during which she kissed them on the cheek. For this "crime" they were sent to the Morrison Training School for Delinquent Boys in Hoffman, North Carolina. With the help of the SWP we hired Conrad Lynn, a radical black lawyer, to represent the two boys. We then organized a defense committee and started circulating petitions demanding the release of Hanover and Fuzzy. Nora wrote the story for the *National Guardian* as well as the *Young Socialist*, and we held a very successful press conference. We also organized a picket line in front of the United Nations.

Through this effort the case finally got some serious publicity in the press. Most significant, the foreign newspapers gave it a big play. In Rotterdam, Holland, fifteen thousand high-school students and teachers signed a petition that they sent to Eleanor Roosevelt, which she in turn forwarded to President Eisenhower. This kind of attention forced Governor Hodges to intervene and free the boys on February 13, 1959.[10]

This was not the end of our connection with Monroe, North Carolina; it was actually the beginning. It was through the Kiss Case that we and the world learned of Rob Williams. Rob, a native of Monroe, had worked in factories in the North and then enlisted in the marines. When he got out of the service he headed back to Monroe, where he, with the support of other militants, took over the NAACP chapter. The town and county was dominated by the Ku Klux Klan, which terrorized the black community. In response Williams enrolled the NAACP members in the National Rifle Association and trained them in self-defense. When the Klan attacked the home of the vice president of the NAACP, Dr. Albert E. Perry, Williams and these armed NAACP members were ready, and they fought off the Klan attack with guns. The relationship of power in the area began to shift. Blacks were no longer afraid, and Williams became a symbol of a new kind of militancy among blacks throughout the country.

In 1961 Williams and his NAACP local began a drive to end segregation in Monroe. The main issue was the integration of the local swimming pool. The KKK organized white mobs to surround the swimming pool, and the local police, as usual, supported the KKK. The town became extremely tense. At the point of greatest tension a white couple drove through the black neighborhood and found themselves surrounded by angry blacks. Williams intervened and rescued the couple, allowing them into his home for safety. For this humanitarian act Williams and several other NAACP activists were prosecuted for kidnapping![11]

Once again we contacted Conrad Lynn and organized the Committee to Aid the Monroe Defendants (CAMD) to raise funds and gain publicity. Williams and his ideas of self-defense became well known throughout the country as an alternative to Martin Luther King, Jr.'s, pacifism. Williams, fearing for his life, fled to Canada and from there to Cuba.

Our work with the Kiss Case prepared us for the next, and far more important, civil rights struggle. This began in the spring of 1960 when students from southern black colleges began sit-ins at lunch counters in Woolworth stores to force integration. These actions soon led to the formation of the Student Non-Violent Coordinating Committee (SNCC), which became the center for several years of black militancy and which, in a later period, was the source of the Black Power movement. At the beginning, however, these southern sit-ins were largely spontaneous and lacked any coherent support in the North.

The YSA's reaction was immediate and highly effective. We discussed the problem with Tom Kerry, National Organization Secretary of the SWP, who gave us the wisdom of his many years of experience in the trade union movement. We decided that we needed to concentrate all our efforts on a mass picket line of youth in front of the Woolworth's on 34th Street, the largest one in New York, at the peak shopping hours on Saturdays. We formed the New York Committee for Integration to organize these demonstrations. The committee was to be open to everyone and would meet after each demonstration to plan for the next one. The officers and policy of the committee would be decided by the mass assembly of participants. We did not want the committee to take any particular political stand. What we fought for was militant mass youth action against Woolworth's as the most effective way to support the southern black students and force integration upon the chain.

The FBI issued a report entitled "Picketing of Woolworth's Stores New York City 3/5/60 Racial Matters," which stated that "informa-

tion set forth in enclosed letterhead memorandum was furnished to Bureau of Special Services, New York City Police Department on 3/3/60."

The April 1960 *Young Socialist* carried the huge headline "Boycott Woolworth's" and announced that our Saturday picket lines were pulling between three hundred and four hundred students. Most of the participants were high-school students, and we were able to recruit some of them to the YSA. Our leader was Fred Mazelis,[12] who was attending CCNY. Using New York as our example, our supporters in different cities organized similar committees and held picket lines in front of their local Woolworth stores. The YSA was completely mobilized nationwide, and we were having an impact!

The YSA had now passed through a series of effective actions. It was beginning to win a militant reputation and was training its members as both activists and propagandists. The YSA was becoming a group with politics and spirit. It was a good period. I was quite optimistic. The demoralizing atmosphere of American radicalism in the mid-fifties was now a dim memory.

The Formation of the YSA

For the SWP, my national campus tour together with our new civil rights activity represented a shift away from a primary concentration on regroupment and toward consolidating a national revolutionary youth organization with a reasonably coherent political perspective. It was a gradual process, uneven nationally, and different members of our group gave somewhat different emphases to the regroupment or, more directly, the organization-building side of our work. But the battle for control of the *Young Socialist* in June 1958 had been decisive.

We were committed to building a youth organization on the basis of Trotskyist politics as we understood those politics. While the Socialist Workers Party could view our youth formation as its possession, as Tom Kerry had expressed it, the actual political relationship between youth and party in that period was far more complex. Partly this was because of the continued participation in the leadership of the *Young Socialist* formation by independents like Dick DeHaan. More important was the independent temper of the youth leaders, who considered themselves Trotskyists and political supporters of the Socialist Workers Party. I was by no means the most cantankerous of the lot. In fact, I worked in that period on a daily basis with the SWP leadership and viewed myself as under party discipline. Shane Mage had his own political ideas, which rarely coincided with those of the SWP or anyone else. Jim Robertson had spent over ten years in Shachtman's camp and was not about to accept what the SWP said or did without critically evaluating it. The true-blue SWPer who unquestioningly accepted the party leadership's views as gospel was, luckily for the vitality of the YSA, a rare creature, especially on the leadership level.

We were all committed to building a youth movement that, while politically aligned with the Socialist Workers Party, remained truly organizationally independent, with its own leadership and deciding its own tactical course. We believed that the organizational independence of the youth from the party was crucial to an active, growing YSA. It was emphatically not a public relations ploy to rope in those more distant from the SWP; nor was it, as some party leaders saw it, a product of the cussedness of the youth leaders.

We needed very much to consolidate our youth forces into an actual national organization. We had the *Young Socialist* newspaper, and our supporters had organized a number of loosely structured local clubs—more geared to regroupment than to coherent propaganda and action. Of course there was the SWP, which was a tightly disciplined national organization. But that—for a number of us—was part of the problem. As long as the youth movement remained decentralized and politically vague, the SWP would in reality run things through its party structure and discipline. We preferred that the young comrades, SWP members and nonmembers, have their own organizational forms for determining their policies and activities. We were convinced that a strong national youth organization would be at the same time a more independent youth organization.

On November 28, 1958 the SWP held a National Committee Plenum in New York City. An FBI informant was present and took extensive, detailed notes of the proceedings. I gave a youth report that summed up, perhaps a bit too optimistically, our accomplishments in this period.

"Work in the youth field has centered primarily around the publication of the 'Young Socialist,' which, according to WOHLFORTH, has been publishing regularly since the first issue was put out in September, 1957. In its first year of publication, close to 70,000 copies of the 'Young Socialist' have been sold or distributed. . . .

"WOHLFORTH said there were functioning groups of supporters of the 'Young Socialist' in some 13 areas throughout the US, and there were good contacts with young people in an additional 10 areas, 'such places as Madison, Wisconsin, Oberlin, Antioch, Earlham College, Portland, Oregon, etc.'

"The development of a national youth cadre, according to WOHLFORTH, was primarily through the young members of the SWP, both those who initiated the youth work and those who joined the SWP through the youth group. . . .

"WOHLFORTH continued that the combined YSL-YPSL have probably, through recruitment, recouped their losses from the split of the YSL left wing. The YPSL had from 200 to 250 members, he estimated. . . .

"A lesser rival of the 'Young Socialist,' WOHLFORTH said, were the youth around the CP. He said there was an attempt on a nation-wide basis to reorganize the CP youth into a young Communist group. . . .

"The important thing as far as the question of rivals, WOHLFORTH said, was the fact that for the first time in the history of Trotskyism, the revolutionary socialist forces were qualitatively the same in strength as their rivals. . . .

"WOHLFORTH said the greatest potential of winning and building a socialist youth movement in America was believed to be work on college campuses. . . . WOHLFORTH said that the main challenge was the ability to combat the YPSL elements on the campus and win over the leftward moving youth."

We all finally agreed to call a conference of *Young Socialist* supporters in Detroit on December 27 and 28, 1958. We planned the conference very carefully to permit us to coalesce our forces around the paper while not cutting off any gains we might still be able to make from our regroupment work. The conference was a modest success.[13] We had fifty-seven delegates representing groups in fourteen cities. Considering the rather elderly group that had initiated our work a little more than a year earlier, the average age of the delegates was an impressively low twenty-two.

The conference was not without its factional excitement. This time the dissidence came from within the Socialist Workers Party rather than from the more healthy source of regroupment forces. A few youth supporters of a party minority faction[14] rather artificially proposed that the *Young Socialist* supporters abandon campus work and turn toward "the proletarian youth." I remember a lot of talk of selling papers in candy stores in poor neighborhoods. I don't remember these young people having much success testing their theories in practice. Perhaps they discovered that most young people who hung out in candy stores liked candy and, in most cases, hadn't graduated from primary school.

The party made a decision—wise in my opinion—to let these youth fight for their views at the conference without fear of party disciplinary action. They gathered no more than one or two votes. It felt strange being part of a leadership instead of a beleaguered opposition! The person who enjoyed it most of all was my acquaintance from Los Angeles, Carl Feingold. Too old to be classified a "youth," Carl turned up at the conference as the Socialist Workers Party's fraternal representative. Carl still had the "Cannon Connection" and called Jim two or three times a day with detailed descriptions of what was going on. Exactly what he told him, I can only guess, since the defeat of this small faction was a foregone conclusion and there was no one else there to give us trouble. In fact, a little more trouble from some open-minded independents would have helped the affair.

The conference organized our supporters into an independent revolutionary youth organization in everything but name. We elected a National Committee of Young Socialist Supporters, and this august body elected the *Young Socialist* Editorial Board to put out the paper and act as the leading body of our youth organization. We even issued membership cards and, of course, collected dues. We adopted a rather minimal political statement that to any politically sophisticated person made it clear we were Trotskyists. It was still a very small organization with under two hundred members. The Socialist Party's youth organization, now controlled by my former YSL comrades, was about the same size.

The FBI took six rolls of film of people attending the Detroit conference. Informants at the conference identified as many people as possible. Unidentified photos were then circulated to the Denver, Chicago, Cleveland, and Los Angeles offices of the FBI. The Atlanta office was sent "two photographs of an unsub male Negro." As a backup, ".16 millimeter motion picture films were also taken at the above conference."

The next year-and-a-half was very fruitful. The national youth leadership we had assembled in New York and in the localities worked, and worked quite well. We turned our people outward to reach the new student generation and to mobilize forces around the civil rights struggle. Our paper was lively, militant, and actually quite interesting. We wrote book reviews, carried on polemics, and analyzed world events. We even published some mimeographed pamphlets with our own meager resources.[15]

A very healthy division of labor emerged. Jim Robertson came to the center in New York and concentrated on organizational matters. He started work on a well-researched constitution for the group. Jim Lambrecht was our recruiter and street speaker. Jim was a man of enthusiasms, whether about his latest "contact," or some world revolutionary event. His approach often lacked caution or subtlety, and at times it bothered my deep sense of Marxist orthodoxy—yet it was a great asset in a youth group. Shane Mage was our thinker, our theoretician. He helped to stimulate discussion and saw to it that we did not suffer too deeply from the American disease of purely organizational activism.

Then there was Sherry Finer, the youngest daughter of SWP National Secretary Farrell Dobbs. Sherry was a pretty young woman of strong will, and she was very willing to pitch in on all the organizational work we had. Unfortunately, however, Sherry was a somewhat rigid thinker. She had been literally born and raised inside the party and had had virtually no contact with nonparty mortals. She usually gave expression to the most formal and narrow interpretation of the party line and thereby tended to repel new recruits and sympathizers. But even Sherry, who could not believe the heresies some of us uttered from time to time, fitted in in her own square way and was very much a part of our youth leadership.[16]

Then there was me. I was the central leader, seeing to it that everything that had to happen, happened. I wrote a lot of letters, talked with a lot of comrades, toured for socialism, consulted, consulted, and then consulted again with our friends in the SWP. I wrote articles, thought a lot about strategy, tried to develop myself theoretically, and learned to work with a fairly mixed lot of people. On the whole I think I did a pretty good job of leading the *Young Socialist* forces in those days. It was some of the healthiest socialist-building work I ever did. It was a happy period for me.

On February 28, 1960, the SWP National Committee held a plenum in New York City, and again I was asked to give a youth report. An FBI informant present provided an extensive summary of this report:

"The past six-month period of the youth movement has been the most fruitful of any other period, other than the original six-month period during 1957. This period has been spent basically intensifying the political work on the campus. . . .

"At the present time, we have a 'Young Socialist' press drive of 4,500, an increase of 1,000. . . . As a whole, 100 to 150 Young Socialist members will be represented at the national conference. . . .

"We have won over members of the Socialist Democratic Youth since the split in the Young Socialist League in Boston, Philadelphia, and Seattle, and will continue with left-wing elements in the YPSL. The YPSL has become demoralized and, among other things, has lost its paper.

"The Communist Party youth have made attempts to organize themselves nationally and in a more concentrated way in New York City. . . . The CP will have a considerable struggle in attempting to catch us in influence."

The next step in our organizational development was the founding conference of the Young Socialist Alliance, which we held on April 15–17, 1960, in Philadelphia.[17] Jim Robertson wrote a very fine—I might say flawless—constitution for the new organization. Shane Mage wrote a somewhat turgid, but absolutely correct, resolution on war; possibly one of the better ones produced since the Zimmerwald conference during World War I. I gave the major-perspectives report. The conference was attended by one hundred delegates and friends. Numerically it did not represent much of a gain over the Detroit conference, but politically it represented an important stage in the maturation of a Trotskyist youth movement in the United States. We declared our political solidarity with the Socialist Workers Party but insisted upon our organizational independence. In practice this meant that the YSA elected a representative (me) to sit on the SWP Political Committee, and the party elected a representative to sit on the YSA's leading committee. I was elected National Chairman and Jim Lambrecht became National Secretary. There was even a touch of regroupment with Annette Rubenstein, a writer with a solid reputation in progressive circles, giving greetings in person and James Aronson of the *National Guardian* sending in written greetings.

A Period of Transition

The period of radicalization in the mid-1960s did not come out of nowhere, and the political movements that dominated that period were affected by past radicalism. The birth of the YSA took place during a period of transition from the conservatism and reaction of the 1950s to the radical activism of the mid-1960s. Changes external to the small radical movement were both shaping the existing radicals and creating conditions for the emergence of a new Left.

It was a period of prosperity and economic growth. With some exceptions, trade union militancy continued to dissipate. Yet a new movement of blacks, who were disproportionately left out of the new prosperity, began with the sit-ins in the South. This movement was partly led by students and it had mass support, which encouraged some among the new generation of students, black and white, to turn toward leftist politics. Many of these new young radicals were the children of the old radicals, particularly of those who had been members or supporters of the Communist Party.

It was international developments, however, that had the biggest impact on the Left and the potential Left in this period. The Hungarian Revolution had brought about a profound crisis within the aging ranks of the Communist Party and its periphery, already partially decimated by persecution and isolation. During the 1957–1961 period the Communist Party remained basically paralyzed politically. The CP was mainly preoccupied with its own survival and was unable to organize an effective youth organization. Perhaps even more important, it entered the 1960s with a banner soiled by the Khrushchev revelations and the invasion of Hungary. The new student radicals, most of them relatively ignorant about past radicalism, began their political lives convinced that they had to chart new ground. For reasons not always clear to even themselves, they knew they could not simply follow in the political footsteps of the dominant force of past American radicalism, the Communist Party.

The fate of my former comrades, now organized as the Young People's Socialist League and affiliated with the Socialist Party, was only marginally better than that of the CP. Once the merger with the Shachtmanites had been completed, the YPSL grew swiftly to the size of the YSA and, I would venture to guess, grew significantly larger than the YSA during the early 1960s. It had the advantage of a democratic openness and lack of Leninist doctrinairism that should have given it appeal to the new generation of leftists. Its problem lay with its connection to the Socialist Party and to the political evolution of the Shachtmanite leaders within that party.

The Shachtmanites had become such embittered anti-Communists that they tended to identify democracy and progressive social change with

American world interests rather than with the independent movements of people, East and West. They interpreted the political immaturity of many New Left students as a sign of Stalinism and feared the generation's militancy, directed as it was toward the government they now felt comfortable with. They were dead wrong about Stalinism and the New Left. The students lacked sophistication on the issue—in fact many were stubbornly determined not to think about the matter at all—and here or there they raised incorrect notions and had illusions. But the thrust of this New Left movement was profoundly democratic, rooted more in American populism and anarchism than in Stalinism. But the Shachtmanites were correct in seeing these students as moving far to the left of their own positions.

Of course most of the YPSL members at that time were on the left within the Socialist Party and were critics of the leadership. For this very reason the group became preoccupied with internal factionalism, and only those who split from the SP seriously affected the student movement at all and even then not much before 1968, when the Peace and Freedom Party was formed.

The YSA did have its impact upon the 1960s student movement. It was able to play a central role, along with such radical pacifists as A. J. Muste, in directing and mobilizing the anti–Vietnam War sentiments into a series of massive demonstrations in Washington and other major cities.

Notes

1. *Young Socialist* (New York, July 1958), p. 3. It was written under the pseudonym William Martin.
2. This faction, which continues to control the Communist Party, is now led by Gus Hall.
3. Steve Max went on to form the Tom Paine Club. Then he took his group into SDS and was present at its Port Huron convention. For several years he actively promoted his realignment politics within SDS.
4. DeHaan did not consider himself a Trotskyist but rather a "libertarian socialist."
5. *Young Socialist* (March 1958, May–June 1958, July 1958). Jim Robertson had been one of the leaders of our faction in the YSL. He later founded the Spartacist League.
6. Farrell Dobbs, *Teamster Rebellion* (New York: Monad Press, 1972).
7. See chapter 5.
8. This is a proposal that makes it illegal for a trade union to require everyone under its jurisdiction who works for an employer with which it has a contract to be a member of the union. It severely weakens the effectiveness of unions.
9. *Young Socialist* (November 1958), p. 2.
10. Robert F. Williams, *Negroes with Guns* (New York: Marzani & Munzell, 1962). *Young Socialist* (December, January, February 1958, 1959).

11. Paul Buhle et al., *Encyclopedia of the American Left* (New York: Garland, 1990), p. 57.
12. Mazelis's parents were workers who had been members of the Communist Party. We recruited him through our ISP election activities. Mazelis would play a prominent role in the Workers League.
13. *Young Socialist* (January 1959).
14. This was the Marcy group. See chapter 4, "In the Mainstream of Trotskyism."
15. These included three pamphlets written or edited by me: *Revolt on the Campus: The Student Movement in the 1930s, Which Road for Socialist Youth—Reformism or Revolutionary Socialism?, History of the International Socialist Youth Movement to 1929*; and two pamphlets by Shane Mage: *Fight against War* and *The Hungarian Revolution.*
16. My last contact with Sherry was in the Bay Area. She was living with Peter Buch, a comrade who had also played an important role in the early YSA as head of our Los Angeles group, and remained a loyal member in the local branch.
17. *Young Socialist* (June 1960).

4

In the Mainstream of Trotskyism

116 University Place

The headquarters of the Socialist Workers Party was a four-story reddish brown building overlooking teeming Union Square. At election time it was festooned with a huge poster of a worker in a thirties-style cap, sweeping away the two capitalist parties with a broom. Across from headquarters was another Smith's, a twin of the Shachtmanite one, with its pastrami, corned beef, and roast beef steam table and the same sorry-looking free-lunch stand. On the ground floor was a fashionable antique shop. A little unmarked gray door next to the antique shop led up to the busy world of mainstream Trotskyism.

Even in those poor days, the SWP headquarters was spacious, clean, and well-staffed compared to the Shachtmanite loft I had come from. Jim Cannon was a great believer in "proletarian" organizational efficiency and an enemy of "bohemian" dirt and disorder, an outlook he held in common with his enemy, American business. On the first floor of the building was a good-sized hall capable of seating 100 to 150 people. The hall was the domain of the New York local, which used it for forums (held every Friday night), weekly branch meetings, and an occasional social. It was freshly painted in New York–loft gray-green-beige and sported a counter to the right of the entrance that was used to serve drinks and beer at parties. Contacts, as well as hard-drinking members, were served Old Pap bourbon, bought at nearby Astor Place Liquor Store, and Old Bohemian beer (price considerations predominated over the objectionable name), purchased on sale at the supermarket. Proceeds from such sales were carefully watched and reported by the New York branch treasurer at the weekly meeting.

The third floor housed a complex of offices linked by a rather long, dark hall. In the front were the offices of National Organizational Secretary Tom Kerry and the New York local organizer (a position with frequent turnover). Down the hall and off to the right was the very small office of Pioneer Publishers, devoted to publishing the works of Trotsky and party leaders. At the end of the hall was the *Militant* circulation office with its old Addressograph and metal plates.

On the fourth floor was the reception area and office of the SWP national secretary, Farrell Dobbs, and his secretary, the extremely efficient Reba Hansen, who was Joseph Hansen's wife. The fourth floor was also the home of the *Militant* editorial staff, which occupied a large, cluttered room that served additionally as the meeting place of the party's highest body, the Political Committee.

The whole operation was staffed by about a dozen people, some of whom worked only part time. To me this was a large bustling political center. The Shachtmanites put out their weekly paper with only Hal Draper working full time; the SWP had at least four full-timers on the *Militant*. Gordon Haskell, a part-time Shachtmanite staffer, tried to do what Dobbs, Kerry, Reba Hansen, and a couple of part-timers did at "116." Although the SWP was incomparably better-organized as a party than the amateurish Shachtmanite ISL, I always felt that *Labor Action* was a much more readable and interesting paper than the *Militant*. In later years the *Militant* staff grew to seven or eight and the paper's size from a modest, large-format four-pager to a twenty-four-page (or more) tabloid, yet the paper remained to me an exceedingly dull one.

The Socialist Workers Party, for all its revolutionary pretensions, was traditionalist in at least one sense: It was led by men and administered by women. Since I spent so much time at 116, I got to know these women quite well. The little room of Pioneer Publishers was staffed by Ann Chertov (Chester). Pioneer published very few books in those days due to lack of funds. Volume 1 of Trotsky's *The First Five Years of the Third International* had been published in 1945; Volume 2 was pending publication during my entire stay in the SWP. Pioneer was able to get out Trotsky's *Third International after Lenin* in 1957 and *The Stalin School of Falsification* in 1962. This all added up to a publishing rate of no more than one book every five years.

Ann always had much to do because she handled orders from branches for books from other publishers and kept track of Pioneer's meager and aging book stock. She was a bit set in her ways, yet for whatever reason, I got along quite well with her and with the other ladies of 116 University Place. Ann and her husband, Bob, had joined the Trotskyists when A. J. Muste's American Workers Party merged with Cannon's group in 1934.[1] Bob made a study of postwar Stalinism and became an expert on East Europe and related theoretical problems that plagued Trotskyism in those days.[2]

Bob's brother, Morris Chertov, was a factory worker in Philadelphia. Morris's wife, Pearl, a very energetic lady, was a key party activist and branch organizer who much more easily than most of the rest of her generation in the party made the transition to the new, younger, and largely student party of the 1960s and 1970s.[3] The story of the Chertovs was not at all atypical in the SWP (and, I suppose, this may also be said of the Communist Party). Whole families joined the party in the 1930s under the impact of the depression. They settled in, married within the party, raised families, and died party members.

Sharing the dark denizens of the third floor with Ann Chertov was Karolyn Kerry, who staffed the *Militant* circulation department. Karolyn, Tom Kerry's wife, was a Texan with a wonderful accent and sense of humor. She, like much of the party of that generation, smoked too much and suffered for it in her declining years. Reba Hansen, like her husband, Joe, and Joe's brother Al, was of Mormon descent. She looked a bit severe and reminded me of the farmer's wife in the Grant Wood painting "American Gothic." I do not want to suggest that she acted severely or was really cold. It is just that she possessed that American pioneer-stock look and was reserved in relating to people. But perhaps most important, she had the strength of character one associates with the Western pioneer. Reba was at party headquarters every day. To save money she packed a lunch and walked to work, where she stayed as long as she was needed. She did this with husband Joe her entire adult life. When I came to know her in 1957, she had been so working for some years. When I returned to the party in 1977 she was still coming to work daily, now to a different headquarters, where she worked in a different department. She was an efficient and orderly worker and she kept her work area very tidy. Once I understood the kind of person she was, we got along fine.

During most of the regroupment period Dick Garza was the New York branch organizer. Dick was a handsome man in his late thirties with a winning smile—a thoroughly nice person. Dick's father was Mexican and his mother Puerto Rican (or was it the other way around?), which made him well-suited for work among Latinos. Dick's brother, Mike, was a worker and a party member in Minneapolis; his sister Virginia married the future leader of the party's antiwar work, Fred Halstead. Yes, the SWP was a family affair in those days! Fred was a rather large fellow—he and Murry Weiss used to hit Chinatown at 3 A.M. for eating binges—and was known in Vietnam-protest days as Big Red Fred. Fred and Virginia—a relatively petite woman—stayed with my wife and me once for a week or two when they were between apartments. We had only a narrow single bed in our spare room and somehow they survived.

Tom Kerry, the party's National Organizational Secretary, was someone toward whom I had mixed feelings. I genuinely liked him and greatly respected his political and tactical judgment. In the fall of 1957, the party leadership decided Tom was to be my party liaison, replacing Murry Weiss. Tom, as our fight for control of the *Young Socialist* illustrated, was a good man to have on your side when conditions required tough factional decisions. And his advice during the sit-in support work revealed a flair for working in a broader milieu. Tom was then in his fifties, somewhere around Farrell Dobbs's age, perhaps a decade older than the bulk of the party membership in that period. He was a dapper-looking man who wore a bow tie, a plaid shirt, and corduroy pants.

The cause for my mixed reaction to Tom came in the faction fight that began in 1961. The fellow approached a political dispute with the subtlety of a barroom brawler. For Tom there was the party, with which he completely identified, and the opposition, which he viewed as riffraff to be summarily dealt with. It was a *Stalinist* approach that, it is hoped, he reconsidered in the last years of his life when he found himself in the San Francisco branch and growing more and more critical of the party leadership.[4]

I had many fewer dealings with Farrell Dobbs, SWP National Secretary. Farrell, a handsome, gray-haired man with a midwestern look and accent, could give a powerful class-struggle speech, evoking the memories of the major labor battles he had experienced—and in some cases led—in the 1930s. Trotsky had personally talked him into leaving an important post in the Teamsters Union to come to New York to become the SWP Labor Secretary. When James P. Cannon decided to retire to the West Coast, Farrell was the obvious choice to replace him as the active leader of the party. He certainly had the credentials to lead a party that prided itself on its proletarian character.

Quite frankly, I found Farrell to be a disappointment. Not every gifted mass leader makes a good party leader. Farrell seemed to spend most of his day in his office on the fourth floor of 116 University Place reading the *New York Times* while the party was really being run by Tom and the youth were being run by myself. Major party policies were formulated by others. Murry Weiss, for example, deserved the credit for encouraging the youth work and for pushing ahead the party's regroupment perspective, and Joe Hansen developed the party's theoretical understanding and orientation toward Cuba. Fred Halstead was the main man behind the party's Vietnam War work in the next period. As is often the case with someone who holds a position at the limit of his capabilities, Farrell had a conservative, almost bureaucratic approach toward the administration of the SWP. I wonder if Trotsky was right in pulling him out of trade union work.

The *Militant* staff served as a kind of general political leadership for the party, and most of its members were also on the Political Committee. Dan Roberts, Nora's father, was editor in those days. Dan was a competent fellow with a slight German accent, but he was not a particularly original thinker or politician. Harry Ring was the one member of the *Militant* staff who was not on the Political Committee. Harry was a short, roundish fellow with glasses that seemed to recede into the folds on his impish face. Harry had a good sense of humor and a light touch, which made his journalism a bit more interesting than the rest of the rather dull writing in the *Militant*. Harry was more than a party stalwart; he was a party enthusiast. Many comrades liked our youth work, but Harry *loved* it. Many comrades were hopeful that regroupment would bring us gains; Harry projected visions of hundreds of Communists embracing Trotskyism due to the great foresight of our party's leadership. Some of us felt the paper went a bit overboard in taking on the coloration of the "progressive" milieu; Harry felt it did not go far enough. It goes without saying that Harry simply adored Fidel Castro! Harry was married to Priscilla, a thin, tall lady who sold subscriptions in housing projects.

Joe Hansen was also on the *Militant* staff and was readily available for other party assignments. Joe was a gentle man, quiet-spoken, giving careful consideration to anything he might say. Yet he was quite capable of rolling up his sleeves and writing effective, even rather bitter, polemics against party enemies. His favorite polemical weapon, however, was humor, and he allowed himself an exaggeration here or there for the sake of an effective gibe. He was also a consummate party tactician. Joe played a supporting role to Murry Weiss in the regroupment work but began in this period to develop more of an interest in the international movement. It was Joe who, step by careful step, developed and carried through the party's reunification efforts in the Fourth International (FI). He also found expression for his theoretical interests, developing the party leadership's position on Cuba in 1960 and 1961. Yet he preferred the role of party adviser and tactician, leaving day-to-day party leadership to Dobbs and Kerry, and in the late 1970s, to Jack Barnes.

From time to time Art Preis would turn up at the office. Art, like the Chesters, was a former member of the Muste group and had been Labor Editor of the *Militant* for many years. Now he had crippling arthritis and would very painfully climb three flights of stairs to a desk in the *Militant* editorial room. There he worked on his book, *Labor's Giant Step*, the story of the formation of the CIO. Each touch of the typewriter hurt him, but he was determined to record the great events of the 1930s as the Trotskyist movement had experienced them. Sherry Finer, when she wasn't earning a living or working with the YSA, set the book in type in the evenings. The Socialist Workers Party lived very much in the past, but it must be said that it was a proud past.

The SWP was much more closely watched than were the Shachtmanites. Recent evidence has revealed that the FBI had placed 301 informers inside the SWP over a sixteen-year period at a cost to the government of $1,683,000.[5] *My files offer ample evidence of the presence of these informers even though great effort was made to black out any information that would reveal their identity. I have already noted reports by FBI informants present at the SWP National Committee Plenums in 1958 and in 1960. An informer was also present at a National Committee Plenum held in 1961.*

In addition to receiving information from informers, the FBI placed its agents outside the unmarked gray door at 116 University Place to note, and occasionally to photograph, those who entered. For example, at the time of the above-mentioned plenum, "On January 14 and 15, 1961, subject was observed by Special Agents of the FBI entering and leaving SWP headquarters, New York City." A photographic surveillance was also conducted at this time, and at least two rolls of film with thirty-six exposures each were taken. These photos were then circulated to FBI offices throughout the country for identification in the same manner as were the previously reported photos taken at the 1957 SWP convention.

This method of circulating photos certainly suggests that the FBI at least sought to place informers inside each local branch of the SWP. It is easy to see how, with the ebb and flow of agents and informants, a figure of 301 was easily reached over a sixteen-year period.

Curiously, the FBI appears to have goofed up its coverage of a plenum it expected to be held in 1959. "It is noted that physical surveillances were conducted in the neighborhood of SWP headquarters, 116 University Place, NYC, on 5/23 and 24/59, and neither the Minneapolis SWP National Committee members or any other out-of-town National Committee member was observed entering or leaving SWP headquarters." This suggests that FBI penetration of the SWP was far from perfect, nor was it necessarily on the highest level. Certainly if the FBI had an agent placed within the Political Committee, such an error could not have taken place.

I was a member of the Political Committee (PC) of the SWP from the fall of 1957 until the summer of 1963. At first I was a member representing the YSA, and from June 1961 on I was a representative of the minority tendency. The PC met once a week from 8 to 10 P.M. (it was either Tuesday or Thursday night) because it had members who worked during the day. The PC included Tom Kerry, Farrell Dobbs, Murry Weiss, Dan Roberts, and Joe Hansen, all of whom the reader has already been introduced to.

Arthur Birch, a somewhat mysterious fellow who never attended any other party meetings, was also on the committee. Arthur, I was told, was a lawyer and had played a critical role in holding the party together during World War II, when the top leaders were imprisoned under the Smith Act. My favorite PC member was Morris (Moishe) Stein. Moishe, who looked so frail, small, and old, still worked each day as a plumber. He had come to the party in the 1930s from the Jewish movement and had once edited a Trotskyist journal in Yiddish. He was bright, political, particularly interested in the international movement, and given to independent thinking. Morris's wife, Sylvia (Bleeker), came to all branch meetings and spoke out on every point on the agenda. Sylvia had a disdain for routinism and bureaucratic procedure and was the bane of local organizers. Al Hansen, Joe's brother, also attended PC meetings from time to time. I believe he was an alternate and not a full member. It didn't really matter, as Al was a "silent worker" type and I do not recall him speaking during the years he did attend the meetings.

Myra Tanner Weiss, married to Murry Weiss, was the only woman on the PC. Myra was a very beautiful woman in her forties. Myra, like Joe Hansen (with whom she did not get along), came from a Mormon family. I believe the Tanners are prominent in the Salt Lake City area. Myra was a very bright woman and an excellent mass speaker. In 1960 Farrell Dobbs was the presidential candidate and Myra was the vice presidential candidate of the party. Myra had a tendency to address small gatherings, including branch meetings, as if they were mass outdoor rallies, a practice that occasionally lost her support. Above all, she was a strong woman who did not approach other party leaders with undue reverence. She was definitely not well liked by the Dobbs section of the leadership.

There was a layer of women in the party who, like Myra, were politically strong and who refused to accept a secondary role because they were women. These early party feminists included Evelyn Reed, George Novack's wife, who made a special study of anthropology,[6] Frances James (Nora's mother), and Clara Fraser (Kaye), a leader of the Seattle branch.

The Political Committee functioned reasonably well in those days; its regular, brief meetings reflected the overall organizational efficiency of the Dobbs-Kerry regime. It published totally incomprehensible minutes due to the security concerns of the McCarthy period. The PC was called the Club Executive, each member had a pseudonym, and motions were recorded with no content. Typical minutes would read something like this: "Wood absent. Preston made Political Report. Accepted." Wood, as I recall, was Birch, and Preston was Dobbs. The minutes were so secure that they were almost totally useless to the National Committee members who received them!

The main problem with the Political Committee was that it was not very political. It concerned itself with organizational matters and dealt with these matters largely in a routine fashion. World events were rarely discussed; one wonders if they were even thought about. Unlike the YSA, the Socialist Workers Party in general in the late 1950s was a dull place, and Dobbs's PC was no different. A typical PC meeting was a two-hour battle to keep awake. I had arrived at the very top of the most revolutionary party in the United States and had trouble not falling asleep!

MOUNTAIN SPRING CAMP

There was more to the Socialist Workers Party than the inhabitants of 116 University Place. I got to know the party, its members, the branches, and its way of life well in those years. Sometimes party life was a chore, but other times it was a pleasure. Mountain Spring Camp fell into the latter category. The camp was built on property given to the party by Connie Weissman. Connie was a very lovely woman—one of those radical recruits from America's aristocracy—who functioned part of the time as Tom Kerry's secretary. Connie's husband, George Weissman (Lavan), played a role similar to that of George Novack in the party, specializing in defense cases and fund-raising. In the late 1950s he worked on the *Militant* staff.

The camp was located in the Pocono Mountains in New Jersey near the Delaware Water Gap. The center of the property was an old farmhouse with a beautiful stone foundation. The basement area had been transformed into a charming bar, Smokey Joe's, with a large stone fireplace.

Sometimes, late at night, someone would go upstairs and cook huge hamburgers that were then served on homemade buns. Smokey Joe's added much to the cohesiveness and warmth of the SWP as a human institution.

On top of the hill above the farmhouse the party had built a large dining hall and a series of open-sided cabins. More recently the party had constructed, with the voluntary labor of its members, a quite comfortable motel-like structure near the farmhouse. Most guests stayed in the farmhouse or this new building, but when the party held conventions there—1959 and 1961—the old cabins were also used. There was a little muddy lake that served, almost adequately, as our swimming hole.

The food at Mountain Spring was usually excellent. This was particularly the case if Paul Montauk, a chef by profession, was in charge. Paul met Mary Lou, the eldest Dobbs sister, in this period. Mary Lou had been deserted by an alcoholic husband and had three children. Paul took on the whole lot and in later years settled in Berkeley, where in time, Farrell also joined the resettled family clan. Sometimes Fred Halstead would cook, and he was equally good. His wife, Virginia, would make homemade tortillas. If there were only a few of us there, we might all go out to a nearby Italian country roadhouse for steamer clams, pizza, and beer and to play shuffleboard.

Mountain Spring Camp served the party in many different ways. On summer weekends comrades and friends would come out from New York for an inexpensive vacation. Full-time party staffers got free vacations there as partial compensation for their small paychecks. Joe Hansen loved the flowers around the place and spent many a peaceful hour wandering around the grounds carrying out gardening tasks. In addition to it being the site of two party conventions, Mountain Spring hosted many a pleasant YSA educational weekend.

The most unusual use of the place was by the Trotsky School. After World War II the SWP leadership decided that the party was sorely in need of a solid Marxist education. Since this need extended to the very top of the party—an implicit recognition that most of the trained intellectuals had left with Shachtman and that that split was, by no means, entirely beneficial—the first six to eight students for the Trotsky School were PC members. Each year a small number of students were chosen to attend a school session that lasted about six months. When I joined the party, the entire National Committee had already passed through the program and the branches had begun to nominate activists to attend the school.

Although I never got to go myself, I got a pretty good idea of what the school was like from my close friend Danny Freeman, who attended a Trotsky School session led by Fred Halstead. The students carried out all chores and cooking, managing to support themselves on something like fifty cents a day per person for food. The food was starchy but edible, and the students led a kind of monastic life separated from party work and devoted to intense study. The main text for the school was Marx's *Capital*, which could keep anybody occupied for six months. However, the impression I got from talking with Danny, and from hearing observations of other graduates of the school, is that Marx was taught in a Talmudic fashion, isolated from contemporary world events and intellectual thought. This was very much in the spirit of the autodidactic origins of the school. It was as if a workers' party had discovered the need for theory yet sought to gain theoretical knowledge without that knowledge being imparted by the "unclean" vessel of the intelligentsia. The resulting lectures focused pointlessly on abstract concepts of "value" and "use value" and lacked connections with the living process of history, research, controversy, and interplay with other intellectual disciplines.

Mountain Spring Camp had one permanent involuntary resident, Carl Skoglund. Carl came to this country from Sweden as a young worker already imbued with socialist ideas. He went, like many Swedes, to Minneapolis, where he joined the Socialist Party before World War I. After the war he supported the Communist faction of the party when it split in 1919. Carl became associated within the Communist Party with the Dunne brothers[7] and James P. Cannon. In 1928 he became a founding member of the American Trotskyist movement. In 1934 he was active with other Trotskyists in the Minneapolis Teamster strike and was one of the leaders of the SWP imprisoned under the Smith Act during World War II. In the McCarthy period the federal government moved against Carl, seeking to invalidate his naturalized citizenship and deport him to Sweden. In the course of these proceedings Carl was confined by court order to Mountain Spring Camp, where he was living at the time. Carl died there on December 11, 1960.

I, like many youth members, got to know Carl pretty well in those years. Carl was a strong, barrel-shaped man with thinning hair and twinkling eyes. He had the kind of smile that encompassed his big wrinkled Scandinavian face and fitted more my childhood image of Santa Claus than that of a subversive to be feared; but then again I was not one to fear subversives! Carl never lost his strong Swedish accent and sometimes was hard to understand. He was a self-educated worker with a deep love for the sciences. He loved to apply his knowledge of the Marxian dialectic to studies he made of astronomy and physics. When I knew him he was well into his seventies and he never stopped gaining new knowledge, which he loved to discuss with everyone. Carl was one of the great pleasures of a trip to Mountain Spring Camp.

Just as the old Socialist Workers Party was giving way in those days to a very different kind of party, so too, Mountain Spring Camp seemed destined to disappear as a symbol of the old party, whose members had lovingly labored to construct it. It happened in 1962 or 1963. The New Jersey State Police had discovered a way to harass "the Commies." They conducted raids against the camp, claiming we were in violation of various state laws by serving liquor without a tavern license. I am not at all sure that we were in violation of any law: We were more like a private club; no money ever passed over a counter—you accumulated a tab that you paid at the end of your stay with your bill. But those who were formulating party policy at the time became convinced that we could no longer serve liquor there and that we could not sustain the place without the profits from liquor sales. So it was sold and the money thus gained was plowed into other party projects. The SWP never built another institution like it. An era passed with the passing of Mountain Spring Camp.

Branch Factionalism

Life in the SWP in this period was no longer dominated by class-struggle activism. The bulk of older party members who had spent decades in the trade unions had more recently drifted into other occupations. One former Teamster militant was selling used trucks in Minneapolis. One of the Trotskyists sent to jail during the war under the Smith Act, Jake Cooper, was operating a supermarket in a small Minnesota town. Others who remained in the unions were inactive or carried out sporadic activity on a kind of free-lance basis.

Branch life in the Socialist Workers Party was a dull and routinized affair. Each branch meeting began with the reading of the minutes from the last meeting. Then came an organizer's report, usually a dry recitation of the various organizational tasks facing the branch. This was followed by a string of subordinate reports concerning the treasury, *Militant* sales, the forum committee, regroupment activity, or what have you. Happenings in the world that week were rarely mentioned, and questions of theory and political line were only discussed once every two years in specified preconvention periods. The apolitical tone of this political party was set at the top in the PC and then expressed faithfully in each branch across the country.

I got to travel around quite a bit, especially during my nationwide campus tour, and I visited most of the branches. What I discovered shocked me, but when I reported my findings back to the PC, the leaders appeared amused that I was so unaware of the state of the party. The years of isolation had taken their toll on the SWP just as they had on the Shachtmanites, but the sickness of the SWP found a unique expression.

Each branch had dutifully maintained its structure, its local institutions, and the flow of funds to the center, but in many cases the branches had degenerated into little personality cults. Where more than one such personality existed, the branch was divided into warring cliques.

I found the most bizarre example of this in Milwaukee. The branch was led by James Boulton, who dressed in an out-of-shape brown suit and always, always wore a soiled hat pressed straight down over his bald head, almost to his ears. The fellow had the Willie Loman look of a traveling salesman. He was convinced he was "well-liked." Out in front of his house was his car, on top of which he had built a huge sign declaring: "James Boulton for Governor! Wayne Leverenz for U.S. Senator!" Wayne, whom I also met, was a clean-cut young man who appeared to be relatively normal but was completely under the thumb of Boulton. The car had a sound system, and Boulton used to cruise the city blasting away in the residential neighborhoods, which certainly did not endear him to the local population. Inside the house Boulton had covered his wall with precinct maps and put a large pin wherever he had received a vote in a previous election. There were not many pins, and I suspect most pins marked spots where buttons on coat cuffs caught the SWP lever while the voter was reaching for the Democratic or Republican line at the top of the machine. The SWP ran election campaigns for two reasons: to make a political point against those groups such as the Communist Party that supported capitalist parties and to gain a little free airtime for propaganda purposes. Boulton, however, was determined to win and could come up with statistics showing that in some precincts he had doubled his vote (from one to two).

Boulton insisted on accompanying me when I visited the *Studies on the Left* crowd that ran the Wisconsin Socialist Club in Madison. There was Boulton, in the apartment of one of our sophisticated intellectual contacts, wearing his hat, puffing a cigar, and handing out his campaign literature. No wonder we never recruited anyone from this group! Boulton was more than just weird; he completely transformed his branch into a faction around himself. At the time I visited Milwaukee, the faction had no political coloration. Yet a year or so later Boulton embraced the Maoist political line of SWP old-timer Arne Swabeck, and the whole branch, of course, also became Maoists.

In Seattle, I found another independent branch/faction led by Dick Fraser and Clara Fraser (Kaye). This group, which would split in 1967 to become the Freedom Socialist Party (FSP), was healthier and more politically responsible than some of the other maverick branches.

The center's ties to Buffalo, New York, however, were perhaps the most attenuated of all. I never visited Buffalo because the branch, headed by Sam Marcy, was so hostile to the student orientation of the YSA that they could not be expected to arrange any speaking engagements for me. Marcy had decided that the Hungarian Revolution was basically a Fascist uprising and that as defenders of the Soviet Union, Trotskyists had a duty to support the Soviet intervention. His whole branch agreed, without exception, with Marcy on this matter. Having a very sizable and economically healthy branch, Marcy sought to geographically expand his faction by exporting branch members. I remember the Marcy group at the 1959 SWP convention, which was held at Mountain Spring Camp. I would see this small mass of people moving like a swarm of bees over the New Jersey hills, engaged in intense discussion. Deep in the center of the mass was a little animated man talking nonstop. I was not very impressed when I heard him speak; he had a high-pitched voice, and I thought he spoke in a completely hysterical manner. Yet I noted that the Marcyites were enthralled by his performance. He was clearly speaking to them and not us; they had become his alter ego and responded to him en masse. It was my first experience with true political cult followers.

In 1959 the Marcy group was no longer talking about Hungary. Instead they made a reasonably accurate critique of the party's regroupment position, a critique I had some sympathy with. But Marcy's alternative turned me off. To the SWP's orientation toward the Gates wing of the Communist Party and the Progressive Party milieu, Marcy counterposed an orientation toward the ultra-Stalinist Foster wing and splinters that were breaking away from Foster. He also pushed a rather generalized "proletarian" orientation.

The Marcyites split from the party the following year. It happened in the middle of a debate on youth work that I was conducting with one of their followers in the New York local. This fellow, I believe it was Mike Kovacs, who had spoken at our Detroit youth conference, got up and shouted something about how we were nought but they would be all and then marched out of the branch meeting with all the Marcy supporters. They formed the left-Stalinist Workers World Party, which is still around and quite active today.

Branches contained warring personal cliques in two cities, a situation that taxed the very considerable diplomatic skills of the party leadership. The Twin Cities branch had been formed by a retrenchment merger of the St. Paul and Minneapolis branches. The former St. Paul comrades continued to look to Henry Schultz, an old electrical worker, for leadership; the Minneapolis comrades owed their loyalties to Ray Dunne, a former leader of the 1934 Teamster strike. The Philadelphia branch was split between comrades close to Dave Weiss, brother of party leader Murry Weiss, and those who supported the Chertov family.

There were many "normal" branches in places like Los Angeles, New York, Cleveland, Detroit, and the San Francisco Bay Area, but even these branches had many older members who had turned inward in reaction to the years of isolation during the 1950s. Yet I believe this branch-faction phenomenon, something unique to the SWP, was not simply the result of bad times. It was also the product of a party that championed organizational functioning over politics and theory. The political life that was absent on a national level sometimes flowered in a perverse way in a particular branch. And as long as dues were sent to the center and the circulation figures for the *Militant* were maintained, the national leadership was perfectly willing to look the other way.

The New York branch had its own factional problems. A group of comrades was seeking some way to turn the party toward meaningful political activity because, outside of the youth and an occasional cocktail party for Morton Sobell, very little was happening. These comrades, like the Marcyites, sought to revive the SWP's traditional orientation to the trade unions. Not able to get the branch as a whole to move, they did secure permission to launch a separate branch in Brooklyn. The new branch plunged into union work and soon recruited two black workers, John and Clarence Franklin.[8] Prominent in this project were Nat Weinstein,[9] a good-looking house painter, and his equally attractive wife, Sylvia, who was also quite an activist. They had several teenage daughters who became active in the YSA. Several other comrades with a number of years of experience in the trade union work of the party were also involved in the Brooklyn effort. Tom Kerry was thought to be sympathetic to the project, seeing it as a counterweight to the overly middle-class milieu of the progressives and of the youth.

After a while the party leadership slowly tried to exercise more control over the Brooklyn branch, and most of its members reacted by coalescing around Joyce Cowley, a very talented writer. The "Cowleyites" opposed the party's regroupment work, were critical of the youth work, and favored an overall "turn toward the working class." They were talented and experienced comrades who were frustrated at having been shut out of the unions by McCarthyism and a boom economy. I believe they held an exaggerated view of what could be done at the time, but nevertheless, the Cowleyites should have been integrated into the party's political work. That they were not was a result of the lethargy and ingrown conservatism of the leadership in Manhattan. The party slowly whittled the group down: Some comrades drifted out of the SWP, Nat and family were drawn back toward the party mainstream by Tom Kerry, and Cowley moved to the West Coast, where she briefly joined our minority a few years later.

Troubles at the Top

The problems of the SWP in the period from 1957 to 1963 were not restricted to the membership alone. I had been recruited by Murry Weiss. I worked with Murry on a daily basis and found him to be personable, tactically wise, and flexible, as well as very open to intellectual and theoretical discussion. My relations with Farrell Dobbs and Tom Kerry were comradely enough, though I did notice just a touch of distance, of formality, on their part. Just a few short months after our group split from Shachtman, I was called in to meet with Farrell Dobbs. Farrell told me that the Political Committee had decided to relieve Murry of his assignment as party representative to the youth and that from now on I should work through Tom Kerry.

Over the next period I began to have disagreements on minor tactical matters with some of the SWP youth who were close to Weiss. Then party members close to Dobbs began to talk informally with me, and I discovered the subterranean Dobbs-Weiss conflict.[10] The Dobbs people saw Murry as the leader of a "petty bourgeois clique," while Murry's supporters saw the Dobbs people as ingrown and conservative. The decision of the Political Committee to have me coordinate youth work with Tom Kerry instead of Murry Weiss was, without a doubt, motivated by Dobbs's fear that the Weissites would gain control of the youth just as the Shachtmanites had in 1940.

The battle between Dobbs and Weiss was, to a large extent, a clique struggle produced by the same unfavorable conditions that led to Boulton's branch/faction and the Marcy group. To the degree that a party is isolated from real-life struggles and growth, the personal element tends to predominate in party life. The very negative experience so many of us passed through in the 1970s testifies to that. Murry Weiss had the kind of personality that cultivated personal as well as political closeness. If Murry had chosen to be a college professor, he would have been the kind you find sitting in the college cafeteria or local bar with a circle of starry-eyed students around him. Farrell was not as personable and warm, yet I felt he enjoyed being looked up to as a class-war hero of the 1930s.

As if the Dobbs-Weiss clique war did not complicate the life of the SWP enough, there was the problem of what was known as the "dual centers." Jim Cannon moved out to the Los Angeles area in the early 1950s. The purpose of Cannon's "retirement" was to allow Farrell Dobbs to develop as a party leader and also to devote more time to writing. But Cannon, an old party leader and fighter, did not retire quite that easily. He assembled around him a group of National Committee members residing in the Los Angeles area. They met regularly, acting as an advisory group to the New

York center. The result, in practice, was a dual party center, for this group—in fact, Cannon alone—had the authority in the party to veto almost anything the New Yorkers tried to do.

During the period I was in the party, this center included, in addition to Cannon, Arne Swabeck, Cecil Frank Glass (Frank Graves, John Liang, Li Fu-jen), George Novack (William F. Warde), and Milt Alvin, a congenial fellow who earned his living as a construction contractor. Arne Swabeck was born in Denmark in 1890 and had been a member of the German Social Democracy before World War I. A founding member of both the American Communist Party and the SWP, Swabeck was an independent thinker. Cecil Frank Glass led a remarkable life, having been a founder of the South African CP in 1921, the Chinese Trotskyist group in the mid-1930s, and the Fourth International itself in 1938.[11]

It was during the regroupment period that I discovered this Los Angeles center and the clout it possessed. Farrell Dobbs and the PC prepared a tepid document for the 1959 party convention that simply restated the current party regroupment policy. On the very eve of the convention, Cannon's West Coast National Committee (NC) group rejected the document and demanded that regroupment be ended. Farrell flew to Los Angeles for consultation, and a new draft was quickly written that put a halt to regroupment. I was most happy about this at the time because of the adaptation to Stalinism that had become rampant throughout the party. There was little time to develop an alternative policy, so the convention was devoted to a kind of abstract assertion of "party building." To fill the void Jim Cannon gave an interesting address on democracy.

I do not wish to suggest that the SWP in this period was some kind of factional jungle. Actually life in the party was peaceful to the point of boredom. Most factionalism was of an underground character, conducted by individuals who claimed to have no political differences with the leadership. Dues were paid and the *Militant* was always sold. The party was run in a modest, but smooth and professional manner. The problem was that the party comprised a generation of workers and intellectuals—those recruited in the 1930s and during World War II—that was getting old and tired. Cannon did a better job than Shachtman in holding on to his aging cadres, and on the whole, he and his followers kept the revolutionary faith. But because will and energy had departed, faith was about all they had left. Cannon could not defy the general trends affecting the working class in the 1950s.

The party had not recruited in any significant numbers in the period between the immediate aftermath of World War II and the arrival of our group at the doorstep of 116 University Place in 1958. A generation had been lost. There were the party members in their middle forties and middle fifties and then there were those of us barely out of college. In the course of the next few years the old generation would almost entirely disappear while the party was completely transformed by the youth. The process was by no means painless, and factional battles flared as the new generation replaced (and in some ways pushed out) the old.

THE FOURTH INTERNATIONAL

The Socialist Workers Party viewed itself as a section of the Fourth International. The anti-Communist Voorhis Act prohibited it from actually being affiliated, but we saw this as a formality. The Fourth International had been established by Leon Trotsky in 1938 and was modeled after the Third International of Lenin. Trotsky believed that Stalin had destroyed the revolutionary character of the latter international organization. The Fourth International, from its inception, has been composed primarily of small ideological groupings in various countries. It has been more an idea and a hope than an international reality. Yet, as we will see, it had an inordinate impact on my life as well as on the lives of many other Trotskyists.

My experience in the Shachtmanite group had not prepared me for life within the Fourth International. The Shachtmanites had political friends in different countries with whom they maintained contact. However, they had not been able to construct an international organization that served as an alternative to the Fourth International. When I first joined the SWP its international relations were moribund and I was not conscious of them. In fact, I accidentally stumbled upon the international arena.

It happened this way. In 1959 I began reading a journal, *Fourth International*, published by a group called the International Secretariat of the Fourth International. It was edited by Sherry Mangan (Patrick O'Daniel), an American living in Paris. Mangan, I later discovered, was a poet of some note and a correspondent for Luce Publications.[12] The journal was very lively and contained interesting attempts to explain the course of world revolution. I began a correspondence with Mangan.[13] Cannon found out about my new pen pal and scheduled a meeting with me while I passed through Los Angeles on a YSA tour.

I went to a small one-story stucco house somewhere in the sprawling Los Angeles area. There Jim lived with his longtime companion Rose Karsner and another comrade who acted as a full-time secretary. Jim was a big, gray-haired man whose Irish good looks evoked the Kansas of days gone by, and although seventy years old in 1960, he retained a certain boyish appearance. He wore thick glasses then, as his eyes were giving him a lot of trouble, a condition he found infuriating because it made it so difficult to get through the mountains of material he felt obliged to read. He had documents all over the place because he was engaged in a correspondence with Theodore Draper about the early Communist Party.[14]

Jim Cannon did not beat around the bush: "I hear you have been corresponding with the Pabloites. Have you ever read my speech to the majority caucus in the Cochranite fight?"[15]

"No," I stuttered.

"Well here it is. You just sit down on that couch and read it. Then we will have a discussion."

I dutifully sat down and read the document while Cannon retreated to some other part of the house to continue with whatever project he was working on when I arrived. Afterward he sat me down and we "talked." More accurately he went on and on about what Michel Raptis (Pablo), International Secretary of the Fourth International in the postwar years, had done to disrupt the SWP and to scatter cadres around the world. He spoke, I believe now quite correctly, about the limits of what a mature international leadership should do in relation to national sections that disagree with the international center. He was no doubt thinking not only about his bitter experience in 1953 when Pablo intervened in the internal life of the SWP to support the minority Cochranite faction against Cannon, but also of the mess the Comintern had made of the American Communist Party in the 1920s. He ended with a not-so-veiled threat that I had damn well better stop writing Sherry Mangan, as he was not about to allow anybody from abroad to mess around in the SWP again.

I told Cannon that I was not in any kind of bloc with the Pablo center and that I knew little about it. I explained that I just liked their magazine and that I completely agreed with him about the importance of party building and the crime of unnecessary splits that dispersed our small forces.

When I returned to New York City I decided to study a bit on international matters. I ordered a stack of yellowed mimeographed bulletins that covered the 1953 faction fight with Cochran and the related international split. I plowed through this material and then discussed it with Shane Mage, who was friendly with the *La Verité* group in France, led by Pierre Lambert. (At the time, this group was kosher in the eyes of the SWP leadership.) I could not make much out of the documents covering the Cochran dispute. Comrades wrote at great length about whether Stalinism was counterrevolutionary "through and through" or simply counterrevolutionary. What was clear to me was that a sizable section of the working-class members of the SWP wanted to get out of the party. I was not shocked that the reactionary mood in the country in the 1950s produced such a tendency within the party.

The international side of the dispute seemed a little clearer to me.

Michel Pablo had become convinced that a revolutionary tide was sweeping the postwar world and that the Stalinists were leading it. While it was difficult to spot such a tide in the United States, certainly Tito's break with the Kremlin, the victory of the Chinese Revolution, and the bitter struggle in Vietnam gave some empirical basis for his view. The problem was, as Pablo saw it, that we, the real revolutionaries, were not a part of the process. Objective conditions were forcing the Stalinists to act in a revolutionary fashion, and we Trotskyists needed to be inside the Stalinist organizations where we could influence this process.

Pablo then sought to utilize the tiny international apparatus of the Fourth International to force the various sections to enter the Communist parties. Where he was successful in convincing comrades to carry out this tactic, the results were disastrous. The difficulty was that while the Stalinists were willing to fight imperialism in different parts of the world, they remained internally rigid and bitterly hostile to the Trotskyists. The majority of the French Trotskyist organization, led by Pierre Lambert, resisted and were expelled from the Fourth International. In England Pablo supported a minority within Gerry Healy's group. Then he tried to advance his scheme by supporting the Cochranite opposition within the American SWP. Jim Cannon simply issued an "Open Letter" declaring independence from Pablo's International Secretariat of the Fourth International (IS). He formed a rival international group called the International Committee of the Fourth International (IC). This new group was composed primarily of Lambert's group, Healy's group, and the SWP.

In 1960 I was sufficiently trusted to be invited to attend an International Committee meeting as part of the SWP delegation. This rare event was held in Toronto.[16] Our delegation was composed of Jim Cannon, Tom Kerry, Farrell Dobbs, Murry Weiss, George Novack, and me. The small Canadian group was represented by its leader, Ross Dowson, an old worker by the name of Pat, and Ernie Tate. I knew Ernie from our early YSA days when he spent a summer in New York and helped us greatly in our work. Then there was Gerry Healy, who represented the Socialist Labour League and was also the secretary of the IC. The French were not able to attend, though they had met with Healy in Europe immediately prior to the conference.

The French were very much the main subject of the discussion. Jim Cannon wanted to resolve the split in the FI. The Lambertist Parti Communiste Internationaliste (PCI) was the main force within the IC resisting any unity moves. Cannon's idea, borrowed from past Comintern experience, was to set up a parity committee between the two factions to run the FI in the interim in preparation for a world congress. As a concession to the French, and also to ease his own worries about Pablo expressed so forcefully to me a year earlier, Cannon agreed that the IC side in any parity committee would not accept Pablo as International Secretary. Throughout these discussions, Gerry Healy was very supportive of the SWP. In return the SWP agreed to run some articles in the *Militant* defending Healy's group, the Socialist Labour League, which at the time was being subjected to a factional attack by the small IS group in England.[17] I gave a report on the very positive growth we were experiencing in our youth work, and Healy reported on similar growth in England, which had led to control of the Labour Party's youth movement, the Young Socialists. No one attending that gathering would have thought that Cannon and Healy would be at each other's throats within a year or that I would be in the thick of the mess—on Healy's side!

Occasionally we SWP Political Committee members would be treated to a visit by a foreign dignitary. There were no more prestigious visitors than those from the Lanka Sama Samaja Party (LSSP) (Equality Party of Sri Lanka). The LSSP was the pride and joy of world Trotskyism for very good reason. It was the only Trotskyist party to win real mass influence and to have at least a bit of a taste of power. At the time I met the LSSP leaders the party had the largest opposition bloc in the Ceylonese parliament.

The first LSSP leader I met was Doric de Souza, a member of the Ceylon parliament who was traveling in the United States as a guest of the Parliamentary Union. Doric, who had joined the LSSP in the 1930s while a student at the university, attended our PC meeting on the fourth floor of 116 University Place. I was rather impressed with the very correct-sounding Marxist assessment of the Ceylonese situation, presented in perhaps too professorial a tone. Doric explained in detail the communalist divisions in Ceylon and attacked Prime Minister Bandaranaike's demagogic exploitation of Sinhalese nationalism. I was told privately by comrades "in the know" that de Souza represented a "center" element that was resisting a more opportunist policy being pressed by N. M. Perara.[18] Four years later I would find that this was not quite the case.

I especially remember Robert Gunawardena, a very large man with a dark complexion. Robert, brother of the more famous Philip,[19] had been among the founders of the party in the 1930s and had a reputation of being one of its most militant leaders. He was staying in the pleasant town house of George and Connie Weissman, who always put up the important foreigners (like Trotsky's grandson Sieva).[20] I interviewed Robert for the *Young Socialist*. He told me all about the LSSP's "youth leagues," which he claimed had some forty thousand members. These appeared to be quite different from the YSA. They really were village organizations made up of peasants of all ages, and they gave the LSSP its mass base. These leagues were Robert's special field of work. He impressed me very much; he was spirited, an effective leader of masses of people.

The SWP leaders greeted Doric and Robert very warmly, and the feelings were obviously mutual. These were men of the same generation, the radicals of the 1930s. While the SWP had, even in its best period, functioned on a much more modest scale than had the LSSP, it had had its taste of mass action, of sharp class struggle, of leadership. In the war period it was SWP seamen who maintained these Asian revolutionaries' contact with the thinking of Trotskyists elsewhere. It is true that in 1953 the LSSP had refused to follow the SWP out of Pablo's International Secretariat. Yet these leaders had made it quite clear that their own sympathies were with the more orthodox views of the Cannonites.

To the extent that old-style Trotskyism had succeeded anywhere, it had succeeded in Ceylon. I did not realize at the time how swiftly old-style Trotskyism would be put to the test. Trotskyism would not only survive in the next period but flourish perhaps to a greater extent than in any other period of its short, stormy history. However, it would be a different Trotskyism, embraced by a different generation.

Notes

1. James P. Cannon, *The History of American Trotskyism* (New York: Pioneer Publishers, 1944), pp. 169–88.
2. Robert Chester, *Workers' and Farmers' Governments Since the Second World War* (New York: Socialist Workers Party, 1978). Bob died of a heart attack in 1975 and Ann went to live in the Bay Area, where she played a somewhat dissident role in the San Francisco branch.
3. I last heard of her in the early 1980s when she was Oakland branch organizer. Pearl's daughter, Eva (who at one point married a Cuban and lived in Cuba), was also active in the party for many years.
4. Jack Barnes was National Secretary then. See chapter 11, "The Prodigal Son."
5. Frank J. Donner, *The Age of Surveillance* (New York: Vintage Books, 1981), p. 137.
6. Her book *Woman's Evolution* (New York: Pathfinder Press, 1975) made quite an impact in the 1970s.
7. There were six brothers who were active in the labor movement. Four became Communists: Bill, Vincent R., Grant, and Miles. Bill Dunne remained in the Communist Party and was closely associated with William Z. Foster. The other three became Trotskyists, Vincent R. (Ray) being the most prominent and the only one I knew personally. See Theodore Draper, *The Roots of American Communism* (New York: Viking Press, 1966), p. 317.
8. The Franklin brothers, John, Clarence, Robert, and William, were the subjects of an FBI COINTELPRO operation. See Nelson Blackstock, *Cointelpro* (New York: Pathfinder Press, 1988), pp. 83–91.

9. Nat led an important split from the party in the 1980s. See chapter 11, "The Prodigal Son."
10. The conflict had its origins during the Cochranite split in 1953. Weiss had taken the lead in fighting the largely working-class Cochran group while Dobbs had dragged his feet, having many personal ties with the group's members. After the split Weiss's young supporters went on a party-building campaign that Dobbs felt threatened his control of the party. Jim Cannon intervened, called a truce in the new factionalism, and got both leaders to agree to work with each other. Weiss had to announce to the party that he was dissolving his "group" even though he claimed he did not have one, and Dobbs was forced to give Murry a leadership role in the party.
11. "Li Fu-jen (Frank Glass, John Liang) 1901–1988," *Revolutionary History* (London, Summer 1988).
12. Alan M. Wald, *The Revolutionary Imagination; The Poetry and Politics of John Wheelwright and Sherry Mangan* (Chapel Hill, NC: University of North Carolina Press, 1985).
13. This correspondence was reprinted in "How Healy and Pablo Blocked Reunification (Documents, 1956–58)" (New York: Education for Socialists, July 1978, National Education Department, Socialist Workers Party), pp. 97–100.
14. Later published as *The First Ten Years of American Communism* (New York: Lyle Stuart, 1962).
15. James P. Cannon, *Speeches to the Party* (New York: Pathfinder Press, 1973), pp. 67–91.
16. This meeting is not mentioned in Robert Alexander's otherwise thorough account of the history of the International Committee. Robert J. Alexander, *International Trotskyism 1929–1985* (Durham, NC: Duke University Press, 1991), pp. 537–39.
17. This group was led by Ted Grant. It is now known as the Militant Group. It has considerable influence within the British Labour Party but has no affiliation with the Fourth International.
18. For background on the LSSP, see George Jan Lerski, *Origins of Trotskyism in Ceylon* (Stanford: Hoover Institution, 1968).
19. Philip by this time had broken from the LSSP and joined the Bandaranaike government on his own.
20. Siéva, who now calls himself Esteban Volkov Bronstein, lives in Mexico City, where he is an engineer. While not interested in politics, he has concerned himself with defending his grandfather's reputation. *New York Times* (November 16, 1987).

5

The Cuban Revolution

THE CUBAN DISCUSSION

In January 1959, the July 26 Movement (M-26), a radical non-Communist peasant guerrilla army, threw out the Batista dictatorship in Cuba and came to power. In the last stage of its struggle it moved beyond guerrilla warfare to lead a mass uprising of the population. M-26 was dominated by the personality of Fidel Castro, a leader in the Latin caudillo mold.[1] At first Castro established a relatively moderate coalition government committed to agrarian reform. Castro tried to maintain good relations with the United States while at the same time pursuing his domestic reforms. The old Communist Party (known as the Popular Socialist Party—PSP) had relatively little influence over Castro because it had had links at one time with Batista and had opposed the guerrilla-warfare strategy.

In 1960 this situation changed dramatically. Fidel Castro pushed forward a very radical course of reform within the country that threatened American economic interests, his coalition government broke up, and the United States responded with a trade embargo. The state declared a monopoly on foreign trade, the land was nationalized, and virtually all U.S. and Cuban-owned capitalist enterprises were expropriated. Castro turned to the Soviet bloc for aid, and the role of the Communists was expanded on all levels within the country.

With these exciting events taking place, the entire Socialist Workers Party turned its attention to this small island in the Caribbean. At first our tasks were clear, and the party approached them with enthusiasm and unanimity; Cuba was under attack by U.S. imperialism, and we did all we could to defend it. It is very much to their credit that the SWP leadership and membership came out right away to defend Cuba. Most of our activity centered on the Fair Play for Cuba Committee, an organization that the SWP did not found but did play a major role in building around the country.

But as Trotskyists, we were obliged to do more than defend Cuba. We had to understand its revolution theoretically and place that understanding within the framework of our overall view of the world revolutionary process. On this basis we would determine the details of our political stance in relation to the revolution. Were we to be more than the *defenders* of Cuba and become its supporters, its advocates? Should we hold up the "Cuban model" as a desirable one for revolutionaries in other countries to follow, as we had done for so many years with the Russian Revolution? Or should we distance ourselves from Cuba's leadership and take a more critical stance?

There was much in the Cuban Revolution that appealed to the SWP. It was non-Stalinist in origins and very radical. Castro appeared to be carrying out in practice Leon Trotsky's theory of the permanent revolution, though he did not use the terminology. This theory holds that in order to carry out "democratic tasks" (national independence and economic development) in a lesser-developed nation, revolutionaries need to pursue a socialist course (the overthrow of capitalism).[2] The revolution also seemed to be highly popular and had politically mobilized masses of people.

Above all the SWP was desperately hungry for a revolution it could wholeheartedly embrace—not just critically defend. Party members had been living on the thin gruel of a degenerated revolution for too long, and their orthodoxy had kept them from giving in to the temptation of too great an enthusiasm for the Stalinist-led Chinese and Vietnamese revolutions. American radicals have always been tempted to seek to overcome the despair brought on by bleak prospects at home by uncritically embracing a foreign revolution.

Cuba became the SWP's revolution. SWP members identified with it and its leadership wholeheartedly and almost uncritically. Jim Cannon was the most enthusiastic. Finally, he felt, he was witness to a revolution comparable to the Russian Revolution, the event that had shaped his adult life. Farrell Dobbs, who was the SWP's presidential candidate at the time, made a trip to the island, donned a sugarcane-cutter's hat, and favorably inspected the revolution firsthand. Murry Weiss could not contain his enthusiasm. For him the implications went beyond the narrow confines of the SWP, a party within which he felt increasingly suffocated. He dreamed of some broader revolutionary reunification that would go beyond Trotskyism and prepared his own departure from the party.

It was Joe Hansen who took over the task of working out the theoretical implications of the Cuban Revolution. The Political Committee (PC), with Joe doing the thinking, decided in the fall of 1960 that Cuba was a "workers' and farmers' government" on its way to becoming a workers' state. Then on December 23, 1960, the PC passed a resolution:

> When the capitalist holdings in the key sectors of Cuban economy were taken over by the government, Cuba entered the transitional phase of a workers' state, although one lacking as yet the forms of democratic proletarian rule.[3]

The PC's main concern was Cuba's character as a workers' state. The lack of democratic forms was seen as a relatively minor problem that would in time be rectified by the Castro leadership, which the PC viewed as being democratically oriented.

I began to discuss this question with my closest friends in the YSA. First I consulted Jim Robertson and Shane Mage, who had led the minority in the Shachtmanites with me. We had shared common experiences then, and we were still politically close within the SWP. Of course, we did not always agree on tactical matters, but we had come to share a kind of common worry about the party. The leadership had seemed to chase after the Stalinists during the regroupment period, watering down our political program for their benefit. We were also dissatisfied with the static, routinized condition of political and theoretical discussion in the party.

It seemed to us that the SWP was embracing Castro a bit too wholeheartedly and uncritically. The necessary defense of a beleaguered nation against imperialist assault was giving way to a process of political identification with its leadership. We could not accept such an identification. We insisted that Cuba must be seen within the framework of our general Trotskyist perspective. So we prepared our own memorandum to the Political Committee, which we felt assessed Castro and Cuba in a more orthodox and balanced manner.

We were not yet ready to declare Cuba a workers' state, a point the majority took as a kind of Shachtmanism. However, the question of whether Cuba was a workers' state was not at the heart of our differences with the majority of the PC. We realized that Cuba was headed in the direction of a society based on the state ownership of the means of production, which we all then called a workers' state. Our main concern was the lack of democratic forms of rule in Cuba.

The single incident that exposed most clearly the problem of the SWP majority's attitude toward Cuba was the suppression of the Trotskyist movement there in 1961. There had been a small Trotskyist group in Cuba since the days of Trotsky. It published a paper supporting the revolution but criticizing Castro from the left, particularly urging the formation of workers' councils. We learned in June 1961 that the government had seized the print shop that published the paper, banned the paper, and broken up the type that was being set in preparation for publishing Trotsky's book *The Permanent Revolution*. Some Argentine Trotskyists, in Cuba to help the group, were expelled from the country, and the leading Cubans were put in jail. (I later met several of these wonderful comrades in Havana in 1983.)

The response of the SWP leadership was mild, indeed. They attributed the action to some middle-level government official and hinted that the Cuban Stalinists had acted without the knowledge and backing of Castro. Yet the act was never reversed. In fact, it was part of a consolidation of monolithic power around Castro that included a purge of the Castroite but anti-Communist trade union leader David Salvador, and in time, the non-Communist group around the paper *Revolution*.[4] Our minority, quite correctly, was incensed by the action and the failure of the SWP majority to draw from it any political lessons. If Castro was throwing Trotskyists in jail in Cuba, what in the world was the meaning of all the SWP's talk about the "objectively" Trotskyist character of the revolution? And further, if the SWP would not defend in any serious way our imprisoned comrades abroad, did this mean that Trotskyism was in danger of being abandoned outside the United States? We in the minority thought so.

In January 1961, the Socialist Labour League (SLL), the major British Trotskyist group headed by Gerry Healy, sent a long letter to the SWP Political Committee sharply criticizing the party's position on Cuba along the same lines as had our minority. The document went further; it related the Cuba debate to the messy factional situation within the Fourth International. Healy's document advocated deepening the split with the International Secretariat (Pablo-Mandel) at a time when the SWP was actively trying to reunite with that group. Not coincidentally, the Pablo-Mandel formation had the same assessment of the Cuban Revolution as did the SWP leadership.

The letter made a deep impact on our group. We had not thought much about the problems of the Fourth International up to that point. Our thinking at the time flowed from our own experiences within the SWP as well as from our attempt to understand the Cuban Revolution within the framework of contemporary Marxist theory. However, it did not take us long to find ourselves in a factional alliance with Healy and the Lambert group, doing battle with the majority of the SWP leadership.

The SWP held a National Committee Plenum in January 1961, which adopted the Political Committee position on Cuba and launched the reunification effort. The meeting was held in New York in our old hall on the second floor of 116 University Place. It was quite an affair. There I was in the middle of a faction fight again. I had been a part of the leadership since 1957 and was not prepared psychologically for being a besieged minority. I was the only comrade on the NC who held any critical ideas on Cuba.

The day I was to speak about Cuba I had a 102-degree fever and my presentation had a slightly hysterical pitch. We had accomplished so much together in the four very busy years since the YSL convention, yet here I was again leading our small group of dissenters in a one-sided struggle. The players and issues were different now, but I had much the same feelings. I had learned a little since 1957 and conducted myself accordingly. I was exhilarated, and the clash of ideas was exciting. Yet I also felt a kind of demoralization that had not been present in 1957. Then the problem had been clear enough: I needed to break with Shachtmanism, the tendency Trotsky himself had denounced, and become part of the mainstream of Trotskyism and all would be well. Now all was not well, and I was finding myself terribly isolated within this mainstream. "Oh well," I thought, "on with the battle; deeper thoughts will have to be put off to later."

The discussion went rather poorly. My views on the Cuban question did not lead members of the majority to evaluate critically the Cuban Revolution. Instead, each speaker tried to outdo the previous one in expressing enthusiasm for the party line. The appeal of a fresh revolution was too great for us to sway a cadre that had waited over thirty years for some kind of breakthrough. Further, the word had quietly gotten around the plenum that unification with the Pablo group was imminent and it was best to find nice things to say about these old enemies. I was most shocked with the remarks of Morris Stein, an old Trotskyist for whom I had great respect. He stated that "the Soviet Union is compelled today, instead of playing a counter-revolutionary role—to place itself on the side of revolution."[5] If this was the case why, I thought, did we bother to break with Pablo to begin with, or for that matter, bother with Trotskyism at all? The party leadership, however, liked the discussion so much that they took the unprecedented step of transcribing it in its entirety and publishing it in a preconvention discussion bulletin.

Between the January plenum and the June convention we recruited our minority faction. Most of the recruiting took place right around the time of the plenum. I have found this to be one of the laws of faction fighting. There is a preciously short period of time when party members are open to any ideas different from those of the leadership. It is in this brief period, usually lasting no more than a week or two, when a minority recruits its support. Then, with forces lined up on both sides, an intense discussion ensues—many discussion bulletins are issued, lengthy debates, lasting weeks, take place in all branches—during which almost all minds are already closed. It is a ritual that affects the outcome very slightly. Sometimes the intensity of the bombardment coming from the leadership rescues a few stray lambs from the clutches of the minority wolves. The results seem to have more to do with the intensity of social pressure than with the brilliance of argumentation—I speak as someone who has been on each side of the battle more than once. This is why most minorities try their best to get an early start, feeling out friends in the party, privately showing them draft documents, and hopefully gaining some adherents before the leadership is even aware a minority is coming into existence. These necessities, I am afraid, tend to give minorities a cliquish structure. All minorities I have observed have such a structure to one degree or another.

The dispute heated up on the eve of the convention when the leadership issued a document attacking us as a petty bourgeois formation similar to the 1940 Shachtman group and linked to it through leading figures such as Robertson, Mage, and me. The document was designed to poison the atmosphere of the discussion, a task it successfully accomplished. Cannon then published a series of letters he had sent to the party center in New York in which he denounced Healy for being on a "sectarian binge," an assessment that was not totally off the mark. In retrospect the discussion was proceeding right on schedule; it reached a point of almost orgasmic frenzy and hysteria on the eve of the convention.

The 1961 convention was the last one to be held at Mountain Spring Camp. The sessions took place in the large dining hall with open sides on the top of a hill. A special National Committee meeting was scheduled in the dining hall on the day before the convention opened. The atmosphere was very tense, and most of us in the minority feared we might be expelled at this convention. Certainly the NC meeting started out badly as Tom Kerry bitterly denounced us for "factionalizing" the youth. Then during a meal break I met with Jim Cannon. We worked out an agreement about control of the YSA in order to create a better atmosphere for the convention and to gain some time to work for our views within the party after the convention.

Cannon came up with the idea that the YSA should add two new members to its leading committee—Peter Camejo and Barry Sheppard[6]—and that the SWP should implement its right as a fraternal organization to appoint a party representative to also sit on the committee. My old buddy Carl Feingold was chosen for this task. The addition of Pete and Barry gave those in the youth leadership who supported the SWP majority on Cuba half the votes. Feingold would have, when he felt it critical to use it, the deciding vote. The rest of the minority leadership was consulted and agreed with me that we needed to make this concession.

The convention then proceeded with a slightly improved tone. At least I was not alone. The Minority Tendency had three delegates, and I had speaking rights as a full member of both the National and Political committees. But the discussion held no surprises and did not influence anyone's views. In the end I was reelected to the NC and PC, but this time to represent the minority rather than the youth.

The FBI took note of my election to the National Committee as a full member representing our Minority Tendency. My Security Index file was reopened on July 6, 1961, to verify my membership on the National Committee and Political Committee and "to designate subject as a Key Figure." On August 25, 1961, I was placed on the Key Figure list. My file was tabbed DETCOM (Detention Communist), which meant I would be among the first to be picked up when the mass raids took place. My home address, place of employment, and related information would now be checked every three months instead of just once a year.

By rights, we were also entitled to a National Committee alternate, a position we did not get. I protested to Jim Cannon, who bluntly said, "You are not entitled to anything. We give you what we want to give to you." Cannon's attitude did not jibe with my reading of the party constitution, nor did I feel it was consistent with the Trotskyist tradition on minority rights. Oh well, it was his party, so I guessed he ought to know.

The YSA Convention

The Cuba discussion did not end at the convention because the YSA had its convention scheduled for December. It was to determine its own attitude toward Cuba. It was unclear what role SWP members within the YSA should play in this discussion, as the SWP—a democratic centralist organization—had a formal position on the matter. I raised the issue on the PC, and the leadership equivocated. I suspected that the minority was being set up for expulsion if we put forward our views during the YSA debate. Finally Morris Stein intervened and agreed with me that the PC had an obligation to clarify whether minority members could speak their minds within the YSA discussion. Stein's position forced Farrell Dobbs and the rest of the leadership to give us permission to present our views within the YSA. Moishe's intervention struck me as a voice from the SWP's proud past and a reflection of its honest, democratic, working-class roots.

That fall we had a repeat discussion within the YSA, and we all knew that the result was a foregone conclusion. The PC's decision to permit a democratic discussion actually served the leadership quite well. It allowed them to rally their forces and to completely isolate us within the YSA, where we still had influence.

The YSA convention was held December 29–31 at a dismal old hall in a decaying section of Chicago near the Loop. The building also served as a single-occupancy hotel. I noticed a Bulgarian anarchist newspaper stuck into a couple of the mail boxes! Outside the wind was blowing and it was snowing.

The FBI was present—hopefully the agents suffered frostbite!—and circulated in their usual fashion "125 photographs obtained by means of a photofisur [surveillance by camera] at the entrance of 777 Adams Street, Chicago, on 12/29–31/61, conducted by SAs [blacked out] during the time the YSA National Convention was in progress at this location."

The setting seemed perfect for the grim proceedings that we knew would take place. Jim Robertson, Shane Mage, and I were not to be allowed to retire peacefully from the youth organization, which we had played such an important role in creating. It was as if the YSA as a body was placing its collective finger down its collective throat and throwing us up.

I gave the main presentation on Cuba, and it was a better speech than I had given at the party convention. When I had finished I walked down the aisle through the hostile delegates of the majority to the section in the back of the hall where our minority delegates were seated. A young woman delegate—I barely knew her—jumped up, threw her arms around me, and gave me a big kiss. It unsettled rather than pleased me. I was reminded of the scene I had witnessed at the 1959 SWP convention when Sam Marcy gave a speech in a fashion that did not touch a single delegate outside his own followers. His followers were, like this young comrade, enthralled! Were we now like the Marcyites were then: a cult totally isolated within a miniscule party that itself had at best marginal influence within the society as a whole?

We were not the only ones removed from the youth leadership at that cold, stormy convention. The key youth who had worked with our group of former Shachtmanites in creating the YSA were, with the important exception of Sherry Finer (Dobbs's daughter), supporters of Murry and Myra

Tanner Weiss. This group, which included Jim Lambrecht (Lamb), Arthur Felberbaum (Phelps), and Nora Roberts, led the attack on us regarding Cuba. Their reward was that they were maneuvered out of the new leadership of the YSA. The victors were Peter Camejo and Barry Sheppard. Jack Barnes, who was in this period organizer of the SWP New York Local, would soon be moved into the youth as YSA National Secretary, an important step in his ascendancy to leadership of the SWP itself.

Hard Times and Despair

After the convention I entered a very difficult and peculiar stage of my political work. By the end of 1961, for the first time since I took up the socialist cause, I was no longer involved in a youth organization. We all grow up, I suppose. The problem was that there was nothing for grown-ups to do in the SWP. With the sole exception of the Fair Play for Cuba Committee—where I was not particularly wanted—the only significant party work was youth work. And because of the factional tensions that had persisted since the convention, the leadership was not particularly anxious to allow me to create new areas of meaningful party work. My political life became the life of our tendency, and since most of our adherents were in the same boat, this life became rather inwardly directed.

Every now and then we minority members of the SWP were able to join our fellow members and carry out some activity: "On 10/27/62, SAs [blacked out] and [blacked out] observed and photographed a picket demonstration which was held between the hours of 3:00 P.M. and 5:00 P.M. on 47th Street and First Avenue, adjacent to the UN." The Fair Play for Cuba Committee was one of the sponsors, and I got my picture taken once again.

I had been carrying on an intense correspondence with Gerry Healy since January 1961. I reported to him in detail on all our activities, thoughts, and what was happening in the party in general. Gerry, as usual, was extremely busy, traveling some 1,200 miles a week, as he reported to me in one of his letters. So I got about one letter from him for every three or four I sent. Each letter was carefully passed around to the other minority comrades and its implications thoroughly discussed. We began to feel very much a part of an international formation, with Gerry the leader.

This international support helped to counteract our deep feeling of isolation within the SWP. Yet though we did not realize the implications, we were paying a price for this support: London was becoming our Moscow.

Healy's letters were warm, supportive, almost fatherly. In style they reminded me very much of Jim Cannon's writing: blunt, mainly practical rather than theoretical, and tough yet tactically wise. A recurrent theme was his shortage of cash. I expect Healy missed the bit of revenue he used to con out of the SWP. At one point we were asked to contribute one thousand dollars toward a trip by an SLL leader to Japan to meet with Trotskyists there and seek to win them over to our positions. We came up with the money but Healy never sent anyone.[7]

Our tactical perspectives got a definite boost when the Fox group joined the Minority Tendency. This very small group of talented comrades was all that remained within the SWP of a faction led by the West Indian intellectual C. L. R. James (J. R. Johnson).[8] When Johnson split from the SWP in 1950 to build his own party, Fox and friends[9] remained, holding to their view that the USSR was a state capitalist country. They were convinced, however, that the SWP was a revolutionary party with a proletarian leadership that in time would come over to their views. They were deeply committed to a "workerist" concept of party building, which, to their credit, they carried out in their own lives.

The FBI placed our Minority Tendency under surveillance: "Unless stated to the contrary, all functions sponsored by the SWP minority faction were held at the WOHLFORTH *residence, 320 West 101st Street, New York City." We can assume that they placed an informant within our tendency. On November 28, 1962, the FBI issued "12 copies of a letterhead memorandum pertaining to the current activities of the SWP Minority Tendency suitable for dissemination."*

My activities as a member of the SWP were also watched: "On the following dates, TIMOTHY WOHLFORTH *was observed leaving SWP headquarters, New York City, by Special Agents of the Federal Bureau of Investigation: October 18, 1962; November 15, 1962; and February 7, 1963."*

Unfortunately, all was not well with our faction, which had swelled to about sixty people. The spirited clash of views in the preconvention period was now in the past. We had to adjust to the dull and suffocating existence of a minority inside a relatively inactive party that was mainly engaged in doing things we disagreed with. The effect—and I have seen it so many times in factional situations—was that many of our members were turned inward to a life of cliquish gossip, developing in the process a very embittered attitude toward the party majority. Many of the majority members in turn felt hostile and suspicious toward us. This pressurized scene set the stage for a sharp clash within the Minority Tendency over perspectives.

A majority of our faction, led by Jim Robertson, no longer considered the SWP a revolutionary party: In their opinion, the SWP's position on Cuba was "liquidationist," and the party was now "centrist." A smaller group of people, who supported me—Danny Freeman, Fred Mazelis, Jack Jersawitz, my wife, Martha, the Foxes (Art, Edie, and their son Steve), and a few others—wanted to remain in the SWP and hopefully win over a majority to our views. While we did share with Robertson a very harsh—overly harsh, in fact—assessment of the SWP, we were not ready to write it off as a revolutionary force. We felt that Robertson's inflexibility could lead to a premature split. So now I led a minority within a minority!

Art Fox was the strongest in our camp on the issue. His group had survived since 1950 through its belief in the working-class character of the SWP. He and his followers were convinced that whatever its momentary political weaknesses, the SWP's proletarian cadre would react in a revolutionary fashion in the long run. Art traveled to England and convinced Healy to support this view. Healy got Lambert's support and, in Comintern fashion, wrote a perspectives statement for us and demanded that each member of the tendency sign it. Only those who signed it would be considered members of a tendency supported by the IC. Robertson, quite understandably, screamed Stalinism, and his people refused to sign. It was in this way that two small tendencies emerged inside the SWP.

The internal battle with Robertson was my third faction fight in six years. The battle with Shachtman had been fresh and exciting, and, within the context of the great changes then taking place on the Left, had filled us with hope. The battle with Cannon and his followers was serious and was conducted with more maturity. Although it centered on reasonably clear political issues, it was somehow sad and depressing. The old party cadres did not listen to us, and we were reduced to a small following among the youth. The conflict with Robertson was personal, intensely bitter, politically confusing, and degenerate. It almost drove me out of politics completely.

Considering the isolation of our tendency within the SWP, Robertson's approach appealed to a majority of our members. Robertson carried the day in part because so many in our tendency were sick of life in the SWP.

My feelings—though not my rational thoughts and perspectives—were with these comrades. Having been removed from the vitality of the YSA, I myself could hardly stand the dull life of a party member. Some of Robertson's backers, such as the Bay Area group around Joyce Cowley, were in the process of leaving politics altogether. Every minority picks up demoralized people and most of us, at some point in our political lives on the left, experience similar feelings, if only momentarily.

LIFE GOES ON

In 1959, a little over a year before the faction struggle broke out in the SWP, my second son, Bill, was born. Of course he was named after Big Bill Haywood, the anarcho-syndicalist leader of the Western Federation of Miners and of the Industrial Workers of the World who died in the Soviet Union. We moved to the Upper West Side to have a bit more room for our growing family. As I was on movement salary, we settled for a tenement building on West 89th Street between Columbus and Amsterdam. We had a railroad apartment, a fifth-floor walk-up. Two large windows made the front room light and bright. As you walked toward the back of the apartment, you passed through a series of perpetually dark rooms without the benefit of any hallways. In the rear was the kitchen and behind it a very small bathroom.

Soon after the 1961 SWP convention Martha and I moved to a new apartment on 101st Street, near Riverside Park. It was an old town house that had been cut up into apartments. We had two immense rooms and a small kitchen. The front room had been given over to the two children, leaving us with a beautifully paneled living room that also served as bedroom and office. It was definitely a step upward from the decaying railroad flat.

It was not an easy time for Martha and me and our small family. We were isolated within the party, relatively demoralized politically, and doing our best to survive financially. Then Martha got pregnant. We knew we did not want another child; we were having enough difficulty making our way with two children. Martha was beginning to get back into music and was planning a career. We decided she must get an abortion. But this was the period before abortions were legal. We had to find someone to perform a safe abortion.

Through friends we discovered an émigré doctor who was willing, for the very large sum at that time of eight hundred dollars, to perform an abortion. We went to a little office at the top of a building on the West Side. The doctor examined Martha, packed her uterus with cotton in preparation for the abortion, collected his eight hundred dollars, and sent us home. The abortion was to be conducted in our apartment! The doctor came with his little black bag on a Saturday morning. The children had been sent away with friends. The doctor instructed us to immediately pull down all window shades. He was a nice enough fellow, but the whole incident was frightening and emotionally disturbing. I was sent into the next room to wait, and Martha was placed on the kitchen table for the abortion. He gave her a local anesthetic and quickly completed the abortion. He told us not to call if there were any problems but to go immediately to a hospital and claim that a miscarriage had taken place. There was some bleeding but no complications. The problem was more emotional than physical, as Martha recovered after a few days' rest. Neither I nor Martha will ever forget this incident.

THE 1963 CONVENTION

The 1963 convention was held in New York City at the Empire Hotel. It was one of those second-class New York hotels that sported a kind of seedy ornateness. The convention turned out to be a very lively event. It revealed new factions emerging from out of the old party cadres, consummated a process of split and reunification on an international level, and began a course that led to the expulsion of the Robertson group from the party.

"TIM WOHLFORTH was observed at the Empire Hotel, New York City, on July 18 and 21, 1963."

It was a convention of minorities; all flowers were blooming but not getting much nourishment. Arne Swabeck, pioneer American Communist and Trotskyist, came forward with his special position on China. Arne was a frail-looking man who must have been in his late sixties at the time. He had a sharpness of wit and cussed independence of spirit that made him a lot tougher than he looked. When I was young I was very much impressed by the movie *Lost Horizons*, which featured a thousand-year-old wrinkled and dried-up Dalai Lama, and that was the image that Arne brought into my mind.

Arne's message was straightforward. He had studied the Chinese Revolution and had become convinced that overall, Mao Tse-tung had done a bang-up job of it. Now that Mao was taking on the USSR, Arne felt this proved that Mao *objectively*, to use a favorite Trotskyist word of those days, was a revolutionary and a Trotskyist (something that Mao himself was not aware of). The SWP leadership had fallen for nearby Castro and his revolution, so Arne looked to the more distant, but much grander, "Red sun rising in the East." Arne did not object to the SWP's Cuban position, it was just that he felt the Chinese events were much more important. He bought the books and read the magazines and became quite an expert on the Far East. He got a lot of help from Cecil Glass (John Liang), who supported his positions. He won over James Boulton and his Milwaukee branch, admittedly not much of a catch, but in faction fights one cannot be overly choosy. It was sad, perhaps, but not unexpected, that Arne lost his battle. He was regarded for a while after that as something of a crank and was eventually expelled from the party in 1967. This was too bad, because Arne deserved better.

Dick Fraser and his Seattle branch came forward with a special position on what was then still called "the Negro question." Fraser had conducted a rather obscure polemic with George Breitman around this issue for a number of years. In 1963 we observed the first indications of the rise of black nationalist views within the black movement. The SWP leadership, with Breitman as point man, warmly greeted this development, seizing upon Trotsky's advocacy of the right of self-determination for American blacks. The leadership interpreted Trotsky's view as advocacy of black nationalism. It felt that the task of the *Militant* was to popularize and encourage black nationalist views without criticism. Soon after this convention the SWP became a strong advocate of Malcolm X, reporting his activities prominently in the *Militant* and publishing his speeches.

Fraser did not dispute the right of blacks to self-determination, only the advocacy of black nationalism. He believed that the migration of blacks from the rural South into the cities, North and South, made any kind of national separation impossible. He did not believe that blacks were a nation but believed rather that they were an oppressed racial minority. He believed that we should have criticized black nationalist leaders for proposing a course that was unrealistic and harmful to the cause of ending racial oppression in the country.[10]

The most important happening at the convention was the decision to move ahead with unification of the Fourth International. The SWP leadership had reached agreement to unite the IC with the IS, now led by Ernest Mandel, to form the United Secretariat of the Fourth International.[11] The cornerstone of the unification was common agreement on Cuba.

As Gerry Healy in England and Pierre Lambert in France would not accept such a unification, a split with these groups was clearly on the agenda. Their positions had many similarities with Cannon's opposition to

Pablo in 1953. A very important ingredient was factional tension in England and France between competing groups affiliated with the IS. At the same time, the Lambert/Healy critique of the past theories of Pablo and Mandel, combined with their opposition over Cuba, gave their position, at least to us in the SWP minority, broader political and theoretical appeal.

Interestingly, the kind of disputes taking place within the SWP were also plaguing the IS. The SWP's unification proposals brought centrifugal forces to the fore. Unification was opposed by Michel Pablo, the International Secretary, and Juan Posados, who headed the Latin American bureau. Pablo believed that a process of de-Stalinization was going on within the USSR and urged an orientation to the Moscow Stalinists, while Ernest Mandel and the IS majority were, like Swabeck (though not in as extreme a manner), sympathetic to China. Pablo was no doubt also aware that reunification would mean loss of the International Secretary post.[12] Posados had built his own privately run little empire in Latin America and equally feared a unification that would bring rival Latin American groups into the FI.[13] Joe Hansen had made a tour of Latin America and had lined up several groups. The most important were Nahuel Moreno's group in Argentina and Luis Vitale's in Chile.[14] This unification and pending split did not bode well for our position in the SWP.

I have said nothing about our "Reorganized Minority Tendency's" participation at the convention for very good reason. It was a dismal affair for both our faction and—this was no solace—for Robertson's "Revolutionary Tendency" (RT) as well. We had hoped that our break with Robertson would allow us to reach more of the party membership. However, this break was overshadowed by the pending unification of the IC with Mandel's IS and the accompanying split from the SWP of Healy and Lambert, our allies.

I was removed from the National Committee and Political Committee at the 1963 convention because the party leadership considered our tendency to be "disloyal." The FBI took note of this demotion and instituted another review of my Security Index status. On November 13, 1963, my SI cards were no longer tabbed DETCOM and I was "deleted as a Key Figure."

The convention set the stage for the expulsion of the Robertson faction. Our faction was to survive one more year. The new National Committee set up a control commission to investigate the RT. This commission took advantage of our internal discussion with Robertson to expel the group, essentially for characterizing the party as centrist and for having what it considered a split orientation.

The 1963 convention proved to be a very important turning point in the history of the SWP. The factional disputes with Fraser and Swabeck were more significant than the small numbers within the party that supported their specific politics. It was the surfacing of a process of political disorientation and personal demoralization that affected a majority of the older party cadre. Dobbs's subterranean war with the supporters of Weiss, which never produced a clear political confrontation, also came to a conclusion following this convention. Murry, wife Myra, brother Dave, Carl Feingold, Bert Deck, their youth supporters such as Jim Lambrecht and Arthur Felberbaum,[15] and many others dropped out. The only prominent supporter of Weiss to remain in the party was Fred Halstead.

Those in the old cadre of the party, which had not aligned with any faction, open or subterranean, continued to leave. A generation was leaving revolutionary politics and a new generation was just beginning to join the movement. Most of us who played the role of linking the old generation to the new through the YSA leadership also dropped away, though one or two, like Peter Camejo and Barry Sheppard, managed to hold on and play important roles in the later 1960s. For a time the loss of older cadres was not countered by the gain of young students. Membership in this period stagnated at less than five hundred, and the party did not significantly grow until 1969.

A Turn to Theory

The one advantage of forced political inactivity is that it gives one time to do some theoretical work. I must say, to my credit, that last year in the SWP was one of my most productive theoretical periods—for which I must thank the party leadership's refusal to let me function productively during this period. Also, I was employed by tobacco trade publishers that year, and my journalistic responsibilities were light. That winter I took a suitcase full of old documents to a Miami Beach kosher hotel. After going across the street to the Fountainbleau to snap a few pictures at a tobacco trade show, I devoted the rest of the week to writing some of my most difficult theoretical material.

My theoretical work began in the summer of 1961. Gerry Healy urged us to focus on the question of Pabloism, which he then considered to be at the heart of the dispute. We were to place the Cuban question in a subordinate position: "Whilst we can continue to discuss the Cuban situation, it is as we have always maintained quite subordinate."[16]

We agreed in general to this approach but found it all but impossible to carry out in practice. We did not determine the agenda of the internal party discussion or what dominated the thinking of most radicals in the United States. Cuba, whether Healy liked it or not, remained at the heart of the party dispute and dominated the thinking and activity of party members.

There was, from a theoretical viewpoint, a more fundamental reason why a discussion of Cuba could not be avoided. It had not proved possible to take Trotsky's theoretical heritage and apply it in a coherent fashion to the postwar world. Unable to lead successful revolutions, the Trotskyists were quite naturally drawn toward those who had. Since the leaders of postwar social change were, in most cases, the Stalinists, and since the resulting regimes were totalitarian, it is not difficult to imagine the confusion and demoralization in world Trotskyist ranks. "Pabloism," the views espoused by Michel Pablo in the 1951 to 1954 period, represented a more extreme expression of this confusion. If we were to combat Pabloism, as Healy urged, we had to develop an alternative theory of postwar Stalinism. We felt that this meant first of all understanding Cuba.

That summer our group began its own discussion on the nature of Cuba. I wrote a document for this purpose declaring that Cuba was a deformed workers' state ruled by an administrative layer around Castro, and that a Trotskyist party was needed to fight for workers' democracy. I suggested that under some circumstances a petty bourgeois formation is theoretically capable of establishing a workers' state but that the price paid for the lack of a working-class leadership is bureaucratic deformation from the very beginning.

The discussion of the document was held in the living room of my new apartment. Jim Robertson loved my document and spoke in support of it. Shane Mage, however, was less enthusiastic. He placed the document within the framework of Trotsky's overall theory of Stalinism and revolution and found it wanting. Shane made two criticisms: (1) Trotsky had insisted that Stalinism was counterrevolutionary—it opposed revolutionary actions and revolutionary victories. Yet my theory held that Stalinists were capable of leading victorious revolutions, though, of course, the product of these revolutions was a far cry from what we called socialism. My theory, therefore, posed a different conception of the nature of Stalinism than did Trotsky's. (2) Trotsky had insisted that only the working class could lead successful revolutions that established workers' states. Yet I was maintaining that a petty bourgeois party and social force—a different class—could, under unusual circumstances, create some kind of workers' state.

Shane suggested that a monistic theory of Stalinism could possibly be evolved if we turned to Trotsky's writings on Poland and Finland in 1940 and Ernest Mandel's (Germain's) development of Trotsky's thought in his theory of *structural assimilation*, which he used to explain East European developments. Shane then dropped the matter and never wrote on the subject, at least to my knowledge, in his years as a member of the Spartacist League. Robertson later published my preliminary document on Cuba, which became the theoretical basis of the Spartacist group's assessment of Cuba and similar revolutionary events. I was intrigued by Shane's suggestions and became determined to try to develop a unitary theory of Stalinism that was consistent with the main body of Trotskyist theory.

I began my thesis, which I later published as *The Theory of Structural Assimilation*,[17] in the fall of 1961 and completed my work on East Europe by the spring of 1962. I had to stop work on the project during the faction fight with Robertson, and then other matters prevented me from returning to it until late 1962, when I worked on the section about Yugoslavia. I was interrupted again and finally completed the document in the summer of 1963.

The remarkable thing about this project was the total lack of interest in it on the part of Healy and his people. I informed him of every step of my work and sent him the draft as I produced it. I got no comments. This seemed strange to me because the heart of Healy's critique of the SWP had been his contention that the party had abandoned Marxist theory. Here I was trying to develop an inclusive theory of postwar Stalinism—the very issue that was at the heart of so many of the disputes and splits in our international movement—and Healy couldn't have cared less. Was my theory off the wall? Did Healy have a better explanation of world Stalinism? He did not criticize my work; he just said nothing. He seemed not to care about it or be aware that the Trotskyist theory of Stalinism was in a total shambles.

When I went to England in 1964, Gerry told me to talk to Cliff Slaughter, his top intellectual, about my project. Slaughter gave me ten minutes on a bench in a railway station. While he did not disagree with my project's overall thrust, Slaughter made some vague methodological points. We went ahead in the winter of 1964 and published the document on our own. I never heard another peep from the Healy people about the theory over the next ten years, one way or another.

My thinking began with a pretty obvious premise: All the existing "socialist" countries were identical in structure—single-party dictatorships in which the means of production were state-owned and centrally directed. It was a reasonable suggestion that this common end product was the result of a common process. I hoped to explain this common process by developing Trotsky's theory of Stalinism. Trotsky viewed Stalinism as a *degenerative* process that infected an existing healthy workers' state. This process led to the triumph of a bureaucratic caste—which could be removed only by revolution—controlling property forms that remained working class in character. I viewed the growth of postwar Stalinist states as the expression of the *defensive expansionism* of this degenerated workers' state.

This explanation worked quite well for East Europe. Here social transformation occurred in an area under the control of Russian troops. Stalin even considered incorporating the area into the USSR and did so with some bordering territories. Soviet consolidation of the region could be explained as a reaction to the Marshall Plan and American consolidation in Western Europe. My document explained—even today I would say quite well—this process in considerable detail: As the petty bourgeois parties were eliminated, the social democratic parties fused with the Communist parties, the new party fused with the state apparatus, new constitutions were written, and trade relations were realigned with the USSR. The societies were thus structurally transformed (a more accurate term than Mandel's "assimilation") after the model of the USSR.

Problems arose when this analysis was applied to Yugoslavia, China, and Cuba, however. Yugoslavia was a product of both the regional military campaigns of the USSR and the indigenous actions of a partisan movement led by the Yugoslav Communists. The Red Army liberated only a very small portion of the country. During the period when Stalin was consolidating his grip on the rest of East Europe, Tito resisted the influence of Stalin's agents within Yugoslavia. In 1948 this led to Yugoslavia's break with the USSR.

The Chinese Revolution represented an even more formidable challenge to my thesis. Stalin viewed China as a kind of strategic buffer protecting his eastern flank, and he sought to secure this flank through the creation of a friendly, though capitalist, government. He pressed the Chinese Communists to work out a power-sharing deal with Chiang Kai-shek. Mao had other ideas and, disregarding Stalin's instructions, led his revolutionary army to power. The Vietnamese Revolution followed the Chinese pattern. However, in defense of my thesis, it was certainly true that the cadres that led these three revolutions were trained in the Stalinist school and had strong links with Soviet bureaucracy during much of their history.

The Cuban Revolution, unlike all the others, was led by a predominantly non-Stalinist group on an island distant from the USSR. However, what really struck me at the time was that when Castro chose to socially transform his country he secured trade links with the USSR and adopted the ideology and organizational structure of Stalinism.[18]

The strength of my structural assimilation thesis was that it maintained consistency with Trotsky's thinking on Stalinism while encompassing all the postwar Stalinist societies. Years later, in the middle 1970s, the Thornett group, which broke away from Healy, discovered my theory and adopted it as its own.[19] My good friend Adam Westoby wrote an introduction to Thornett's reissue of my document, but in it he disputed my theory's application to China. He had a point, as the thesis did not give sufficient weight to the *indigenous independent thrust for power* expressed in Yugoslavia, China, Vietnam, and Cuba.

The central theoretical problem, I now believe, is one that is inherent in Trotskyist theory. It goes back to Trotsky's struggle with the Stalin faction in the 1920s. Trotsky viewed Stalin, then in a bloc with Nikolay Bukharin, as representing a tendency on the part of the bureaucracy to encourage the *degeneration* of the revolution back toward *capitalism*. In 1929 Stalin broke with Bukharin and adopted many of the positions of the Trotskyist opposition in an extremist fashion, carrying through a rapid and bloody forced collectivization of agriculture and a brutal industrialization drive. Trotsky, to his credit, opposed this process and deepened his opposition to the resultant bureaucratic regime. However, he was unable to *rethink* completely his theoretical understanding of Stalinism. He could not recognize Stalinism as a *revolutionary* yet profoundly antidemocratic and anti-working-class tendency. The postwar experience has proved that the Stalinists *are seekers of power for their own purposes*. This suggests that the "confusion" within postwar Trotskyism could have been rooted, at least in part, in the appeal that this revolutionary side of Stalinism has for many revolutionary intellectuals. I am reminded of George Orwell's phrase about "intellectuals with the whip." Let it be said, as my description of the American Trotskyists I knew amply illustrates, that a conflicting democratic and humanist tendency was also strongly present.

My second major theoretical project was the result of a secret trip I took to England in February 1964—the same trip that produced my ten-minute discussion with Slaughter on structural assimilation. Gerry Healy had become convinced that the central problem with the SWP was that it had abandoned Marxism for American pragmatism. When Trotsky was alive the SWP relied on the Old Man for Marxist theory and turned its attention entirely to day-to-day practical work. In the postwar period the SWP leadership, so the thesis went, tried to recreate this relationship using Pablo and the International Secretariat as the theoreticians. That ended in disaster: The leadership was left to its own resources, and over time its views degenerated into the same kind of revisionist views that Pablo had developed.

I was very impressed with this conception of the SWP and immediately set to work to write my own history of the party. This occupied my time during the summer and fall of 1964. The Socialist Labour League started to print the results in their magazine, *Fourth International*, in the winter of 1964 and concluded the series in the summer of 1966. We published the whole manuscript in 1971 as *The Struggle for Marxism in the United States: A History of American Trotskyism*. The book, in its own small way, made its mark over the years, as it was the only extant history of the SWP that went beyond 1940.

The book was marred by a tendentious factionalism, since its aim was to explain and justify our break with the SWP in 1964. Yet overall, the book was a reasonably honest history of the party and recounted a very interesting story that needed to be told. Where else could one learn about the party's reaction to the Smith Act prosecution, its thinking in the aftermath of the postwar labor upsurge, the unity negotiations with Shachtman, the Cochranite fight, the role of Murry Weiss within the party, etc.? While most people could live reasonably well without this hidden history, the thousands of young Trotskyists produced by the 1960s upsurge were certainly interested.

I believe my central theoretical argument, while exaggerated, continues to have merit. Cannon's party reflected not only the strengths but also the weaknesses of the American workers' movement. This movement has had great difficulty rising above the general theoretical and philosophical level of the nation as a whole. Jim Cannon built solidly, practically. His party was organizationally strong and, during much of its existence, well-rooted within the American working class. Nevertheless, the party was built upon theoretical ideas imported from Europe.

Many American intellectuals have criticized American Trotskyism as well as its Communist cousin for dependence on a foreign ideology. The problem is that American intellectuals have not produced an American revolutionary ideology or made significant contributions to international Marxist theory. We remain a pragmatic people, good at engineering and building. We are net importers of ideas and ideologues. The main change in this situation recently is that we are no longer as good as we once were at building. Now we import Toyotas as well as theories.

The Final Split

We lived a life of political limbo that year between the 1963 convention and our expulsion in September 1964. Blocked from party work by the leadership and therefore having some spare time on our hands, we did our best to implement our perspective of reaching out to the working-class cadres of the party.

In May 1964 the Fox group broke from our tendency. They felt we were not sufficiently committed to a long-term perspective of winning over the proletarian kernel of the party (a kernel, as the above account indicates, that was getting increasingly difficult to find). They were right about this.

In our own way, a year later than Robertson, we were becoming quite demoralized about life in the SWP. The cause of our demoralization was twofold. We were partly the victims of the leadership's obsession with homogeneity, which encouraged all but the most hearty to either capitulate or leave. We were also becoming more and more embittered toward the SWP as we absorbed the positions of the polemics of our international allies.

Our break with the Fox group was not bitter. They simply went their way and we, ours. Art lasted inside the SWP only one more year. He got the opportunity to take a minor full-time union position for a while, and the SWP moved in with its discipline, accusing him of opportunism and demanding that he give up the position. Art was no opportunist and was quite rightly hurt by the factional attack. In later years Art and Steve Zeluck played important roles in international socialist circles.

Developments in Cuba continued, in our opinion, to give further evidence of the correctness of our critical approach. One little tidbit made it into my FBI file: "The NYO forwarded to the Bureau a newspaper clipping from the Late City Edition of the 'NY Times' of 7/13/64, which concerned the arrest in Cuba of 5 Trotskyites. This article also contained a certain amount of background material on the organization of the international Trotskyist movement."

The final break with the SWP came over the summer of 1964. By that time our tendency had been reduced to a modest nine people. The issue around which we were expelled was the crisis in the Ceylonese LSSP. That summer the LSSP voted in its overwhelming majority to join the Bandaranaike government. This was in clear violation of the central Trotskyist tenet of opposition to coalition governments with capitalist parties. What made it even worse was that the Bandaranaike government was committed to a Sinhalese communalist, Buddhist, and anti-Tamil orientation. The LSSP from its origins had stood alone in Ceylon, opposing the conflict between the two communities and defending the rights of the Tamil minority. The old and rather well-to-do parliamentarians of the LSSP leadership had grown tired in their own way and felt that they had to take the only opportunity they might ever have to taste even shared power.

We blamed the capitulation of the LSSP upon the recent reunification of the Fourth International and its leading body, the United Secretariat

(USec). In hindsight I must say this was a bit unfair as the USec also denounced the LSSP majority and supported a small opposition group led by old-timer Edmund Samarakoddy and trade unionist Bela Tampoe.[20] For us, however, the entire degenerative process that had affected the Trotskyist cadres had one name, Pabloism, and one source, the USec.

We were correct, I feel, in sensing that the entry of the LSSP into the Ceylonese government was a watershed in the history of the Trotskyist movement. The old Trotskyism, with its proletarian roots and support, represented by leaders of the caliber of N. M. Perera and Leslie Gunawardena in Ceylon, Guillermo Lora in Bolivia,[21] and Jim Cannon in the United States, had become played out. The LSSP crisis was the crisis of a generation, not simply of a party or an international leadership. It was also the crisis of a movement that clung to an almost fifty-year-old revolution and the ideas of a man then dead almost twenty-five years.

Surprisingly, a new generation of students would rescue this dying movement and give it a second life, though they would change its character in the course of resuscitation.

Notes

1. Edward Gonzalez, *Cuba under Castro: The Limits of Charisma* (Boston: Houghton Mifflin, 1974). Mario Llerena, *The Unsuspected Revolution: The Birth and Rise of Castroism* (Ithaca, NY: Cornell University Press, 1978).
2. For a contemporary exposition of this theory, see Michael Löwy, *The Politics of Combined and Uneven Development: The Theory of Permanent Revolution* (London: Verso, 1981).
3. "Draft Thesis on the Cuban Revolution," point 10, in *The Nature of the Cuban Revolution* (New York: Education for Socialists, April 1968).
4. See Carlos Franqui, *Family Portrait with Fidel* (New York: Vintage Books, 1985).
5. *Discussion Bulletin* 22, no. 17 (June 1961).
6. Barry Sheppard had been a member at large of the old Shachtmanite Young Socialist League but had not supported us at the time of our split. Later, Peter Camejo and Jim Robertson recruited him to the YSA. He was a prominent leader of the SWP for many years and is now a member of Socialist Action.
7. Jim Robertson has recently confirmed this. See "Healy Implodes," *Spartacist* no. 36–37 (New York, Winter 1985–1986), p. 7.
8. James is a fascinating character. Born in Trinidad in 1901, he traveled to England in the 1930s as a cricket journalist. A contemporary of Jomo Kenyatta and Kwame Nkrumah, he was drawn to Trotskyism and joined the SWP. He split from the SWP in 1940 with Shachtman. He left Shachtman in 1947 and rejoined the SWP only to leave again in 1950. In 1958 he was invited back to Trinidad by his old classmate, Prime Minister Eric Williams. When Williams turned toward American imperialism, James broke with him. James is the author of a fine book on Toussaint L'Ouverture and the Haitian Revolution,

The Black Jacobins (New York: Vintage Books, 1962). See Paul Buhle, *CLR James: The Artist as Revolutionary* (London: Verso, 1989). James died in May 1989. "CLR James (1901–1989)" *Revolutionary History* 2, no. 3 (London, Autumn 1989).

9. This group was composed of Art Fox, a union activist in UAW Local 600, his wife Edie, who was also an auto worker, their son Steve, who was active in the YSA, Steve Zeluck (Dave Miller), and his wife Barbara. Zeluck lived in New York City and was involved in the life of our little tendency. He was also active in the United Federation of Teachers. Barbara Zeluck, who came from a wealthy southern Jewish family, was recruited to the SWP during the regroupment period. Evelyn Sell, a prominent SWP woman, was once part of this group, as well as several people in the Chicago area, including Ed Calnek, who was in our original Left Wing Caucus in the YSL.
10. The Seattle branch of the SWP, led by Dick and Clara Fraser, split from the SWP in 1967 to form the Freedom Socialist Party. Almost immediately a factional struggle broke out between Dick and Clara linked to a very messy divorce the two were going through. It seems branch members had to line up with one of the two litigants. The group under Clara's leadership has since played a fairly active role in feminist and gay circles. In 1979 Murry and Myra Weiss joined them. See *Freedom Socialist* (Seattle, Summer 1979). Dick moved to Los Angeles, where he became a supporter of Dorothy Healy's New American Movement and eventually a member of the Democratic Socialists of America. He died in 1987 after a long illness.
11. Mandel, in the process of seeking unification with the SWP, faced the splitting-away of a group led by Michel Pablo, the International Secretary of the Fourth International during the postwar period. Pablo's group at this time tilted politically toward the USSR; Mandel's sympathies were with China. Pablo was deeply involved with Ben Bella in Algeria at the time. Another group, the Latin American bureau headed by Juan Posados, also split away. Posados, to his credit, was active in trying to build a group in Cuba, and it was his people who were arrested there. He also was supported by the well-known journalist Adolfo Gilly. However, his group was well along the road to becoming an exotic personal cult and would largely disappear as a meaningful factor in Latin America during the next decade.
12. Michel Raptis (Pablo) was born in Egypt in 1911, educated in Greece, and has spent most of his life since 1938 in France. Soon after his split from the IS he became an economic adviser to the Algerian government of Ben Bella. He heads a group called the International Revolutionary Marxist Tendency, is active within the Unified Socialist Party (PSU) in France, and has become a strong advocate of self-management. See his *Socialism, Democracy and Self-Management* (London: Allison & Busby, 1980).
13. Posados had groups in a number of countries, each named Partido Obrero Revolutionario (POR—Revolutionary Workers Party). It was Posados who took the initiative to build a group in Cuba and to reinforce it with Argentines. The well-known journalist Adolfo Gilly, an Argentine, was a supporter. (See his *Inside the Cuban Revolution* (New York: Monthly Review Press, 1964), and *The Mexican Revolution* (London: Verso, 1983). In the recent period his groups have all but disappeared; Posados himself has become interested in flying saucers.
14. Nahuel Moreno had a relatively sizable group at the time working within the

Peronist movement. He subsequently built a number of groups throughout Latin America (including a sizable organization in Colombia), became an ally of the SWP in factional disputes within the united FI, and then split from the FI. He recently died. Perhaps his most famous recruit was the Peruvian peasant leader Hugo Blanco. Luis Vitale has been active for many years within the Chilean Left.

15. Arthur Felberbaum (Phelps) was an important leader of the early YSA heading our Philadelphia branch. It was the hope of Arthur, and other supporters of Weiss such as Jim Lambrecht and Nora Roberts, that with our demise in the youth, they would became the new leadership. Instead Dobbs and Kerry brought in Camejo and Sheppard from Boston, as well as Jack Barnes from Minneapolis. Arthur was personally and politically close to Murry's brother, Dave. Arthur went on to play a prominent role in the New York Marxist School. He died at a relatively young age.
16. Letter from Gerry Healy to Tim Wohlforth dated July 24, 1961, in the author's possession.
17. Published by our group in mimeographed form in late 1964. Republished in *'Communists' against Revolution*, edited by Adam Westoby (London: Folrose Books, 1978).
18. This is how my thinking on Cuba started out; in fact, the entire project began with my attempt to explain theoretically how Cuba became a deformed workers' state (to use our old terminology). However, Healy was pressing us on the matter; he stubbornly insisted that Cuba remained a capitalist state. Sometime prior to the 1963 convention I accepted Healy's view on the matter, developing a highly convoluted explanation of Cuba as a capitalist state in transition to becoming a deformed workers' state.
19. They were responsible for publishing *'Communists' against Revolution*. See also John Lister, *Cuba: Radical Face of Stalinism* (London: Left View Books, 1985).
20. The two soon parted, with Samarakoddy moving toward Spartacist and Tampoe sticking with the USec.
21. Lora and his supporters played an important role within the union of tin miners and during the 1952 Bolivian Revolution.

6

On My Own

THE MIMEO ON 95TH STREET

The SWP expelled our not-so-mighty band of nine people in the fall of 1964. We were finally on our own. Right up to the moment of our expulsion we were preoccupied with the political fight within the SWP. We had not seriously thought about existence in the outside world. It was a very cold world, a world made up of people preoccupied with matters other than our arrival on the scene.

Years of factional activity had scarred our little group. We were turned inward, speaking a language incomprehensible to most of the Left, not to mention to the rest of the population. We were skilled in polemics and factional survival and had little recent experience in working with nonparty people. We were a demoralized lot. The fight within the SWP had not worked out as we had envisioned it. It seemed the harder we fought and the clearer we became in our ideas, the smaller we got. It was not supposed to work out that way. Correct theory was supposed to reward its practitioners with some degree of success.

I was as demoralized as the rest. But I was the leader and had to hold the little circle together and counter the pessimism I shared with them. I was afraid to vocalize my inner doubts, even to Martha, my wife. Why did I keep going in those days? How did I keep going? The answer is summed up in one word: *belief*. I believed in Marxism, that our theory and politics represented Marxism, and, like many before me, that persistence in these views, combined with their practical application, would lead in time to victory. Within me a battle raged between this belief and a mood of demoralization based on the so far miserable results of the interaction of my beliefs with the real world.

Considering this difficult circumstance, I did make a few reasonably correct decisions. The first was to recognize squarely that we would be able to accomplish only limited tasks. We were, whether we liked it or not, a very small propaganda group held together by a very specific set of ideas. For the moment it was best to concentrate on developing those ideas and propagating them among the very few in our immediate political periphery. These ideas were very much tied to our belief in the *international* movement. We believed that we were part of an international party; we had our specific assessment of international developments, particularly Cuba; and we looked to the relative success of our international collaborators, especially the British. Therefore we decided to call ourselves by a somewhat clumsy name, which we felt expressed our current size and objectives: The American Committee for the Fourth International (ACFI).

On September 24, 1964, we started to publish a modest, mimeographed, sixteen-page newsletter, which we called the *Bulletin of International Socialism*. So that no one would mistake exactly what we stood for, we dug up and placed on our masthead in blazing red the old emblem of the Fourth International: a hammer and sickle with a "4" superimposed on it. The emblem had never been popular in anti-Communist America. The Communist Party had long since abandoned the plain hammer and sickle, and the SWP likewise did away with the Trotskyist variant. Few workers used a hammer any more in the course of their work, and no farmers used sickles. But we were not trying to appeal to workers or farmers at the moment. Our modest task was to reach just a few politicized radicals to reinforce our tired little troops so that we would have the strength to do a bit more later on. We might not have gained many readers with the emblem, but I doubt if we lost any either.

What we did do was a really nice, professional job of mimeographing. The newsletter looked neat, was very readable, and featured two colors and an occasional photo. We pooled our resources and bought a brand new Gestetner mimeograph—the best there was—and churned out our publication every two weeks without fail.

The *Bulletin* was a modest success. We slowly built up its subscription based in the course of two years to over one thousand, a figure that severely strained our duplicating and collating capabilities. We became known among those leftist radicals who were interested in Trotskyist politics. We did not expect more from a mimeographed publication. Occasionally we did sell copies at meetings or at demonstrations, particularly antiwar protests. Jack Jersawitz went to the South and joined the freedom riders and wrote of his experiences for our little journal. But, in the main, we wrote relatively high-level political commentary on world events and on the politics of the Left. Most of our copies went to subscribers.

The FBI was one of our subscribers. Our expulsion from the SWP elevated us in their eyes. On November 30, 1964, the New York office reported to J. Edgar Hoover: "Subject is being considered a Key Figure of the New York Office in view of his leadership in the newly formed American Committee for the Fourth International, made up of members of his faction expelled from the Socialist Workers Party. Subject was previously a Key Figure of the NYO and photographs and handwriting specimens have been furnished to the Bureau. FD-122 is being forwarded tabbing subject's SI Card as DETCOM."

Further review revealed that somehow they had messed up and did not have a handwriting specimen and that photographs of me "appear to be rather poor." These matters were swiftly remedied. Sufficient material had been gathered on me by this time to require that it be placed in "Red Rope Folders" (nice touch) and kept in a "Bulky Exhibit Vault."

Martha and I, together with our two children, Carl and Bill, were living in a five-room apartment on 95th Street between Columbus and Amsterdam on New York's Upper West Side. It was a nice apartment in an oldish elevator building. There was a miniscule room off the kitchen, not counted in the five, with the remnants of a buzzer system on the wall. Once a maid was supposed to live there. There were two bedrooms in the back of the apartment. Martha and I were in one while Carl and Bill shared the other with bunk beds.

One room was set aside for ACFI and the *Bulletin*. We placed a long narrow table made out of a flush door in front of a window overlooking West Side apartment buildings. We put a collating rack on this table while the Gestetner sat on its own stand nearby. Every other week the clan would gather in this room to collate and staple the *Bulletin*. I had a reel-to-reel tape recorder and had taped Ed Beech's jazz program from WRVR, the radio station of William Sloan Coffin's Riverside Church. While Coleman Hawkins played on by the hour, we would slowly circle the narrow table gathering up the pages of the *Bulletin*. Carl and Bill would join in; they were great collators and they enjoyed the social side of the process. We also held our internal party meetings in this room. However, the living room was reserved for our class series. The activities of the ACFI were certainly homey in those days.

The Progressive Labor Party

We continued, of course, to follow events in the Socialist Workers Party quite closely, commenting on them in the *Bulletin*. But we had no illusions that we would recruit many more from that party. We had said our piece for a number of years there and I believe reached everyone we could. We knew we needed a new milieu if we were to grow in the immediate future. The broad layers of the American people were not quite ready for us—or we for them. We had to grow within American radicalism first. We chose a special orientation toward Progressive Labor (PL).

PL was founded in July 1962 by a left split from the Foster wing of the Communist Party. It was headed by Milt Rosen, a white worker and ideologue; Bill Epton, a prominent black militant; and Mort Scheer, as well as two Communist youth leaders, Jake Rosen and Fred Jerome. Fred Jerome's father had been a longtime Communist Party intellectual. PL was an extremely militant organization, sharply critical of the CP's reformist and pro–Democratic Party politics, yet still quite Stalinist, leaning toward Maoism. Political organizations have *personalities* as well as politics, and sometimes these personalities stand in contrast to the politics. Individuals, for example, may hold very radical ideas in their heads yet dress and act very conservatively. The SWP had (and has) a quite conservative personality while adhering to extremely radical positions. PL, however, had politics still affected by the reformism of Stalinism and had a very radical, and at times adventuristic, personality.

Our very first political statement, "The Crisis of American Socialism," published in the first issue of the *Bulletin*, contained an important appeal to the "new radicals" in and around Progressive Labor.[1] This was followed by more detailed and serious material. We carefully traced the current reformism of the official Communists back to its roots under Stalin and linked it to the bureaucratization of the USSR. This approach permitted us to pose Trotsky's struggle against Stalin and the politics of Trotskyism as the alternative to Stalinist reformism. Then we explained how the Chinese continued to cling to Stalinism while rejecting the contemporary leadership of the USSR and how they persisted in bureaucratism internally. It was a reasonably intelligent and well-argued polemic, and the tone was both friendly and serious. It had its impact.

In the early sixties, Progressive Labor was still somewhat fluid and was beginning to attract young people. We sent Danny Freeman down to PL's Lower East Side Club, which was run by Fred Jerome's mother. Danny, who did not hide his affiliation with us, was most welcome and soon became a leading salesman of their paper *Challenge*. Danny met Jeff Goldstein (Sebastian Gato), who had gone to Cuba that summer with a PL group headed by Philip Abbot Luce. Jeff had an inquiring mind and came to the first class series we held in our apartment on 95th Street. He soon became convinced by our Trotskyist ideas and resigned from PL in September 1965.[2]

Jeff played an important role in ACFI and its successor, the Workers League. He was an intensely political person, representative of many of the student radicals of the 1960s. He had a brilliant academic record in mathematics, a subject he had simply lost interest in. The movement and Marxist ideas became his sole passion. He loved to talk all night and he slept as little as possible. Jeff took over a lot of our mimeograph work even though he was not mechanically inclined. He would battle the poor machine through the night, scattering paper and ink everywhere in order to produce our newsletter. Jeff was thin with a bushy brown mustache and intense brown eyes that, especially when he hadn't slept in days, would burn right through you. Our small group with very big ideas had a natural attraction for his radical intellect.

PL went through an explosive and rapid development. It was able to capture some of the same aura of militancy and freshness that contributed to SDS's growth in the same period. While clearly descended from the Old Left and maintaining a "Leninist" structure, it was able to attract New Left students in a way the official Communists could not. PL followed up its Cuba trip by organizing the May Second Movement (M2M), which then carried out a series of somewhat adventuristic, highly publicized actions against the Vietnam War. Hundreds of students joined M2M, and the government countered by prosecuting Phil Luce for his trip to Cuba. Luce, who came from a southern upper-class background, moved swiftly into a leadership position in PL, editing its magazine *Progressive Labor*. In February 1965 he broke with PL and wrote an anti-Communist exposé in the May 8, 1965, *Saturday Evening Post*.[3] Luce then wrote a book on his PL experiences, which took a conservative anti-Communist point of view. We got a small mention in the book for being the most consistent and intelligent critics PL had on the left.

The group quickly closed the door on Trotskyism and spent several years seeking to define for itself a distinctive set of political views. It started with a stridently Maoist international position and then became increasingly critical of the Chinese. Yet it refused to question Soviet history prior to 1935. At the same time the group became more Stalinist in its internal regime. PL dissolved M2M in February 1966 and immediately turned its attention to SDS. Many former M2Mers joined SDS, and by April 1967, PL supporters could emerge within SDS as the Worker-Student Alliance, a powerful minority faction.

I continued to correspond almost daily with Gerry Healy, and he wrote us back around once a week. The main subject of our correspondence in that period was the internal factional dispute between our International Committee and Ernest Mandel's United Secretariat, supported by the SWP. I was not the only one to read Gerry Healy's letters. The evidence suggests that the U.S. Customs Service routinely steamed open Healy's letters, photocopied the contents as well as the envelope, and sent copies to the FBI. I have in my possession one such letter, postmarked January 29, 1965, which was produced in the course of discovery during the SWP suit against the FBI. The letter is devoted to Healy's rather factional opinion of USec groups in Belgium, England, and France.

Our little group slowly grew during 1965. It was a matter of recruiting one person here and another there who were attracted to our theoretical seriousness, and to the promise of future growth posed by the successes of our British allies. We began some very modest trade union work. Comrades, after all, had to go to work every day. Even Jeff finally signed up with the city as a welfare investigator. His job permitted him to begin building a group of supporters within the Social Services Employees Union (SSEU). This was an ideal place to start union work because so many of the members of that union were college-educated and radically inclined. Judy Mage, wife of my collaborator of many years, Shane, became president of the SSEU in this period. The union was governed by wide-open, democratic delegate assemblies where politics as well as union matters were debated on a grand scale. Jeff soon recruited Dennis Cribben (O'Casey) and his wife, Lucy (St. John). The two had been close to PL and quickly became leading members of ACFI as well as respected union activists.

Fred Mazelis, who had just graduated from City College of New York (CCNY) with a chemistry degree, got a lab job in a hospital and became a member of the militant hospital union, Local 1199, led by the "progressive" Leon Davis. This was right at the time when Davis successfully organized New York's volunteer hospitals and won an extremely militant strike. ACFI had little impact upon 1199. After all it was not easy to build a "left" caucus within a union led by leftists who were actually doing a pretty good job of organizing minority workers and militantly defending them.

Fred had impact, as he was a good union militant, and the rest of us got some feeling of being part of struggles broader than our little group.

Despite our slow progress we continued to command the attention of the FBI: "Subject was personally observed in the vicinity of his residence on 6/15/65 and the writer, who observed subject, recorded description on (FD-186) attached. SA [blacked out] also ascertained that the photo appearing on the SI cards bears a current likeness of the subject."

Also, beginning on June 18, 1965, the FBI routinely furnished the Secret Service with updates of my SI file because I was "believed to be covered by the agreement between the FBI and Secret Service concerning Presidential protection." The reasons cited as to why the FBI thought I might endanger the president included the accusation that I was "a member or participant in a communist movement," and that I fell under the category of "subversives, ultra rightists, racists and fascists" who express "strong or violent anti-U.S. sentiment." Each time the FBI furnished the Secret Service with a photo of me.

The last communication was sent on January 27, 1976. My description was pared down to "potentially dangerous because of background, emotional instability or activity in groups engaged in activities inimical to U.S."

In the fall of 1965, one year after our expulsion from the Socialist Workers Party, we moved into our first office at 339 Lafayette Street. It was a narrow little room on the second floor of a seamy-looking red brick building a half-block from Houston Street. We were also conveniently close to the Bowery should anyone be interested in muscatel or a soup kitchen. It was definitely not an inspiring location, but we got few callers at our office anyway in those days.

Our next-door neighbor was the Libertarian League. It was the only existing anarchist group in the United States in those days and was headed by a very nice fellow named Russell Blackwell. I had met Russ in my Shachtmanite days, as the Libertarian League had a world outlook quite close to Shachtman's. Russ had once been a Trotskyist and had helped organize the first Trotskyist group in Mexico in the 1930s. The Libertarian League was emphatically not a lively neighbor; in fact months went by without our hearing a sound from its room. Then one day Russ showed up with a couple of young people and began taking out files and furniture. The Libertarian League was going out of business! If Russ had held out a few more years he would probably have done a roaring trade. Many of the SDSers were anarchists in their approach to life and culture but were simply unaware of the existence of such a tendency. The collapse of our neighbors was not a good sign for us.

By far our liveliest and most entertaining member was Dave Van Ronk, the folksinger. Dave had joined the SWP and our faction both in the last months before our split. He had been active earlier around the Libertarian League and as part of a faction in YPSL. Dave was really an anarchist in personal and political spirit, though he was with us intellectually. He was a very political person and participated fully in the internal life of ACFI. He had learned his music from folksingers and hung out in musical circles that included Bob Dylan and Tom Paxton. Shaggy hair flopped over his face; he had a gravelly voice and drank Irish whiskey.

ENTER LYNDON LAROUCHE, JR.

That year we got our next wave of recruits from the SWP, and we could not have done worse. We began discussions with Lyndon H. LaRouche, Jr. (Lyn Marcus). I had known Lyn just a little when I was an SWP member. He lived in a nice apartment on Central Park West with his wife, Janice, and small child. Lyn earned his living at the time as an economic consultant. He was a close friend of Murry Weiss and was totally inactive in the party, playing no role at all in the party discussions in the 1961 to 1964 period. After we had all left, LaRouche suddenly stirred from his slumbers and started submitting lengthy documents to the SWP discussion bulletin. He developed positions that at least appeared to be close to ours, and we began a collaboration. He had by then left his Central Park West wife and was living in the Village with Carol Larrabee (Schnitzer, White), a woman who had joined the SWP during the regroupment period.

LaRouche had a gargantuan ego. A very talented, brilliant fellow, he was convinced he was a genius. He combined a strong conviction in his own abilities with an upperclass arrogance that, happily, I rarely encountered in radical circles. He assumed that the famous comment in the *Communist Manifesto*, that a "small section of the ruling class cuts itself adrift, and joins the revolutionary class" was written specifically for him.

The characteristics of LaRouche's thinking process, which he would later develop to such reactionary extremes, were already present when I knew him in 1965. He possessed a marvelous ability to place any event in the world within a larger perspective, a talent that seemed to give the event meaning. The problem was that his thinking was schematic and lacking in factual detail, and ignored contradictory considerations. His explanations were just a bit too perfect and his mind worked so quickly that I always suspected that his bravado covered superficiality.

LaRouche had the "solution" to anything and everything. It was almost like a parlor game. Just present a problem to LaRouche, no matter how petty, and without so much as blinking his eyes, he would come up with the solution, usually prefacing his remarks with "of course."

I remember private discussions I had with LaRouche in 1965 when he went on at length about Kennedy, Rockefeller, and the Tri-lateral Commission. LaRouche held to a view that there existed a network of foundations and agents of the more moderate, internationalist-oriented, Eastern-based capitalists who sought to avoid unrest at home through reform projects and to avoid revolution abroad through development programs like the Alliance for Progress. He was very much a believer in conspiracy theories. I, even in my most ultraleft days, was a bit of a sceptic. For LaRouche, even as a radical, the *liberals were the main enemy*.

I was disturbed by LaRouche's thinking process in those days. I do not claim to have realized then where he would end up, but he definitely made me uncomfortable. He seemed to be an elitist with little interest in the plight of ordinary people. His ideas were too schematic and mechanical for my taste. I could not agree with the position he expounded in that period that the Vietnam War was a battle over Vietnam's capabilities of becoming the breadbasket for the industrialization of Asia. I also was suspicious of conspiracy theories.

LaRouche stayed with us only six months—I think our little group was not big enough to contain him—and he moved on to Robertson's Spartacist League. Unable to win this group over to "LaRouchism," Lyn and Carol left after a few months. Sometime later we got a letter from him in which he announced that all factions and sections of the Trotskyist Fourth International were dead and that he and Carol were going to build the Fifth International. I suppose, in a way, this is what he thinks he has done.

I continued to follow LaRouche's political evolution after he left our group. Dennis King, who has made a study of LaRouche, has noted that I was "one of the first observers to spot something amiss."[4] In the beginning of 1967 LaRouche and his wife joined a relatively broad coalition of New Left intellectuals called the Committee for Independent Political Action

(CIPA). He gained control of the West Village CIPA branch and started gathering a coterie of young intellectuals. He had finally discovered his milieu, and success swiftly came his way. Through a combination of rather high-level classes and spirited polemics, LaRouche won over a group of graduate students, most of whom were members or sympathizers of Progressive Labor. Progressive Labor was in that period at the height of its strength within SDS. LaRouche's gifted young intellectuals included Ed Spannaus (who is still with him), Nancy Spannaus, Tony Papert and Steve Fraser (two who led his work at Columbia), Paul Milkman, Paul Gallagher, Leif Johnson, and Tony Chaitkin.

It was the Columbia University occupation and student strike in 1968 that established LaRouche on the left. The student movement there was being led by SDS. There were two main factions in SDS, reflecting a split developing in the national organization: Mark Rudd's Action Faction, and a somewhat more moderate group known as the Praxis Axis. The rather appropriate names were coined by LaRouche. The Rudd group was interested only in provocative demonstrations and punch-ups with the cops. It would soon emerge as the Weatherman group of underground terrorists. The Praxis group was influenced by the French intellectual André Gorz, who held that a new working class was being created by modern technology. The students were the vanguard of this new working class. Gorz's ideas gave the group a kind of mainstream "student power" perspective.

LaRouche captured most of the PL-SDS group at Columbia and was able to come forward as a relatively strong third alternative. He presented a plausible program for linking the struggles of the students with the struggles of the surrounding poor black community. This was a period when many students radicalized by the Vietnam War and the black struggle were beginning to look for a way to carry the leftist struggle beyond the campus gates. LaRouche appeared to some to have a program that could fulfill this wish.

After quickly regrouping his followers into the SDS Labor Committee (later to become the National Caucus of Labor Committees), LaRouche began to hold meetings in the Columbia area. From time to time I attended these meetings. Some twenty to thirty students would gather in a large apartment not far from Columbia. They would sit on the floor surrounding LaRouche, by now sporting a very shaggy beard. The meeting would go on at great length, sometimes for as long as seven hours. It was difficult to tell where discussions of tactics left off and an educational presentation began. The students were given quite esoteric assignments, such as searching through the writings of Sorel to discover the anarchistic origins of Rudd, or studying Rosa Luxemburg's *The Accumulation of Capital.* For some reason, perhaps because the SDS movement was strong on spirit and action but rather bereft of theory, LaRouche's ruminations found a home.

LaRouche in this period developed a series of ideas by extracting and distorting some theories from the Marxist tradition. Even today, from his right-wing position, he retains this element in his thinking. He held these ideas, in an elementary way, even in the period of his membership in our organization. Most important was his *Theory of Hegemony*. He wrote in 1970:

> One must start with the recruitment and education of a revolutionary intelligentsia. By necessity rather than choice, the source of such cadres is mainly a minority of the young intellectuals, such as student radicals, rather than the working class, black militant layers, etc., themselves. . . . The selection from the ranks of (mainly) radical-student intellectuals (as distinct from merely "educated" radical students in general) is necessary on the basis of those persons who are willing to commit themselves to a total re-education and life of the most intensive study as well as activism.[5]

LaRouche drew this notion from his own interpretation of Lenin's *What Is to Be Done?*, where Lenin speaks of intellectuals bringing socialist consciousness to the workers. He then expanded it by drawing from Gramsci's notion of hegemony. LaRouche's goal was to forge an intellectual elite corps that would gain hegemony on the left and then capture from on high the allegiance of the masses. I am not arguing that LaRouche's interpretation of Lenin and of Gramsci was in any way an accurate one—Gramsci, for example, was a strong believer in an autonomous working-class movement—but only showing which strands of the Marxist tradition appealed to LaRouche and motivated him and his followers in his radical period.

A necessary corollary of LaRouche's concept of a superior intellectual revolutionary elite is the concept of an inferior class. Here LaRouche distorted Marx's distinction between the class in itself (ordinary consciousness) and the class *for* itself (socialist consciousness). He also made heavy use of Lenin's polemics against the "economists" in Russia who, in Lenin's opinion, were adapting to the backwardness or ordinary consciousness of the workers. It appeared that LaRouche and his followers, even in their radical stage, had a low opinion of ordinary human beings. In 1969, for example, LaRouche followers Steve Fraser and Tony Papert wrote about forcing "working people and other groups to begin to part with their habitual swinish outlooks."[6]

The second strand of LaRouche's thought was his *Theory of Reindustrialization*. This concept remains the heart of his current economic theory and rightist agitation. LaRouche began with a rather orthodox theory of capitalist crisis derived from Marx's *Capital* and Luxemburg's *The Accumulation of Capital*. He was convinced that capitalism had ceased to grow, or at least ceased to grow sufficiently to meet the needs of the country's poor. This created an economic crisis that would only worsen. He believed international capitalism was on the brink of entering what he called the "third stage of imperialism" (see his pamphlet by the same name published in 1967). The "third stage of imperialism" was an attempt by the developed nations to overcome stagnation at home and revolution abroad by fomenting a new industrial revolution in the third world. LaRouche expected this to take place in India. His idea was that the advanced nations would use their unused capacity to make capital goods and export them to India, setting up factories that would employ the country's surplus work force.

At this point in the argument LaRouche borrowed from his Trotskyist background to develop a *transitional program* that would, he hoped, motivate the masses to support him so that he could resolve this worldwide crisis of capitalism. Trotsky proposed a program that addressed the immediate needs of masses of people in the hope that the struggle around these demands would lead the people to realize the need for socialism. LaRouche hoped to win the support of American workers by promising that his program would supply jobs. For example, during the Vietnam War his idea was to reconvert the war industries to this peaceful reindustrialization process.

This entire economic schema, which made up the bulk of LaRoucheite writings and agitation in the late 1960s and early 1970s, was presented in an increasingly frenetic manner, bolstered by predictions of economic doom. LaRouche was a crisis-monger of the first order—though our group gave him a run for his money. LaRouche and his followers became increasingly convinced that the fate of the world rested with their group and with their leader, Lyndon LaRouche, Jr. The resources, both technological and human, were present for this glorious economic transformation. The problem lay with the cussed stupidness of the nation's leaders and the swinishness of the masses. If only LaRouche were in power all the world's problems would be dealt with swiftly.

In the early 1970s, as the Left in the United States shrank under the impact of conservative times, LaRouche lashed out with a series of attacks on the SWP and the CP. Soon his group was denouncing all leftists and seeking support from extreme right-wingers. The LaRoucheites began mouthing anti-Semitic phraseology, promoting the nuclear power and arms industry, advocating a Star Wars defense, and baiting gay people. The old Trotskyist, a member of my own small organization, had emerged as a Fascist! Shocking as the political evolution has been, I am most struck by the elements of *continuity* in LaRouche's thinking. This is where I believe there are lessons for the Left.[7]

Most important is LaRouche's *elitism*. Ordinary human beings were viewed by LaRouche the leftist and by LaRouche the Fascist as a swinish element to be manipulated. LaRouche never absorbed the *humanist* and *compassionate* side of the Marxian socialist tradition. He is not alone in expressing this defect. We need only think of Stalin, who could ruthlessly permit the death of millions of peasants and consciously purge and murder hundreds of thousands of his own Communist cadres, all in the ostensible interests of "history." A more recent example is Pol Pot's conduct in Cambodia. Only socialism rooted in humanism can any longer be considered socialism. Once an individual, party, or state is no longer anchored in this view, then terms like "left" and "right" lose any significance.

In fact it is quite remarkable how the "new" LaRouche organizes his followers in a Leninist cadre fashion, drives them with a vision of their historic tasks and the necessity of their actions, and successfully reaches layers of society with "transitional" slogans that appeal to economic needs or old prejudices.

An Interlude with the Spartacist League

In the fall of 1965, Healy and Lambert began to plan for a conference of the International Committee. They felt a need to counter the attractive power of the United Secretariat, and they began to look around for possible new allies to bring to the conference. Healy struck upon the idea of Robertson's group, the Spartacist League. Our own growth since the split in the Minority Tendency had been modest, and we now had a little group of just over thirty supporters. Robertson, who had been expelled from the SWP a year earlier with a larger group, now had about sixty members. The group appeared attractive to Healy, who suddenly proposed that we unite with the Spartacist League.

I was less than enthusiastic about the idea. I was not convinced that there was a political basis for such a unification. The two groups had clashed that summer over tactics in the antiwar movement. A broad umbrella organization had been formed called the Fifth Avenue Peace Parade Committee. It was headed by A. J. Muste but had been created primarily as a result of the very hard work of the Socialist Workers Party. I felt it was a reasonably principled coalition, as it was committed to the demand "End the war in Vietnam now." I favored a more radical approach, seeking to connect the war to other issues affecting the American working class, but I felt it was principled for us to join the committee and press our views within it.

The group organized a powerful march on 5th Avenue of around thirty thousand people. We participated in the march along with the Tompkins Square Neighbors for Peace. This local group on the Lower East Side contained some talented artists and had made signs and banners with large dollar signs and skeletons that through symbolism linked the war with capitalism. This way we got around the restriction of limiting the march to only the one agreed-upon slogan. It was a good beginning for us as a small group participating in a broad coalition yet beginning to put forward our more specifically radical policies. We had already become the dominant element in the Tompkins Square group.

The Spartacists denounced the Fifth Avenue Committee as a "popular front," an unprincipled coalition with capitalists. We were attacked for participating in the committee. I was convinced they were dead wrong and were displaying a sectarianism that was deadly to a small group, a sectarianism they had also expressed in their extremist attitude toward the SWP during the internal party discussion. I was afraid that unification, with Robertson's people in a majority, could hurt our ability to grow.

I was also worried about the deep animosity between the two groups. The Spartacist members had absorbed many highly factional documents concerning our break in 1962 and were deeply embittered toward us and, of course, toward me in particular. It was the kind of group that learned to hate the most intensely those closest to it politically. This meant that in any unified organization I would find myself a minority in a hostile, cliquish political atmosphere.

There were, in addition, problems within our own small group. We remained very isolated, just beginning to grow and to find ways to participate in political life outside our circle. We recruited people who were attracted to *ideas* and did not mind an isolated existence given to propagating ideas. The problem is that some of those we recruited *preferred* such an existence and were therefore much like the members of the Spartacist League. A kind of ill-defined semifactionalism was developing within the group with some comrades largely hanging out among themselves and developing criticisms of our group that had little or no political content.

Most disturbing was the way Gerry Healy organized his unification campaign. He approached Robertson directly, without first discussing the proposal with our group. It was as if our four-and-a-half years of extremely loyal support meant nothing to the man. I felt deeply hurt and undercut, and I suspected that Gerry was dealing with Robertson behind my back.

Healy decided to come to Montreal to meet one weekend with our group and the next with the Spartacist group to spur on the unification. Our whole New York group got into cars and drove up to Canada. LaRouche and his wife volunteered to pick up Healy at the airport in their beat-up old Volkswagen, no doubt hoping to gain his ear before he met with the rest of us. Carol smoked a pipe while Lyn lectured Gerry about his various theories as if he were talking to a schoolboy. It was a long ride in from the airport, and, as Healy reported the incident to me that day, he almost decided to head back to London.

Healy made his presentation and then I spoke. I agreed to proceed with unity discussions but I insisted that we had to realize that Robertson was not a Marxist. Healy jumped all over me for making this statement, suggesting that I was trying to sabotage unification. He went on to take up the Spartacist's position on the Fifth Avenue Peace Parade Committee. He then spent the rest of the weekend quietly meeting individually with the other comrades, encouraging those who were critical of me and sympathetic to Spartacist. Dave Van Ronk told me years later that Healy had attacked both Robertson and myself as "Shachtmanites," saying that the only difference between us was that I had been more loyal to the International Committee.

I returned to the United States thoroughly demoralized. I went through the motions of unity negotiations, letting the comrades who most favored unification take the lead. I became convinced that I must have been wrong on the Fifth Avenue Committee position, I confessed my error, and we withdrew from the group. At the same time, for the first time in my life I was actually enjoying my job. I was working for a trade magazine dealing with diesel trucks, of all things.

I received my instructions from England and was told I must make plans to go to London in April to attend the conference of the International Committee. I had not earned time yet on my job for vacation and I was afraid I might endanger it if I pressed the point. I decided I would not go to England, and our group sent Fred Mazelis instead. I know that the real reason I did not go to that conference was that I had become deeply demoralized by the whole process leading up to it. I could not stomach being thrown back into the kind of bitter personal factional atmosphere that had characterized the Minority Tendency during the battle with Robertson in 1962. I felt I could not openly oppose the unification, but I did not believe in it, I did not really wish it success. I came as close as I had in years to simply dropping out of the movement.

The State Department has its own intelligence and surveillance apparatus. This will not come as news to those who followed closely the 1992 presidential election campaign. Clinton accused the Bush administration of violating normal procedures to rush through an FOIA search of the files on both Clinton and his mother held at the Passport Office and at consular offices.

My files suggest that the main repository for political files on American citizens maintained by the State Department are held by the Passport Office. There also exists a deputy assistant secretary of security and a Bureau of Intelligence.

The State Department was closely watching the preparations for the 1966 International Committee meeting. On February 21, 1966, a special AIRGRAM was sent to the embassies in London and Moscow signed by "RUSK" (presumably the then Secretary of State Dean Rusk). I was the subject.

"The Department has been advised that the subject, head of the American Committee for the Fourth International and a former member of the Socialist Workers Party's National Committee, has been invited to participate in an international Trotskyist conference to be held in London, England, originally scheduled for January 1966, at which time consideration would be given to the proposed unification of the ACFI and the Revolutionary Committee of the Fourth International (RCFI) in the United States. According to an informant, the conference has been rescheduled for April, 1966 and Wohlforth will probably attend.

"In the event pertinent information is received concerning Wohlforth's activities, Embassy London notify your Legal Attaché and Moscow notify the Department."

The conference of the International Committee turned out to be a disaster.[8] It was attended by Lambert and Stephen Just for the OCI,[9] Gerry Healy, Mike Banda, and Cliff Slaughter for the SLL, an old-timer from the war period from Greece, a group from France known as Voix Ouvrière,[10] our group, and Spartacist. One morning Robertson took the floor and presented his views. He made a number of critical comments on the SLL's positions in relation to the immediacy of the economic crisis, Cuba, and American blacks. He was no doubt right on some matters and wrong on others. He then retired from the afternoon session, claiming to be tired from being sick and from staying up all night working on a resolution. His absence infuriated Healy, who took it as a direct insult to the conference. Healy had a point. If Robertson felt ill or tired he should have excused himself from *both* morning and evening sessions. It is a bit arrogant to give a presentation and then not attend the session immediately after your presentation when others wish to comment on your views.

I also believe that Healy was just as infuriated by Robertson's political criticisms of his group. He had suddenly become aware that the Robertson group had a mind of its own (to its credit) and did not worship at the feet of the SLL. Just as impetuously as he had embraced unification with Robertson, he decided to expel him from the conference. Voix Ouvrière believed that the Fourth International had been totally destroyed and had to be rebuilt from scratch—on the basis, of course, of its own politics and organizational methods—and walked out of the conference, leaving the IC where it had been prior to the unification process.

Fred Mazelis returned home with a full report on the Spartacist expulsion and special instructions for me. I was to quit my job and forthwith work for the party full time. It seems that the break with Robertson was "planned" from the beginning; after all, everybody knew Robertson was not a Marxist! We were to take up the struggle for internationalism against this "petty bourgeois" pragmatic American sect. LaRouche immediately went into a fury of activity, accusing Healy of sabotaging the unity. He did his best to win Van Ronk and Jeff over to his viewpoint and bring them into Spartacist. He failed, and Lyn and Carol joined Spartacist on their own, only to leave a few months later in order to launch their "Fifth International" project.

THE EARLY DAYS OF THE WORKERS LEAGUE

Over Thanksgiving weekend of 1966, following this fiasco, we held the founding conference of the Workers League. We had not grown much that year, but the change in name meant we were going to try to act a little differently. We wished to be a bit more like a real party rather than the small circle that we actually were. We now had a modest, printed paper and a new, more presentable office. We had ambitious plans to develop some trade union work and to begin a youth movement. Our conference noted that "the world capitalist system is in a fundamental crisis." And we quoted Healy to the effect that "the more you penetrate the trade unions the more you are called upon to tackle the basic questions of the application of dialectical materialism."

We were determined to do just that, to send our essentially intellectual group into unions and somehow develop theory in the process. We passed a resolution proposing to campaign for a labor party in the United States and one calling for an orientation toward teenage youth. Although the former proposal was quite correct in the abstract, it did not flow from a clear analysis of political reality: At that time there was no movement within the AFL-CIO ranks in the direction of political independence. Neither did we have the forces in 1966 to implement the latter proposal.[11]

We started 1967 with a big political bang. Taking our cue from the SLL in England, we decided to give critical support to the Red Guards and the Chinese Cultural Revolution. The Red Guards had a special appeal for our British comrades, so many of whom were youth members. Also it appeared to us that Mao was utilizing the students as a battering ram to reform the bureaucratized party and apparatus. Mao was certainly doing this, *but* (and this is a huge "but," which we blindly overlooked) his aim was to regain his own personal power over Chinese society. Further, the Red Guards carried out their campaigns in a thoroughly reactionary way, assaulting factory workers, pillorying intellectuals, and setting back Chinese science and industry for years to come. Years later it occurred to me that Healy's love affair with the Red Guards reflected a Stalinist element in his own thinking, and that the basis for the IC/IS break in the Fourth International was not at all as clear as we thought it was. If an adaptation to Stalinism can be considered "revisionist" within the framework of Trotskyist thinking—and I believe it can be—then "revisionism" existed in *both* the main international camps of Trotskyism.

Yet the Red Guard campaign did give the Workers League a bit of color and created some excitement around us. We ran huge headlines: "Hands Off the Chinese Revolution" and "Conditional Support to the Red Guards" and held some rousing meetings with beautiful red banners draped all over the place. It is too bad that we were so politically wrong, as it was a very exciting and effective campaign!

The Second National Convention of the Workers League was held on Thanksgiving weekend in 1967. It was not a healthy affair. We had hardly grown from the preceding year despite what appeared to be a favorable political atmosphere in the country for radicalism. As happened so many times in small political groups, when we did not understand what was holding us back from the growth we felt we deserved, we turned against each other as factionalism broke out.

We had a sharp faction fight with a comrade from San Francisco, Earl Gilman (Owens). Earl wanted us to build caucuses in the unions, but we were determined to electrify the working class more directly with our paper sales at the factories and docks, and we also wanted to reach "the revolutionary youth." It was a tempest in a very little teapot, which led to Earl walking out of the group. Dave Van Ronk quite correctly opposed our attack on Earl and chose to resign in protest. In any event, he was getting more deeply involved in his musical career.

Once in this period our whole New York group went out of town for a conference. When we returned several of us went straight to our office. We opened the door and the place was empty! We had lost our typewriters and our precious Gestetner mimeograph machine. We called the police, who quickly concluded that it was an "inside job" because the door had not been tampered with. I believed then, as I do now, that either the FBI or some other government agency had carried out a "black bag" raid. Another time, when I returned from a trip, the nice superintendent at our apartment told me the FBI had been around asking if they could look through my garbage. Now we know one source for the files in "Red Rope Folders" that were placed in the "Bulky Exhibit Vault"!

From 1967 until 1969 the Workers League grew slowly, painfully slowly. But our modest growth gave substance to that optimism so essential for the survival of little sects. By the time of our second convention in late 1967, we had perhaps sixty members, but by the end of 1969 we were approaching one hundred. Only then did serious growth take place. We were recruiting by ones and twos the politicos, the intellectuals.

Two key recruits from this period were Juan and Helena Farinas. One day a handsome young Latino man walked into our office at 10th Street and bought material on Trotsky. He asked a couple of questions, pointedly did not give his name, and left. Then he started coming by regularly, once or twice a week, each time talking a little more freely. Finally he gave me his name and told me his story. Juan and his wife, Helena, edited the Spanish portion of Progressive Labor's weekly paper *Challenge/Desafio*. These were important positions within PL, as their paper had a large circulation, and they put a lot of energy into selling it in Spanish-speaking areas of New York.

Juan and Helena had developed differences with the PL leaders, who had taken an extremely sectarian attitude toward the Puerto Rican independence movement and generally were acting in a rigid and bureaucratic way. At the same time the leadership had begun a discussion on the historical roots of Stalinism and was beginning to move away from its support for China. Juan had found its theoretical efforts very superficial and had seen the material we specifically addressed to PL that critiqued its documents from a Trotskyist point of view.

When Juan was still a member of PL, he was drafted into the military. On PL's advice, when he entered the induction center on Whitehall Street in New York City, he gave an antiwar speech to all his fellow inductees. He did not refuse to be inducted, but he had no chance to continue the induction process, as the security guards hustled him out. He was arrested and charged by the federal government with impeding the induction process and refusing to be inducted, neither of which were true. So matters rested, since PL did nothing about it for two years or so. When Juan joined our group the court had finally gotten around to his case.

We immediately went to work to organize a defense, receiving help from the American Civil Liberties Union. We organized a defense committee, and Fred Mazelis, falling back on his SWP training, did an extremely competent job of raising funds and publicizing the case. We got quite a bit of support, including support from a number of unions, key figures in the Latin music scene such as Ray Baretto and Santana, and various notables. Even the YSA backed the case. We sent Juan on tours around the country, and the case definitely helped build the Workers League.

However, legally Juan's situation was very difficult. He lost in court and we made an appeal, which we also lost. Juan had to go to Danbury Federal Penitentiary, where he served about a year. I used to drive Helena to Danbury along with their absolutely darling little two-year-old girl, Marianna, who spoke only Spanish.

Juan arranged with the educational department of the prison for me to teach a course there on philosophy. I was admitted behind the bars and passed through the exercise area in the center of the prison, where inmates were keeping themselves in excellent physical shape so as to be prepared for their return to the outside and, in most cases, to their former professions. About a dozen prisoners gathered for my lectures, mostly Latinos and blacks radicalized by the events of that era, and a few antiwar activists. These latter included one of the famous Berrigan brothers, Catholic priests who had openly burned draft records. I gave my standard lectures on dialectics and revolution, which got a good reception.

It was in this period that we went through our stage of prisoner work. We began sending our paper to prisoners, and we also sent books to the more-interested readers. One prisoner, I will call him Victor, called us upon his release and promised to give us an interview on the "revolution" within the prisons. We sent a comrade to stand on a particular street corner, where she was picked up by a cruising van. The comrade then interviewed Victor in the back of the moving van while his companion continued to cruise Manhattan's streets, weaving in and out to avoid being followed. I really doubt if anyone was interested in following the van, but it was most exciting.

We received marvelous letters from these prisoners. They were quite enthusiastic about Marxism, and many were especially attracted to its philosophical side. Yet we built nothing stable out of this work. The prisoners too often fell back into drugs and petty crime once they left prison. The dreamy idealistic and utopian side of Marxism had a tremendous appeal while they were in prison. Yet harsh realities in the ghettos and myopic drug dreams proved more powerful than revolutionary conviction.

BLACK NATIONALISM AND MARXIST THEORY

We made very little progress in recruiting blacks prior to 1970. However, we followed the changes taking place within the black movement, and these became the subject for some theoretical development. I believe our thinking on what we then called the Negro question was among the most original in that period. More important, in general outline, the approach remains valid today.

The SWP 1963 resolution on the matter stated:

> Revolutionary socialists welcome the growth of . . . Negro nationalism and give its participants whole hearted collaboration in the fight against our common enemies. For us, Negro nationalism and revolutionary socialism are not only compatible but complementary forces that should be welded closer together in thought and action.[12]

The resolution did not claim that the blacks were a nation but rather stated that if blacks chose separation, the SWP would defend their right to do so. The SWP implemented this position through articles friendly to nationalism in its press. With Malcom's break from Elijah Muhammed, the *Militant* became a major avenue for the publication of his speeches. In 1968 the YSA went further and declared that "Black people make up what is known as an intracolonized nation" and by 1969 both the SWP and YSA referred to themselves as "multinational organizations."[13]

I approached the question quite differently. It seemed to me that the starting point for Marxists should be the understanding of the *nature* of the American black. Once this was understood, a proper political approach to the existing black movement could be developed. I felt that the SWP was approaching the matter in the opposite way: It was seeking to find a theoretical justification for a predetermined positive political attitude.

In March 1965 we put out a special issue of the *Bulletin* devoted totally to black nationalism.[14] In this issue I rejected the idea that the blacks made up a separate nation, arguing that they lacked a separate language and a territory of their own. The majority of blacks had left the rural southern "black belt" and migrated to southern and northern cities where they became integrated into the industrial economy alongside whites. Geographical separation was therefore not a real option for blacks.

However, blacks were not simply a *race*. They had been forced to live in segregated communities, to endure manifold varieties of discrimination, and were, on the whole, economically oppressed in a more severe manner than whites. This had given them an identity and cohesiveness that, while based upon their skin color, went far deeper. This was why black nationalism was appealing to so many politicalized blacks.

I drew an analogy with the Jewish people. I turned to a fascinating theory developed by Abraham Leon, a Belgian Trotskyist who died during World War II in a Nazi concentration camp.[15] Leon felt that Jews were more than just a religious group. They were a "people-class" created by the unique economic role they had been forced to play during the Middle Ages. Barred from integration into the Christian feudal structure, left to survive primarily through money lending, Jews preserved their own culture and language. With the rise of capitalism, Jews were only partially integrated and therefore maintained much of their old culture and identity. This contradictory situation gave rise to the dream of Zionism.

The parallel with American blacks was striking. Black Africans were brought to the United States to be slaves on the southern plantations. Racism developed to justify the perpetuation of this system. With the abolition of slavery following the Civil War, segregation was imposed upon blacks and their separatism preserved. However, this separateness lost its original economic specificity with the destruction of the slave system. As a result, the American blacks were partially integrated economically into capitalist production and left culturally and socially separated. This is why their political history involves both periods of integrationist activity followed by pursuit of the dream of black nationalism (read Zionism). Thus blacks are neither a nation nor simply a race but, as I awkwardly put it at the time, *a race-class in the process of disintegration*.

This view does not necessarily lead to a specific political program. Yet it does suggest that the black nationalist movement needed to be approached in a critical manner because it promoted a utopian "solution" to the problems of American blacks. I did not reject the idea that the black movement needed its own leadership and organization, but my inescapable conclusion was (and still is) that American black liberation can be achieved only in common struggle with the working class as a whole. Those aspects of black nationalist propaganda—antiwhite agitation and sometimes even anti-Semitism—that impede that common struggle should be rejected.

The East Village Days

When we moved our offices to the East Village in 1967 I did not realize that the neighborhood was to become, with the Haight-Ashbury in San Francisco, the source of the new countercultural ferment in America. It was the Age of Aquarius to all those around us, even though we thought we were living in the era of Lenin and Trotsky. We actually got along well with our flower-child neighbors, and it could be that they influenced us more than we influenced them. They were a tolerant lot, and in time we became accepted as a kind of new-age Trotskyists. We may have dreamed different dreams, but we were all dreamers.

We found a sunny room on the second floor of a little two-story building on the corner of 10th Street and 1st Avenue. It was a wonderful area. At the corner of 1st and 11th streets was a great pizza stand (actually run by Italians) and just a few steps up 11th Street was an Italian cheese store that sold fresh mozzarella soaking in trays of brine. Across 1st Avenue was a spice store specializing in imported Hungarian paprika and other ethnic rarities. Directly across from our office, on 10th Street, an enterprising black woman had opened the Princess' Cafe, a little restaurant with barely four or five tables in it, specializing in soul food.

In a small studio down the hall from our office, an artist labored away day and night. One of our comrades, Marty Jakovsky (Jonas) recognized his name. Marty, who was an expert on comic books and had a fabulous collection of Marvel Comics, told us the fellow used to draw for Marvel, especially the mystical Dr. Strange series. More recently, he had been recruited by the Hare Krishnas, who loved our neighborhood and had a commune down the street near the Hell's Angels' compound. Our Marvel illustrator was now creating beautifully complex, mystical drawings for the Krishna's magazine, *Back to Godhead*.

Only a few blocks away on 2nd Avenue, the Fillmore East was housed in an old movie theater. The best of the psychedelic rock groups performed there each weekend. Holdover enterprises from a Yiddish past, such as the B&H dairy restaurant and the Second Avenue Delicatessen, enjoyed new business, while small vegetarian Indian restaurants sprouted under tenements housing Puerto Ricans, elderly Jews and Italians, and hippie communes. In those days it was so much fun to look out the window that it could distract me from my many revolutionary chores. Every now and then I would catch a glimpse of a large lady with a huge broad-brimmed hat standing on the corner and shaking everyone's hand. The East Village was part of Bella Abzug's district, and this was when she got her start.

We were just a couple of blocks from Tompkins Square, where the first mass socialist demonstrations against unemployment had been held a century earlier. Now, while here and there you would see an aged East European face, the area was largely Puerto Rican. Unfortunately it was also quickly becoming a drug hangout where heroin brought together a degenerating section of the flower children and some impoverished Puerto Rican youths. Tompkins Square Neighbors for Peace had a small storefront on a side street between our headquarters and the square, where our comrades mingled with the more political elements from among the East Village's artists and intellectuals.

Deborah Goldstein was at the center of our little group on 10th Street. She quickly mastered the words and the mystique of our group, if not its content. She was, more than any of us, a part of her generation, a child of the 1960s and the East Village. Deborah was an attractive young woman with blue eyes and lots of blond hair descending around a smallish round head.

Deborah did not work, and in this period she lived with Jeff Goldstein and spent her time doing political assignments.

Though she had no formal training, Deborah had considerable artistic talent and quite an imagination. It was Deborah who created Captain Bolshevik, a figure who rapidly became our informal symbol in the East Village. Captain Bolshevik was modeled after Marvel's Captain America: He was clothed completely in red and sported a large hammer and sickle and "4" on his shield. Captain Bolshevik was featured on leaflets and posters advertising our parties, and he drew a good crowd. We made money from those parties, but we made few recruits. They were social occasions where we were accepted by our bohemian friends, but few of them were serious about politics.

Deborah spent days creating party leaflets and posters. Her posters were particularly spectacular. We held our parties in Jeff and Deborah's apartment, which was at the top of a seven-floor walk-up on Stuyvesant Street overlooking the picturesque St. Marks-in-the Bowery Church. She once painstakingly created an accurate color picture of that tenement with a little castle way on the top sporting a red flag with our hammer and sickle. Everything Deborah did had hammers, sickles, and fours. Yet she used such symbols in a style as acceptable in the East Village as a flower or a dove. The problem was that the posters were so good people would steal them soon after they were put up in East Village hangouts.

Deborah loved the Peanuts comic strip. What particularly struck her fancy was Linus and his belief in the Great Pumpkin. Linus believed so strongly that the Great Pumpkin would turn up on Halloween that he was able to convince all his friends to stay up with him and await the Great Pumpkin's arrival. Yet he was disappointed every year. I became a bit disturbed when Deborah starting mentioning me in the same breath as the Great Pumpkin. In her dreamy mind there was some connection, some link. Was she believing in me, worshiping me? It was all so unscientific, nonmaterialist, and disturbing.

Deborah's imagination captivated our little group, and soon we all fell to one degree or another under her spell. I was among the last to fall, but I fell the hardest. Without any of us realizing it, she transformed our group into a circle around herself and her own very dreamy vision of socialism. I suspect we were vulnerable because of our political isolation and rather abstract way of thinking about theory. Deborah *sounded* very good and was most enthusiastic. Yet I knew she did not read, and I wondered if there was any substance behind her speech. But it was not a period for substance in any event; it was a time of color and feelings, and especially dreams.

It was in this period that we ran into a whole group of cultural anarchists, the extreme wing of what became the yippies, a radical prefigurement of the punks. The group was succinctly known as the Mother Fuckers, and they spent most of their time, when they were not high on something and lying around on a tenement floor, painting appropriately obscene slogans on the walls of the East Village.

The Mother Fuckers liked us. They would come to our weekly class series in our small office on 10th Street and stand in the back (even if there were empty seats) as we went on and on about imperialism and revisionism and internationalism and several other isms, combined with a very heavy dose of contradictions and opposites within opposites and transitions and leaps. Then came the discussion period, and up went the hand of the leading Mother Fucker. We would recognize him and he would shout out in his loudest, proudest voice: "Up against the wall, Mother Fucker!" The group shouted their agreement and then they left. They never said anything more or anything less.

This was a period of considerable personal turmoil for me. For some time Martha and I had drifted apart. She was no longer interested in politics. I had my life down on 10th Street, while she had returned to school and was studying music. Our relationship had always had a lot of tension and conflict within it, and I would often come home and put on my earphones and listen to music to cut myself off. I was thirty-four years old, which at the time felt like middle age. I thought then that I had already used up close to half my life, and I began to wonder if I was living as I really wished to live. I had my mid-life crisis just a bit early. Then there was the period, the spirit of the times, the climate of the East Village. It was time for me to change personally, to experience what most experience at a much earlier age.

It was the summer of 1967, and Deborah had been working with me in the office for some time. Then she did not show up for a full week, claiming that she had a cold. Finally, she called and asked if I would come and see her, as she was still too sick to come to the office. So I went the short block and a half from the office to her apartment at the top of 48 Stuyvesant Street. She was resting on the couch, clearly not that sick. I went over the latest happenings in our little group with her just staring at me. Then she started to speak:

"I haven't been coming to the office even though I am not really that sick because I can't stand being near you. I love you! I can't help it but I can't hide it any longer. I love you! I love you! I love you!" She started crying.

There she was: blond hair, blue eyes, that infectious dreamy romantic quality, so different from my wife, from the life I was leading. Her emotion swept through me and I could not think. I just felt, and what I felt was this tremendous, uncontrollable desire for that crazy little girl. I said nothing, but Deborah could sense the way I was feeling.

She got up from the couch and we both walked very slowly toward the door. Before I reached it, I turned toward her and took her into my arms and we kissed passionately and started to undress each other. We staggered to her bed and were soon making passionate sweaty love. I was lost. I could no longer view Deborah with any objectivity. I was totally, madly in love with her.

I left Deborah in bed, naked, dozing off, and I got dressed and walked to the door of her apartment. Then I heard the phone ring.

"Hello, Trina," it was Deborah's best friend, a dressmaker for the flower children who had a small storefront in the neighborhood. "Guess what? I just fucked the Great Pumpkin!"

I heard her words but I did not comprehend them. If I had I would have known then what I know so well now. It was the Great Pumpkin she had made love to, not me. We all were in love with dreams that summer. Some of us dreamed of community, or socialism, others of love itself. Belief, love, was real, very tangible. What we loved, what we believed in, was less so.

I left the apartment in a daze. I just could not go back to my wife, Martha, as if nothing had happened. I had to tell her the truth, to break up a fourteen-year marriage. I told her that night as we went for a walk in a slight rain in our West Side neighborhood. At first she was tearful, begging me to stay and then bitter and hostile, urging me to leave. I tried to wall myself off from her emotions so that I could be free to pursue my dream.

Exhausted we went to bed and the next day, with relief, I went off to work at 10th Street.

Politics called me away to England, so for a while, I could escape my personal turmoil. When I returned I found that Martha had organized Carl and Bill to help her gather all my possessions and then had had comrades take them to Deborah's place. It must have been very hard on the children.

Life with Deborah quickly turned into its own kind of nightmare. There was, after all, Jeff Goldstein, her husband. Jeff quite sensibly left for the West Coast to build us a branch in San Francisco. Soon after I moved into Stuyvesant Street, Deborah was on the phone to Jeff. She suddenly discovered that she truly loved Jeff and had to be with him immediately. Because she had no resources of her own, I found myself giving her the bus fare for the long trip to the Coast. A few days after her arrival on the Coast, my phone rang. It was Deborah. Having returned to Jeff, she now knew with certainty that she loved me deeply and had to be with me. Anxious to see her, I sent her airfare in spite of the meagerness of my resources. I remember her walking down the corridor from the plane at Kennedy Airport, deeply engrossed in a discussion with a young soldier. No doubt, I thought to myself, she is carrying out revolutionary antiwar work. I swept her into my arms and all was forgiven.

But all was not over. Deborah went back and forth between coasts and lovers three times that summer and fall. Then one evening reality broke into my thick head almost as forcefully as dreamy love had. I could see Deborah as she really was. I was free of her and I could now lead my own life. But I did not go back to Martha. My life had changed too much.

That winter we recruited a graduate student, Karen Finkel (Frankel). Karen was an attractive woman with a full figure, carrying just a bit of weight. Karen loved ice cream and would eat a pint of rich Haagan Dazs all by herself without stopping. She had dark curly hair, which she was always struggling to straighten. She tended to wear jumpers and loose sweaters. She was extremely bright, aggressive, good at reaching new people.

I invited her to my apartment one evening to talk about politics. We sat on my couch and were soon deep in conversation. Starting on politics, we soon shifted to anthropology—a side interest of mine and her major—and the discussion got animated. Karen came alive in that discussion, her whole personality beaming through her face. I found myself falling in love with her, a kind of mingling of an attraction for her mind and for her body. It was most pleasant, and there was no guilt involved. Certainly I owed nothing to Deborah, with whom I had had no contact for months. Karen had no responsibility for my break with Martha. The situation had potential. I walked Karen to the subway and got up the nerve to ask her out. All very proper behavior, and more mature than my fling with Deborah. In a week or two Karen and I had a relationship going.

Very soon after Karen and I got together, Carl had to go into the hospital for a heart operation. He had been born with a fused heart valve, which meant that he did not grow quite as fast as other children. In time he would die if it was not surgically opened. We put him in Lenox Hill Hospital, and they performed open-heart surgery. I remember visiting him there after the operation. He was so very small with tubes coming out of him and his heart throbbing away on a television screen. I was convinced that I had to watch the screen to be sure it continued to pulse, as none of the nurses were paying the least attention. No one told me that a buzzer went off if there was a failure. So I could hardly concentrate on Carl, so preoccupied was I with the screen. Martha was there too and we hugged, the last time we ever touched each other.

Karen and I lived together quite well for about five years. After two years we decided to get married, primarily at my urging, a reflection of my fear of losing a woman. My father, quite unexpectedly, treated us to a honeymoon in Bermuda. We had a wonderful time in a little cottage right on the beach at the Elbow Beach Club and whipped around the small island on rented mopeds. Afterward we moved out of Stuyvesant Street to Brooklyn, where Karen felt more comfortable. By then the Workers League had also moved its offices to 14th Street. Our East Village Days had come to an end.

Notes

1. *Bulletin of International Socialism* (New York, September 14, 1964).
2. *Bulletin of International Socialism* (New York, September 6, 1965).
3. Kirkpatrick Sale, *SDS* (New York: Vintage Books, 1974), pp. 196–97.
4. Dennis King, *Lyndon LaRouche and the New American Fascism* (New York: Doubleday, 1989), p. 19.
5. *Campaigner* 3, no. 1 (New York).
6. *Campaigner* 2, no. 2 (New York).
7. I agree with Dennis King's assessment that the LaRouche group reflects a unique form of American Fascism. See Dennis King, *Lyndon LaRouche and the New American Fascism* (New York: Doubleday, 1989), pp. 39–46, 274–85.
8. Joseph Hansen, ed. *Marxism vs. Ultraleftism: The Record of Healy's Break with Trotskyism* (New York: Socialist Workers Party, January, 1974), pp. 75–101.
9. Organisation Communiste Internationaliste. Formerly known as the Parti Communiste Internationaliste, the Lambert group took this name in 1965.
10. This group was founded by a Romanian Communist named Barta who passed through France on his way to fight in the Spanish civil war. He was recruited to Trotskyism and never made it to Spain. Just prior to World War II Barta's

supporters withdrew from the factionalized Trotskyist movement and devoted themselves to clandestine work in factories. Trotskyists outside of France lost sight of them until they emerged in 1956 with a small but well-organized group. They began to recruit substantial numbers of *students* attracted to their workerist orientation and activity. They became a sizable group on the extreme left in France, not quite as large as the OCI or La Ligue Communiste Révolutionaire (the section close to Mandel). Among their distinctive political views was the notion that all of East Europe remained capitalist because it was not, like the USSR, the product of a genuine workers' revolution. Rose Jersawitz (Kay Ellens) formed a small group within Spartacist supporting their politics. See A. Belden Fields, *Trotskyism and Maoism: Theory and Practice in France and the United States* (Brooklyn: Autonomedia, 1988), pp. 73–84.

11. *Bulletin* (New York, November 7, 1966).
12. "Freedom Now: The New Stage in the Struggle for Negro Emancipation and the Tasks of the SWP" SWP *Discussion Bulletin* 24, no. 13 (New York, May 1963), p. 7.
13. *Young Socialist Discussion Bulletin* (New York, 1989 and 1969).
14. *Bulletin* 2, no. 6 (New York, March 22, 1965).
15. *The Jewish Question—A Marxist Interpretation* (Mexico City: Ediciones Pioneras, 1950).

7

The Vietnam War

THE YEAR OF REVOLUTION

In 1968 our little group and the rest of the American Left were swept up in the revolutionary tide that spread throughout the world. No single year in the whole post–World War II period witnessed as many rebellions and revolutionary events as did that year. It was a year when ferment in one country encouraged ferment in another. It was an 1848 *with television*![1]

The year began with the Tet Offensive in Vietnam. This heroic coordinated mass offensive of the National Liberation Front (NLF) is now credited as the beginning of the end of America's invasion of Vietnam. While the NLF failed to hold a single position it captured, the political impact of the action upon the American and world public was decisive. It was no longer possible to question the support the NLF received from the majority of the Vietnamese people. Just as important, the heroism of the NLF troops and cadres convinced many thinking people that this force would never give up its fight this side of victory. Many Americans began to question whether they wished to continue to see Americans die in a war that could not be won.

The NLF became the hero, the inspiration for the entire American Left and a whole generation. Our personal sacrifices as political activists seemed minor and our work insignificant in comparison. The temper of a movement shifted dramatically leftward. The stage was being set for militancy to move into adventurism, for New Leftism to be abruptly replaced by Marxism-Leninism, and for a few to adopt terrorism and an underground existence.

Next came the Prague Spring. In January, old-time Stalinist leader Antonin Novotny resigned as first secretary of the Communist Party of Czechoslovakia. Ferment among the country's students and intellectuals led to reformer Alexander Dubcek's rise to power. Hundreds of dissident voices spoke out, and great cultural creativity sprang up in a rebellion centered in radio, television, and cultural circles. Soon the workers joined in support of the revolt and the country appeared to be on the road to the humanist and democratic form of socialism so close to the hearts of we Trotskyists. The Prague Spring ended abruptly with the Soviet invasion in August. Once again our assessment of Stalinism was reaffirmed by world events, and the worldwide Communist movement sustained heavy losses. At the same time, given the international character of the revolutionary turmoil, we viewed this setback as temporary.

As if these events were not enough for one year, in May the French students took to the barricades in the Latin Quarter of Paris. The police brutally stormed the barricades, causing many injuries and arrests. Then—we could hardly believe our eyes as we watched it on television—the French working class went on strike in defense of the students, occupying factories throughout the country. We were elated! Our fantasies appeared to become reality, and we believed we were witnesses to genuine proletarian revolution in an advanced nation in the very heart of Europe!

The French student movement had swept right past the Communist Party and was being led by what in Europe became known as the Far Left, a coalition of anarchists and Trotskyists. The French youth, supported by the United Secretariat and the SWP, as well as Lambert's youth, grew overnight into organizations with several thousand members and a huge periphery. The problem was that the Communist Party still dominated the major section of the working class and succeeded in negotiating an economic settlement that got the occupying workers out of the plants. The Far Left groups were then banned and their members made subject to arrest. This, we felt, was one more lesson in the treachery of Stalinism for the world's working class.

We joined the SWP-YSA and many independents from Columbia University, then experiencing its own insurrection, for a march in New York in defense of the French students and to protest the bans. It was a marvelous affair; we carried huge red banners with the slogans of the French groups we supported, and red flags were everywhere. American student struggles had played a role in inspiring the French students, and now we were being inspired by France's own rich revolutionary history. The result was the largest concentration of red banners in New York City since the demise of the Communist Party and its old May Day parades.

There were many other rebellions in other countries that year. Most significant were the demonstrations by the Mexican students, which were brutally repressed by the police as a bloody preparation for holding the summer Olympics in that country.

As I look back twenty-five years later, it is obvious that 1968 did *not* usher in a period of triumphal worldwide revolution. The Vietnam War had given the student movement throughout the world a common focus, while the new technology of television had visually linked these diverse movements. Here and there the student ferment connected with other layers of the population and gave expression to more fundamental rebellions: those of intellectuals and workers in Czechoslovakia and workers in France. However, one can understand the events on the American Left that were to follow only by understanding the impact world events in 1968 had on all of us. The year 1968 may not have been the beginning of world revolution, but it certainly *seemed* that way to most of us. Older radicals like me felt vindicated, and our energies were renewed. We had passed through a period of darkness touched by the shadow of the death of radicalism only to enter a new period of rebellion and revolution. Thousands of students new to politics, some brought into the struggle only in the course of that year, made decisions to devote their entire lives to the grand cause of socialism and revolution. As they made that choice, they did not feel isolated and alone as I did making the same choice at Oberlin College in 1953. They felt they were part of a worldwide struggle. They were the future!

The Antiwar Movement

Beginning in 1965 tens of thousands of American students turned to radical activism. The main factor producing this radicalization was the Vietnam War, which meant that students faced the draft and possible death. At the same time, the Americanization of the war created a sense of moral outrage among many students who objected to their government fighting a force that appeared to have the support of the people in Vietnam. There were other concerns. The civil rights struggle, which in this period became largely transformed into an expression of black consciousness and power, not only radicalized black students but had its moral appeal to many white students. Also, the growth of the university system to meet the needs of the baby boom generation created a university bureaucracy very distant from the needs of its students. The resulting malaise encouraged student-power protests.

The antiwar movement was also a generational and cultural conflict, and these dimensions tended to add color to the basically political protests. There is always a conflict between generations, but it is not so easy to explain why the generational conflict of the 1960s was so profound, so universal. It was *the* generational rebellion of the postwar era. Everywhere students rejected the values of their parents, abandoning, at least for a time, a career orientation and embracing rock, drugs, peace, and communal living. Love replaced war, cooperation replaced competition, and a little later, spiritualism replaced materialism. The generational rebellion was so profound that it has never been fully reversed. While today's students are very career-oriented, a youth culture persists, and the ecology and peace concerns of the 1960s generation continue to have great currency in the nation. I believe the generational side of the rebellion gave the more strictly political struggles a wider base of support than they would have otherwise had. Even totally apolitical students felt that the peace marches were a genuine expression of their generation.

The student movement followed two main paths: broad massive demonstrations against the war and localized, militant, bitter campus struggles usually directed against ROTC and various forms of campus complicity in the war effort. The mass antiwar demonstrations were organized through a broad coalition of forces in which the Socialist Workers Party, the Communist Party, and pacifists such as Sidney Peck, Dave Dellinger, and A. J. Muste played critical roles. Local protests were led primarily by SDS, which, after organizing a successful march in 1965, largely abandoned the mass-march strategy. Of course many of the same students participated in both kinds of activities.

The SWP concentrated its forces and almost all its energy on the mass demonstrations. Its strategy was straightforward and widely appealing. It proposed that the broadest possible coalition be formed to build the largest possible peaceful demonstrations around the one simple, but basically radical, slogan: Out Now! The SWP's major competitor in this work was the Communist Party. The CP's strategy was a bit different. While favoring an end to the war, it sought to utilize antiwar sentiment to build a liberal political coalition within the Democratic Party. Thus for the Stalinists, the peace marches were a vehicle to bring about a realignment within the Democratic Party.

A key figure in this organizational struggle was the Reverend A. J. Muste, whom I had met in regroupment days. His prestige and integrity were essential to getting broad backing for the marches from community, church, and labor circles. Most of the time the CP was forced to work in a common coalition with the SWP and around the SWP's strategy.[2] The key SWP figure in building these coalitions was Fred Halstead. I had known Fred quite well in my SWP days, and I was impressed by the way he came forward in the antiwar movement, utilizing all his tactical abilities and political charm to hold together fragile coalitions under great stress. He then utilized the coalitions to mobilize tens of thousands and, in time, hundreds of thousands of participants.

I do believe that the SWP deserves the major credit, along with certain political independents like A. J. Muste, for the success of the many mass antiwar demonstrations. I would not claim that the SWP did not make mistakes, perhaps compromising too much with liberal politicians, and here and there acting out of its desire to control groups organizationally. But on the whole, its strategy was principled and successful. I believe the mass demonstrations were critically important in awakening ever-larger layers of the American population to the nature of the Vietnam War and, in the end, contributed to ending that war. The SWP and its members can be justly proud of having affected world history positively in the 1960s.

Yet it must be mentioned that in choosing to concentrate its energies on the antiwar movement, the SWP chose to neglect the equally important growth of SDS. In part I am sure this neglect was a matter of scarce resources, as the SWP entered this period severely weakened by a series of splits, including ours and Robertson's, as well as the defection of older, tired cadres. It had around four hundred members during most of the 1960s and did not seriously grow until the 1970s.[3] But the choice in favor of mass antiwar work was also due to the party's political personality. The SWP felt comfortable working with those politically to its right on massive peaceful demonstrations. It was decidedly uncomfortable when approaching groups such as SDS that were to the left of it and whose chosen form of activity was more spontaneous and, occasionally, adventuristic. Just as the SWP had ignored Progressive Labor's rise, so too did it abstain from intervening in SDS, which soon had a loose membership of around thirty thousand students. The SWP recruited almost no one from the SDS milieu.

There were two aspects of the antiwar movement with which we were mainly concerned: the conferences that determined policies and the mass demonstrations. They were equally important and could be equally exciting. The conferences were gatherings of virtually the entire Left for the purpose of debating and deciding policy in relation to the struggle against the Vietnam War. There were so many of them, mostly held in Cleveland at Case Western Reserve University, that they become a kind of blur in the mind, a memory of one continuous conference. The Workers League, of course, was represented at all of them. We sold papers and we put forward our political positions, but we were not a major actor. We were, for the most part, observers and ideologues propagating views that were not held by most of the participants.

Two conferences do stand out a bit in my mind. The first was held in Cleveland in July 1969. It was a gathering of around a thousand people who filled the bleachers of a large gymnasium. I remember one whole bleacher was dominated by the Revolutionary Youth Movement (RYM) faction of SDS; RYM members wildly cheered their leader, Mark Rudd, when he spoke from the platform in favor of an adventuristic policy of street confrontation. Everyone was there: PL's SDS, the SWP-YSA in great force, the Communist Party and its youth arm, the DuBois Clubs,

Above: With Henry Wallace in 1950, two years after he lost the presidential election as the Progressive Party candidate. *Left*: Future leaders of the Young Socialist Alliance gather at a Socialist Workers Party educational weekend, Mountain Springs Camp, Washington, NJ, June 1957. *Top*: Giving the main talk. *Center*: Murry Weiss, a leading member of the SWP's Political Committee and instrumental in the formation of the YSA. *Bottom (left to right)*: Rose Jersawitz (Kay Ellens), who later led her own split off from Robertson's Spartacist League; Bert Wainer (Deck), key leader of the New York YSA; and his wife at the time, Renee.

Max Shachtman

James P. Cannon

Carl Skoglund

Farrell Dobbs (*far right*) visits a state farm in Cuba during his 1960 election campaign.

Building the Workers League. *Above*: Seeking to raise funds to launch a twice-weekly *Bulletin*, Dayton, Ohio, 1970. *Above right*: Staffing a literature table during an antiwar demonstration, Sheep Meadow, New York City, April 1968. *Below right*: Addressing a rally launching the twice-weekly *Bulletin*, New York City, 1973.

Answering Gerry Healy's slanders of SWP leaders before 1,150 people at a London rally, January 14, 1977. *Left to right*: Ernest Mandel, United Secretariat of the Fourth International; George Novack (head partially blocked), Socialist Workers Party; Tariq Ali, International Marxist Group; me; François Demassot, Organisation Communiste Internationaliste; Pierre Lambert, OCI; Betty Hamilton, veteran Trotskyist and longtime associate of Gerry Healy; Tamara Deutscher, wife of author Isaac Deutscher.

Leaders of the Workers Revolutionary Party (*left to right*): Gerry Healy, Mike Banda, and Cliff Slaughter, London, 1983.

Left to right: Alex Mitchell, former editor of the WRP's paper *News Line*, Corin Redgrave, and Vanessa Redgrave defend Gerry Healy after the WRP Central Committee expelled him, following a sex scandal in 1985.

and various pacifists and other individuals. I remember a young, earnest, clearly middle-class woman getting up and speaking for PL-SDS. "We must ally with the workers and not the liberals," she said in a kind of singsong fashion. "I have been working in this factory for the past three weeks and all the workers believe we must break with the liberals and fight for socialism."

There were motions and countermotions, battles over credentials, and lots of corridor negotiations. In the end the SWP-YSA carried the day and another Washington march was set. The issues changed but little from conference to conference. The SWP-YSA always, in one form or another, favored broad, mass demonstrations around the immediate-withdrawal slogan. The opposition posed various alternatives, and many of them sounded much more radical than the SWP-YSA program. There was a lot of discussion of grass-roots organizing, of linking the Vietnam issue to other working-class issues, of confrontationist tactics, some pacifist in origins, others more anarchistic. Many on the left were drawn from time to time to opposing the SWP strategy out of a feeling that "one more march" would be futile, that "something more" was needed. Yet people could rarely come up with a meaningful "something more," so we all ended up marching that one more time.

Not all the antiwar opponents of the SWP were to its left, however. In most cases these left-sounding opposition coalitions included the Communist Party. The CP in one way or another found a way of including support for the liberal wing of the Democratic Party in the opposition's program. The CP would use left-sounding rhetoric to do this, such as criticizing the single demand for immediate withdrawal as too narrow a focus for a mass movement. We never felt able to support this opposition and were drawn toward the positions of the SWP-YSA. Yet we could not entirely accept these either because of our predisposition to view that group's policies as "revisionist." We ended up tailing the SWP-YSA while urging upon it greater emphasis on the role of the labor movement in ending the war and more distance from liberal Democratic politicians.

The second conference I remember well was held in July 1971 at Hunter College in New York and had well over two thousand participants. It was called by the National Peace Action Coalition (NPAC), which the SWP-YSA had organized and which was the major organization in the antiwar movement. Featured speakers of the conference were Democratic senator Vance Hartke and UAW vice president Victor Reuther. NPAC looked upon Reuther's attendance as a real coup, since at that time even many of the more liberal labor leaders had not yet come out against the war.

Progressive Labor, through its SDS, mobilized heavily for the conference in its stronghold, Boston. The PLers made it plain that they would attempt a disruption. From the moment the conference opened, the PLers did their best to break it up. They almost succeeded in shouting down Vance Hartke. When Reuther appeared, pandemonium broke out. Clearly Reuther would not be able to speak unless PL was removed. We did not agree in any way with PL's tactics. While we were opposed to Hartke's presence because we did not believe Democratic Party politicians should be part of the movement, we felt that the conference participants had a right to determine whom they wished to listen to. We were particularly incensed over the attempt to disrupt Reuther; while we were critical of Reuther, we believed he was a representative of the labor movement, and his presence at the conference was an important step forward.

We were rather proud of our delegation to the conference. We had mobilized almost one hundred delegates, and most of them were young blacks and Puerto Ricans, reflecting the successes we were beginning to have in building a working-class youth movement. Spartacist had a much smaller group there and they were allied with PL, also trying to break up the meeting. The decision was made by the conference leadership to clear the hall of the disrupters. From where I was seated I had my eyes on two people, Big Red Fred Halstead and Mike Zagarell, a former CP youth leader and now with District 65 of the UAW, also a rather large fellow. They carefully and determinedly moved on the PLers. Fred just picked one up bodily without hurting him and walked him out of the conference—as someone might pick up a dog who made a mistake on the living room rug—while other PLers rushed him. We, as well as others in the audience, happily joined in the action and started moving the PLers and Sparts out. It was great fun, and those in the audience were so unanimous in their hatred of this attempt to break up a democratic conference that the hall was clear in ten minutes and the rest of the conference went ahead peacefully.

The peace marches soon became part of our lives. There was at least one a year, and sometimes two or more. We never missed one. Sometimes we concentrated on selling our paper, while other times we built a contingent complete with colorful banners, bullhorns, and chants. Once we sold over two thousand papers, and another time we mobilized a contingent of five hundred. We chartered our own buses to Washington, and the trip there and back offered ample opportunity to talk with and sometimes recruit nonparty members who came along. We were cautious in our tactics and avoided, most of the time, street battles and other adventures that a few at these marches would sometimes attempt.

The FBI was now devoting considerable energy to spying on those active in the antiwar movement. This became reflected in my own file: "On March 26, 1966, subject was observed marching in a parade down Fifth Avenue designated 'International Days of Protest,' placards for which indicated the parade was a protest of United States policy in Viet Nam. . . . On April 15, 1967, a Special Agent of the Federal Bureau of Investigation (FBI) observed Wohlforth participating in a demonstration at Central Park, New York City, called to protest the United States policy in Vietnam."

On one trip we brought down some yippie kids who clearly were using our buses for the ride only. As soon as we hit Washington they went off on their own, seeking the action. They evidently found it, for when they returned to the bus their clothes were permeated with tear gas. They got on and soon everyone was in tears, so we had to remove them from the bus.

The Pentagon march in October 1967 was a favorite. We had a small contingent of perhaps sixty or seventy people, but we were well organized and had our own buses. We made beautiful banners and spent most of the time chanting for a labor party. We felt then (and we were partly right) that the strong sentiment building in late 1967 to break with the Democrats due to Johnson's escalation of the war would soon spread to the labor movement. These were the days of the chant, "Hey! Hey! LBJ! How many kids did you kill today?" The SWP was doing a good job promoting a presidential ticket of Fred Halstead and Paul Boutelle, and the process had begun that would soon launch the Peace and Freedom Party.

The demonstration of a hundred thousand or so snaked its way for a few miles, crossed a bridge over the Potomac River, and arrived right at the wall of the Pentagon. We all felt like Davids coming up against Goliath. There we were with our banners, leaflets, ideas, and general goodwill. There "they" were with barbed wire surrounding the place and troops with rifles pointed at us from the roofs. We all wanted to stop "them," and we were not at all sure how to do it. The climate was set for some to try a more direct form of confrontation with the armed state. We saw it start but we did not participate. We did not believe students could stop armed men with street scuffles. I guess, when it came to tactics, we were closer to the SWP than any of us wished to realize.

There was another New York march that has remained in my memory. The year was 1969, and some 200,000 marched in a light drizzle down the west side of Central Park in New York, directed by the police to remain as much as possible out of the view of the public (though there was an awful lot of the "public" marching). A separate contingent of several thousand had been organized in Harlem by Black Power militants. It joined the main march close to the southwestern corner of the park, where we were supposed to end and disperse into the Sheep Meadow. The black contingent just kept right on going down Broadway into the center of the city. We and a few thousand others from the main march joined them.

The cops were caught by surprise as the march proceeded through Times Square without any interference. We got a great welcome from people on the sidewalks and caused no difficulties except for a minor traffic snarl. Then the march turned down 42nd Street and headed for the UN. Around 3rd Avenue the cops had regrouped and set up barricades, which at first only slowed us down. I found myself against a barricade, nose to nose with a cop. I smiled and said, "They are pushing me from behind," and with one shove we crashed through the barricade and were headed for the next clash with the cops.

Suddenly I stopped to think for a moment. What in the hell was I doing? So far it had been fun, and we had made a political point in the center of New York City. Now was the time to get our people out of there somehow before anybody got hurt or arrested. So we hid our banners under our shirts, regrouped, and snuck out of there without injury or arrest. It was our only "adventure" in the entire antiwar period.

The biggest peace march of all was held in Washington in November 1969. We brought a contingent of over one hundred with a number of college students. The New Jersey Turnpike was packed with thousands of buses with banners streaming out the windows and students waving at each other. It was like one long New York City traffic jam. Every now and then a Howard Johnson Restaurant would appear and literally hundreds of buses would stop so people could go to the bathroom. It was fantastic: three or four thousand students seeking to piss at the same time. As was usual in such situations, hundreds moved through the men's room at a reasonable speed while the line for the ladies' facility snaked out almost into the four-lane highway. Soon the women were pouring into the men's room, turning it into a unisex facility. This liberation was not enough. Hundreds just ran into the nearby woods.

We arrived in Washington and the city was a complete snarl. It was not used to 500,000 additional people. We finally made it to the assembly area and everyone was in good spirit, people were hugging each other, a few of the more exuberant stripping off their clothes and dancing. The atmosphere was not particularly conducive to selling papers, which did not matter because we were determined to march with the half-million. We had to wait three hours for our turn, so we held a little rally in the meantime. Then most of the half-million were back again on the turnpikes, wending their way to New York and beyond, tired but happy at this display of our common strength, our common opposition to the hated war.

THE STUDENT UPSURGE

For better or for worse, SDS captured the American student's imagination in the 1960s. The movement was organized in a very open, participatory, democratic fashion and usually operated in a free, sloppy way that irritated anyone trained in a Leninist organization. Organizationally it was a political expression of the way a generation of middle-class youth were keeping their rooms. While its politics varied from campus chapter to campus chapter, it did have an overall coloration. It combined a reformism, almost a liberalism, in its attitude to the Democratic Party and its programmatic ideas of social change with a tendency toward very radical direct action. Counterculturalism grew within the movement, and a greater and greater hostility toward the "capitalist state" developed—at first empirically—as the war in Vietnam intensified and conflicts grew on individual campuses.

Until 1969 and 1970 we did not connect with SDS. We were not alone in this. Groups much larger than we, such as the SWP and the CP, never made a connection. SDSers believed they were a New Left. They were uninterested in the "Old Left," Leninism, history, and even political theory (it was amazing how anti-intellectual American students could be). They did retain, however, a hostility to Trotskyism inherited from the Social Democratic and Stalinist backgrounds of the parents of some of the SDS leaders. Only PL made inroads. Milt Rosen's left-Stalinist party appealed to the mood of radical adventurism in many of these students while at the same time satisfied their need for a programmatic connection to the working class. The result was that PL won over perhaps a third of SDS's active members and recruited them directly into its own organization.

The student movement was explosive, and we were swept up in it even though we were in no position to lead it. The Columbia strike in April 1968 was the high point, at least for me. Here students had occupied buildings in a protest not only against university complicity in the war effort but also in defense of the nearby black community. The concrete issue was the proposal by the administration to build a gymnasium on a portion of Morningside Park. Yet somehow the rebellion was about more than this; it had for a moment passed beyond specifics to a general rebellion against society, the state, the system—the life that an older generation had prepared for the students.

I went to Columbia each day of the building occupation and resulting strike. There was excitement, tension, in the air. Mark Rudd, who was leading the struggle, was pushing for action and adventuristic confrontation. He combined this appetite with a very patronizing view of the black struggle. For Rudd the struggle of blacks and minorities was part of an anti-imperialist struggle that paralleled that of the Vietnamese. All whites were oppressors and part of the imperialist system. All white radicals could do was prove their worth to blacks by battling the cops. Of course, the black students were very unimpressed with all this. They had occupied their own building and were acting in a most arrogant manner toward the rest of the students.

A key future member of the Workers League and my future wife, Nancy Freuden (Fields), was inside one of the buildings. She was one of the few occupiers who worked for a living, and she would crawl out of a window early each morning and go to work at *Time* magazine and crawl back in each evening. We did not know her then.

We had no members who were students at Columbia, so we were not present when, late one night, the police stormed the buildings and then proceeded to riot, beating up the students and dragging them off to jail. We were there the next day when the entire campus went on strike. It was an impressive event of great solidarity and militancy, pitting generation against generation. Of course we knew it was only a student struggle, but it felt a little like the classic revolutionary events we had studied so closely. The Hungarian Revolution or even moments in the Russian Revolution came easily to mind. If a revolution could succeed in one square block of a city, it would have then, at Broadway and 116th Street.

We were even more involved when in reaction to the renewed bombing of North Vietnam and the invasion of Cambodia in May 1970, students went on strike all over the nation, occupying campus buildings in the process. This time college administrations, sensing the tremendous unpopularity of the government's actions and having seen the bitterness created at Columbia and elsewhere by heavy-handed police intervention, simply turned the campuses over to the students. We were part of the occupations at Cooper Union and City College in New York City, as well as at other colleges in other parts of the country. Everywhere the facilities of the university were made available to churn out antiwar material. Huge meetings of over one thousand students were held daily at Columbia, which we were able to address. Ad hoc committees sprung up, which we participated in, to coordinate the struggle at different campuses. Our little office at 10th Street became a nerve center, with the phone constantly ringing as we sought to coordinate our people on different campuses.

This time we had a simple and distinct proposal to make—and that is the key to any effective intervention when there is real ferment—and we gained considerable support. We proposed that the students urge the trade union movement to call a demonstration against the war. It made a lot of sense, particularly because the more reactionary sections of the labor movement, the building-trades unions, had recently held a jingoistic pro-war demonstration of fifty thousand, and the liberal sections of the labor leadership felt pressured to do something. The proposal flowed from our Marxist orthodoxy, which held that only the working class had the power to stop the war. It also struck a chord among leftist students who felt they had reached the limits of a student power movement and had to find ways to reach outside the university to more powerful social forces.

We succeeded in getting our position carried at virtually all SMC[4] meetings, at the ad hoc coordinating committees, and at other mass gatherings. I do believe we made more of an impact than the much larger YSA. The YSA restricted its work to talk of transforming the universities into antiwar centers. But the question was, what should these antiwar universities *do*? The YSA did not do well in such radical mass situations; it had, for example, played almost no role in the Columbia rebellion.

Soon the New York City Labor Council called such a demonstration. Some twenty-five thousand unionists turned out for the first labor demonstration held against the war. No doubt it could have been more massive if the union leadership had put in half as much effort as did its right-wing building-trades rivals. Of course there were many others besides the Workers League also working for such a demonstration, including the SWP, and we cannot take all the credit for it. Yet we did feel our efforts made a difference. For once we were able to connect our theories with the sentiments of a significant layer of people.

The year 1968 marked the high point of the student power movement. It was then that SDS went into a deep crisis.[5] The founding leadership played little role any more. The problem was that this leadership had done little to prepare a new leadership for the movement. There were no longer many advocates for its vision of a democratic participatory movement that would promote in a radical fashion a democratic socialist society. The failure of the New Left to encourage a serious study of the Old Left had disarmed SDS members. They had rejected the past without understanding it, making them prone to repeating past mistakes. The application of participatory democracy internally had created an anarchistic state of affairs that paralyzed SDS as a national entity. Little thought had been given to the *future*, to how student radicalism could contribute to a movement that could transform American society at large. At the same time, SDS's members had become swept up in a mood of radicalism, encouraged not only by their own experiences in the United States but by the world events of 1968 as well.

The leadership group, facing a serious challenge from PL and reflecting the radicalization of many of its members, organized the Revolutionary Youth Movement faction. The faction soon split into RYM I, the Weatherman group headed by Mark Rudd and Bernadine Dohrne, and RYM II, headed by Bob Avakian and Mike Klonsky. Both factions professed to embrace Marxism-Leninism in a Maoist form. Soon Weathermen went underground while RYM II broke into warring Maoist parties, primarily Avakian's Revolutionary Union (later called the Revolutionary Communist Party) and Klonsky's October League (later called Workers Viewpoint). Several thousand former SDSers followed the Maoists into what was known as a New Communist Movement, which produced no unity and many further groupings. The PL-SDS formation itself slowly shriveled into a small sect. By 1972 SDS, once a powerful movement of over thirty thousand, was no more.

Was this madness inevitable? Is it all to be blamed on outside "invaders" from the Old Left? *Or to pose it bluntly, where in the world were the old SDS leaders when all this was going on? What alternatives did they have to offer at the time*? Where was Todd Gitlin, Carl Ogelsby, Paul Booth, and Tom Hayden? Tom Hayden continued to play a prominant role in SDS and American Left politics. However, he was part of the problem rather than part of the solution. He joined the Weathermen during the Days of Rage at the Chicago Democratic Party Convention that fall.

I am well aware of being a Monday-morning quarterback. I was around at the time, and what I had to say then was in its way as off the wall and sectarian as the antics of those more intimately involved with SDS. Yet there is little purpose in studying history if we cannot learn from the mistakes we all made. Was there an alternative road for SDS and, most important, its graduates, a road that was practical at that time, a road none of the prominent actors advocated? I believe there was.

It is insufficient to blame the implosion totally on PL. One must ask why PL was so successful within SDS that it not only gained a majority at a convention but forced the opposition to mimic its Marxism-Leninism. It was a deeper matter than just good faction organization. I believe PL swept through SDS because it represented an alternative, a way for students seeking to build a permanent leftist movement in the United States. PL identified the working class as the force capable of bringing socialism to America; it popularized the classical Marxist methodology and scenario; it counterposed party organization to the paralysis of consensus anarchy. This alternative was certainly *not* a scientifically correct one. While the natural constituency for socialist ideas in the United States must include the working class, socialism requires a broader definition, as the older SDS leadership had for many years correctly, if a bit one-sidedly, pointed out. There is a world of difference between mouthing Marxist phraseology and developing the Marxist methodology in a new world situation. A party can have an organizational form that is open, pluralistic, broad, or it can become a narrow, elitist, personally dominated sect. My point is that PL had a perspective. The SDS membership was not offered a meaningful alternative perspective.

What could have been proposed in 1969? It is *now* very clear to me that what was needed was a broad socialist party in the Debsian tradition, staunchly anti-imperialist, radically democratic and pluralistic, a bit messy and sloppy internally, capable of absorbing and reflecting the leftist activists as they and their movements evolved.[6] Such a party would have been a home for the black activists, the feminist movement, which was only then coming into being, and militants from the trade unions and would have been capable of "greening" as the ecological movement developed. Yes, it would have been somewhat like the Democratic Socialists of America launched over a decade later but positioned to the DSA's left, reflecting the political temper of the 1960s.

Let us continue for a moment with our dreamy speculations in the realm of the "could have." If the New Left had consciously negated the Old Left, that is, had studied its history and thought through where it had gone wrong rather than simply turning its back upon that experience, it might have been able to educate a new generation. Instead, the questions that were ignored simply burst forth a few years later as a new generation rediscovered Marxism-Leninism. To paraphrase Marx from the *Eighteenth Brumaire*, the second time around it was true farce. The first generation of SDS leaders has some responsibility for this appalling backwardness.

This entire process was the political expression of the collapse of a movement and the maturity of a generation. The movement continued in spurts into 1973, ending when the United States withdrew from Vietnam. No other issue rekindled the kind of dynamic mass upsurge of students as did Vietnam. Prior to the collapse of the broader movement, the layer of students who chose a radical socialist worldview because of their experiences in this movement became aware of the limitations of a purely student activism. Thousands began searching for a general theory to support their continued radicalism and a strategy to reach from the campuses to the American masses. Many of these people were no longer students; graduation does, in time, finally come. In one manner or another these young radicals embraced Marxism and sought to build a party that would link them with the American working class.

THE WORKERS LEAGUE RECRUITS

Growth came to the Workers League in late 1969 and in 1970. Our politics, finally, began to make sense to many students who had passed through the SDS experience. Our Trotskyist theories gave us an appealing worldview and a historical accounting of the causes of the bureaucratization of the socialist countries. At the same time we had a concrete orientation toward constructing a base in the trade unions that centered around the labor party demand. Many student radicals had become disillusioned with the Democrats, who had been the chief engineers of the escalation of the Vietnam War. Our labor party propaganda therefore had some appeal even though there was little appetite for such a party in the AFL-CIO itself.

Our politics did not, of course, appeal to all former SDSers. Those caught up in Maoism, for example, were completely hostile to us. Most of our new recruits came from around PL, a party that had no consistent theoretical understanding of Stalinism and was acting in a bureaucratic fashion toward many of its less-committed followers in SDS. We appealed mainly to those students most interested in theory as well as to those who wanted to reach the American working class.

We did not compete with the SWP for these students. Its base was elsewhere, among those antiwar activists on campuses who had not been part of the SDS experience. The SWP, too, began a fast pace of growth by recruiting through the YSA the best militants from the SMC. Our competitors, in addition to PL, were Spartacists and the left-Shachtmanite International Socialists (IS). Both groups claimed an adherence to Trotskyism and grew in this period. Spartacists fared the worst, as they were not much interested in the labor movement, and their rather rude factionalism and sectarianism got in their way. For the entire crucial year of 1968, for example, Spartacist suspended most of its public work to have an obscure internal faction fight. As a result of that battle, Rose Jersawitz (Kay Ellens) and Harry Tanzer (Turner) split from that group.[7] The IS, however, did quite well, recruiting a serious layer of activists.

One of the more peculiar discoveries I have made from my FOIA request to the FBI pertains to Spartacist in this period. My files contained minutes from two different meetings of the Political Bureau of the Spartacist League, on April 28, 1970, and June 15, 1970. The minutes were supplied to the FBI by U.S. Army Intelligence! This indicates that Army Intelligence had its own informant rather highly placed in the Spartacist League. My guess is that the army connection could have been related to antiwar work Spartacist may have been conducting among soldiers in that period.

The minutes ended up in my file because of brief references in them to the Workers League and myself.

Interestingly, the main preoccupation of Spartacist in that period was work with and within PL-SDS.

We developed an original tactic to draw new members to the Workers League, and it worked amazingly well. We gave our new audience the full treatment. We held a series of regional conferences devoted to Trotskyism with a capital "T" at which we explained over the course of a weekend the entire history of the world Communist movement and our specific place therein. Our first one, the Eastern Regional Conference, was held in January 1970 at the Hotel Diplomat in New York City. We covered the walls with banners and photo displays on the history of the workers' movement. Dany Sylveire was there representing our British comrades, and we showed a propaganda film outlining their progress. About a hundred people attended.

When the sessions came to an end, I asked everyone to stay who was interested in joining the Workers League. We convinced about twenty to stick around, and I gave them my best pitch. They *all* agreed to join! Of course a few changed their minds when they returned home, but we were on our way; we were on a roll. We held a Western Regional Conference in San Francisco in late February and drew seventy people. Some drove up from Los Angeles on their own to attend. We reached a group of students and intellectuals at San Francisco State, started our branch in Los Angeles, and recruited through one representative a whole SDS chapter in San Diego. It took us until October to organize a Midwestern Regional Conference at Madison, which also drew seventy people and led to new branches there and in Chicago and St. Louis as well.

Another form our recruitment efforts took was the educational weekend school. We sponsored our first in September 1969 at Tishler's in Kerhonkson, New York, deep in the Catskill Mountains. Tishler's was an old farmhouse that had been a small Jewish resort for many years and catered mainly to the once-large Communist Party periphery. When we discovered the place, it was surviving on folk-dance fans in their forties and fifties who had once been part of the same milieu but were now apolitical. The school combined pleasant scenery, hearty Jewish cooking, and a Saturday-night dance with some pretty heavy-duty indoctrination courses. As we did at the conferences, we ended the weekend with a recruitment session and always got a group to join. This became an annual event until we outgrew the facility. That first year we had about 60 people, but in 1971 we had 150 and recruited 30 new members.

We held similar schools on the West Coast. Our first, and by far the most spectacular, was held in November 1970 at Asilomar, a YWCA conference facility at Monterey. The place was gorgeous, right on the water, with surf thundering over beautiful rock formations, and it featured the famous twisted Monterey cypress trees. We had a good turnout from the San Francisco Bay Area and a few people from Los Angeles. In the middle of the first session a shiny new Cadillac drove up, followed by a pick-up truck, and out piled a whole commune from Orange County. The SDSers explained they had just borrowed daddy's limo for the trip and were soon in the thick of the discussions on revolution and the working class. The following year the YWCA tore down the old cabins we stayed in, and the place was no longer affordable. We found a very nice facility in the Redwoods near Sebastopol, which we rented several years in a row from the Catholic church!

L'il Joe had to be our most unusual recruit on the West Coast. At the time of our Western Regional Conference, the UCLA campus was occupied by the students as part of the upsurge over the U.S. invasion of Cambodia. In an act apparently motivated by white guilt, the mainly white demonstrators immediately handed over administrative power to their black classmates, a group that included L'il Joe (who was not actually a student at UCLA, or anywhere for that matter). L'il Joe obtained in this fashion a university car and some gas and headed up to our conference together with a group of black militants. L'il Joe, brought up in the poor neighborhoods of Watts and Compton, was the product of the entire Black Power experience. He was, as his name suggests (and I never learned any other), short and very skinny. Indoors and out he always wore a round derbylike hat. He never smiled but rather glared at you with intense brown eyes that reminded me of Jeff Goldstein's.

I went to Compton and spent a few days with L'il Joe in a little apartment right in the heart of a black area that stretched for miles in all directions. Joe was living with a small black woman who never spoke, at least when I was around, and who had a baby. Joe told me some of his political history. He had read the famous Little Red Book and had become a Maoist. But he did more than wave Mao's book; he took it literally, as a guide for his political activity. Mao said revolutionaries were to start a movement by building nuclei among the peasantry. So, living in the middle of a Los Angeles ghetto, L'il Joe searched for peasants. He actually found some small plots being farmed along the freeway, and he preached from the Red Book to the half-dozen startled Japanese farmers who were assembled there.

L'il Joe was a completely self-educated worker whose thirst for knowledge was accompanied by a doctrinal intensity that inclined him toward the more exotic and sectlike political groups. For a period he had been one of the few members of Michael Laski's CPUSA-ML.[8] This extreme Maoist sect almost blew up literally when founder Laski took the party's treasury to Las Vegas, expecting to double it at the roulette tables. He came back empty-handed and was scolded sharply by his Central Committee. In the heated exchange that followed, Laski reputedly pulled a pistol on his critics and threatened to shoot them.

L'il Joe, who was a cult of one, did not last long with us. Later he was a member of the International Socialists for a short while and then I lost track of him. I hope he found his way into teaching or some other intellectual occupation because he was, without question, a brilliant fellow.

The year 1970 marked two anniversaries, thirty years since the assassination of Leon Trotsky and the centennial of Lenin's birth. We borrowed the idea from the British of making big events out of these anniversaries, utilizing them to explain the theories of the two revolutionaries and our own role as their self-appointed interpreters. The SWP ignored these anniversaries, which gave us an opportunity to challenge publicly the SWP's hegemony over Trotskyism in the United States. Also, our commemorations were in keeping with the mood of the times among radical students, many of whom were quite curious about both figures. In May 1970 we held our Lenin meeting in New York City and drew 150 people. In November we held a lecture series on Trotsky drawing between 100 and 150 people.

The growth of the Workers League brought about an increased surveillance on the part of the FBI. However, there was a superficial concession to the new atmosphere in the nation. Congress repealed the detention portion of the MacCarran Act in 1971. This meant that the FBI was supposed to abolish the Security Index. However, the FBI simply renamed SI the Administrative Index (ADEX), and DETCOM tabbing was replaced by Priority 1. This change is reflected in my file. The idea was to keep the file up-to-date so that should Congress change its mind, there would be no delay in the detention process. By 1976 the list had been reduced to 1,250 people. I remained one of these 1,250 people.

The Workers League's successes in recruiting students and former students gave me an opportunity to return to the campus lecture circuit. It was a kind of work I really excelled in, and it reminded me of the exciting days of 1959 to 1961 when we built the YSA. The campuses were far more radical now, but our meetings were smaller than my first campus tour because we were now one among many radical groups competing for a hearing among the students. We did not organize the kind of independent student organization that had been so successful in that earlier period. Perhaps we should have, though I do not think our lack of a specific perspective for students hurt us much. The *party* question was what was on the minds of most radicalized students in that period.

Years later I discovered that my exhortative activities caught the attention of William F. Buckley, Jr., and actually made it into one of his books. This took the form of a letter to Buckley from an admiring right-wing woman student, which he printed in full and which I quote to give a little bit of the feel of our work in those days:

> I went to a lecture in New Haven given by Tim Wohlforth of the Workers' League, supposedly a more radical split with the American Communist Party. Granted that his speech was directed to people who know the subject and are involved in the Communist effort, people that were directly concerned with the Trotsky split and the problems of revisionism; granted too that the question of Dialectics is vital to the growth of the Communist movement in this country. Correcting for all this, Tim Wohlforth still comes across as ineffectively and pedantically as my most ineffective and pedantic English professor. Furthermore, as a conservative escorted by a young communist (I had picked him up on a street corner selling [party] papers in the best Horatio Alger tradition), instead of being threatened or even ideologically roused by the lecture, I found myself not only totally unimpressed by the Red Menace, but, God help me, my maternal instincts raised by the kind of poor but honest idealism and the unquestionable reassurance that with communists such as these we need never tap another phone. Their project for the next day was covering an auto plant, this was before the GM strike was resolved, and I knew then and know now that their objective of selling dialectical materialism to auto workers in Framington was doomed to failure by boredom, or, the All-American Huh?[9]

Oh well, we did not win over *all* students in those days, and I do suspect at times that we were a bit pedantic and heavy-handed in our presentations. Yet soon our membership exceeded two hundred—all members were extremely active—and we had branches in New York (several), Boston, New Haven, Baltimore, Washington, D.C., Philadelphia, State College (Pennsylvania), Detroit, Chicago, Madison, Twin Cities, Northfield (Minnesota), Los Angeles, San Francisco, San José, Palo Alto, San Diego, Portland, as well as Toronto and Montreal. It wasn't a revolution and not even a mass party, but it was a lot more than the nine faction-weary comrades who stumbled out of the SWP in 1964.

Notes

1. David Caute, *The Year of the Barricades; A Journey through 1968* (New York: Harper & Row, 1988). George Katsiaficas, *The Imagination of the New Left: A Global Analysis of 1968* (Boston: South End Press, 1987). Tim Wohlforth, "The Sixties in America" *New Left Review* 178 (London, November, December 1989).
2. See Fred Halstead, *Out Now!* (New York: Monad Press, 1978); Nancy Zaroulis and Gerald Sullivan, *Who Spoke Up?* (New York: Holt, Rinehart, Winston, 1984).
3. See the chart on SWP membership, p. 253.
4. Student Mobilization Committee. This was established as a student arm of the national antiwar coalition and was dominated by the YSA.
5. Todd Gitlin, *The Sixties* (New York: Bantam, 1987). James Miller, *Democracy Is in the Streets* (New York: Simon and Schuster, 1987). Kirkpatrick Sale, *SDS* (New York: Vintage Press, 1973). Wohlforth, "The Sixties in America."
6. One of the very few people thinking along these lines at the time was James Weinstein. See *The Decline of Socialism in America 1919–1925* (New York: Monthly Review Press, 1967).
7. On Kay Ellens see note 8 in chapter 6. Harry Turner split from Ellens and continued a sectarian existence in groups of rarely more than six members. I remember one such group was called the Trotskyist Organizing Committee (TOC).
8. Communist Party of the United States of America—Marxist-Leninist.
9. William F. Buckley, Jr. *Cruising Speed* (New York: Putnam, 1971), pp. 95–96.

8

To the Masses!

Into the Ghettos

We, like our competitors, sought to bring the socialist message to the working class. While we had some modest successes in the trade unions, our main focus was different, and our results actually were quite rewarding. We sought to construct a working-class youth movement. Our Young Socialists, as we named the group, was based primarily on minority youth and was an expression of ghetto rebelliousness directed against racism and class oppression. The Young Socialists was overwhelmingly a movement of black and Puerto Rican youth, led by black and Puerto Rican youth, yet devoted to the socialist cause and reflecting the politics of the Workers League.

Our successes among minority youth were as much due to the period we were passing through as our recruitment of white students was. The black movement began as a pacifist-led civil rights struggle. This movement succeeded in achieving basic legal rights for blacks and in removing Jim Crow barriers. By gaining some preferential hiring schemes, the civil rights movement also gained economic advancement for a thin layer of blacks. The mass of blacks remained economically impoverished, however, with many unemployed and on welfare in disproportionate numbers. Their frustrations found expression in the ghetto uprisings in Watts, Newark, Detroit, and other cities, and also in the black nationalist movement.

The black nationalists gained domination over the black movement following the collapse of SNCC, a process well under way by 1966. But by 1970 the black nationalist movement faced its own crisis. The ghetto rebellions had died down, and the government, with the Ford and Rockefeller foundations also participating, began doling out money to "poverty programs." These programs had quite limited funds and changed very little the day-to-day lives of blacks. However, they provided employment for many black nationalist militants, thus pacifying them. Factionalism, some of it based on unprincipled struggles over control of poverty funds, broke out among the various nationalist groups. Further, many blacks began to realize that control of their own impoverished ghettos did not in itself bring about a real change in their inferior position. Somehow they needed to participate with others in efforts to change the nation as a whole.

The long-range effects of these processes would be the decline of all sections of the black movement, marginalizing both the remnants of the black nationalists and the remaining traditional civil rights organizations, as well as isolating the Left almost totally from blacks. A significant layer of talented—or just plain lucky—blacks took advantage of affirmative action programs and entered the middle class. An underclass remained untouched and sank into lethargy, the welfare system, drugs, crime, and poverty. The stage was set for the conservatives' neglect of minorities and the encouragement of racism, which has dominated national politics since the election of Ronald Reagan in 1980 and which created the conditions that exploded in the Los Angeles riots of 1992.

However, for a brief period in the early 1970s a radical sentiment lingered among ghetto youth, and some hope for change persisted. To some, we appeared to offer a way out with our hopes for socialism. Our strategy was based on a revival of the labor movement and on building a new political party, a labor party, in the United States.

We began to make headway when we recruited a few college-age blacks, and these comrades were then able to reach a younger layer. Our first recruits came from New York City Community College (NYCCC) in downtown Brooklyn, where we reached students by selling our paper. Our first recruit was John Holmes, and he was soon followed by Ernie McIntyre. John was an intellectual fellow, very thin, and sporting a mustache. I can see John as a small child, bookish, shy, not quite fitting in on his working-class block in Bedford-Stuyvesant. Ernie was another matter. His parents had been full-timers with the Salvation Army, and Ernie had been brought up in the thick of Salvation Army work, playing a trombone in a marching band at an early age. He was a big fellow who always wore, summer and winter, a long, very hip leather coat that came down almost to the ground. Ernie knew everybody at NYCCC and was most helpful. We convinced the pair to turn away from a black nationalist outlook with long discussions and some sharp conflict.

The Black Panthers were dominant in this period. This group represented a development beyond the Black Muslim kind of nationalism, even beyond Malcolm X. For one thing, the Panthers were not religious. More important, they were influenced by Marxism, even if primarily in the cruder Maoist form. The Black Panthers viewed themselves as revolutionaries who were seeking to mobilize the masses of poor blacks. They sought, in their own fashion, to address the economic plight of blacks in addition to the more traditional nationalist preoccupation with consciousness and self-identity. This was the meaning of their free-breakfast program. Certainly the Panther's open advocacy and practice of armed self-defense caused the American power structure to view them as a revolutionary threat. We were particularly impressed when Huey P. Newton began writing about dialectics and Marxist philosophy in his paper the *Black Panther*.

We remained critical of the nationalist side of the Panther program as well as aspects of it that seemed to us to be reformist. Yet we were able to engage some of the members, particularly the small following in New York, in discussions. The SWP, however, made no attempt to reach Panther members and took a generally hostile attitude toward them. I feel the Panthers were too radical, too dangerous for the SWP. Looking back at this period, I now see that the growth of the Panthers, their popularity in the black ghettos, as well as developments like the prison rebellions in Attica, reflected a radicalism that was affecting many black and other minority youth and helped to explain our own success in reaching some of them. It was a kind of last heroic gasp of the movement that had begun with SNCC in 1960.

While our Panther contact was quite minimal, we got a little further with the Young Lords. This group, made up of Puerto Rican youth recruited from street gangs, was modeled after the Black Panthers. For a brief period it enjoyed considerable popularity in New York City. One day I was invited to meet with the leaders. I went to their headquarters, an abandoned building in the Bronx, which the group had simply commandeered. The building had boarded-up windows, and guards let me in through the barricaded door. Clearly the Lords felt themselves to be under siege. Who could blame them, after the murderous attack of Chicago's police on the Panthers, which led to the death of Fred Hampton? Once I entered the building, I found myself in a darkened room with a number of heavily armed Puerto Ricans standing around. I was then ushered into the next room to meet the leaders, who appeared to be former college students in their late twenties. I actually had a good discussion with them. Though coming from a mixed nationalist Maoist background, they were open to Trotskyism. They invited us to march with them in a special Puerto Rican independence demonstration the next week.

We turned up with our banners and found ourselves marching right through the bombed-out streets of the South Bronx behind a contingent of several hundred Young Lords in full uniform complete with red bandanas. The kids were soon doing a combination march and dance step as they chanted, "Pick up the gun! Cha, Cha, Cha!" The tenement residents, hanging out their windows, loved it, though nobody had any intention of following their advice.

Soon we arrived at a small square where a meeting was planned. We found ourselves surrounded by a group from the MPI[1] and the Communist Party, who pushed us out of the square. The Lords were not about to stick their necks out in our defense. It was in this same period that three of our comrades were beaten up, including our new recruits John and Ernie, when they attempted to speak at an MPI meeting.

We soon recruited several other key black comrades. Most important was Helen Halyard. Helen was an attractive, bespectacled woman in her mid-twenties. She had a look of competence about her, and she became one of our most capable party members. She was working as head teller at a bank when we first met her. She clearly had leadership ability, was a good speaker, and soon was playing an important role in our youth work. The youth had a lot of respect for her. She came on our full-time staff as treasurer and was a member of our leading committee.

Helen's boyfriend, a very handsome black man, Tyrone, soon joined as well. Tyrone worked for Brooklyn Union Gas (BUG) as a meter reader, as did John Holmes after he graduated from NYCCC. Tyrone was a quiet, extremely hardworking comrade, yet I never felt comfortable with him. We held a trade union conference in Chicago once, and just before the session was to begin Helen called saying that she would not be able to attend. A couple of us rushed to her room to find her face all swollen. She was covered with black-and-blue marks. Tyrone had gotten drunk and beat her up. Was he jealous because she was now a key leader of the party and he was just a rank-and-filer? We never learned his reasons, as he would say nothing. We expelled him on the spot and rushed Helen to a hospital, where she was treated for what were, luckily, superficial wounds. It is one thing to win a person over intellectually to a revolutionary point of view, but sometimes it is quite another to break him from reactionary and sometimes brutal behavior.

On a happier note, we recruited Jacques Gagnon, a Haitian who also worked at BUG. Jacques was a very political person and played an important role in the Workers League. Dave Neita, another new member, was a large and thoroughly nice fellow, a teddy bear of a man who looked somewhat like a black Dave Van Ronk. He could have been a marvelous director of youth activities for a poverty agency or the YMCA. Whether because of his size or because of a kind of bluster and bravado he had, the youth loved him. Dave's girlfriend was Esther Galen.

The next step in building our youth movement was contacting the

Brownsville–East New York Third World Coalition, a group made up primarily of young Puerto Ricans. The contact was made through Ernie, who had been around the Panthers. Our key black comrades simply went to their meetings and engaged them in a no-holds-barred battle over nationalism. We counterposed as an alternative to the nationalist outlook of the group our perspective of socialist revolution, a revitalization of the labor movement brought about by the deepening economic crisis, and the building of a labor party as a political expression of workers and minorities. The group members were impressed because they all sensed the crisis the nationalist movement was in, and they were not used to socialists who advocated their ideas openly and who were willing to flatly counter the theories of nationalism with their ideas.

Our comrades brought a group of Third World Coalition members down to our hall, and we all pitched into the discussion. Through this process we won over Gil Gonzales. Gil, a short, handsome fellow in his mid-twenties, soon also went to work at BUG. He was politically sharp, a natural leader who, however, appeared to need to have acolytes at all times. Interestingly, he brought with him his Catholic upbringing. Whenever he came under criticism, and the Workers League was a great place for criticism and self-criticism sessions, he readily confessed to every and all charges, just as he would have in a church confessional, and then proceeded to act just as he had acted prior to the criticism session. Yet Gil was the key link to a layer of high-school youth who would be the first cadre and leaders of our Young Socialists.

Prior to our recruitment of Gil and his supporters, I had only the vaguest idea where Brownsville and East New York were. I soon discovered these areas on the outskirts of Brooklyn, areas without character that had once been populated by Italian immigrants who owned small homes. Now, although some Italians remained in one area, most of the sprawling, poor slum was populated by blacks and Puerto Ricans, with the latter more concentrated in East New York and the former in Brownsville. It was an area of crime, drugs, and abandoned buildings. But it was also an area of industrious working-class families who owned their own small homes. We recruited the brightest children of these families, who attended the special-track classes at Jefferson, the neighborhood high school that was almost 100 percent minority.

I cannot think of these youth without a warm smile; they were so bright, spirited, talented, and idealistic. There was Abbie Rodriguez (Mendez), small, extremely bright, the leader of the younger group. Abbie became the editor of the *Young Socialist* newspaper, launched in 1973, and our main recruiter. His sister Kiki, smaller still and very pretty, could sock it to 'em in a speech. There was also his brother, quiet but loyal to the group.

Their father worked at an auto plant in New Jersey and was also the minister of a Pentecostal church in East New York. Abbie's girlfriend, Nancy Vasquez, was taller, bigger than Abbie, and looked older than her age. She had long, straight hair and was a very good writer. There was Gil Gonzales's sister, Millie, a beautiful girl who was a bit quieter and an excellent student. She attended CCNY and dated a large, well-built fellow who was not that political but extremely handy to have around, should difficulties arise, as they occasionally did.

We recruited Gil during the spring of 1971, and that summer Gil and his group went into the streets of East New York, rapped with the unemployed youth hanging around, sold papers, and, one by one, convinced some of them to join a Young Socialists' (YS) club. This was the basic way in which we carried out all our youth work from then on. We spent many hours in the streets, the parks, and the housing projects, talking with youth, getting their agreement to attend youth meetings, and then picking each of them up to be sure they came. It took a great deal of energy and patience, and a willingness to accept hundreds of refusals for every new recruit. More than that, it took an ability to communicate with youth without either talking over their heads or talking down to them. A comrade had to be able to make our ideas live, to make them seem real to a young teenager without much education but with plenty of street knowledge of the ills of capitalism. Some comrades never succeeded at this. Most places it was necessary to use older white comrades in this work, as we did not have that many minority cadres. Some of these white comrades proved to be extremely good at this work.

It did not take us long to learn that we had to combine politics with other activities to give youth a more rounded social life in our YS clubs. I will never forget our first dance in East New York, at the beginning of our work there, in the summer of 1971. We got hold of a hall right in the center of East New York, where the Third World Coalition held their dances. We had a sound system, records, and a good disc jockey. The place was packed with hundreds of black and Puerto Rican youth. Then our sound system blew the electricity in the place and we had to run an extension cord across the city street to a pizza stand run by an Italian (Spike Lee's movie *Do the Right Thing* comes to mind). Comrades and local youth helped direct traffic over the cord so we could keep the dance going. Tension began to develop between the blacks and Puerto Ricans over whether to play soul music or salsa. Gil had to call the dance to a halt, get up on a chair, and give a speech about the unity of the working class against our oppressors. The eloquent and quite political address was concluded with the proposal to alternate salsa and soul records, and he was loudly cheered. The dance proceeded without incident and was a great success for us.

We had many other dances, and our conferences always featured a dance with a popular live band. It was often The Rare Experience, a funky, hard-driving band that was a favorite of the local kids then. It was quite a sight to see a floor full of teenagers rocking to the rhythms at an event organized by an openly socialist party. It was enough to make us old fogies learn how to dance. We always kept these dances orderly, thanks especially to comrades like Ernie, Dave, and Tyrone. At one dance, for example, held in Washington in conjunction with our mobilization for an antiwar march, Ernie convinced a group of youth to flush rather expensive pot down the toilet in the interests of security!

A little later we also held a number of sports activities. Basketball was the real favorite, as it was by far the most popular sport in the ghetto neighborhoods. Besides, there were few fields available for football or softball. We set up leagues and had games between various YS clubs. I believe our conception of building a working-class youth movement with more than a strictly political appeal was correct. Church groups had realized long ago the importance of athletics and dances in reaching youth, and they were the only real competition we met in the ghettos. I would be quick to add, however, that socialist youth organizations should not fall into the trap of *substituting* sports and entertainment for politics as an opportunistic way of holding on to the membership. In the later period of our youth work, this is exactly what happened to us, and our British comrades had a similar experience.

The main political activity of our youth clubs was holding their own meetings, each of which always included an educational presentation. We placed great emphasis on theory and philosophy and actually learned to present some pretty big ideas to youth with little education. I got heavily involved in this side of the work, not only in New York but across the country as well. I loved to teach classes to young people, whom I found lively and stimulating. Socialist ideas have to be presented very concretely to young people, in terms of their own lives, and the youth need to be encouraged to speak about their own experiences. Whenever we discussed philosophy, the young blacks would bring up their religious beliefs. This led to exciting and fruitful discussions of materialism and idealism, which unfolded in a manner relevant to the actual thought and daily lives of the participants.

We also organized youth unemployment marches and demonstrations. I do not believe most of these events came off that well, as our forces were small and the demonstrations rather abstractly called for "jobs." We unfortunately did not indicate how or from whom these jobs could be obtained. I believe many times we lost members because of these demonstrations. Youth could sense the futility of marching through the streets of poor neighborhoods, with red flags, shouting about jobs.

We established our YS clubs on a neighborhood basis—there is no other way to reach teenage working-class youth—and soon had a number of small clubs throughout New York City. As this youth work became more and more a preoccupation of our party branches, we broke up our branches into smaller units, each in charge of one or two YS clubs.

We had a lot of fun. We discovered Arrow Park in the Catskills around Monroe, New York, close enough for a day's outing. It was run by the remnants of the Russian, Ukrainian, and Polish-speaking Communist Party groups. While still of a "progressive" bent, the camp's sponsors had turned in a cultural direction. It was amazing to see three huge statues of Slavic writers and poets—one was Pushkin—constructed in the middle of the woods and to hear symphonic music playing on loudspeakers. Nearby was a very pretty little lake for swimming and boating. We went there each summer for about three years in a row, bringing busloads of ghetto youth for a day of swimming, picnicking, and, of course, lectures on world events. We brought 350 to Arrow Park in June 1973. Most impressive was when Ronnie Roberts—our SSEU recruit and our film critic—showed up with two buses filled with seventy people from the Bronx, mostly ghetto youth, and a few SSEU members. Not only did I give the lecture that day but I also had to feed the mob! Since the Arrow Park management would not let us use their kitchen facilities, I set up two hibachis and cooked hundreds of hot dogs for the lot.

In 1973, with the recent reelection of Nixon being undercut by the Watergate revelations, we launched an intensive campaign to force his resignation. It was, quite understandably, an extremely popular campaign in the ghetto neighborhoods of the United States and contributed greatly to the success of our YS work and our newspaper sales in that period. We got a great idea for a fund-raiser. We would hold a "Barbecue Nixon" feast, and we featured a picture of a roasting pig with Nixon's face on it in our ads.

We held one of these barbecues in the all-black section of Bushwick in Brooklyn, in an old house that belonged to Helen Halyard's father. We set up a barbecue pit in the backyard by getting some cinder blocks from a nearby construction project and covering the top with grates from comrades' ovens. The homemade grill must have been at least eight feet long. We had in excess of three hundred people in the place and I, again, was in charge of the cooking. This time I roasted huge slabs of ribs doused with beer and special barbecue sauce. So much smoke was created that it looked as if the house were on fire. I thought I was going to keel over from smoke inhalation and the heat, so I kept drinking beer to keep going. I was not in great shape when I stumbled into the house to introduce Helen, whom we were running for Congress in that district, to the crowd. But it was a great event, the kind of function that someday in America will become commonplace as part of building a mass-based people's party.

Work in the ghettos was not without its dangers. They were dangerous enough for the local inhabitants; white radicals could very well be targets of racial resentment as well as ordinary crime. I am amazed that so many of our comrades worked in those neighborhoods daily without the slightest problem. It was a tribute both to the courage of our comrades and to their ability to develop a relationship with the people in the neighborhoods. There were, however, some bad moments.

Once we were holding a dance in the basement of one of the buildings at the Fort Greene housing project in Brooklyn, not a particularly safe place even in daylight hours. It was about eight o'clock on a dark night, and Ronnie Roberts headed toward the building alone to help out on the dance after work. He noticed a gang of black youths on the sidewalk whose ages ranged from ten to fourteen, but he paid no attention. As he crossed the grassy area in the shadow of a building, they all dashed after him and jumped him. Before he knew what was happening, a young boy stabbed him with a knife. They grabbed his wallet and ran. Luckily some tenants saw what happened and called the police. Ronnie was rushed to the hospital and the doctor discovered the knife had come within one-sixteenth of an inch of his heart! He recovered completely, but things were not quite the same after that, for Ronnie or any of us. We learned caution and traveled only in groups.

I had two close calls. One was in Youngstown, Ohio. We organized a joint educational evening, bringing comrades and contacts from Dayton and Pittsburgh, as well as from Youngstown. Two college girls—one of them inappropriately named Prudence—were starting to build a branch for us in Pittsburgh with the help of some local people. They had little money and not much street sense. A black man in his thirties seemed to befriend them and take an interest in their politics. He volunteered to drive them to Youngstown. They turned up while the class was in session and immediately the man started demanding money for the trip. We refused to pay anything but a share of the gas, and he left the meeting furious. We figured that was the end of him. Suddenly there was a knock at the door. I opened the door and there he was, gun in hand, threatening to shoot if he did not get his money. For some reason I did not lose my cool but carefully explained to the fellow that he was not getting any additional money; he would have to shoot all of us, which would not be a paying proposition as somebody would surely call the cops. The guy finally left, and shaken, we returned to our class.

The second incident was in Watts. Sheila and Dennis—two former Peace Corps members whom we had recruited in New Haven and sent to Los Angeles to build a branch—had done a fine job building a meeting for me among Los Angeles black teenagers and had gotten the permission of a poverty group in Watts to use its hall. The place was on "Charcoal Alley," the block that had been burned to the ground during the riots and that was now almost bereft of buildings. It was a rather dark night, and we arrived with several carloads of youth and party members. We were greeted very coldly by several large black men who worked in the center. What Sheila and Dennis had not realized was that the center was controlled by one of the most reactionary and corrupt of the black nationalist groups in the Los Angeles area. It had been accused of the murders of several members of the Black Panthers.

I began my presentation on our perspectives. I did not get very far, for the men from the center had entered the hall and started arguing with me from the back. To make matters worse, a fellow had shown up from LaRouche's Labor Committee. Their group had an extremely hostile attitude toward community control and black nationalism—more so than we had—and he was not very subtle about putting his position forward. It did not take long for the meeting to get completely out of hand, and we frantically tried to figure out a way to end it quickly.

Finally we just closed it down and hurried our supporters out. As we headed down the stairs, the nationalists started hitting us. We made it somehow to the parking lot, which was almost pitch dark. I could make out only a large, sinister guy in a white suit who was pointing a gun at us. I do not know if he was from the original group or was a police provocateur. I pushed our people into the cars and van. Dennis got a blow or two in the face, but somehow we all got out of there in one piece. At Dennis and Sheila's home, out of breath and shaken, we did our best to explain to the youth the meaning of what had happened, that the incident was a result of the reactionary and corrupt turn that many nationalists had by then made.

For each of these incidents of terror, there were hundreds that still warm my heart. The very same Dennis and Sheila brought several carloads of contacts, including a few huge black longshoremen and their families from San Pedro, on a long drive in the mountains to Bear Lake for a picnic. It was there that I learned how to make *real* barbecue sauce. On the whole it was the kind of work that gave you a glimmer of what a real revolutionary movement could be like in the United States. Two Australian comrades, Howard and Carol Morris, organized a wonderful YS group in St. Louis led by Willie, a natural leader. Two Peruvian students built a group in the middle of the South Bronx, which had to be the worst slum in America. Helena Farinas, while her husband was in federal prison because of his draft protest, campaigned daily among Lower East Side Puerto Rican youth.

In December 1971 we held our first East Coast Young Socialist Conference to launch the campaign for the Young Socialists. We had three hundred at the conference, representing clubs in East New York, Brownsville, Jefferson High School, Carnarsie High School, Fort Greene, Brooklyn College, Seward High School, Stuyvesant High School, the Lower East Side, Cooper Union, CCNY, the Bronx High School of Science, the Upper West Side, and Queens. Dany Sylveire was there to give greetings from the British Young Socialists. The key speaker was Adele Sinclair. Adele was a very pretty black woman with a round face and a huge Afro. One side of Adele's family in Bedford-Stuyvesant traced its ancestry back to Louisiana Creoles, and there was a slight French look in her features. Adele was a Brooklyn College student who had been a leader in the black students' organization there. She was a fine speaker and writer and soon became a key leader in our national efforts.

The conference was a powerful beginning for the Young Socialists and encouraged our comrades in other cities to direct their energies into the ghettos and construct Young Socialist clubs. We did so with mixed success. In some cities, such as St. Louis and Cleveland, we did quite well, while in others, such as the Twin Cities (where there were fewer blacks), we reached only a layer of white students. In all areas the work had its ups and downs, and only in New York City did it really take root.

Some 350 youth attended the Founding Conference of the Young Socialists in the spring of 1973. Eight of the sixteen youth elected to the National Committee were black or Puerto Rican. Our largest youth conference was held in New York City in May 1974. This was our second National Conference and it had an attendance of 550 youth. It would be fair to say that the YS, at its height, had a membership that fluctuated between 500 and 700. With the possible exception of the Communist Party, I do not believe any socialist group ever built a youth movement of our size with such an overwhelmingly minority composition. I know it impressed the SWP when we would turn up at SMC conferences with over 150 ghetto youth supporting our positions.

There are some important lessons to be learned from this youth work. We recruited far more blacks in this period than did the SWP or any leftist organization with the possible exception of the CP. It would seem at first to be a paradox, because the SWP's political position of full support to black nationalism should have given them an edge over us. However, the SWP did not give a potential black recruit any reason to join. If black nationalism was as progressive as the SWP said it was, then why not, the potential recruit would reason, remain in one's black nationalist organization? This became a more severe problem in the early 1970s, when many young blacks began to look critically at the shortcomings of the black nationalist movement.

Our Young Socialist activity was most successful when it was combined with continued recruitment of college students, black and white. These students, particularly minority ones, became the link to the younger high-school students. Among teenagers, the bright college-oriented students from working-class homes were able in turn to reach others whose lives were less blessed. This whole process depended on our ability to *politically develop* youth leaders. In our healthiest period, we were able to do this not only by holding classes in Marxism but, more important, by involving these youth in the political life of the Left, particularly the antiwar movement. Also, we took them to Europe with us, to British summer camps where they came to feel themselves a part of an international movement, and in other ways we involved them fully in party life.

Our Young Socialist work suffered when we withdrew from the college campuses, had less contact with the rest of the Left, and turned to frenetic activity with less political youth. To make matters worse, this course, like the rest of our activity, was harmed by a sectarian political approach that substituted abstract agitation for concrete and practical programs aimed at alleviating the conditions working-class youth faced. And we were not helped when the political climate in the nation shifted dramatically to the right.

To the Workers!

We were very "workerist" in those days, devoting much energy to trying to build a base in the trade unions. For some reason we had a fixation on the docks. It could be that we were all impressed with Marlon Brando's performance in *On the Waterfront*. Every morning comrades would get up in the dark and make it to the piers as dawn was breaking. In San Francisco, this was a safe exercise, even sociable and jovial, as the union had a radical leadership and the dockers were happy to see anybody up at that hour. In Brooklyn it was a bit scary. Not many papers were sold when the proceedings were being watched from a Cadillac stretch limosine by large men in suits. Surprisingly, we never got seriously hurt. Perhaps the mob, which controlled the International Longshoremen's Association (ILA), just didn't think we were worth the bad publicity. Not so surprising, even though we met a friendly individual here or there, we never built a base among the dockers on either coast.

I have previously mentioned our work in the less romantic, more middle-class Social Service Employees Union (SSEU). Jeff Goldstein, before he went to the West Coast, worked in welfare and recruited Dennis Cribbins (O'Casey) and Lucy Flynn (St. John), a couple who eventually got married. Dennis, sandy-haired and freckled-faced, looked like a cross between Mike Harrington and Van Johnson. He was a principled, moral person, and he became a good spokesman for the party. His only problem was that he was a little stiff and formal (and our rather rigid politics did not help). Lucy was a very attractive woman, politically very bright and an excellent writer and organizer to boot. During a major SSEU strike, the *New York Daily News* featured on its front page a picture of Lucy jumping across a snowbank in a fur hat, high boots, and a miniskirt, carrying a picket sign. She did a better job of reaching people than did Dennis.

The SSEU was first headed by Judy Mage, a former member of our tendency in the SWP, as well as part of our original group in the Shachtmanites. Judy was succeeded by Marty Morgenstern, who had been part of her leadership group. Both Mage and Morgenstern were "lefts" as union leaders go, but they advocated compromises that we, as well as a section of the membership, felt went too far. We built a caucus in the union, the Committee for a New Leadership, which existed continuously for a number of years and was the main grouping to the left of the union leaders. Over the years, we slowly recruited some of our union supporters, such as Ronnie Roberts, who helped us in our youth work and many other activities.

Here or there we made some labor gains outside our base in the SSEU. First, we recruited some already-political workers. Two autoworkers, Rudy Sulenta and Tom Cagle, who had been members of the SWP, joined us. Rudy worked at Southgate in the Los Angeles area and Tom at the General Motors Fremont plant in the San Francisco Bay Area. Both had many years behind them in the United Auto Workers (UAW) and they were opposed to the SWP's abandonment of trade union work. These two found our propaganda for a labor party quite appealing. We also recruited Steve Cherkoss, a former PL member who was a steelworker.

Our best work was done in Dayton, Ohio. Here we recruited an older couple, the aunt and uncle of a young comrade in Minneapolis. These two people went out to the plants in Dayton day after day after day, selling papers and talking with workers. They finally made a breakthrough and began to meet with two black autoworkers at the Delco-Moraine plant, John Austin and Jim Lawrence. These workers had been deeply affected by black nationalism as well as by trade union issues and were building a black caucus within the local. We soon convinced them of our political perspectives—we did not favor black caucuses—and in a short while they joined our party and became extremely valuable members.

Jim was a big man with a round face. He had a good sense of humor and was the kind of worker who had many friends. He was not quite as committed politically as John, but he was more popular in the plant. Jim's main problem was that he was an avid softball player. We did not understand why he dropped out of the party every spring only to rejoin in the fall until John finally explained to us that he played every day through the summer in a softball league. He was also a family man and had only so much time for either socialism or softball! John was a thin, handsome man with a small, neat mustache and a goatee. He always wore a seaman's watch cap. He, too, was married, and had a small child. John was very intense and serious, and he studied our material carefully and participated in our educational work. He was a rounded political person, not just a trade union activist. If Jim and John made little progress in reaching other workers in the plant, I believe we shared a responsibility for this, as we trained them more as propagandists than as union activists.

It was at the Lordstown GM plant, also in Ohio, that we met a group of young, militant, white autoworkers. When we were in Cleveland on a subscription drive, we noticed a small item in the local paper. It reported that three workers had turned up at the Lordstown plant to picket, hoping to close it down as a protest against the speed-up going on. They came with picket signs but put bags over their heads so that management could not identify them and fire them. They closed down the entire sprawling plant for the shift, but the police moved in and arrested them, using an old law from the Reconstruction period aimed at the Ku Klux Klan that made it illegal to appear in public with a hood on one's head. We immediately sent a comrade down to interview them for the paper. They were extremely open and quite interested in our group and our ideas.

I then went down to visit the two younger, more politically inclined of the three. I entered a small apartment over a store in a poor, white, working-class section of Youngstown to find one of the workers sitting cross-legged on a bare floor, burning incense, smoking pot, and listening to psychedelic rock. This was my first introduction to the new young worker. He was a radicalized Vietnam vet and was hostile to the system and the assembly line. He would like to come to our meeting, he stated, but he had to go to Kent State that weekend for the first anniversary of the slayings there. He did, however, come to some of our other activities.

The other worker, Richard Welsh, was a bit more straight. He came to a number of our events and helped us organize a meeting of about twenty or so autoworkers. The meeting was held in the very nice home of a young worker, a former teacher who was forced to work in the plant to make a decent living. It took the form of a class on Marxism, and the discussion was very lively. Unfortunately, the group withered away after the ex-teacher, whom everyone looked to as their leader, left our classes to take a union post. Although we did not get much out of the Lordstown work, our experience there was evidence that there were some young white workers who were becoming radicalized by processes affecting all youth, and who were thus open to socialist ideas. Up to that time, most radical whites we encountered in the plants were former college students sent into the unions by some leftist party or other.

We held two national trade union conferences, one in Chicago to found our Trade Union Alliance for a Labor Party (TUALP), and a follow-up conference in St. Louis. The purpose of the TUALP was to promote the idea of a labor party within the trade union movement. This was a good idea and received some support among more politically advanced workers. However, the organization was too closely controlled by the Workers League and therefore never took on a life of its own. Sectarianism is particularly deadly in the trade unions. It is important to be willing to make alliances with other leftist tendencies as well as with previously nonpolitical workers on the basis of the membership's desire for a militant, democratic, and revitalized labor movement.

Our conferences were successful despite these severe limitations, reflecting some political ferment in the unions and quite a bit of agitation on the part of the Workers League. The St. Louis affair drew 275 people. Rudy Sulenta was there, as were Jim Lawrence and John Austin. We held workshops in the labor arenas of transportation, government, health care, auto, steel, construction, communications, and electrical. We also held a conference of around seventy autoworkers in Dayton that Tom Cagle came to. This conference was built by a combination of our union contacts and door-to-door canvassing with the *Bulletin* in the black neighborhoods where many autoworkers lived. However, no permanent national auto caucus emerged from it.

Our best trade union work remained in the SSEU, where we operated over a long period of time, were known to a layer of militants, and, from time to time, could express the interests of broad layers of union members. If we had conducted similarly patient union work with some of our new recruits, especially those in the UAW, I believe we would have had more success in the unions.

Building the Press and Apparatus

We moved to a new office at 135 West 14th Street in 1970. It was almost directly across from the Shachtmanite headquarters where I had started my New York political career in 1955. I must say it was a brighter, lighter, more cheerful place than the old Shachtmanite offices, and we kept it a lot neater. We rented the place from two brothers who were garment manufacturers. They had been, they informed us, socialists in their youth, but their youth had been a long, long time ago.

It was a very good office, convenient to the subways, in an elevator building, and just about the right size for us. We had outgrown our 10th Street offices even after expanding into an adjoining room. On 14th Street, we had a whole floor with a meeting area that could seat about 150, a small bookstore, and our offices. As we grew over the next few years we took over another floor and a half in the building. We developed an apparatus at 14th Street that fitted well the size of our organization: We acquired phototypesetting equipment and a small printing press.

We placed a good deal of emphasis on our paper, the *Bulletin*. Selling the paper was important to every aspect of our work: our successful efforts at reaching college students, our political interventions in the antiwar movement and in competition with other groups on the left, our efforts to reach trade unionists, and finally, our new campaign to build a youth movement in America's ghettos. We built our apparatus primarily in order to expand our press. The *Bulletin* became a twelve-page weekly in November 1969. By the time we moved into 14th Street we had a circulation of around five thousand. (As late as 1968 we were still striving to reach a circulation of two thousand!) In April 1971 we put our masthead in color and expanded the paper to sixteen pages. I believe at this point we had a paper of sufficient length and frequency for our size and tasks. It is not difficult to fill pages with copy. Our largely student membership was reasonably literate and their writing tended toward the verbose. It is harder to fill a paper with *quality* journalism, something more than socialist rewrites of stories from the *New York Times*.

The paper had its moments. Danny Freeman (Dan Fried) was our labor correspondent, and he did a very good job visiting striking miners and interviewing laid-off steelworkers. We pulled off some reasonably professional reporting with nice photo spreads on poverty among Chicanos in San Ysidro on the border or on young striking Borax workers in the middle of the desert. We carried a heavy load of polemical material, which nevertheless had some good content. We also had lighter material, such as our film reviews. Overall, we did a good job, but I think we had the talent to make the *Bulletin* a more effective journal. In retrospect I can see that we could have easily improved our product by being more selective in what we published, and by not getting so carried away with the push to expand.

The circulation of the *Bulletin* had reached ten thousand by the fall of 1971. By this time almost all our sales were in ghetto neighborhoods, and our circulation was increasingly based on subscriptions we got going door-to-door. This subscription base then became a contact list for our various activities, especially for increasing the membership of the Young Socialists. In the fall of 1972 we tried something very different, something distinctive to the Workers League. We sent out our first trailblazing team, a group of six comrades who sold subscriptions full time in a new area for two weeks. For our first team we rented a beat-up old trailer and chose the Michigan–Ohio area. Nancy Freuden (Fields) led the team. Nancy was an attractive woman in her middle twenties with long, straight, brown hair who usually wore a white shirt and jeans. She had previously been around SDS and the Peace and Freedom Party.

Nancy was good at working in neighborhoods with black youth, but she was phenomenal when it came to subscription work. She could get any door to open and, once inside, find a way to engage the person in a discussion that led inevitably to the sale of a subscription. She combined this activism and willingness to get out on the street with a very sharp political mind and good writing skills. Nancy quickly rose to the central leadership of the Workers League.

Nancy was accompanied on this first foray by Danny Freeman, not our best salesman, but a hard worker; Nancy Russell, a girl from Madison with a wonderful spirit; John Holmes; and a couple of others. The team sold 217 subscriptions in the first week and ended up with a total of 522 for the two weeks, well over the quota we had set for them. Over the next year and a half we organized trailblazing campaigns every two months or so in conjunction with subscription drives. We soon learned that a trailer was a waste of money, and that to cover an area larger than a single city was a waste of time. We also found out that we could sell one thousand subscriptions in a two-week period.

These drives sometimes enabled us to start a branch in a new area. Cleveland was our most successful effort of this combined sort. We had gotten such a good response from our team's short stay in Cleveland on that first drive that we organized a special team to work just in the black community of East Cleveland. As the team sold subscriptions, the names were collected and return visits made to those who seemed the most politically interested. The team obtained a place for the meeting—this was the team that had first contacted the Lordstown militants—and I flew out for it. We had gathered about thirty people for the meeting, I gave my talk, and we collected names of those interested in joining. Then we left behind permanently three comrades from the team to pull together the contacts into a functioning branch.

By October 1973, through these fantastic forced marches, we had built up our circulation to the twenty thousand mark. At the same time the SWP reported a circulation for the *Militant* of under fourteen thousand. It was an amazing achievement for which, I now understand, we paid too high a price in wear and tear on the comrades. But our success did reflect a political period—the period of Watergate and the fall of Nixon—when some ferment persisted in the minority communities, a period just before the political conservatization of America.

Our frenetic circulation drives were motivated by a desire to build our circulation to the point where we could justify publishing the *Bulletin* twice weekly. A twice-weekly *Bulletin* was seen as an important concrete step toward a daily paper. This scenario was borrowed from the British and it served the same purpose for us as it did for them. Increasing our circulation became a concrete goal for *driving* the membership and bore no relationship to the needs of our small group. We wanted to have something our competitors on the left did not have. It was as if we believed that if we could only accumulate the technical accouterments of a mass party we would *be* a mass party.

We felt we needed to have our own professional web press if we were to be able to put out a twice-weekly paper efficiently. We settled on a four-unit model that, together with related equipment, would cost us in excess of $100,000. Now where could we, a group with a little over two hundred members and a large but poor youth periphery, expect to get such a sum of money? We got it the way all our competitors on the left did in that period, particularly the SWP, and the way the British comrades did as well. The layer of students who were the basis for our growth, and for that of all left organizations, had some money. Many individuals came into reasonably sized trust funds at the age of twenty-one. These were committed, dedicated people who were used to living on very little money. It was not hard for us to convince them to give all, or a portion, of this money to the party.

The commitment and wealth of these leftist students permitted us (and our competitors as well) to make the mistake of expanding our apparatus out of proportion to our growth and support within the working class. We could and did create a small bureaucracy of full-time comrades who represented a significant portion of the most committed membership in the New York area. By the time we had assembled a work force sufficient to staff a web press, a camera department, and a typesetting department and to fulfill all our other needs, we had to hire about twenty of our members full time.

In March 1973 we moved the bulk of our operation to 540 West 29th Street. This was a very nice building that had housed a construction firm. The ground floor garage area was perfect for our web press. We developed an efficient system in which papers came right off the press and were fed into a Cheshire labeler near the door, tied in bundles by zip code, thrown into mailbags, and taken out the door into a waiting van and to the post office. The second floor on 29th Street had been very nicely converted into offices by the former tenant and we just moved into them, saving the back room for the typesetting and camera departments.

The new press arrived in March and we launched the twice-weekly *Bulletin* on October 4, 1973. We organized an impressive rally of 450 to celebrate the occasion. It was a great moment for us all and we were very proud of our achievement. We really did seem to be on a roll, headed toward becoming the kind of mass-based party I had dreamed about since I had first become a socialist at Oberlin College in 1953. It was such an advance over our poor mimeographed newsletter of the 1964–1966 period, and we achieved it in only seven years. There was no telling what great gains were now possible in the next seven years! I not only spoke at the rally but afterward rushed to the back of the hall to serve the sangria. And did I ever make a sangria that night, combining the wine, fruit juices, and soda with perhaps a bit too much brandy. People loved it, though; and it was a memorable evening.

Owning our own press enabled us to start a monthly youth paper, so once again I found myself publishing a journal called *Young Socialist*. It was in full color (long before *USA Today!*) and we eventually built up its circulation to twelve thousand. At first, we did have to run an inordinate amount of paper through the press to get the colors right, but our technical skills benefited from the experience, and I do believe the *YS* was the sharpest-looking left-wing youth paper ever.

The Disease of Sectarianism

The Workers League was plagued from the start by a need to justify its own existence separate from the SWP. We did not accept that the league was necessary merely because we held a special view of the Cuban Revolution or because we functioned better politically than the SWP. We had to try to prove that the continuity of Marxism passed through our formation, and that the future revolution was largely dependent upon our leadership for its success. Conversely, it was insufficient to assert that the SWP had a wrong assessment on Cuba, had a stifling internal regime, and, here or there, acted in too conservative a manner. We had to attempt to prove that the organization was "revisionist" and would act in a "counterrevolutionary" fashion during a revolutionary upsurge. We did not invent this approach to politics. We inherited it from Trotsky, who had learned it from Lenin during their period of collaboration, particularly in the construction of the Third International.

I would describe this kind of politics as *sectarianism*, and it is clear to me that the Workers League never fully escaped from the grip of this disease. The term *sect* originates from the Latin noun *secta*, which means "a following" and is derived from the Latin verb *sequi*, which means "to follow." It was first used to describe small religious groups that break away from the established religions and adhere to a rigid doctrine and/or follow a specific leader. The political sect, like the religious one, maintains its following by preserving its doctrine and justifying the importance of this doctrine through a continuous critique of competing doctrines. So it was with us.

The sectarian stance can lead a well-intentioned group to act as if it is on an exclusive historical mission. The biggest problem occurs when a competing group does something *right*. It is very difficult for the sectarian to recognize the complexity of politics, to give credit where it is due, and to recognize that an organization that may be dead wrong on one matter might be very right on another. This was our problem in our relationship with the SWP. The SWP carried on a principled campaign against the Vietnam War that permitted it to aid in mobilizing millions of Americans in effective action against that war. This conduct was inconsistent with our judgment of the SWP as "revisionist" and "counterrevolutionary." With more than a little help from our British friends, we felt compelled to oppose the SWP's Vietnam strategy. This made our own actions ineffectual. In addition, this opposition affected the kind of people we recruited, particularly in the first few years of our independent existence. We became a home for critics and web-spinners rather than creative thinkers, doers, and leaders.

It would have made more political sense if we had supported the positive actions of the SWP, remained always open to a principled unification with them, while maintaining our criticisms of that organization's shortcomings. Such a course, if carried out consistently, would have brought us into conflict with our international allies and raised among us some very big questions about our Leninist-Trotskyist heritage. We did not, could not, consider such a course in those days. We were the defenders of a heritage, of a doctrine; we were still relatively young followers of an Old Left tradition in a New Left political world. We had our own set of political blinders and could only look straight ahead and straight back into history.

We were not the only ones with blinders in those days. The New Left had its own theoretical weak spots. New Lefters had freed themselves of the narrowness of our tradition—a tradition shared in differing ways with such diffuse groups as the SWP and the CP—but at the high cost of ignoring history and having only the vaguest idea of what the future should be like. What the New Leftists did grasp was the present, and they knew how to be effective within it, way beyond the wildest dreams of the 1950s leftists. The Workers League floundered in that present until the time came when the broader Left could not avoid the question of the *future* of the movement. Concern with the future required an assessment of the past. The stage was set for the collapse of the New Left, which incidentally made the growth of our little group possible. This process began in 1969 and ended as a new wave of conservatism swept the country in the middle 1970s.

Note

1. Movement for Puerto Rican Independence, later called the Puerto Rican Socialist Party (PSP). It was headed by Juan Mari Bras and, while independent of the Communist Party, was politically close to Fidel Castro.

9

The World Movement

INTERNATIONALISM

Socialists since Marx's day have believed in internationalism, but success in building an international socialist movement has been limited. The First International succumbed primarily to factionalism. The Second International was the victim of the successes of key sections that could not resist the temptation to put patriotism first. The Third International became essentially an extension of the foreign interests of a single nation, the Soviet Union. The Fourth International has never been more than a collection of small ideological groupings. In the period under consideration in this book, to make matters worse, a series of Fourth Internationals sprouted.

Yet it would be a grave mistake to dismiss internationalism as a conceptual approach to the modern world or, for that matter, to treat lightly efforts of socialists to live by its precepts. There is a reason why every nation with world-power pretensions seeks to project its specific national interests as if they were international interests. There is no higher moral ground than the claim that a particular course of action is in the interests of all the world's peoples and not just a policy that would lead to the subjugation of one nation for the benefit of another.

Trotskyists have taken internationalism more seriously than any other section of the Left. Their efforts in constructing an international center to advance the Trotskyist program have largely been unsuccessful. The International Committee of the Fourth International, with which I was affiliated, was among the most fruitless of efforts.[1]

Most Trotskyists, however, will remember their international experiences as among the richest in their political lives. So it is with me. We not only met leading figures from organizations in other countries but we *experienced* the life of those parties. In this fashion we learned much about political life in other nations. We became, if only partially, international citizens.

Rosa Luxemburg expressed our sentiment the best: "I feel at home in the entire world wherever there are clouds and birds and human tears."[2]

LIFE AT 186A CLAPHAM HIGH STREET

My first trip to London to visit Gerry Healy and the Socialist Labour League took place in February 1964, while I was still a member of the Socialist Workers Party. I took one of those overnight flights and arrived at Heathrow at the crack of dawn with almost no sleep and totally spaced out. An SLL comrade drove me to Clapham Common just as it was getting light. I did not get a memorable look at the place that morning, but over the years I got to know the area quite well. Clapham was considered an archetypical petty bourgeois area of London. It was a place of seemingly endless drab but neat row houses surrounding a pleasant common, or square, which was the hub of diverse activity. Each day, rain or shine (usually rain), the common was invaded by an armada of prams with pale, unattractive babies in them, pushed by women who looked a bit young to be mothers. There were also the pubs, whose clientele simply rolled out onto the sidewalk at closing time. There was a snooty tobacco store aimed at the upper layer of the lower layers and a very good Indian restaurant on High Street, where Healy's lieutenant Mike Banda would easily eat two dishes of curry at one sitting.

Wherever it was in England that Healy had his influence, I could tell it was definitely not in Clapham. Its residents appeared to be totally oblivious to the presence of their very radical neighbors at 186A. This fact, combined perhaps with jet lag and the dreary London weather, gave my trips to England an otherworldliness I felt but could not verbalize. An occasional glance out a dirty window at the passing prams on High Street just at the climax of a powerful presentation on the imminence of world revolution sometimes made me feel like I was in the twilight zone.

The entrance to 186A was narrowly squeezed between a branch of Barclay's Bank and a prosperous butcher shop just down from a Lyon's tea shop. To get in, you had to knock once—since Healy was always concerned with security—and then walk up a narrow, dark stairway to a series of offices and meeting rooms that filled the next two floors. Healy's own office was to the left, at the top of the stairs. The front office, with its large panes of glass looking out over High Street, was always a busy place with people coming and going with bundles of *Newsletters* and *Keep Left*s to sell.

The place struck me as very different from the SWP's headquarters at 116 University Place, where sober veterans of the party quietly watched over the humdrum activities of the party's branches. Shachtman's 114 West 14th Street was different still, its cluttered innards largely bereft of any life at all. Healy's operation may have been isolated from the pram-pushing existence in the common, but his office bustled with youthful activity nearly twenty-four hours a day.

The morning I arrived, the front office was reserved for a meeting of Healy's Central Committee, and I was to be the special guest. I can recall very clearly the way Gerry Healy looked that day. He was a short man whose Irish descent could not be missed. He was overweight, and he had almost no neck and an unusually large head. His eyes were rather small for such a big head, and he wore glasses. He had very little hair and the madder he got, the redder his head got. For all his weight, he was sturdily constructed with relatively short but powerful legs and arms. He always dressed the same, in a shapeless dark suit with a white shirt and a pair of old-fashioned suspenders holding up the pants. If he wore a tie it was loosely draped around an open collar. If he became overheated, he would strip down to an old fashioned tank-style undershirt.

I was gruffly greeted for one who had carried out a grueling three-year faction fight for Healy's politics. In fact, I was rather treated as the colonist who would now be straightened out by the masters from the mother country. The meeting began without ceremony (or anything that suggested rules of order, minutes, and other formalities). Gerry gave a long lecture on the SWP. He was now convinced that the SWP leaders were not Marxists. According to Healy, in the past they had been good revolutionaries only because they listened to Trotsky, but they had never mastered Marxism. Cliff Slaughter was then called upon to explain the question in terms of philosophy. Slaughter stated that Jim Cannon was an American pragmatist and had never absorbed Marxist philosophy, in particular dialectics. The struggle with revisionism now, Slaughter explained, was a struggle for dialectical materialism against the American pragmatic deviation. It was thus that Healy's preoccupation with dialectics began. As time went on this preoccupation became a disease in Healy's movement, which replaced the *content* of politics with the *form* of dialectics.

At first I was at sea. I was not sure what Healy was driving at. Certainly, I thought, the SWP had always been very weak on matters of theory and its reaction to Cuba had been very superficial and impressionistic. Yet up until this moment the SLL comrades had insisted that the SWP was a revolutionary party despite its current revisionist course, and that we should fight to remain part of it and hope to win over its cadres. If the SWP was now viewed as non-Marxist, how could we hold that it was still revolutionary, and what future did we of the minority tendency have inside it?

I tentatively raised these questions, and the comrades were appalled by my thickheadedness. I was also accused of being a pragmatist unable to grasp dialectically how the SWP was simultaneously not Marxist and still a potentially revolutionary party. It was necessary for me to study philosophy further and study the history of American Trotskyism. At that point the meeting came abruptly to a halt as it became clear Healy had other plans for the rest of the day. In fact he had plans for most of the week, so he handed me over to his chief theoretician, Cliff Slaughter, who was to drive me to Leeds where I would spend a few days before being sent off to Hull for a couple of days with another important SLL academic, Tom Kemp.

When I returned to Clapham I got a better chance to look the place over. I discovered the print shop, which was behind the Clapham High offices. Since there was no connecting door, to get in you had to go around the corner from the bank to an alley and down the alley to the shop. It was a small and crowded shop but well equipped and very busy. Healy had just installed two flatbed Heidelberg presses with rotary units that printed a second color. It was all letterpress in those days, but the best of that kind of equipment. There I met Mike Banda, Healy's closest collaborator for many, many years and the man who ran the shop. Mike was a Ceylonese comrade who had been with Healy since the early 1950s. Rather overweight, he could be very open, jovial, and friendly. At the same time he had a reputation as a "heavy," a fellow who did not mind getting into a punch-up, and certainly not particularly sensitive to democratic procedures. This character trait found a political expression in a considerable bent toward Stalinism, unusual for a member of an orthodox Trotskyist group. Mike believed that the Chinese Trotskyists should have gone into the countryside with Mao Tse-tung, he was quite sympathetic to Ho Chi Minh, and during the Cultural Revolution he became a great supporter of the Chinese Red Guards.

He spent much of his time in the print shop working on Healy's presses. Mike had played a major role in the 1950s in building up a printing plant in that difficult period of isolation. Even in the 1970s it was not uncommon to find that he had worked through the night on some printing project and had fallen asleep on the rubber conveyor belt at the end of the web press. In fact, for whole periods Mike seemed to retreat into this printing work to get relief from his political responsibilities in the organization. Mike also organized Healy's big summer camps for the youth. While raucous rock and roll dominated the camps to attract the working-class youth, Mike tuned his portable radio to the BBC and listened to classical music.

Healy's front office was staffed by energetic women who balanced the books, assigned the papers, kept track of the branches in the field (especially how much money they owed the center), and then in the evening went off to their own Young Socialists branches to work with the youth. In this period Janet Sutton was still working in the office. Janet was the one I had corresponded with in 1960 and 1961, and she had played an important role in the youth work within the Labour Party.

Janet was assisted by Sheila Torrance, who worked in that office right through the 1970s, in fact, right up to the recent period. Sheila had a pleasant, oval face and wore large glasses that gave her an owlish look. She had the appearance of a middle-class student, slightly disheveled but extremely competent. She ably held all the threads of a relatively large and unbelievably active party in her hands and was understandably prone to chronic headaches. She was at once sharp and tough, but somehow she could be pleasant as well.

When I was in London I usually stayed at the flat, situated in Victoria, of Healy's oldest collaborator, Betty Hamilton. Betty was Swiss and had lived in England since the 1930s. She still loved espresso coffee served with hot milk and spoke with a French accent. She was married to a very pleasant, nonpolitical architect who provided the nice flat in Victoria. Betty had been with Gerry during World War II and told me of going out to the mines in Yorkshire, in the snow at the crack of dawn, to sell their little paper. She had gotten frostbite in her feet, which still troubled her. Betty, when I knew her, was still a member of the party's Central Committee and would contribute money. She would do anything for the movement *but* sell papers!

Sometimes in my early years of association with Gerry Healy I stayed at his home. Healy lived in a modest house located no more than ten minutes from Clapham Common. Gerry and I would be driven there by Aileen Jennings, in those days the editor of *Keep Left*, and already Healy's almost inseparable personal aide. It was always very late at night, say eleven or twelve, as Healy worked incredibly long hours. Healy pointed out an empty lot across the street, a result of the bombing of London during World War II. We climbed up a flight of stairs to a large kitchen where Healy's wife, Betty, had left out some freshly baked whole wheat bread, butter, and jam. We could therefore have a little late tea before going to bed.

After our snack we would go downstairs to Healy's bedroom, where I slept on a spare couch. Healy would stay up for a while reading a spy story—I am afraid he may have read a few too many spy stories—then we would sleep for four or five hours to be picked up at seven A.M. by dutiful Aileen to make an eight A.M. editorial board meeting. Gerry then usually headed out of town for a branch meeting or an appointment with an important comrade in Oxford or Reading. He might return around two P.M. to check copy for the paper or for other meetings only to dash off again in the evening for a meeting in some other part of the country. He was not exaggerating much when he had written to me that he traveled 1,200 miles a week!

Healy's style of party leadership could not have been more different from that of Farrell Dobbs of the SWP. By the time Dobbs finished reading the *New York Times* in his quiet isolated office in New York, Healy would have had his editorial board meeting, traveled to Oxford to consult over trade union tactics at the Cowley plant of British Leyland, and be back in London for another meeting. Healy's approach was personal and energetic. He was deeply involved in every aspect of party and youth work and he got to know almost every comrade pretty well, even when the movement had one thousand or more members. No man ever personally drove an organization the way Healy did. Healy could claim quite rightly much of the credit for the growth and successes of the SLL in the 1960s. At the same time the party, and each and every member in it, became dependent on Gerry Healy the individual. His strength was also his weakness: He built an impressive movement, yet that movement was the creature of his personality, suffering from the idiosyncrasies that any strong person has. When Healy was wrong there was no way internally to correct him, to even check him—and Healy could be very wrong!

When I made my first trip to England in 1964, the Passport Office was informed of my pending voyage. This office then informed the FBI when I actually left the country and when I returned. The FBI also contacted the Bureau of Intelligence and Research, Department of State (prior to receiving my FBI files I had never heard of such a body!) and the Legal Attaché in London (sometimes called the Foreign Liaison Unit). This attaché was asked to inform British intelligence and request that a report be made back to the FBI on my contacts and conduct in England.

On January 10, 1966, the FBI informed not only "Legal Attaché at London" but also requested a report from the Central Intelligence Agency. It further noted that the FBI had furnished reports in the past to both the Department of State and the CIA. A letter on February 13, 1967, requested Legat "to alert appropriate British Security Services."

THE YOUNG SOCIALISTS

When I encountered it in the 1960s, the Socialist Labour League was already a movement of young people. Outside of Healy, Banda, Bob Shaw, Bill Hunter, Betty Hamilton, a layer of intellectual refugees from the Communist Party, and very few others, everyone in the SLL was under thirty years old. These young Trotskyists had been recruited in the hundreds from the Young Socialists (YS), originally the official youth section of the British Labour Party (BLP). Healy had worked within the BLP since World War II and by the 1950s had successfully built a base of support within Aneurin Bevan's left wing. In the early 1960s, supporters of the SLL gained a majority within the YS, which grew into an organization with hundreds of branches throughout Britain and which now advocated policies and programs far to the left of Transport House, headquarters of the Gaitskill leadership of the BLP. Hugh Gaitskill moved in 1963 and the BLP disbanded entire branches and expelled the democratically elected leadership of the YS. Supporters of Healy's youth paper within the YS, *Keep Left*, counterattacked and in 1964 again won a majority of the leadership of the YS. Gaitskill expelled the newly elected leadership once again. Late in 1964, well after my visit to the country, Healy instructed his people in control of the YS to refuse to accept expulsion and to withdraw the YS from the Labour Party. All SLL members quit the BLP, ending a twenty-five-year internal intervention. Gaitskill then reorganized the loyalist sections of the YS as the Labour Party Young Socialists (LPYS).

Tony Whelan, a critic of Healy's, claimed that contrary to Healy's mythology, the SLL actually recruited its youth from the middle class.[3] Whelan is only partially correct. Healy recruited many middle-class students, who made up the bulk of his youth *leaders*. Everywhere I went in the SLL I met these young, competent, middle-class people who were running things—Sheila Torrance, Jean Kerrigan, Dave Ashby, Dany Sylveire. This kind of recruitment continued throughout the later 1960s and 1970s, even when Healy was denouncing his opponents on the left for being petty bourgeois. My opinion is that the bulk of *party members* were composed of middle-class students. Yet the vast majority of Young Socialists *members* were recruited from the working class. No one else in Great Britain could make this claim.

The Young Socialists, while its membership was always in flux and Healy had a terrible tendency to exaggerate membership figures, certainly had in excess of one thousand members throughout the 1960s. Much of the energy of SLL members—and they had a fantastic amount of energy—went into building and sustaining the YS. In return the YS members were Healy's shock troops. They made up the bulk of the attendance at all rallies, camps, and demonstrations, and they were responsible for most of the circulation of the party press.

Healy soon became an expert in the techniques of working-class-youth recruitment by relying heavily on football matches and dances. Yet, in my opinion, these techniques would not have succeeded if there had not been a real *political* basis for this recruitment. The many critics of Healy's youth movement, while raising valid points, miss this essential one. I believe Healy's success was rooted in the fact that millions of British youth were disenchanted with capitalist society. The sustained postwar boom certainly kept adult workers within the limits of political reformism, but many youth felt left out of the good times and were not overly optimistic about their future. It was not simply a matter of youth unemployment, which certainly did exist; it was also a question of the decay going on at the very heart of British manufacturing, which relegated many young people to extremely low-paying service jobs. The powerful rebellious youth culture of Britain has also reflected these persisting, harsh realities. In pop music, it has yielded up an unending stream of creativity, from the Beatles through the punk-rockers, and in cinema, the "angry young man" and "kitchen sink" films of the early 1960s. Unfortunately, the violent "teddy boy" and "skin head" gangs were also products of the depressed condition of the British working-class youth.

In March 1967 I came to England and was able to get a pretty good firsthand impression of both Healy's youth movement and the competing official Labour Party Young Socialists. A group of us led by Mark Jenkins piled into the back of a van to take a very bumpy trip to Llandudno, Wales, to attend the LPYS convention. For me it was a crazy trip because the van had no windows in it and I traveled across England without seeing a thing. After several hours I found myself in this picturesque town on the Welsh coast with Mount Snowden in the background. We went out on a dock to the pavilion and somehow got hold of tickets to get inside. There, around six hundred to seven hundred student youth were assembled, and the kind of debates and political struggle with which I was more than familiar were going on.

By 1967, the LPYS was controlled by Tony Cliff's International Socialists, and the main opposition was led by Ted Grant's Militant Group. The Labour Party officialdom had succeeded in ridding itself of one Trotskyist group only to have another take its place at the head of its youth. This seems to have been the fate of social democracy in England, and to some extent also in the United States. Cliff's people were being quite militant, and various threats were coming down from Transport House. A youth radicalization was beginning to seriously develop quite outside of the BLP, particularly around the Vietnam War, and the IS was attracted to this movement and grew considerably from it. Soon after this conference, it abandoned British Labour Party work for open work in the universities and in the trade unions.

Healy's forces were totally outside this political process. We held a small meeting of our own that attracted only a handful of people. At the time, of course, I felt that Healy had been right to abandon this "middle-class swamp" for "healthy" work among working-class youth. Yet I felt a little uneasy about it all the same. Here was the kind of political struggle, the conflict of differing ideas that educate youth, and here too were many students who could play a role in a healthy revolutionary movement.

The next weekend I was off to Morecambe for the annual conference of Healy's independent Young Socialists. This was another seaside town and we stayed in bed-and-breakfast places right on the edge of a cliff overlooking the Irish Sea. Then we went down the steep hill to the large pavilion called the Winter Palace, where the conference was being held. Buses full of working-class youth were pouring in from all over England. Soon the pavilion was packed with around a thousand youth. Reports were given from different areas, a discussion held on the problems of youth and on politics in general, yet Morecambe felt more like a rally or a demonstration than a policy-making convention.

That evening we had a dance. A reggae band played at a deafening volume and a thousand youth danced nonstop until we were literally thrown out of the place in the wee hours of the morning. It was such a different world from the Llandudno conference, less political perhaps, but impressive nonetheless. It had a dynamic that permitted an imaginative person to grasp, if only for a moment, the feeling of a mass working-class movement. No doubt that was its purpose. Such rallies—at once massive and politically hollow—were mainly aimed at impressing not only foreign visitors like me but the average SLL member, to give that member a sense that this movement had potential and could actually affect society at large.

Trade Unionists

One day, I believe the year was 1967, Gerry took me on a trip to Oxford. After dark, we reached the working-class part of town far from the university, parked, and walked down an alley to a little red brick building set behind other houses. Inside the Oxford Trade Union Liaison Committee was in session. There were between thirty and forty workers present. The platform had been taken by an older worker in a cardigan sweater smoking a pipe, who was expounding upon all sorts of diagrams on a blackboard. He was painstakingly showing the audience exactly how Measured Day

Work would operate in the motor car industry and why he felt it was not in the workers' interests to accept it.

Then came the discussion period. At one side of the hall a tall worker approaching middle age was waving a rolled-up pamphlet to get the speaker's attention while on the other side of the hall another worker, perhaps a couple of years younger, was also gesticulating. I noticed he had the same pamphlet—white cover with black and red type—thrust into his back pocket. I soon recognized the pamphlet as *Leon Trotsky on the Trade Unions*, which had been recently published by the Socialist Labour League. The two workers were Reg Parsons (pamphlet in hand) and Alan Thornett (pamphlet in pocket), both workers from British Leyland's Cowley plant. After the meeting both men, plus two or three of their mates, piled into Gerry's car and we drove them home, picking up some fish and chips on the way. Over this traditional workers' fare I learned what the British comrades were doing in the factories.

England has had a very strong trade union movement. The heart of this strength has been the ability of shop stewards to enforce agreements through strike action. In the 1960s the decay of British manufacturing, under conditions of tough international competition, placed British workers in a defensive position. The employers, with the help of the Labour government, launched a campaign to break the power of the local stewards and at the same time to introduce productivity schemes such as Measured Day Work. This was the beginning of a process that has led to the present weakened state of the trade unions and the low living standards of British workers when compared to their European counterparts. An important center of the resistance to these attacks on British labor was the British Leyland assembly plant in Cowley, an industrial suburb of Oxford.

The SLL's intervention at Oxford began with the Young Socialists, who started selling papers and campaigning around the Cowley plant. After initial contact was made with workers, Healy moved in, driving to Oxford daily in some periods, meeting with various workers, attending branch meetings, and teaching a class of workers. The trade union strategy of the SLL in the situation was straightforward: to confront and oppose directly all productivity schemes, defend the shop conditions of the workers as well as the power of the stewards to negotiate these conditions in their areas. The trade union leadership, however, accepted the productivity schemes and sought to negotiate within the government's framework. The Communist Party, which had a strong base in the Engineering Union, hedged and sought to avoid a head-on collision over the employers' schemes. Healy was thus able to make his politics distinct and meaningful—even for a time broadly popular—in the plant. The SLL began to attract bright and very political workers, and Healy was able to provide them with a Trotskyist explanation for the treacherous behavior of the trade union and BLP leaders. They began to understand the nature of Stalinism through this combination of actual experience with the Communist Party on the factory floor with theoretical discussions and reading.

In that period liaison committees were established to bring together workers in different plants to resist this employer and government offensive. The Communist Party had taken the lead in establishing these committees and dominated most of them. The committees became an arena where competing tendencies within the shop stewards' movement put forward conflicting strategies of how to fight back.

Healy was remarkably successful at Cowley. He recruited both the Convener and the Deputy Convener (Thornett) in the plant, as well as dozens of other shop stewards and militant workers. For a time, Healy's supporters controlled the Cowley plant, which was central to the Leyland industrial empire. At one point a big witch-hunt was launched against Thornett, who became known in the press as "The Mole." The workers resisted for a while the combined pressure of the government, the press, the British Labour Party leadership, and the trade union leadership. In the long run Measured Day Work and far worse schemes were introduced under conditions of a government takeover of Leyland and the virtual collapse of the British automobile industry.

Healy built up serious forces throughout the Midlands (Britain's industrial heartland) with a party membership there of around two hundred, and these were mostly industrial workers. He constructed exclusively trade union branches at Cowley, Pressed Steel, and other plants, and he developed working-class strength in Swindon and Reading. Some of these workers developed a serious interest in Marxist theory. Alan Thornett, who had joined the Communist Party in 1959,[4] began to play a leadership role in the SLL. At one point in the early 1970s, Gerry told me he was considering Thornett as a possible future General Secretary. At other times Gerry told me he was considering Sheila Torrance for that post, as well as the man who ended up with the title, Mike Banda. In Swindon the main figure was an older trade unionist, Frank Willis, who worked in a plant that made locomotives. Reading was led by a dynamic, beautiful woman, Kate Blakeney.

Healy attempted to pull together his national trade union strength into an organization he called the All Trade Union Alliance (ATUA). It was openly run by the SLL, and Healy and others would cajole those who attended its conferences to join the revolutionary party. Today it is obvious to me that the ATUA was a sectarian operation that could only have hurt Trotskyist work in the trade unions in the long run. The ATUA was not at all like the multitendency Liaison Committee, which had the endorsement of serious forces in different unions throughout Britain. Instead, it was the SLL acting as if it were a mass party.

Yet ATUA conferences could be quite impressive. In fact they were very much *meant* to be impressive, reflecting a new period in the SLL when images were more and more replacing content. Politics was becoming a game of mirrors! I attended the ATUA meeting in Manchester in 1973. Healy's press claimed four thousand present, which may have been a bit of an exaggeration, but not much of one. The amphitheater was packed with workers from all over England. Just listening to the speakers with their strong regional accents—many I could barely understand—impressed me greatly. Healy had already entered his multimedia period; a huge television projection screen hung over the podium. It was a bit much to see Healy's head projected onto that mammoth screen. Vanessa Redgrave was there and performed a cabaret skit entitled "Tories Are a Girl's Best Friend." Amid all the hoopla, Alan Thornett spoke seriously and well about the problems of workers in England, and various delegations from isolated strikes made their appeals for solidarity actions.

Healy had plainly built something in the trade unions. By the 1970s there was beginning to be more glitter than substance, but there was substance. He had built the best trade union base that Trotskyists in any country had in that particular period. It is easy to understand why Healy held such an appeal for me in those days.

Vanessa Redgrave and Friends

At the same time as this trade union work was developing, Healy made his breakthrough on the cultural front. It began very modestly. A group of producers, directors, playwrights, and actors radicalized by the Vietnam War and by Cuba began discussions with people around various Trotskyist groups, including the SLL. The key figure was David Mercer, who wrote the movie *Morgan!* Mercer never joined the SLL, but he played an important role in encouraging others to listen to Healy.

Healy approached these people very carefully and on a very high level. He began a wide-open class that met each Friday in a fashionable apartment in one of the better areas of London. The class was conducted on a reasonably high theoretical level with a strong emphasis on philosophy. The class went on without interruption for about ten years.

The group was attracted by Marxist theory but also by the SLL as a tough party with working-class support. Involvement with the SLL permitted these artists to feel that they were part of the British working-class movement. Yet, quite pleasantly, the extent of their involvement tended to be classes with fellow artists in a comfortable and familiar setting. They were able to feel that they were part of the working class and also part of a stimulating milieu of fellow artists, much like their Hollywood forebears who were in the orbit of the American Communist Party in the 1930s and 1940s.

There was also "guilt gelt": These artists felt separated from the working class and they were assisted in feeling guilty about their relative prosperity by Healy, who managed to obtain from them considerable sums of money. At the same time there were many moments of genuine interconnection of artist and young worker at various camps and rallies, of artistic contributions to movement events and the stimulation of talented artists by their association with a broader movement.

I attended several of these classes over the years. I remember one held in Roy Battersby's apartment. I knew Roy's American wife, Liz, pretty well, as her sister and brother were active in the movement in the United States and Canada. There were between thirty and forty people present, some from television, and a number of stage and movie actors and actresses. The presentation I heard was on the economic crisis, and it was given by Geoff Pillings (Peter Jeffreys), one of Healy's on-again, off-again academics. Geoff was quite active at this moment and was deeply convinced that international monetary problems would shortly bring down the entire world capitalist system. This was exactly what Gerry wanted his members to think so that they would redouble their activism. The discussion was quite serious. There was always give-and-take at these meetings, much more so than at regular party events. The cultural people received kid-gloves treatment from Healy, who spent many, many hours with each person in this milieu, carefully nurturing their development and support.

I met Corin Redgrave in this period, before his sister Vanessa had any contact with the movement. Corin impressed me. He seemed extremely interested in Marxist theory and quite willing to do everything other members did. He would go out at 5 A.M. to sell papers at plant gates and deliver papers door-to-door in working-class neighborhoods. It was Corin who brought his more famous sister around the organization. I met Vanessa on several occasions and she seemed just as serious as her brother and more than willing to carry out any party task she was asked to do. Both of them projected a kind of intense, fervent, burning sincerity, which was almost frightening and otherworldly.

Trotskyism under Tent

Gerry Healy was, without question, the world's foremost radical showman. He put on demos, rallies, pageants, and conferences with a finesse that would have made P. T. Barnum jealous. It was quite natural, then, that his talents would find their most powerful expression under tent. Healy's summer camps began, Mike Banda once told me, many, many years ago in the early British Labour Party days.

I well remember my first summer camp, which was in 1966. It was held on a hilly field in Sussex in the midst of rolling farm country. I suppose there were two hundred to three hundred present. The camp consisted of a series of large circus tents together with a scattering of smaller ones. There was the main tent used for eating and for meetings of the whole camp. A smaller tent just outside it was the cook tent. I was impressed with a series of large stainless steel kettles heated by propane gas. These were the mainstay of the camp, as they were used to cook hundreds of pounds of potatoes and large sticky mounds of porridge, the two substances that largely sustained us. There were a couple of middle-sized tents for mass dormitories for boys and girls (separate, of course, and these camps were rigidly policed) and a few scattered tents for couples.

The camp was lined with trenches to drain water and keep the camp from simply washing away. Yes, it was raining at that camp. In fact, it rained almost constantly the whole week, and the major battle at the camp was with the rains; crews were constantly clearing the trenches and building new ones. The camp was surrounded by guards who patrolled twenty-four hours a day. One year, Cliff Slaughter was in charge of the guards, to prove, I suppose, that he was more than an intellectual, that he was capable of being what in Healy's group was called a "heavy." He literally did not sleep for days. I never saw a more tired and bedraggled person. He was so wiped out you could barely communicate with him, and therefore his intellectual contribution to the camp was largely missing. I wonder if he rested after the camp by dropping out of the movement for six months or so.

One night we were all awakened at midnight and summoned by the guards to the main tent. There we were, bleary-eyed, with Gerry Healy on the podium, face bright red and sporting his sternest expression. One kid had threatened another one with a knife and the two had been separated just in time. It appears there was a very rough crew from Glasgow there that year. There was always a rough crew at the camp from some place or other, usually Glasgow, occasionally Liverpool. The security of the camp was threatened. There could be a police raid at any moment. Sussex was Tory turf. The revolutionary party itself was on the line. The crisis of capitalism was deepening, and never had the revolutionary party been so needed or its opportunities so bright. So we stood there wet, shivering, with visions of revolution and counterrevolution flowing through our heads while guards meticulously searched each tent and everybody's bags for weapons. Finally off to bed we went, to be awakened at 6 A.M. by a guard pounding on the tent pole shouting, "Wakey, wakey."

As I attended more summer camps, I soon learned that there was *always* a crisis at the camp. In Healy's mind a camp without some sort of crisis was a failure. Healy once told me privately that the purpose of these crises was to bring out the real contradictions within the camp. "If one doesn't develop naturally, then I create one," he said in that smug manner of his. In this fashion each comrade is made to feel the urgency of his or her tasks; it was as if a minirevolution was held within the confines of the campgrounds, complete with barricades. Thus the concept of revolution was supposed to take on real life. It really worked. In Healy's party, and especially at his camps, you felt, *you really felt* that your revolutionary ideas had concrete meaning in the immediate period. It was, of course, a trick with mirrors, an illusion created in the hot-house atmosphere of a camp under tent and aided by the slight delirium that comes with lack of sleep.

My next camp was the International Youth Camp, organized by the International Committee of the Fourth International in the summer of 1967. Actually this was a two-stage event; the first week was strictly an SLL/YS affair; for the second week we were joined by our comrades from abroad. The camp was held on that same wet, hilly field, though the weather was slightly better this time. We Americans had made a big effort to participate, and we brought over sixteen comrades all at considerable cost. There were close to four hundred present during the first British week.

I fully expected a crisis to take place during the first week, but what I didn't expect was that I would be in the middle of it. That was the long hot summer of the black uprisings in Newark and Detroit, and the news of these events came to us through the papers delivered each day to the camp. Of course we had to discuss the meaning of the uprisings, and I talked about them in my general presentation in the big tent. I said that in the midst of the ghetto rebellions, the black nationalist message had gained a widespread appeal that should not be ignored. I reaffirmed my belief that American blacks did not constitute a separate nation in a Marxian sense, yet their special oppression and segregation over so many years had affected their consciousness. I suggested that we should give some thought to proposing the construction of a black revolutionary movement as a way of tapping this consciousness, bringing it to a socialist level, and linking it to the working-class movement as a whole.

Mike Banda immediately got up and launched a bitter attack against my views. I was accused of—sin of sins—"Pabloism" and of capitulating to black nationalism. Black consciousness is completely reactionary and petty bourgeois, Banda insisted, as it divides the working class. We must make no concessions whatsoever to these reactionary ideas. I was reflecting the views of the petty bourgeoisie, of American pragmatism, and of American exceptionalism. Suddenly it became a political punch-up, with speaker after speaker getting up to denounce my deviations. Comrades from Scotland and Ireland in particular spoke to prove to Healy and Banda that they, unlike me, made no concessions whatsoever to nationalist sentiments. (The result of their sectarian approach to national problems was that the SLL remained organizationally very weak in these regions, particularly in Ireland.) I persisted, however, in my views. I was yet to become a completely docile servant of Healy's and was able for a short while longer to sustain some independent thought. No doubt it was this independence, more than the content of the dispute, that irritated Healy and encouraged him to exaggerate our differences.

It was what happened after this session that disturbed me the most. Banda, Slaughter, and Healy met separately with each of the leading members of the American delegation and won them over to their point of view. I wandered around that camp totally alone and isolated. To make matters worse, this happened during my year of personal turmoil. Deborah had told me she was returning to her husband, Jeff, on the West Coast "for good." However, she stayed on with me long enough that she was at the summer camp with me. We shared a little two-person tent supplied by the British that looked like it was left over from the Afghan wars. Deborah had an ulcer and kept bringing small bottles of milk from the cook tent and storing them, without refrigeration, in our little home. Soon the tent began to stink of spoiled milk. Deborah, of course, sided with Healy and Banda in this dispute. It was one of the worst couple of days in my life.

The campaign against me soon passed, however, not because the matter was resolved but because the French were due to arrive shortly, and Healy was getting a bit worried. The French did not unquestioningly accept Healy's authority, so he had to be on his toes. He needed me.

Then the French came and camped on the top of a little hill overlooking the main body of the camp. There were over three hundred of them, and they brought their own brightly colored two-person mountain tents. It was a hill full of color, chatter in French, clouds of Gauloise smoke, and couples necking and rolling around in the wet grass in a most un-British manner, all overlooking the drab dirty white tents of Healy's Model Army.

There were now a total of eight hundred people at that camp, representing some twelve countries. Of course the bulk of the people were brought by the SLL/YS and by Pierre Lambert's OCI (Organisation Communiste Internationaliste) and its youth organization, Révoltes. There were also twenty or thirty Greek émigrés from London who had their own IC section. Then our small German group brought some German students who were part of SDS there. These students were led by a fellow we called Red Rudi, who was *not* the more famous SDS leader Rudi Dutschke. This less-famous Rudi shared many of Dutschke's views, and the group had a kind of semianarchist outlook that immediately clashed with the camp rules and the presence everywhere of guards. They also believed strongly in sexual freedom and in the theories of Wilhelm Reich.

Healy did not like this German group much. He insisted privately that if you went into their tent and clicked your heels, they would all snap to attention and salute. But this was far from the case. They represented an oppositional, participatory democratic, almost communitarian kind of rebel that persists in Germany today as one of the trends within the Green Party. I was given the quite impossible task of convincing these free thinkers of Leninism and, if I failed on the theoretical level, at least of convincing them to accept camp rules for the week. I had several meetings with the group and got exactly no place. Their rejection of camp rules had become a matter of principle with them and a symbol of their struggle against all authority. While Healy tended to apply rules a bit too rigorously and overdo guard patrols, some form of regulation was definitely needed when eight hundred radical youth gathered in the British conservative countryside.

One day the matter came up at a meeting of the whole body in the main tent. Healy was in the middle of a lengthy explanation on the nature of the capitalist state, the dangers stemming from its repressive apparatus, and the necessity, therefore, for vigilance and discipline on the part of the revolutionary forces. Suddenly there was a great whirling noise. We ran outside, and there was an unmarked helicopter landing in the adjacent field, and two men, probably from MI-5, carrying cameras equipped with telephoto lenses, were running toward it. They got in and the helicopter lifted off. We went back to conclude the debate on camp rules. Healy could not have asked for better assistance from the capitalist state in making his point, but the Germans were rather stubborn fellows and did not change their minds. That afternoon they put on their lederhosen and backpacks, left the camp, and started hitchhiking back to Germany.

The remainder of the camp was quite uneventful. The main document to be passed, a manifesto calling for an international youth organization, had been negotiated ahead of time between the British and the French. This did not prevent the French, in particular, from speaking on it at great length and in considerable detail, but there was no controversy. In the end the document was unanimously passed, but the international youth organization it projected never came into being.

This international youth camp was just a bit too big for the Sussex downs, and the farmer who rented his fields to Gerry was not at all sure the downs would recover in time for the haying season. The next few camps were therefore held on a large, flat field on the Blackwater Estuary near South End. I attended three camps there from 1970 to 1972. I remember most clearly the 1972 summer camp, Healy's largest, most spectacular, and last camp.

We Americans again made a big effort, got our own charter flight and brought over one hundred people to the camp. The charter plane was provided by the Israeli government airline El Al. The Israelis were just a little nervous when they discovered the political nature of their passengers. They never said anything, but they did place on the plane with us two handsome young men in suits with conspicuous bulges in their armpits.

There were over one thousand under tent at the camp, an expression of the strength of the movement in that period. (Healy had been able to mobilize only a little over four hundred in 1967.) Of course the bulk of those in attendance were the working-class youth. Yet this time there were a substantial number of older industrial workers and also actors. The Workers League had a pretty impressive delegation including a large number of black and Puerto Rican youth whose presence reflected the new work we were doing. The camp was a cultural shock for these youth, many of whom had never been out of New York City, not to mention across the ocean.

Healy gave these kids a real scare when, in one of his more flamboyant speeches, he suggested that the entire country might close down in a general strike, thus preventing our delegation from returning home. Such a strike, Healy claimed, could be the opening gun of the revolution itself. These kids, rather than being impressed that they might soon, like John Reed and Louise Bryant, be witnesses to an actual revolution, were more concerned about not getting back to their homes in East New York! It was my ticklish job, without appearing to "underestimate the depth of the crisis," about as heinous a political crime as one could commit in those days, to reassure them that in all probability, they would get back to Brooklyn safely.

The excitement that year was provided by the press. They had gotten wind of the camp and the *London Telegraph* hired a plane, flew over the place, and ran a huge photo of our tents on its front page, claiming it was all a training camp for armed insurrection. Then the rest of the press descended upon the place, climbing trees and sticking telephoto lenses through the fences around the property. It was sufficient publicity to convince Healy that this should be his last camp. So passed an exciting, if at times nightmarish and otherworldly, institution.

The French Connection

I first met the French section of the International Committee in 1964 during my first trip to Europe. Gerry arranged one of those cheap midnight flights to Paris for me. As we flew low over Paris it was all lit up, full of life at an hour when London had long since gone to bed. I was met at the airport by a sleepy François Demassot. François was a middle-aged man, considered a young leader by the standards in the French movement in those days. His mother had been British, and he spoke perfect Oxford English. François took me to a little hotel situated off some steps that went between two streets; it was a very picturesque location.

After some sleep and a little breakfast I was taken to an apartment to meet the leadership of the French group. When the group was founded in 1944, it was called the Parti Communiste Internationaliste (PCI), but in 1966 Lambert changed the name to Organisation Communiste Internationaliste (OCI). The PCI published a well-known journal, *La Verité*, which had been founded by France's first Trotskyists in the 1930s. Lambert's followers had been the majority group in the French section of the Fourth International in 1952, when Pablo supported the minority opposition and had them expelled. François had joined the group soon after this split and told me that they were at the time extremely isolated and decimated. In a short while they lost most of their members through demoralization, with perhaps seventy surviving out of a group of several hundred. They had slowly grown since that time and in 1964 were finally beginning to recruit students and show some vitality. They were orthodox people, deeply committed to the Trotskyist tradition, and strongly anti-Stalinist in a country where a mass Communist Party existed and controlled the major trade union organization, the CGT (Confédération Générale du Travail).

I was greeted by Pierre Lambert, the PCI's leader. Lambert was a nice-looking fellow of around fifty years old. He wore a vested suit and his hair was just touched with gray. He worked in some government job and had been extremely active for years in the union of government employees, which was affiliated with the Force Ouvrière (FO), the Socialist Party–controlled union federation. Lambert always had a Gauloise dangling from the corner of his mouth and spoke exhuberantly and incessantly. His English was extremely poor and François had to translate.

Also present was Gerard Bloch, who was around the same age as Lambert but clearly in very poor health. He wore glasses and was partially bald. He walked hunched over and breathed with difficulty, although his wheezing did not prevent him from smoking a pipe. Gerard was Jewish and had barely survived the war in concentration camps. He was an intellectual and had contributed greatly to assisting the survival of Trotskyist ideas in the hostile environment of France of the 1950s. I also met Daniel Renard, the other major figure in the PCI from the time of its split with Pablo. Renard wore a black leather jacket and sported a beret, looking very much like the French worker that he was. He worked in the Renault plant just outside Paris and had played an important role in the plant occupations right after World War II. Stephen Just, the other major leader of the PCI/OCI, was not present. Just, who was a Metro worker, went through periods when he would feud with Lambert and drop out of activity. This must have been one of those periods.

We all sat down and I reported on the current state of the Socialist Workers Party as well as on my discussions with the SLL leaders. I explained, as best I could, Healy's new theory that the SWP leadership was not Marxist. The French, to their credit, did not buy it. They had known Jim Cannon over many years and respected the old working-class cadre of that party. They continued to view the SWP as a revolutionary party that had gone astray, and they favored a continued fight to win it back to a true orthodox course. They did not extend this attitude to their competing French group, led by Pierre Frank, which was affiliated with the new United Secretariat of the Fourth International. They viewed that group, then also called the PCI, as hopelessly "petty bourgeois" as well as pro-Stalinist and refused to have anything to do with it.

I liked the French comrades. They were very solid people, extremely active in the trade unions, without, in that period, any full-time staff, any office, any apparatus. I respected their history, their tenacity. They had survived the war, had gone on to promote an antibureaucratic radicalism in an inhospitable postwar world only to be torn apart by factionalism supported by Michel Pablo's Fourth International leadership. Yet they persisted in their views, in their faith.

In 1967, following the international youth camp I visited France again and was taken to the new center of the OCI. This headquarters was a good place to see what made Lambert's OCI different from Healy's SLL. It had a bank of at least eight mimeo machines, and all day long people poured in from different parts of Paris to mimeograph leaflets, newsletters, and minutes. Each one of these comrades was active in some trade union branch or section of the national student federation, or some other kind of mass organization. The OCI was particularly active in the teachers' union and the students' union. The party had a relatively weak press of its own, and a very small staff, but it had an active membership, well implanted in other organizations. I saw far less of the party-building stress that so dominated everything Healy did.

I spent most of a week attending a party cadre school. The school was held in a loft facing a small courtyard surrounded by old buildings where various kinds of small manufacturing was going on. You entered the courtyard through a narrow alley from a very busy street full of cafés and *boulangeries* and bustling with pedestrian and automobile traffic. Gathered in the loft were around thirty young comrades, each and every one smoking Gauloises nonstop as if their main task in life was to sustain this state tobacco monopoly. I gagged, and no doubt that week took several months off my life span.

The school was devoted to a painfully detailed and somewhat schematically presented study of the overall party perspective, illustrated with diagrams on a blackboard. The perspective was clearly a triumph of French rationalism and the logical minds of the French people. The method was quite different from Healy's. There was no boasting, no exaggeration of the crisis, or illusions that our movement could swiftly win the leadership of millions of French workers. Instead, the central theme of the school was *united front* activities. The party's strategy was to urge the Communist Party and the Socialist Party to break politically from the capitalist parties and to unite to form a workers' government in France. Such a development was seen as the next step forward for the French working class. The Trotskyists then posed certain socialist measures for such a united workers' government to carry out. It was hoped that in the course of a struggle for a united-front government, the masses could be won away from the opportunist leaders of both mass workers parties. In this fashion, the Trotskyists might, at some distant point in time, gain leadership of the working masses in France. The same general strategy was also posed within the trade unions, as OCI supporters sought to unite in action the Communist Party's CGT, the Socialist Party's FO, and even the Christian Democratic and independent unions.

The OCI had a different structure from the SLL or the organizations I was familiar with in the United States. It was divided into a series of quite small *cells* in the Communist tradition. Most of these cells were organized on an industrial or occupational basis rather than by geographical district, as was common with party branches in the United States and England. I visited several of these cells during that week in Paris. They were simply groups of about half-a-dozen comrades meeting in someone's living room. The cells had little contact with each other and were connected with the party by a centralized pyramid structure. Such a structure is useful in underground conditions—each comrade, at least theoretically, only knows a half-a-dozen people, plus his party representative—but I believe it can hamper the democratic life of a movement.

The French approached recruitment in a very different fashion as well. While by the early 1970s the British were literally signing up members at street corners, it took a potential recruit at least a year to become a member of the OCI. The candidate was required to attend cadre classes constantly during that year. Once someone actually became a member, he or she was well indoctrinated in the party line and perspectives.

I next visited Paris in 1969, one year after the May–June events. The OCI and Révoltes were still banned, though the movement was operating openly with a change in name (Organisation Trotskyiste). Yet a clandestine atmosphere still prevailed, and the leading French comrades could not travel out of the country. Therefore Gerry Healy, Cliff Slaughter, and I went to Paris to hold a meeting of the International Committee. May–June 1968 had not been the kind of revolutionary victory we wanted, yet it had not been a real defeat either. The political mood in Paris continued to be quite radical. Posters were still evident all over the place. Every now and then a motorist would honk his horn to beat out the first notes of the "Internationale," and soon the whole street was ablast.

We traveled to an old part of Paris, walking the last few blocks toward a café. Gerry wrinkled his nose, sniffing the air, as if he had stepped in something he shouldn't have. "This is Pab country," he said. "This is where I always used to meet with Pablo in the old days." I don't know whether he recognized a building or street or just the smell in the air. Soon we arrived at the café. The owner was an old personal friend of Lambert's who used to harbor resistance people during World War II. He led us to the rear of the café and up a narrow spiral staircase to a small room above it: a perfect spot for a clandestine meeting!

When we took our long lunch break, I began to wonder whether all this conspiracy was really necessary. We went to a nearby restaurant, and the French gathered at one table and we at another. Soon the French comrades were involved in a spirited political discussion, which got louder and louder as the wine flowed more and more freely. A policeman a block away could have taken it all down. That was the French: open, garrulous, spirited, urbane, given to continuously poking fun at each other, capable of consuming large quantities of wine, yet intensely political. How different from the British comrades with their characteristic reserve, their love for the stern expression, of viewing anything light or frivolous as downright treachery, a kind of self-righteous "Model Army." My heart went out to the French, but, I am afraid, my political head was with the British in those days.

The OCI soon was a legal party again (with its old name back) and continued to grow at a very rapid rate. Soon, like the SLL, it moved to larger quarters, created a full-time staff, bought a press, and began publishing well-edited and reasonably widely circulated publications. It reached a height of about four thousand members by the middle of the 1970s. Pierre Frank's group, Ligue Communiste, also grew almost as much. Its student leader, Alain Krivine, was well known throughout France. A third group, originally called Voix Ouvrière but later known as Lutte Ouvrière, also grew, with a membership in the thousands.[5] Trotskyism had become an important force in student circles and in what was known in France as the Far Left.

I traveled to France in February 1970 to attend a major rally organized by the new youth organization of the OCI, the Alliance des Jeunes pour le Socialisme (AJS). The French comrades had rented a large hangar at the Le Bourget airport for the rally. When we arrived hundreds of buses were pulling up in front of the huge building. Long red streamers attached to flagpoles were blowing in the wind, and a huge sign announcing the conference covered the facade of the structure. It was quite a sight. As delegations arrived they marched into the hall in groups, usually singing the "Internationale" or other traditional revolutionary songs. We passed through registration in a smaller hangar attached to the main one, and each of us was given a paper bag containing lunch. Inside the bag was a small bottle of wine, a sandwich made out of some paté and French bread, a piece of cheese, and an apple. Much superior to the cucumber sandwiches of my British friends!

We entered the immense hall, which had a long, elevated platform in the front. Behind the platform there were huge portraits, at least twenty feet high, of Lenin and Trotsky. As we waited for everyone to arrive and the rally to start, teenage French girls wearing red scarves, each holding a corner of large red flags, literally skipped up and down the aisles singing while people threw coins into the flags. There were ten thousand people present, the largest indoor political rally of any kind I had ever attended, and without question, the largest Trotskyist rally ever held in Europe. As the rally started everyone got on their feet, and with fists clenched as only the French can (Americans and British at similar rallies tend to meekly raise their barely closed hands as if embarrassed at this departure from political liberalism), started chanting in unison: "Vive Lenine! Vive Trotsky! Vive le Quatrieme Internationale!!!" Being a sentimental type, I was moved to tears by the event.

THE INTERNATIONAL COMMITTEE

As leader of the International Committee's American affiliate, the Workers League, I believed deeply in the International Committee of the Fourth International. I believed that the IC was the true continuator of world Trotskyism, and that its competing organization, the United Secretariat of the Fourth International (USec), had eschewed Marxism for opportunism. None of us on either side of the international split questioned for a moment that Trotskyism was the true continuator of the Third International and of the revolutionary Marxist heritage going all the way back to Marx and Engels.

After 1963, the IC functioned mainly as a bloc between the SLL and the OCI. But since the two groups had little in common, except their hostility toward the rival USec, the IC was basically paralyzed as a functioning entity. None of the many disputes that erupted within the IC after 1963 were ever put to a vote. A compromise solution always had to be negotiated between the British and the French. The IC survived in those days because the two big parties were about evenly matched, and neither could dismiss out of hand a position held by the other. This edgy balance was the source of some long, careful discussion at times, and although the OCI/SLL symbiosis could not last forever, it did sputter along for almost ten years.

Cliff Slaughter had replaced Healy as IC Secretary in 1964, but this was a position with little authority, as the IC had no office, no staff, and no formal structure. Its one congress after the break of the SWP, the April 1966 affair held in London, was less than successful, to say the least (see chapter 6, "On My Own"). And in spite of some successful collaboration in 1966 and 1967,[6] tensions between the British and French persisted.

Ironically, the remarkable growth of both groups after the events of May and June 1968 only exacerbated these tensions. Each became convinced that its way of building a revolutionary party was *the* way and should be adopted by all other groups within the IC. Both the OCI and the SLL began to foster different IC affiliates, and in this way two separate ICs were being built. This ethnocentric approach was stated (and practiced) most clearly by Gerry Healy:

> A period of unparalleled revolutionary conflict lies ahead. The Socialist Labour League now shoulders an enormous responsibility—that of constructing the mass revolutionary party which will lead the working class to power. By so doing it will inspire revolutionists in all countries to build similar parties to do the same.[7]

Robin Blick called this outlook "Trotskyism in One Country."[8] Healy thought he would make the revolution in our own country and revolutionaries in other countries would be permitted to learn from our experiences and build parties modeled on ours.

When I went to Paris in 1969 for the IC meeting I described earlier in this chapter, I could not quite identify the substance of the preexisting tension. At most, it seemed to me that the French wanted the IC to be more of an organization and to act more aggressively in seeking to regroup revolutionaries around the world. The French had the notion that the Fourth

International needed to be "reorganized" or "rebuilt" through this regroupment process. The British, however, felt that the core of the FI was already in place, that this core was the existing IC, and that it just needed to be added to. We mulled over this disagreement a lot in Paris, but we in no sense resolved it.

In June 1970 a "preconference" meeting of the International Committee was held in London. The purpose of the gathering was to organize the long-postponed Fourth Conference of the International Committee. I flew over especially for the meeting at Gerry's request. I believe he felt he needed every bit of support he could muster. I remember that Healy went to some lengths to make his foreign guests feel at home, even supplying wine and French bread for our midday meal.

I was elected to chair the session, no doubt because neither of the two main groups thought it appropriate that one of its own should chair. Outside of the SLL and OCI, the only other representatives present were an emaciated-looking fellow from our minuscule Irish section, a group of Greeks who worked closely with the SLL, and Balazs Nagy (Michel Varga), representing the Hungarian section. Varga had been a member of the Hungarian Communist Party's Political Bureau and one of the intellectuals who had organized the Petofi Circle, whose discussions played an important role in touching off the Hungarian Revolution. Now in exile in Paris, he had gathered together a small group of Hungarians and, with the assistance of the OCI, had organized among exiles from other East European countries. I never really got to know the man, but his presence was then considered to be of great symbolic importance to the International Committee.[9]

The British were able to steer the discussions to the abstract level of Marxist philosophy. The more wild and apocalyptic Healy's politics became, the greater he stressed dialectics. The cadre, who might be missing the coming revolution in the empirical events surrounding them, were urged to probe beneath the surface to grasp the essential contradictions. The discussion was, of course, a trap. Since Healy had already established—at least to his own followers—that the "revisionism" of the Socialist Workers Party was rooted in its abandonment of dialectics for pragmatism, he was setting the stage for accusing the French of a philosophical deviation at least as grave.

Slaughter explained at length that Marxism was a "theory of knowledge" and that its study was absolutely essential for the preparation of the International Committee cadres for the imminent revolution. First Nagy and then the French comrades rose to the challenge and, in relatively polite language, dismissed Slaughter's remarks as idealist rubbish. For them Marxism was the reflection of the class struggle codified in the Transitional

Program of the Fourth International. Perhaps they were right and perhaps they were wrong, but I don't think it is right for an international political body to seek to decide views on philosophical matters. At the time, however, I was enthralled by the discussion. I loved philosophy then, and I truly believed that we had found the root cause of our differences with the French. The discussion became tense, and the hour was approaching when the French and Nagy needed to leave to catch their plane back to the continent. At the last minute matters were patched up so that the International Committee could go forward in preparing its Fourth Conference.

In July of 1971 the OCI organized, with the formal endorsement of the International Committee, a large rally in favor of a united socialist Europe. Over five thousand young people from thirty-two countries gathered in Essen, West Germany. The British sent a token delegation led by Dany Sylveire. Sylveire sought to amend the general resolution of the conference to add a call for the study of dialectics. Once more, Healy was seeking to maneuver the French into putting forward a position that would appear to rank-and-file SLL members as an opposition to dialectics. The French bit and prevented the amendment from coming up for a vote. Healy became enraged. The climate was well prepared for a break between the two organizations. It occurred that fall, and quite unexpectedly, over an issue never discussed at the preconference or any other IC meeting: *Bolivia*. I have to admit that I myself was the catalyst for the split.

In 1969, due to the efforts of the OCI, which was working very hard to widen the base of the IC, Guillermo Lora and his POR (Partido Obrero Revolutionario) was recruited. Lora's group had played a major role in the Bolivian Revolution of 1952,[10] though his influence in the country had been greatly reduced in the following two decades. I met him in the summer of 1970 when he and the leader of his youth group, Victor Sossa, spent a day at one of Healy's summer camps. He gave a short talk on Bolivia to our delegation at the camp. That year a leftist group in the military under Juan José Torres had taken over the government. Largely at the initiative of the POR, Torres agreed to organize the Asamblea Popular (People's Assembly) made up of the representatives of all the key unions and peasant organizations. Lora functioned in this assembly, where he had considerable influence, seeking to transform it into a soviet.[11]

There was, however, a serious problem. Torres, unlike the leaders of the 1952 revolution, did not distribute arms to the workers and peasants, and I am afraid Lora, perhaps feeling too weak to do so, did not press him on the point. It turned out to be a critical matter, for a right-wing military coup ousted Torres in late August 1971 and easily dispersed Lora's People's Assembly. I then wrote an assessment of the Bolivian events, which was sharply critical of Lora. I believed Lora was wrong in extending any kind of political support to Torres and for not pressing for arms for the workers. Whatever may be the merits of my argument, I believe my tone was much too sharp. I paid too little attention to Lora's long years of experience as a mass leader in Bolivia, the heroic role of his party during those years, and failed to recognize the difficulties a small party faced in Bolivia with its long history of military coups.

The British found the issue tailor-made for their factional purposes and immediately published my *Bulletin* article in their paper. The French sided with Lora by publicly distributing a leaflet in Paris attacking the SLL and me. Healy responded by issuing a statement in the name of the "majority" of the IC, splitting with the OCI. It was signed by the Irish group, the Greek group, and a small group in Ceylon, as well as by the SLL and the Workers League. From October 1971 on, the OCI functioned within its own international formation, Le Comité d'Organisation pour la Reconstruction de la Quatrième Internationale (CORQI), which has had some influence in Quebec, Peru, and some African countries. (Lora and his POR, supported by Política Obrera in Argentina, soon split away.)[12] The International Committee was now the personal possession of Gerry Healy.

I attended two meetings of the IC following the split with the OCI—in 1972 and in April 1974. All I remember about the 1972 affair was that it was held at a British summer camp as an afterthought, since international comrades were coming to the camp anyway, and that our group received the brunt of Healy's criticisms. I remember the 1974 IC meeting the best. Healy had gotten us all reservations in a little hotel near Clapham, where we got a typical English breakfast of fried bread, fried tomatoes, thick, greasy, bacon, and meal-filled sausage along with fried eggs. It was certainly a lot of food, if not too wholesome, and better fare than we had ever gotten at the camps.

Our always-sad Irish supporters were on hand to explain why, once again, everything had gone so poorly in their little group. Dimitri Toubanis represented the Greek section. This was a meaningful group that had its own life and put out a monthly paper. Although these comrades were still in exile and largely living in London, many of them spoke no English, and the group carried on its work in Greek, a fact that insulated them some from Healy's influence. Uhli was at the meeting representing a small, deeply sectarian, German group that had split away from Lambert's German followers. Two Australian comrades were also there: young energetic men who published a journal almost identical to that of Healy's in England, and who in every other way acted the colonials mimicking the mother country's party.

The most romantic participant at the conference was Sergio Barrios, the leader of a Peruvian group, the Liga Comunista (LC), which enjoyed a certain success in that period. Sergio, a dashing-looking fellow from an upper-class family, had traveled by peasant buses to the Ecuadorian border, crossed the border on foot, taken another bus and then a plane from Quito to London. I do not know whether such conspiracy was really necessary (perhaps it was because his paper had been suppressed), but it added a touch of glamor to the proceedings. The British delegation had its own form of glamor, since it was headed by stars Vanessa and Corin Redgrave.

There had been no documents circulated to the sections prior to the meeting, no prepared agenda, and no concrete proposals were before the gathering. Cliff Slaughter (still the International Secretary) and Gerry Healy were in fact at a loss as to what to do. So they ran it like one of their Central Committee meetings, with reports on the work of the various sections. Ironically, considering the explosion that would take place within our organization in just a few short months, the American group was held up to the other sections as a model to follow. For once we received nothing but praise, while the other, smaller groups were criticized for their "propagandism" and general weaknesses.

Internationalism has its dark side. Just as a party can fall under the dictatorial rule of a strong individual or clique, an international organization can extend such control over parties in many countries. This was how the Third International worked under Stalin. I would shortly experience personally the wrath of a petty tyrant with global ambitions.

Notes

1. After 1963 the IC was composed primarily of the British Trotskyists led by Gerry Healy and the French Trotskyists led by Pierre Lambert. Other affiliated groups tended to be satellites of the two main groups. In 1971 Healy and Lambert had a political falling-out, and the IC split into two formations.
2. J. P. Nettl, *Rosa Luxemburg* (New York: Oxford University Press, 1966), p. 860.
3. Tony Whelan, *The Credibility Gap—The Politics of the SLL* (London: International Marxist Group, 1970), p. 6.
4. Workers Socialist League, *The Battle for Trotskyism* (London: 1979), p. 82.
5. Fields, *Trotskyism and Maoism*, pp. 41–86.
6. I have already described the successful joint summer camp in Sussex in 1967. In the autumn of the previous year, the OCI and the SLL/YS decided to send contingents to an anti-NATO demonstration being organized by the USec and other groups, including the Communist Party. Together, the British and French groups mobilized nearly a thousand youth, almost equaling the numbers brought by the USec.
7. Gerry Healy, *Problems of the Fourth International* (London: New Park, 1967).

8. Robert Black, *Fascism in Germany* (London: Steyne Publications, 1975), p. 1109.
9. Varga parted company with the OCI in 1972. At one time he had a minute group of supporters in the United States who published a journal called *Truth*.
10. Robert J. Alexander, *The Bolivian Revolution* (New Brunswick, NJ: Rutgers University Press, 1958).
11. James Dunkerley, *Rebellion in the Veins* (London: Verso, 1984), pp. 177–200.
12. For a full account of CORQI see Alexander, *International Trotskyism*, pp. 634–36.

10

The Nemesis

Frenzy Seizes the Workers League

The year 1973 marked the beginning of the end. It was as much a turning point for the American Left, and for me personally, as was 1968. None of us understood this at the time. We were experiencing a marvelous high: We were selling papers, people were joining the Workers League, money was flowing in, we were buying new equipment and adding to our staff. What we did not realize was that we were like vultures, living off of the flesh of a decaying radicalization. Soon there would be nothing left but bones.

There was remarkable agreement on the left on perspectives in this period. Of course no one would admit our programmatic common ground, as we were a tendentious lot. Yet it is fair to say that we were, all of us, completely off-base. The Workers League could claim credit for being the most off-base, for we made the most noise about the economic crisis. Yet each group, in its own way, projected *the continuation and deepening of the radicalization process of the 1960s.* Every group, with the exception of the SWP, believed this radicalization process would spread from the student movement into the working class. This expansion would strengthen the movement, give it a solid class basis, and we would be well on our way toward an American revolution. This led groups as different as the Shachtmanite International Socialists and the Maoist Revolutionary Communist Party to send their student cadres into the trade unions. Even Spartacist made an attempt at this. Our own main effort, though based on an assessment similar to the other groups' was devoted to work among working-class youth.

The Socialist Workers Party shared the same perspective of the 1960s radicalization, broadening to involve ever-larger sections of the population. However, the SWP saw radicalization as taking place within "movement" arenas rather than within the trade unions. In particular it hoped that the new women's movement would be a substitute for the dying antiwar movement. The women's movement did continue to have vitality for some years; it was the exception to the rule and in any case did not change the character of political life on the left in the 1970s.

The Paris Accords reached in January 1973 meant the end of American involvement in the Vietnam War. With this agreement came, quite logically, the end of the movement that opposed that war (even though the Vietnamese had to fight on for over two more years). The civil rights movement had petered out before this date after winning its legal victories. The Black Power movement persisted into the 1970s, but each year its influence was less, its leadership more bitterly antiwhite and sectarian. For a short while the Left got a breather furnished by another product of the 1960s, "Tricky Dick" Nixon. The Watergate scandal and the resignation of Nixon was the last moment in the 1970s when the ideas of the Left were broadly popular in the United States and those of the Right held in disrepute.

Most important, however, the predicted growth in labor militancy simply did not occur. The 1960s were *not* followed by a classic labor radicalization such as occurred in the 1930s. There were, of course, strikes and plenty of opportunities for socialists to function as militants in specific trade union locals. But the union movement as a whole experienced a growing conservatization, rather than radicalization, of its ranks. The economic crisis, which was supposed to have precipitated the radicalization, simply did not take place. The 1970s were relatively prosperous years for the majority of Americans, including a majority of the members of the trade unions.

The American Left became an increasingly isolated and aging group of radicals recruited during the 1960s. As part of the baby boom generation, many of these leftists also found prosperity as academics with some Marxist credentials, as trade unionists pulling pretty good wages, or as members of the professions. The remarkable thing was not the desertions that occurred in the ranks of all leftist groups but that so many leftists remained true to their radical vision in one fashion or another. This is testament to the extent to which people's lives were transformed by the events of that period.

We in the Workers League were among the most disoriented of those on the left. We were deeply convinced that world capitalism was in its deepest crisis ever. This meant that "revolution" was more than an abstract notion or a moral ideal. We felt we needed to prepare in a practical way for revolutionary events that would soon take place on American soil as well as throughout the world. Our little group would then flourish and become the leadership of the American working class. This leadership would be critical to the success or failure of the revolution. The fate of humanity depended on the outcome of this battle. Therefore, quite logically, we felt that no personal sacrifice for the party was too great. These notions possessed us and shaped our very beings. We became *driven* by them. The more our vision clashed with reality, the more frenzied we became.

I imagine that it is not easy for someone who has not been involved in a "movement" to picture this. Our typical member worked a full day at his or her job and then, instead of going home, headed for the party office, bringing a slice of pizza or a hamburger for supper. Then, together with one or two others, the comrade would go to a dangerous poor neighborhood to sell papers, knock on doors for subscriptions, perhaps pick up half-a-dozen teenagers to hold a youth meeting, organize a dance or a basketball game or just to talk at great length to try to convince someone to do something. Then it was back to the office to talk it all over and finally head for home. Sometimes even at home the comrade would have to try to keep awake to work up a small article for the newspaper. This wearying schedule was not kept only one night a week, either; it could be every night!

From the vantage point of these conservative times, it may be hard to believe how successful we were that year. Our largely middle-class membership went to the ghettos of America and received a response to our revolutionary rantings. Watergate helped us a great deal, and the receding tide of the 1960s radicalization left little pools of protest and hope here and there. We could convince others to believe as we did, if only a little bit or for a moment. People came to our meetings, bought our papers, contributed money, and some even joined. These little successes—so pitifully small when one thinks of our revolutionary ambitions—encouraged us in our dreaming. We followed up each successful campaign with a new and more ambitious one. Comrades pushed harder, draining their bank accounts and their energies. We were all so proud of our accomplishments. But each of us was burning fuel that could not be replenished. Somewhere way in the back of our minds we said to ourselves, "I can do this just a little while longer. Just one more campaign. Soon our dream will come true, very soon because I can't go on this way forever. This is for the duration, but the duration cannot last too much longer."

As time went by our views clashed increasingly with comrades' experiences in the real world. How did we explain this to the members? Since the ever-deepening crisis was taken as a given, we did not see the problems of our organization as *objectively based*. We could not simply recognize that we were having difficulties because the times were not quite as grim as we painted them; there were openings for personal advancement, and many who were once interested in leftist politics were becoming more interested in personal success. We thought our problems were *subjectively rooted*. We believed that the crisis had gotten so deep that the middle classes (for Marxists, the "petty bourgeoisie") were in retreat. Therefore our own cadres, which were of middle-class origins, were resisting reaching out to the young workers, whom the ever-deepening crisis was radicalizing. Those who resisted the most left the organization. We were thus seeing a "class struggle" within the Workers League as the majority fought the middle-class element's resistance to reaching out to the ever more receptive workers.

As we increased the pace of our activities, we stepped up the internal struggle within the organization. Each branch meeting was dominated by attacks against comrades who failed to sell sufficient tickets to an event or to sell papers or subscriptions, or who failed in some other fashion. The comrades were forced to confess their own middle-class weaknesses, even their purported hostility to the working class and to the party. A physically exhausted membership found itself under continuous attack. Believing in the party and our ideals as we all did, each of us became preoccupied with our own internal demons. These kept most of us, at least for a while, from questioning the party's perspective. It was, as I can now see clearly, a highly effective method of brainwashing and thought control. We held on to and inspired a hardworking membership at the cost of becoming—*a political cult!*

GERRY HEALY: THE DARK SIDE

Gerry Healy's movement also changed in the 1970s. The process of change was already under way during the 1960s, and there were antecedents that went back even to the 1950s. Yet by the middle 1970s, quantity had been transformed into quality; the idiosyncratic had become the grotesque; a tendency toward overconfidence and exaggeration was now accompanied by personal corruption and internal terror. It was success, above all, that spoiled Gerry Healy.

It started with the daily paper. The Socialist Labour League campaigned throughout the 1960s in favor of launching the daily paper. The campaign was a way for Healy to distinguish himself on the left: Only the far-larger British Communist Party put out a daily paper. Healy felt that if the SLL could produce such a journal, it would be a great forward step for Trotskyism. And since no other Trotskyist group had ever had a daily paper, Healy's accomplishment would be a kind of concrete proof of the superiority of his brand of Trotskyism. The campaign was also useful for Healy because achieving its goal required raising large sums of money. Gerry was able to utilize his great persuasive powers to raise this money from members and supporters.

The big problems a daily paper can create for a movement were ignored by Healy. The British Stalinists were having a lot of difficulty maintaining their paper, and there is little doubt that the *Morning Star* would have had to drop back to a weekly if it hadn't had such wide circulation in East Europe and the Soviet Union. Nor was it mentioned that the most successful Trotskyist party, the LSSP, had been able to win over the support of the majority of the Ceylonese working class without a daily paper.

No matter, Healy was not concerned. The daily paper was a prestige project, his Aswan Dam. I spoke with Healy within weeks of the launching of the daily, called the *Workers Press*, in September 1969, and he had not yet figured out how he was going to distribute it. Almost to the last day he was considering a commercial newsstand distribution. He appeared to be unaware that the physical *production* of a daily paper was the easy part of it, especially with modern web offset printing. The real problems were how to sustain such a paper financially and how to maintain a circulation that would make the effort worthwhile.

The *Workers Press* required a new plant and a large expansion of the full-time staff. Healy abandoned the cramped quarters in the alley behind 186A Clapham High Street and moved his plant a few blocks down High Street and further down Old Town Road. It was situated in a maze of interconnected red-brick factory buildings around a courtyard behind a large black metal gate. While the party still occupied the old offices at 186A, this new shop area had become the real hub of the SLL's activity, and much time was spent walking back and forth between the two facilities.

Gerry used the new daily paper to recruit professional journalists to put it out. The key journalist was Alex Mitchell, a good-looking but slightly overweight Australian who had trained on the big dailies back home. He was technically competent and had produced some important investigative reporting. I found him to be a bit aloof. Healy treated him as he did his important cultural people like Corin and Vanessa. Shortly after joining the party, Mitchell found himself on the Political Committee and treated as if he were a central political leader of the organization. At the same time he worked very regular hours, going home each evening while party regulars like Paul Jennings, Jack Gale, and David Maude continued work.

One day while I was visiting England, David Maude was absent from the 8 A.M. editorial board meeting. A little later someone found a signed statement of resignation on his desk. It was soon discovered that David had met a woman reporter in the course of his work, fallen in love with her, and decided to resign from the party and get a job as a labor reporter with a provincial daily. Healy was livid. He was most upset because the action was unexpected. He had not even known of the girlfriend. Healy had not penetrated deeply enough into Maude's thinking processes. "They all keep two sets of books," Healy ranted to me. "They tell you one thing and they think another." Healy wrinkled his nose and concluded: "You can never trust the British middle class."

In spite of an enormous daily effort by rank-and-file party members, the press run was rarely over six thousand during the week and ten thousand on weekends. It was an uneconomical operation. Low circulation meant that much of Healy's efforts for the next fifteen years went into raising the funds to sustain the paper. Why did he bother? Clearly the daily paper was critical to Healy's whole mythological concept of the mass revolutionary party. He needed it to sustain his image among his own members. The paper also justified the sizable layer of full-time party employees—eventually more than ninety people—and these full-timers became an important internal base of support for his regime. The party apparatus became more and more an end in itself; the revolutionary objectives of the movement were transformed into rhetoric and in this fashion utilized to justify the apparatus. The means became an end and the end, the means. This state of affairs was in microcosm what had happened on a vast scale with the mass socialist parties in Europe before World War I as well as with Stalinism in the USSR and East Europe.

On November 4, 1973, the Socialist Labour League was "transformed" into the Workers Revolutionary Party (WRP). Like the establishment of the daily paper, the transformation of the SLL into a mass revolutionary party was the result of a long campaign. Healy acted as if a small propaganda group can become a mass party through the same *exhortative* techniques employed in building up the party's press. Comrades went out with membership blanks and simply signed up people on the flimsiest bases, usually by muttering something about fighting the Tories. At one Central Committee meeting Healy proposed that the party recruit three thousand new members in the next ten days, and the proposal was passed without discussion![1] The new members recruited in such a fashion were seldom seen after they were signed up. The truth is that there was no appreciable growth in *permanent* party membership during the campaign for the Workers Revolutionary Party.

I attended briefly one session of the founding convention of the WRP and remember very little of it. Alan Thornett was the chair that day, at a time when Healy was considering him as a possible successor. About six hundred people were at the convention. An accurate measure of Healy's strength among the masses of British workers came when the WRP ran ten candidates in the October 1974 elections. Only three of these candidates got over 1 percent of the vote, and the ten candidates' votes averaged 1.4

percent of the vote that went to the Labour Party.[2] The Workers Revolutionary Party obviously had a way to go to become a mass party.

Along with its technical advances and its increasingly intense party recruitment campaigns, the party developed a more deformed internal life. As the SLL/WRP's perspectives became more and more optimistic and the predictions of the coming revolution more wild, the internal regime became more brutal. I remember well a typical Central Committee meeting. Healy as usual was running the meeting, without minutes, procedures, or a chair (if there was a chair, he or she was not evident to me). "I wish to make a motion," Healy started out, "to expel Cliff Slaughter from the Central Committee and from the party. He has been acting consciously to destroy our movement and to aid the class enemy at a critical juncture in the crisis of capitalism. Never before have the opportunities for the revolutionary movement been brighter. This only makes Slaughter's treachery all the more intolerable."

Although I was quite used to hyperbole by that time, I was shocked, and physically shaking inside myself. Cliff Slaughter, to me the key leader of the SLL after Healy, must have acted in some manner that seriously endangered the entire movement. I waited anxiously to hear about his crimes.

Jean Kerrigan, a youth comrade who was a bit on the heavy side and had a very Irish face topped by curly red hair, was called upon to furnish the ammunition. She worked in the area of the country under Slaughter's authority, the Northwest. Apparently, the Northwest had not gotten enough youth, compared to other areas, to participate in the most recent SLL event. Kerrigan held Slaughter wholely responsible for this, even though it occurred to me at the time that she might have modestly shouldered some of the blame, as she was in charge of the youth movement in the region.

Then all and sundry spoke up to rake Cliff over the coals. He was characterized as petty bourgeois, not only distant from the working-class youth but hostile to them, hating them. Since clearly his actions jeopardized the party, it was fair to conclude that he was consciously acting against the party, which he also hated. This meant that he sided with the class enemy, for—as everyone knows—there are but two classes and you are either on one side or the other. On and on went the discussion, the level of acrimony increasing the whole time. Gerry went into Cliff's personal life. It seemed the entire Central Committee was aware that Slaughter felt it necessary to devote some time to his wife, who was thought to be unwell. This domestic situation proved beyond a shadow of a doubt to the Central Committee that Slaughter put his personal difficulties above the party, the working class, and the revolution.

Slaughter then spoke, confessing to every crime he had been accused of.

He apologized to the committee for not leaving his wife, but, he stated, he was just not strong enough to do that. He accepted full responsibility for the weaknesses in the Northwest and agreed that he had a petty bourgeois character. He spoke with a hollow voice, as a shattered man, and without real conviction. I got the impression that this kind of torture had become relatively routine for him; that the scene I was witnessing had been repeated over and over and over again.

Healy then stated that Slaughter's confession had been meaningless. It was just so many words. It changed nothing. Yet clearly the meeting was running out of steam. What more could be said against Slaughter? What more could Slaughter do but admit to everything he was charged with? At the last minute Healy spoke: "I do not accept in any way Slaughter's hollow, empty confessions. I should push my motion to a vote right now. But, for this meeting, I propose we table it. It will be the first point on the agenda of the next meeting of the Central Committee."

As Slaughter stumbled out the door, Healy stopped him and asked him to meet with me. It seems the International Committee needed a manifesto on some subject or other, so Slaughter was assigned to work on it with me. This broken man, labeled by the Central Committee of the Socialist Labour League as a class enemy, was assigned the critically important task of writing a basic document for the international movement.

Healy's attacks on his members did not stop at the verbal level. Perhaps because he had used up his abusive vocabulary without producing the desired results, he progressed to physical attack. I was totally unaware that such things were going on at the time and was deeply shocked when I learned about the attacks after I broke with Healy in 1974. But the evidence is incontrovertible and comes from several sources. There is the report from the group of trade unionists around Alan Thornett (who also broke with Healy in 1974). This incident involved one of the leaders of the group, Tony Richardson:

> He was called to Clapham for "discussions" in Clapham at 9:00 P.M. on Tuesday evening. The interview was . . . in Healy's flat. Alex Mitchell was present and so was Aileen Jennings. At his interview considerable physical violence was used on him. . . . These methods were only used on the most loyal members.[3]

No doubt Healy reserved such treatment for his most loyal members out of fear that those less committed to him would do the sensible thing and resign from the party on the spot and take a protest to the membership and to others in the leftist public.

I received further evidence from Robin Blick and Mark Jenkins, both members of Healy's group for many years. They had both, on separate occasions, been beaten by Healy. One of these occasions occurred in Healy's tent late at night at one of the summer camps: grim happenings behind the circus facade. More recent evidence comes from the new leadership of the Workers Revolutionary Party, Mike Banda and Cliff Slaughter, who expelled Healy in the fall of 1985. They report, "Victims of Healy's behavior came forward to tell their own appalling stories of his brutality."[4]

How is it possible that intelligent and talented people with personal strength and courage allowed themselves to be verbally and physically abused in this manner? The SLL/WRP members deeply *believed* that revolutionary events could happen in their lifetimes. Individual members might have doubted some of Healy's hyperbole about the imminence of the revolution, but on the whole, they all—I should say we all—accepted the general outlook. We all wished so much to be a part of *history*, the triumph of good over evil, as we saw it. We believed that the SLL/WRP was *the* chosen instrument to make that revolution successful, and therefore it was extremely important to us to be part of that party.

There was an additional factor. Gerry Healy had convinced us that being born to the middle class was a form of original sin. We all believed, to one degree or another, that our middle-class nature impeded our ability to recruit young workers and trade unionists, or even to carry out various party tasks. If some party project did not go too well, we were easily convinced that the fault lay in our own middle-class weaknesses. This blinded us to failures that could more legitimately be laid at Healy's door because often his projects were fantastic, the product of his unreal perspectives. Therefore, when attacked, we assumed—at least to some extent—that we were *guilty*. While most comrades no doubt felt deep inside themselves that Healy was exaggerating their crime, they accepted *some* criminal responsibility. It was better, comrades rationalized, to take one's medicine and try to do better next time than to argue over the extent of criminal responsibility or who else might also have acted criminally.

There was a definite method in Healy's madness. It was a kind of preventive medicine against faction formation or any other form of challenge to Healy's personal rule. Comrades were kept inwardly turned, separated from each other, concentrating on their own purported weaknesses and thus blind to those of the leadership. Those comrades who could not adapt to Healy's methods found themselves forced out of the party *individually* before they could organize an opposition. Should a comrade wish to form an opposition, he would soon find out that he had already confessed to sufficient "crimes" to give Healy the ammunition he needed to isolate the person. This trick worked well, as Healy had no oppositions from 1960 until 1974.

The Storm Clouds Gathered

I had much to think about by the summer of 1974. It had been a very difficult year. The figures looked good. The Workers League was selling more papers and subscriptions than it had during the previous year. Our various conferences and rallies had been numerical successes. Preliminary figures indicated that this year's summer camp would be bigger than last year's. Yet it was becoming harder to achieve our targets, and the strain on our forces had become almost unbearable.

This year we were having to do more to achieve results that were more fragile, superficial. We held youth, many times, more through basketball and parties than through politics. The cadres were getting tired. One by one people who had been with us for many years dropped away. These people did not leave for any political reason—at least this was not clear to us or to them—yet I was aware that some kind of crisis was brewing in our little group.

During the spring of 1973, in accordance with our youth activity, we decided to hold a class series on the history of the International Committee. We opened the classes to people outside our organization. This meant that our main rival for the not-very-large political space to the left of the SWP, the Spartacist League, could attend, and the class series evolved into a pretty thorough polemic with this tendency. We published the running debate in our paper. We hoped in this fashion to educate our own members as well as the youth around us. In late June I was called to England for a week of consultations. This class series was the center of the discussion.

The discussion began with an attack on me and the Workers League for opening up the class series to Spartacist. This was seen as a turn back into the "sick" radical milieu, a turn away from the fresh healthy work among the youth. Then attention was focused on a single sentence in one of the articles in the series that dealt with the relations between Healy's group and the French Trotskyist group headed by Pierre Lambert. The sentence simply asserted that when the two groups were both part of the IC, relations had been based on compromise. It neither said nor meant that these compromises were unprincipled. That didn't matter to Healy. He took the single sentence out of context and insisted that it was an attack on the honor of the WRP. It proved that the Workers League under my leadership had totally capitulated to American imperialist pressures and had developed a deep hostility to the English movement. The British would fight the Workers League to the end; it would forthwith break all relations with us.

It is hard to describe the tension, the hyperbole that mounted as the week progressed. I can remember taking a most uncomfortable trip to the

Midlands with Healy. On the way back we stopped along the road in a desolate spot with rolling hills in all directions, black soil, and nothing growing except for some brownish grass; there were no houses or habitation, just cars and lorries zipping by on the motorway. I felt the urge to run, to escape across those moors. The attacks were so intense that I actually felt physical fear, fear for my life.

The night before I was to fly back, the discussion—actually a one-way shouting match—went on until 2:30 A.M. I was sent to bed with all political relations broken. A public statement would appear in Healy's paper, the *Workers Press*. So deeply did I believe in the British movement, so committed was my whole life to building what I thought to be a revolutionary movement, that I fell asleep crying. Then at 5:30 A.M. I was awakened for one last meeting with Healy, at which I was told I would be given one last chance. I was to fight for the very life of the league against centrism within it. All the work of the past period was now in jeopardy. I had to break with the centrist elements around me in the leadership and drive the movement forward into the working class.

You can imagine the condition I was in when I returned to the United States. I immediately launched a campaign against the "centrist" layer in the organization. I went on a national branch tour devoted solely to this struggle. We brought younger activists, mainly women, into more prominent positions in the organization. At first, it seemed as if the campaign aided our ability to carry on our work in the ghetto neighborhoods and added an urgency, a sharpness, to our work. Eventually, the state of hysteria we were creating in our membership would lead to widespread demoralization, since this hysteria was not validated by comrades' own interaction with young workers in the wider world. We were nevertheless blind to the impending collapse, and we pushed on. Healy was informed of each development in this campaign, and his response was supportive. As far as we could perceive, we were doing just what his June battle with me had been aimed at getting us to do.

The losses in late 1973 and early 1974 came from the central leadership of the Workers League, people who had been with us for years. They included my former wife, Karen, Dennis Cribben, Lucy Flynn (St. John), Jeff Goldstein, and Danny Freeman. No wonder I was sick with worry. I had struggled for years in difficult times alongside these comrades, these friends, and none of them could or would explain why they were dropping out. Perhaps they did not know themselves. Still accepting the perspectives of the Workers League, they may have seen their own resignations as personal failures rather than as the result of too much frenetic activity in the service of a false perspective.

My Last Meeting in London

It was August 1974 and I was on a plane preparing to land in Cleveland, Ohio. It was a rather routine event in my life in that period. I seemed to spend as much time outside New York as I did in the city and often flew around the country for one or another purpose related to the work of our organization. This trip was part of our campaign to build the 1974 summer camp to be held in early September in Canada. The camp was to be the culmination of the political work we had been carrying out throughout the year.

I was met at the arrivals gate by Perry Iverson, our Cleveland organizer. Perry was a handsome blond young man with a clean-cut American look. We had recruited him from the campus of St. Olaf's College in Northfield, Minnesota. The town's other college, Carleton, provided much of the current leadership of our rival, the SWP.

"We just received a phone call from New York," Perry blurted out excitedly, not even taking time to say hello or ask about my trip. "You are to return immediately to New York and then catch the next plane to London. Gerry called. It's an emergency and you must go immediately."

I was dumbfounded, and I felt a deep resistance growing inside me. I was trained to accept whatever came from Britain as truth and any resistance I felt as an expression of the middle-class American chauvinist side of me. But this call did not make any sense. In two or three weeks Healy would be over here and could say to me or to the group anything he wanted. He would, no doubt, as was his usual custom, denounce me or somebody else or the group as a whole. But right now the important thing was to hold this meeting in Cleveland, because the success of the camp depended very much on the last-minute efforts in an area where we continued to have some strength. All this went on in my head. What I said to Perry was more limited.

"Well, whatever it is, it can wait a few hours. This meeting is important. I will look into the trip to England as soon as I return to New York."

"You must return right now," Perry spoke with the proxied authority of the British master. "I've gotten you reservations on a plane that leaves for New York in twenty minutes. You have your bag with you, so if we rush we can still make it."

It looked as if I was trapped, as I could not openly defy Healy. Then, with great relief, I remembered that my passport had expired. This would give me some time to get my head together, to try to figure out what in the world could require such an expensive trip so close to a planned visit. I could also proceed with the pressing work of organizing this camp, a project so fragilely put together this year that it could easily fall apart in the last weeks. I explained the circumstances to Perry and we headed off for the Cleveland meeting. The comrades appeared very tired, but their reports were upbeat. We went over the figures from each branch. I gave my little talk, but my mind kept returning to Healy and his emergency. My resentment would not go away, though I did not vocalize it. The next day I flew back to New York and headed to the Passport Office. In three days I was winging my way across the Atlantic for a meeting that would change the course of my life.

I was met at Heathrow Airport by Mike Banda, who had a grim look on his face. It was meaningful to be met by a stern Mike rather than an expansive, jovial Mike. I was clearly in disfavor and could expect a real working-over when we reached the headquarters. I still could not for the life of me figure out what my sin could possibly be this time around. I consoled myself with the thought that this was going to be a very short trip. I was scheduled to head back the next day, as the preparations for the camp were urgent. Somehow I could survive a day. And, once again, I repeated what had become my catechism, that Healy was the leader of our international tendency and had built, with his methods, an impressive movement in England. I had much to learn from the British and had to prepare myself to be receptive to whatever they had to say.

Soon, after a completely silent ride, we arrived at 186A Clapham High Street. I was rushed up to a meeting room and almost immediately the session started. Present were Gerry Healy, Mike Banda, and two or three other members of the WRP. Healy began the attack. He informed me that he had been visited by Jacques Gagnon, who represented a group of former members of the Workers League. This group claimed it had been forced out of the organization by me and by Nancy Fields, my new companion and future wife.

What was shocking about this meeting was that Healy, who had supported—more accurately, urged and promoted—the course the Workers League had followed over the past period, suddenly endorsed the position of those who were the victims of his own strategy and used their position against me and Nancy Fields. He stated that all of the past year had been a mistake. It had been a turn to community politics and a retreat from the working class. The former party members had been driven out of the party by Fields and myself and therefore we were guilty of liquidating the movement. The national conference, scheduled to be held at the time of the summer camp, was to be called off and the group of former party members was to be brought back into the organization and participate in discussions at the camp. These were my orders from Healy.[5]

Then Healy added his own bombshell. The liquidation of the movement over the past year was the work of the CIA! After all, as he saw it, the Workers League was breaking up. The CIA would like to see the league break up. Therefore, the CIA must be at work. The task, therefore, was to discover the CIA agent in the league leadership. Fields was relatively new to the leadership, had been closely associated over the whole past year with the drive into the youth and was directly involved in the forced marches that had led to people leaving the organization. Fields was therefore Healy's number one nominee for CIA agent. The fact that Fields was personally associated with me fitted his conspiracy theory well. It seems that I myself had fallen under the influence of the CIA. My task, should I accept it, was simply to reverse political course, admit to being solely at fault for the wrong orientation and the liquidation of the movement, and then attack my companion as a CIA agent and break with her.

At this point in the proceedings, Jacques was brought into the meeting to repeat what he had privately reported to Healy and others. Of course, neither Jacques nor any of his collaborators had mentioned anything about the CIA. He became choked up, started to cry, then embraced me and declared his deep personal devotion to me. I stammered my disagreement about the CIA charge but expressed my willingness to carry out the reversal that Healy had ordered: I was well trained. So ended the most bizarre trip I had ever taken to England. I returned to the United States the next morning rather shell-shocked.

The summer camp was less than a week away. I had no time to sort out the meaning of the new turn that was being forced upon us by Healy. Most important, I was deeply disturbed over Healy's accusation that Nancy Fields was a CIA agent. I knew this matter was not likely to be dropped. Healy had become increasingly concerned with "security," and this concern had already added a kind of conspiratorial atmosphere to our movements. After giving a report of the London meeting to the Political Committee, I headed off to Canada with two other comrades to set up the camp.

The Fateful Canadian Camp

Our camp was held in the Laurentian Mountains about sixty miles north of Montreal near the town of St. Agathe. In the middle of the summer it was a children's camp serving Montreal's Jewish community. There was both a boys' and a girls' camp, situated on opposite sides of a pretty little private lake surrounded by pine woods. The camp had fallen on hard times, as parents were less inclined to send their children to camp, and when they did, they preferred specialized facilities such as computer camps, baseball camps, and music camps. Now the camp filled only one side of the lake, so the boys and girls were in a little closer proximity to each other.

The rafters in the dining room had been decorated by generations of Montreal's Jewish youth—"Rachel loves Daniel," "Ruth + Michael"—graffiti that seemed so innocent, so out of keeping with the atmosphere we generated at our camps. The children of a relatively privileged layer of Montreal's English-speaking population seemed to have matters other than world crises on their minds.

The previous year we had held our first camp at this same location; in prior years we had sent large contingents to camps in England.[6] It had been quite eventful. I remember that early on I was working in the kitchen while other comrades were working in the dining room. We were setting things up and listening to music on a little portable radio while we worked. Suddenly I began hearing the comrades from the dining room speaking clearly over the radio. It didn't take me long to figure out that the dining room must be bugged. We instituted a search and found an object about the size of a cigar box on top of one of the rafters. It contained a microphone, a transmitter, and batteries. It was American-made and we speculated it was placed there by the FBI in collaboration with the RCMP (Royal Canadian Mounted Police). Someone put it there, and that someone was no doubt a government agent. We searched the whole camp and discovered another one in a large barn we used for lectures and dances. We did not know much about electronics, but it certainly appeared to be a simple device with a very limited radio range. Some backup unit had to be receiving the signal and recording it on tape. Therefore we assumed some agents were hidden in the dense woods or perhaps posing as fishermen down the road.

You can imagine the atmosphere these discoveries created at the camp. We were convinced that the crisis was deepening and that our group would have a critical leadership role to play in the next period. It appeared that certain governments agreed with our perspective, at least to the point of keeping a close eye on us!

The 1973 camp ended as dramatically as it had opened. On the last evening of the camp, a very foggy one, seven police cars pulled up at the front gate. Included in this muster were the provincial police, the RCMP, and some unidentified Americans. They demanded the right to enter the property. No doubt, after the removal of their listening devices, they expected to find weapons and military training going on. Our resourceful comrades calmly informed them that the camp was private property, that we had a binding lease to it, and that they had no legal right to enter it. We produced the owner, who lived across the lake, and the lease. After consulting among themselves, and checking in by radios with various headquarters, they gave up the effort and dispersed.

Then we made the decision to move out as many people as we could in case they returned with some kind of court order. While we were doing nothing illegal, we had a number of guests there from different countries and saw no point in giving the police information on them or anyone else attending our camp. We packed with amazing speed, and a string of cars started to depart after midnight in dense fog, heading back across the country to Detroit, Chicago, Los Angeles, San Francisco, Minneapolis, St. Louis, and New York. The somewhat melodramatic events of the 1973 summer camp influenced, in their own way, the atmosphere in the 1974 camp, held at the same location the following year. The melodrama of the 1974 camp, although artificially generated, would prove to be much more destructive.

Gerry Healy was not present when the camp opened in the same deceptively peaceful Canadian surroundings. He sent Cliff Slaughter on ahead to check out whether it was possible for Healy to attend the camp without risking his life. Slaughter was to call Healy, and then the Political Committee of the WRP would decide whether to chance it and send the master. Such was the hysterical atmosphere Healy already had begun to whip up.

In 1974 our summer camp was bigger than it had been the previous year, and we had a harder time running it. The preceding year we had lost some of our most experienced comrades, and this weakened the camp leadership. At least as important was a change in the mood of the youth themselves. They reflected the process of depoliticalization, which was already under way in the black and Puerto Rican communities. Therefore, the first few days of the camp were difficult, and we had to concentrate on camp rules and discipline. The camp was just about under control and the educational work was beginning to develop when Gerry Healy arrived on the scene. It appeared that Slaughter's phone calls encouraged the WRP to believe that Healy would be relatively safe in Canada.

Cliff Slaughter had gone to the airport to pick him up. I can clearly recall Gerry Healy's arrival at the camp. He came walking up the small path leading to our little cabin. His beady eyes missed nothing. He wore shapeless dark-colored pants with a white shirt and a pair of old-fashioned suspenders holding up the pants. Droplets of sweat were on his face; he wore no jacket and his blue tie was loose around his neck.

On his left side walked Cliff, a slender man with receding brown hair, a rather large British nose, wearing brown plastic eyeglasses and carrying Healy's jacket in one hand and Healy's worn black briefcase with papers sticking out in the other hand. Aileen Jennings was on Healy's right. In contrast to Healy and Cliff, Aileen was crisply dressed in a blue suit with a white blouse. Her eyes never left Healy.

My companion, Nancy, beside me in the doorway, was clearly nervous, like a prospective bride meeting the new in-laws for the first time. We had been together only a year, and although she had already met Healy, she knew this meeting was going to be different. Suddenly our small gray mutt, Huey, darted between our legs and headed straight for Healy's left leg, barking with maddened abandon. We had never seen him act this way, and I rushed to pull him off. Healy was laughing hysterically.

"That's the American middle-class hippies for you," he managed to mutter between guffaws. "They all have dogs!" Aileen smiled at Healy. Cliff ignored the scene.

I said nothing, as I had learned it was more than useless to argue a point with Gerry. It could be dangerous. I had noticed a number of dogs in working-class homes and I did not take kindly to the hippie charge. Healy seemed to think that a serious revolutionary would not have time to feed an animal or take it for walks.

I glanced at Nancy, and I could sense she felt it was a personal attack on her and was having a hard time suppressing her reaction. Healy was clearly pleased with the element of strain he had created within minutes of his arrival. Huey, who had entered my life the previous year along with Nancy, had been named after Huey P. Newton and had, Nancy claimed, not missed a peace march since his birth in 1968 during the Peace and Freedom Party Convention. I was to learn very soon that Huey understood the situation we faced much better than either of us.

"We need to talk, my boy," Healy declared as he entered the cabin. "Is this place secure?"

"Well, I suspect it is. We haven't noticed anything out of the ordinary."

"Noticed? You don't notice bugs. Has it been swept?"

"We don't have any equipment like that."

Healy chuckled. "Still a game with you, my boy. You don't take things seriously yet, do you? Still campus politics. Why don't we go outside some place . . . in the shade? Leave her here." He was positively glaring at Nancy.

The four of us strolled past the dining hall, where most of the camp was assembled attending a lecture on the Russian Revolution, toward a small shaded knoll overlooking the lake and most of the camp facilities. The summer of 1974 had been a hot one and the warmth could still be felt in September. I was happy that Healy was finally silent and that his two acolytes had fallen in with him. I could think, could try to prepare myself for the grilling ahead of me. What did Healy want to discuss with me? His hostility toward Nancy suggested the worst. I was tired, not so much physically as emotionally, in spirit. I could sense that the rest of the comrades also felt tired and were carrying out their tasks more out of routine and duty than conviction.

My deep ruminations contrasted with the scene around us. It was a peaceful sight of rolling hills covered with fir trees, a pretty lake with rowboats tied to a small dock, while behind us lay the green lawn and buildings of the camp. A fence separated the camp property from a small tarred road that led, eventually, to Montreal and civilization. I could see two of our guards standing by the gate to the camp while two others slowly walked along the property's periphery. At the far end of the lake, where it abutted the road for a short stretch, a lone fisherman was casting in the water.

"RCMP or FBI? What do you think?" Healy had spotted the fisherman.

"I should think it's RCMP. That's the way they work. Of course they share information."

Healy smiled approvingly. I had finally said the right thing. Then his face turned grave. "Cliff, hand me my notes there in my briefcase. It's all here, my boy. The full story. I asked Comrade Jacques to prepare a full report on Nancy and, with Comrade Karen's help, we have it all here. (He slapped his notebook.) CIA, my boy! Just as I suspected. You can't hide anything from me. It is out of my hands now, Tim. There is nothing I can do for you. I must, I simply must place these facts before the International Committee. It will be up to them to act. But because of our long association I wanted you to know ahead of time. You can prepare your own report. This is the most serious security breech in the history of our international movement! Now get me out of here! This place is not safe!" Without waiting for me to say a word, he stomped past me toward his car, with Cliff and Aileen almost running to keep up with him. Healy and Jennings left immediately for a motel in the nearby town of St. Agathe.

The next day was quiet and the camp program proceeded without major incident. All appeared the same, but everything was swiftly changing. Healy barely talked to me, yet his presence was everywhere. I could see him slowly walking around the camp grounds with his little entourage, talking to little knots of comrades. Fred Mazelis had joined Cliff and Aileen, following the Great Man about the place. Introducing Healy to the troops and hanging on his words of wisdom had been my role. Reliable Fred had been my assistant, the second in command all those years. His very loyalty, his unquestioning support for whatever I proposed, used to disturb me. What else did I expect? I had trained him that way just as Healy had trained me. Fred was my friend. Friend? Were any of us really friends?

When Nancy returned from her rounds, I was standing on the porch of the cabin, watching one of the little knots of people respectfully listening as Healy talked in an animated way. She was in charge of camp organization and had just checked out the kitchen and the guards. Her tanned face was drained, wrinkled, and she looked ten years older than her thirty years. As I recall, our conversation went something like this:

"It's terrible, Tim, terrible. They all know; the whole camp knows. I can feel it. I'm supposed to be directing the guards but they're guarding me. Healy is behind this. When I was by the front gate I reached out to check the lock of the chain and a comrade actually lunged for me. I guess he thought I was going to run away. Now that's not a bad idea. I want to get out of here, Tim. It's spooky. I feel like I'm a captive."

She noticed the little scene on the camp green I had been watching.

"So that's it. Fred is taking over. Healy is preparing the succession already. Let's get out of here, Tim. While we can!"

"Nancy, I know how you feel. . . ."

"You don't know; you don't know at all. They still accept you. I'm the one they're hounding."

"I know, I know, but don't exaggerate. It won't help. It's all a game. Healy's just using you to test me, to test my loyalty to the movement. He does this kind of thing all the time. We need to reassure him, to let him know that we're party people. It's my whole life, Nancy, my whole life. Today's Thursday and Saturday night he flies back to England. Sunday we break camp and after that we'll take a few days off to sort things out. All we've got to do is survive two more days. That's all."

"That's all? You're wrong this time. You're damn wrong! I sense it. Something's changed. It's more than a game. He's flipped or something. You're blind where Healy's concerned. You know I'm loyal. You know how hard I work. He goes prancing around the camp chatting with comrades who held back, who sabotaged this camp. I fought a lot of those people so that we could have this camp. Now they're bending his ear about me, happy to get back at me. That's what's going on. You know the truth, Tim."

"Of course, I know. We've got to make him understand. That means we've got to take a bit from him. It's no good getting in a shouting match with Healy. That's just the way to ruin everything. We've got to hold our tongues and bide our time. Try to reason with him."

Nancy began shivering, even though it was another hot day. She pulled me into the cabin with her. She was crying, clinging to me, pressing her head on my shoulder. I stroked her long brown hair. Suddenly she stiffened and pulled herself away from me.

"Where are you, Tim? Where do you stand? Are you going to dump me to please Healy? Is that what you're planning? Karen's behind this. I'm all alone. I can see that now. All alone! Alone."

She ran into the bedroom of the cabin and locked the door. I did not know what to do. I stood there for a moment. Why didn't I bang on that bedroom door, take her in my arms, give her the support she needed? Something inside me held me back. I knew I was relieved when that door closed, when I had an excuse to get away from her. It was Healy! He was there inside me. Not just the man but the movement, my life.

As all this politicking was going on, we were also trying to run a camp of more than three hundred not particularly disciplined or even politically interested young people who were only days out of some of the worst neighborhoods in the United States. Healy decided to make a theoretical contribution to the camp. Therefore we gathered all these youth together in the dining hall for a series of lectures on philosophy. Healy had become increasingly interested in dialectics, and Lenin's *Philosophical Notebooks* was required reading now for all serious members. As Healy's movement became more and more out of touch with reality, his philosophical doctrine became more and more abstract. His lectures at the camp centered on contradiction, the unity of opposites, and such matters. He based his remarks on Hegel, whom he obviously had read only in the short excerpts Lenin quoted. He scribbled all over a blackboard and discovered opposites within opposites within opposites.

You can imagine the response to such a lecture from the youth out of Bedford-Stuyvesant, particularly as the room heated up and the outdoors seemed so appealing. It was not possible to keep order in the hall. Healy then came up with the brilliant suggestion of letting all who were uninterested in the lecture leave. Three-quarters of the audience walked out. With all the comrades inside and all the youth outside it was inevitable that before long fights would break out on the lawn. We had to give up the lecture to reinforce order. Needless to say, I was held personally responsible for the whole situation. This was further evidence of my liquidationism and my petty bourgeois hatred of the working class.

A Central Committee meeting was called for midnight on Saturday, when the camp would be settled down. The sky was pitch black and the camp eerily quiet as almost forty people gathered in the old dining hall. Healy, ignoring proper procedure—this was, after all, a meeting of the Workers League's Central Committee, I was still party secretary, and Healy was just an international guest—called the meeting to order.

"Well, comrades, let's hear it. I have talked to many of you individually and now is your chance to speak out. I want to hear it all. I want to know what has been going on at this camp and what happened in preparing this camp. Speak up, speak up."

Comrade after comrade spoke criticizing Nancy and myself. No complaint was too minor to be left out, no feeling too petty to express. All the problems, the strain, the difficulties in building a camp attended by working-class youth were blamed on our poor leadership. Over and over again I heard the same litany: the "objective situation" could not be more promising and the "world crisis" had gotten even deeper, yet results were poorer and the quality of our campers lower than in previous years. Clearly, comrade after comrade repeated, the problem lay with the failure of our leadership.

Cliff decided that his moment had come to raise the theoretical level of the discussion:

"We have here," he pontificated, "a clear example of the effects of the American pragmatic method. Pragmatists can understand only surface phenomena. On the surface the United States appears to be calm, even conservative. Yet if you use the dialectical method to probe beneath the surface, you will discover the depth of the capitalist crisis. It is like an earthquake in preparation. Only with this method can you steer a revolutionary course and train a new generation of militants."

"Good, Cliff, good. That is exactly what I was proving in my lecture, which Tim sabotaged. But let's get on with it. Speak up comrades, speak up!" He was sitting there with his white shirt open, sleeves rolled up, suspenders holding up his blue pants, grinning in delight, and rubbing his hands together. The man was in his element. He was having fun. "It's Christmas! Let's hear it all!"

Nancy and I just sat there and took it. What else could we do? We knew from experience that to protest, to seek to deflect the criticism, would only make matters worse, would only intensify the pressures on us. We were all seated there in a circle with the graffiti-covered old beams above us, and I could look each comrade in the eyes as he or she denounced us. These people had been my friends. I had recruited most of them personally. It was hard to believe they all could turn on me. Here and there was a flicker of recognition, a turning away of eyes, which suggested that an old friend felt a bit uncomfortable as part of the lynch mob.

Comrades began to repeat themselves. They were running out of steam, out of gossip, out of complaints. Healy sensed this loss in momentum in the discussion and suddenly stood up, right in the middle of a rather long, particularly vicious, speech from Uhli, a young German woman comrade.

"Excuse me, comrade, excuse me. But we cannot get to the root of this problem this way. I understand how deeply comrades feel, how they resent having been betrayed. But we must probe this matter even deeper.

"Let me ask a simple question. Comrades, put yourselves in the enemy's shoes. Suppose you are sitting in a plush office in Langley, Virginia, at CIA headquarters. You want to see this movement destroyed, for you fear what will happen when the American working class finally has true revolutionary leadership. What is it that you would like to have happen within this movement?

"Yes, that's right! Exactly, precisely what has been happening! Isn't that curious now? Isn't that curious?" Healy was back in stride.

"I beg the comrades' indulgence, but we have a comrade here tonight who can shed some light on this matter." He was starring directly at Karen. All eyes followed Healy's and were riveted on her. I couldn't, just couldn't glance at Nancy, but I could sense her reaction next to me.

"Now let's review the facts," Healy spoke softly before his mesmerized audience. "I arrived at this camp and immediately was made aware of the crisis of the movement. Old-time comrades had left, the group was not making gains commensurate with the opportunities in the objective situation, and this camp was on the brink of disaster. That is fact number one.

"You will remember that last year the police agencies had the place bugged. They also tried to raid the camp. They were aware of our presence and they feared we might be successful in our work. This year there is no sign of them. Perhaps they have no need for *external* surveillance. That is fact number two.

"I was aware that we had a new person in the leadership, Comrade Nancy. I knew nothing of Comrade Nancy except that she was an active comrade and that she was Comrade Tim's companion. It struck me as interesting that the arrival of this comrade into the top party leadership coincided with the crisis in the party. That is fact number three.

"My curiosity was piqued. I decided to probe the matter a little bit with Comrade Tim. Tim is an old comrade of mine. We have known each other for many years. Yet there is no secret about the fact that I have had to be critical of Tim in the past. I sometimes feel he approaches things in an American way rather than an international one. Revolution is an idea, a thought, but never, never a *reality*." Healy's voice was beginning to rise; the pace was quickening. "I simply asked Comrade Tim if he had vetted Nancy. It was a simple question. In a serious revolutionary organization no one is allowed to enter the top leadership without a vetting. We must know who we are. We must know.

"I was astounded to discover that there had been no such vetting. Comrade Nancy was permitted access to our vital international correspondence, to information on our work all over the world. Comrade Nancy was allowed to travel to all branches, and from what we heard tonight, boss around the comrades, old comrades, loyal comrades. But no questions were asked of Comrade Nancy. That is fact number four!"

Tension was mounting in the hall as all eyes shifted from Karen to Nancy and me. The comrades had been up since 6 A.M. or earlier, were clearly bleary-eyed, dazed, and caught up in the isolated world of the camp with its tensions, guards, and continuous discussion of the outside world in terms ever more stark and unreal. An atmosphere of complete hysteria dominated the meeting.

"I was forced to do a bit of vetting myself." Once again Healy had assumed the tone of calm reasonableness. "Comrade Tim informed me that Comrade Karen, his former companion. . . . No, no comrades, we do not condemn Comrade Tim for his personal life. We are revolutionists, not moralists. I am just stating the facts as I discovered them. Comrade Karen, a comrade we all know well, is one of the comrades who has left us over this past year. It was Comrade Karen who had recruited Comrade Nancy to the party. I thought I would contact her to get a bit of background on Nancy. What I learned confirmed my worst suspicions! I have asked Comrade Karen to tell us the story in her own words. Tell us, Karen, tell us about Nancy's uncle!"

"Nancy and I were roommates at college." Karen spoke so low it was difficult to understand all of her words. She looked at no one, speaking with her head down and her hands clenched together in her lap. "We knew each other extremely well. She told me about her working-class family in Milwaukee. We were both radicals then. I was around the party while Nancy was close to SDS, and she was quite proud of her proletarian credentials. I asked her how she could afford to go to college. It was then that she mentioned her uncle.

"This uncle and aunt had always wanted a daughter, but they were unable to have children. He was the one member of her mother's family who had gone to college and done well for himself. He had recently retired from some highly placed government job and had sort of adopted Nancy. He was helping to send her to school."

"Did she tell you anything more about her uncle? Did she say what kind of work he did for the government?"

"Well, she said in an offhand manner, 'Oh, you know. He's CIA or something.' But I didn't take her seriously at the time. In those days we used to refer to our conservative parents that way, 'My father's a capitalist pig!' That sort of thing. But then I met him.

"It was during spring vacation and Nancy invited me to go with her to her uncle's home in the country. I remember well his study lined with beautiful leather-bound books from floor to ceiling. On the wall behind his large mahogany desk was a plaque. It had the CIA emblem on it and it marked his twenty years' of service with the CIA and its predecessor, the OSS!"

Healy turned toward Nancy and walked over to her, his two fists clenched and his belly almost touching her face. "Is it true?"

"Of course it's true. I never hid it from anybody." Her face was swollen from tears, from anger. "Tell the rest of it, Karen! Tell it all! We had a fight right there in that room, didn't we, Karen? You witnessed it. I denounced him for the scum he was. I let him know I was in SDS and was fighting everything he stood for. I told him I would not take another dirty penny from him. Didn't I, Karen? Didn't I?"

"You don't need to answer her, Karen. This is not a personal matter. Yes, Nancy, I believe you. I believe you did just that. I would have done the same if I were in your shoes. Karen knew too much. The time had come to activate you on the left. You had to clear up this indiscretion of yours. Yes, good acting, Nancy."

At this point Nancy asked permission to go to the ladies' room. Healy insisted that she be accompanied by two guards. Nancy told me later that one of the guards wanted to enter the booth with her, but she was finally allowed a minute or two of solitude.

"These are facts, comrades, facts," Healy proceeded during Nancy's absence. "We are in revolutionary times, comrades, revolutionary times. As the crisis gets deeper, the importance of leadership, of the revolutionary party, becomes all the more critical. There can be no victory without that leadership. Our enemies know this and they are stepping up their attacks upon us—externally and internally. We can see this plainly in this case. It is happening right now. The future of humanity therefore depends upon us and how we respond to this threat. Security of the revolutionary movement has become key to the future of humanity.

"We have here a proven CIA connection. We have here proof of negligence, of a rotten liberal [he spit out the word] attitude on the part of Comrade Tim. Yes, he has been turned. He has permitted personal relations to blind him to revolutionary responsibilities. His refusal to vet Nancy is unforgivable. He has threatened the security of our world movement. This cannot be tolerated."

Healy, with his face getting ever redder and in an extreme emotional state, stood in the center of the circle, directly facing me. Finally, it was just too much for me. I stood up.

"I . . . I disagree with the entire proceedings," I stammered.

Healy rushed up to me and shook his fists within an inch of my face shouting: "I will destroy you." I became faint but I stood there. I somehow had distanced myself from the scene and felt as if I were in another world very far away, peering in on the meeting with some kind of long-distance telescope, watching myself.

"I will entertain a motion," it was Healy's voice again, "to suspend Miss Nancy Fields from party membership pending a full investigation by a control commission of her CIA connection and to remove Tim Wohlforth as party secretary due to his failure to follow proper security procedures and therefore endangering the world movement."

"So moved." It was Mazelis, my old friend and comrade. "All in favor raise your hands." The hands went up, all of them. All eyes were upon Nancy and me. Then Nancy slowly raised her own hand. My hand followed. I do not know why. It just went up in the air. It was 2 A.M. and the meeting was over. We helped each other leave the hall, as our legs were wobbly, and in a dreamlike state we managed the short distance from the dining hall to our little cabin. Huey was cowering in the corner. He knew.

Once back in the cabin we knew we did not agree with what we had just voted for. Cliff Slaughter was there with us, and we talked with him until the light of dawn began to break over the camp. Cliff made it clear that not for a moment did he think that Nancy was a CIA agent. He urged, however, that we recognize the authority of the party and go along with the proceedings in the higher interests of the party. He gave us the lecture he no doubt had given to himself hundreds of times when his intelligence told him he was being falsely, or at least exaggeratedly, accused by Healy.

Nancy and I at this point just wanted to get out of the place. Somehow we went through the motions of closing down the camp and headed back to New York City on Monday. Nancy, who had been on the full-time staff of the WL, started job hunting. I dutifully went to work at party headquarters, having been moved out of the national office area. I tried to write material for the paper, but everything came out hollow. I found I was brooding over and over the events from the August meeting in London through the camp. I was paralyzed because I no longer *believed*. One day I just didn't show up at the party headquarters. I sent instead a letter of resignation.

That time in the fall and winter of 1974 was the hardest period in my life. Nancy and I were almost penniless. We had worked, as had all the comrades on the party payroll, for almost nothing. The car we used was a party car. We had been working that way for years, so we had no job history. Since I had learned something about printing by setting up the *Bulletin*, I was applying for a job in printing production. Luckily I got the job, and soon thereafter Nancy found clerical work with a union. Thus enough money came in for us to survive.

It was the isolation that was the worst part of it. We had been so dedicated, so intensely involved in our cadre-oriented political life that we had lost any friends we had outside the movement and not a soul in the organization would talk to us now. Here we were in a city of eight million people and we had no one. The phone literally did not ring for weeks.

Then one night the phone actually rang in our Brooklyn apartment. I ran to pick it up.

"That you Tim? Aileen here. Gerry wants to talk with you."

"Tim. This is Gerry. I want you to do something for me personally. You must know how I feel about you, but, my boy, politics is a very hard business. I want you on the platform for the commemoration meeting of the *Bulletin* this month."

I felt fear inside me—caution. Well, I thought quickly, damn, I would go there and say what I wanted.

"OK, Gerry. I will prepare a short presentation on the paper's history, its early days."

"Oh, we don't want you to speak; just to sit there and show solidarity so our enemies don't take advantage of your leaving."

"No thanks, Gerry." I hung up. That was my last conversation with the man.

A couple of weeks later the doorbell rang and when I opened the door, there stood three of the larger members of the Workers League. They wanted me to sign over some papers, since the corporation that owned the party's equipment was in my name. It was just too much for me to take. Here were some of my former comrades, my former friends, and all they cared about were these papers. I shut the door in their faces.

Notes

1. Workers Socialist League, *The Battle for Trotskyism* (London: Golrose, 1979), p. 91.
2. *Bulletin* no. 7 (London, December 1974), p. 2.
3. Workers Socialist League, *The Battle for Trotskyism*, p. 94.
4. *The News Line* (London, October 30, 1985).
5. For an account of these events, written within months of their occurrence, see *Intercontinental Press* (New York, February 24, 1975; March 3, 1975; March 10, 1975; March 17, 1975).
6. *Bulletin* (New York, September 17, 1983), pp. 8, 9.

11

The Prodigal Son

THE PRODIGAL SON RETURNS

There were a number of reasons that Nancy and I, during the fall and winter of 1974–1975, began to think about returning to the Socialist Workers Party. Although we had been deeply hurt by Healy, we were still committed to socialist ideas. We still lived and breathed politics, devoting most of our waking hours to mulling over the experience we had passed through, trying to understand this experience with the same set of ideas we had held in Healy's movement. We were convinced that we were the victims of a combination of undemocratic practices and sectarian politics. We saw this as a violation of the basic tenets of Trotskyism, which were democratic and nonsectarian. We were still searching for the *true* Trotskyism.

Nancy and I finally completed our lengthy document on the break with Healy, and we sent it to all the leftist organizations and publications. Our only response came from the SWP, which at first wished to verify its authenticity. Then in February 1975, Joe Hansen started publishing our statement in *Intercontinental Press* along with his own friendly, but somewhat factional, comments. We decided to contact the Socialist Workers Party to thank them for publishing our document and to suggest discussions. Soon we were on the dinner circuit, a very pleasant recruitment process that, I am afraid, ends when you join. It started with a dinner at Joe and Reba Hansen's apartment, chicken-wing curry. Jack Barnes, the new National Secretary, and his companion at the time, Mary Alice Waters, were also present. It was a pleasant affair and we had a good discussion covering the points of our agreement and disagreement with the party. Then came a dinner with George Novack and his wife of thirty or so years, Evelyn Reed. This was a more informal and relaxed affair. All in all we were impressed by the objective and friendly way we were being welcomed back into the fold considering the many bitter incidents and exaggerated polemics that had occurred over the past ten years.

Of course we realized that our return to the SWP was very useful to the party and its international allies. It was a blow against Healy, who was, without a doubt, the most intransigent foe of the SWP and USec. Our return also helped give the SWP the aura of an organization open to regroupment at a time when there was still quite a bit of ferment on the left. It was hoped—and this hope was not in vain—that our recruitment would encourage others on the Trotskyist left to join the party.

My break with the Workers League combined with my decision to rejoin the Socialist Workers Party confused my watchers within the FBI. The New York office of the FBI had read the attacks on me that appeared in the press of the Workers League and accepted them at face value. They therefore recommended that I be removed from the ADEX. Washington protested, pointing out that the SWP supported me, which meant that I remained a dangerous "subversive." Washington prevailed and I remained on the ADEX. A document I received, dated July 21, 1976, ends: "Subject's activities continue to warrant further investigation."

Nancy and I were soon in the thick of party life. I was assigned to the Lower East Side branch and Nancy joined the Brooklyn branch. The Lower East Side branch was led by Linda Jenness, a national party leader. I guess they felt they needed to put me in a branch with a strong party loyalist in case I caused any trouble. Actually I was most cooperative and began my second term of SWP membership with optimism and a willingness to learn what I could from this party that had changed so much since my previous tenure. It was almost an entirely new party, and only a few faces survived from the past. I was happy to see Dick Garza, whom we ran the following fall for some local elective office, in our branch.

The mid-1970s was a period of change, of flux for the SWP. The leadership and membership had been forced to recognize that the "new radicalization," as they had called it, had come to an end. The party needed a new orientation, and the leadership decided to return to a perspective closer to the one it originally had held before the student radicalization: the building of a "proletarian party." The leadership had written a resolution that reasserted the central importance of the working class and that spoke (in a more restrained tone than I used to!) of the capitalist crisis. The ranks of the party were then asked to make a "turn" into the working class. The exact nature of this turn, which was continuously talked about by all the members, was not defined. The SWP was preparing to take the kinds of steps and develop the kind of orientation that the rest of the Left, including the Workers League, had taken about five years earlier. Unfortunately, the party leadership thought it was embarking on an uncharted course and thus was not able to learn much from the experience of those who had "turned" before them.

We did our very best, of course, to convince them to turn the way we in the Workers League had turned. We were then very strong partisans of our community-oriented work and had yet to make a serious critique of its weaknesses. It is just possible that our discussions made some impact on the leadership, for the first stage of the SWP's turn to the workers resembled in many respects our earlier experiences. Such a development certainly helped to make us feel at home in the party, and to have some hope that we could make a contribution to it.

The party took two steps to implement the turn. First it divided its branches into smaller branches oriented toward specific minority communities. The SWP had a tradition of having gargantuan branches, many with over one hundred members, that had little local bureaucracies and structures. Of course they did not get down to the branch of a half-dozen or so members that was common in the Workers League and that was similar to the cells in European Communist-style parties. Branches of twenty or thirty members were a radical departure for them. Next they began to carry out serious and largely successful subscription work with the *Militant* newspaper in these neighborhoods. Needless to say, Nancy was a great help and sold a lot of subscriptions.

Yet the party was a bit at a loss about what else to do in these neighborhoods. It was not about to conduct the kind of youth work we had been doing, and we did not press this point. The SWP's own antiracist work had petered out after a probusing march in Boston. It did run some local election campaigns, and these at least provided an opportunity for some street meetings in the community. But on the whole, the advocates of the turn had no appetite or strategy to develop lasting roots in black and Puerto Rican neighborhoods.

I do want to say a word about SWP election campaigns. I participated in one of the best, the Garza campaign in the Lower East Side, while Nancy campaigned for Pat Wright, a black comrade, in Brooklyn. We both were also part of the national presidential campaign in 1976. The SWP was very skilled at running effective petition campaigns to get candidates on the ballot. Its members put in hundreds of hours each, collecting signatures and then carrying through with all the paperwork required to get ballot status. The problem was that as soon as a candidate made it onto the ballot, the SWP *stopped* campaigning. At best one or two street meetings were held. The candidate might get an opportunity to speak at a union or a college. Then a banquet was held for the candidate, which was attended largely by party members. And that was about it.

The party never *campaigned* in the sense of going door-to-door, shaking hands, giving out literature, and trying to actually convince people to vote for its candidates. I was convinced then and am convinced now that concentrated campaigning, possibly for a lesser office such as in the state assembly, could lead to a victory here or there. Then, a party member in a state legislature or city council could do a very good job propagating the party's political views. Further, the process of campaigning in this intensive fashion, if combined with work on housing, schools, and other neighborhood projects, could yield a political base in communities and lead to serious recruitment of working-class people. The SWP, however, viewed elections as a way of gaining a little publicity and showing the world we were opposed to the Democratic Party.

In August 1976, Nancy and I went, full of enthusiasm, to the SWP convention in Oberlin, Ohio. I must say life for me had taken on a circular pattern of returning to the past. Not only had I rejoined a party I had definitively broken with ten years earlier but now that party was holding a convention at the college I had attended over twenty years earlier, at the exact spot where I had first become converted to socialism. The convention elected me a full member of the National Committee. I had become a symbol of the party's broadness, a token to encourage others to join or return to the fold.

Near the end of the convention Jack Barnes had a special meeting with Nancy and me. Jack can be a very persuasive fellow, especially when his audience is only one or two people. He insisted that we join the SWP's full-time staff in New York. Such a move, he explained, would permit me to function on the party's Political Committee and allow both of us to play a national role and become more "integrated" into the party. It may be difficult for someone who has not been caught up in Marxist politics to understand what a temptation it is to become a full-timer. It is not a matter of money or privilege. In fact it almost always means a great financial sacrifice for the person involved. For a true political person, the opportunity to devote oneself fully to politics is a great privilege in itself, an extremely enjoyable way to spend one's life. Bureaucracies in small parties are sustained by offering the privilege of just such full-time politicking rather than any kind of material privilege.

Nancy and I insisted on a day to think over the proposition. We then spent a number of hours debating its pros and cons. We were far from being politically fresh and had just passed through an extremely difficult experience with Healy. We had, with great difficulty, patched together our lives and developed modest careers that at least supported us. We honestly admitted to wanting a private life as well as a political life. No one would easily sway us with "Bolshevization" sloganeering. We now believed the best socialists were those who had some life outside of the party and, thus, some connection with reality. But the lure of full-time politics was too much. We had to give it another chance.

THE NEW SOCIALIST WORKERS PARTY

We went to work that fall at the West Street offices of the SWP, beside the West Side Highway and within convenient walking distance of Greenwich Village. The contrast with the old office at 116 University Place could not have been greater. A lot of money and effort had been put into West Street. It was not much on the outside, but inside the place was modern, had flourescent lighting everywhere, as well as tiled floors: It was the very model of an efficient office complex. The place was quite large: The ground floor housed a web press and other equipment; there were second and third floors of offices and meeting rooms. The top floor was a very pleasant lunchroom that opened on to the roof, where on pleasant days one could relax in the fresh air and sunshine.

Almost *one hundred* comrades worked at West Street when we first started there! What a contrast from life at 116 University Place with its staff of under a dozen! Success had definitely come to the SWP. It was a very different party than the one I had known. Perhaps this was more apparent to me than to most members precisely because I had been on the outside during the critical years of its growth and transformation. This new SWP illustrated very clearly the way in which the 1960s radicalization had transformed the entire Left in this country and in many other countries.

It can be useful to look at some statistics of SWP membership. There are several very interesting matters revealed in the chart on page 253.[1] Party membership in 1976 was at an all-time high, reaching 1,610, higher even than at the 1938 founding convention, held in the midst of the depression. Yet between 1954 and 1970 membership stayed relatively stable, between 400 and 500. The low point was actually reached in 1966, when membership dropped to 385, several years *after* the passing of the real isolation of the party in the 1950s. Behind this stagnation in total membership, a dynamic process was at work. A series of splits—with Bert Cochran, Marcy, Robertson, our group, Fox, Fraser, Swabeck—and a numerically

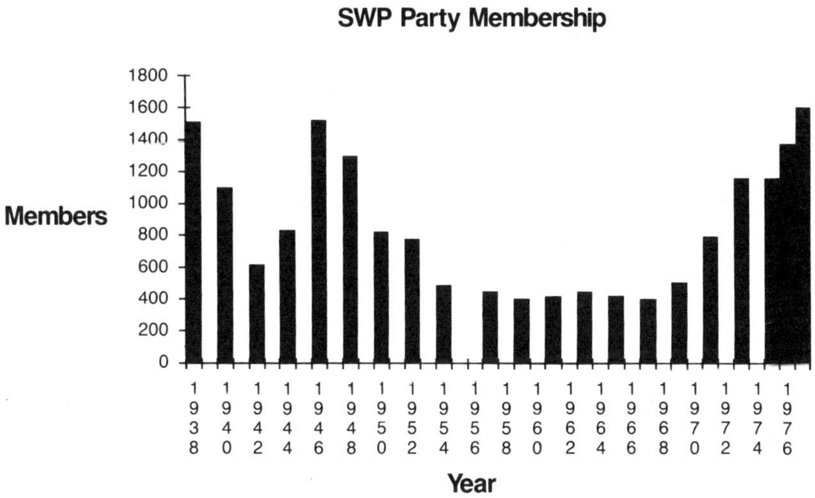

greater draining of old cadre through death and just plain tiredness resulted in the loss of hundreds of comrades. At the same time, recruitment proceeded at a slow but steady rate; nearly all our new members were students from the Young Socialist Alliance. Thus the relatively stable membership figures actually masked the loss of most of the old cadre of the SWP, the product of the struggles of the 1930s and 1940s.

Real growth in SWP membership began in 1970, after the departure of the older comrades. Then between 1971 and 1976, *when the antiwar work and the student upsurge were almost over*, the SWP more than doubled its membership. The party recruited in much the same manner as the Workers League, in a kind of mop-up operation after the 1960s radicalization. A section of those whose thinking was transformed by the events of that period chose the SWP as a party expression of that thinking.

The new SWPers were *not*, by and large, former SDS members. In most cases they were former activists from the SMC and other antiwar groups or simply radicalized individuals on scattered campuses across the nation. The SWP did very well recruiting from smaller college campuses, and I met quite a few members who came from small towns and farms in the Midwest. My own view is that a preponderance of recruits from the American interior made the SWP the most "WASPy" of the radical groups. Of course there were many Jewish members in the SWP, and I noted no anti-Semitism. Yet on the whole, the SWP seemed less Jewish and urban than the International Socialists, the Communist Party, Spartacist, or our organization.

Some 90 percent of the party membership was white and only 28 percent had union jobs. The party had fared poorly in minority recruitment despite (or perhaps because of) its strong support of black nationalism. The union-affiliation figures reflect the beginning of efforts to send comrades into unions. Only a few party members were recruited *from* the working class. Over the next few years most of the members were "colonized," that is, sent into the unions. The point is that the party was overwhelmingly white and middle-class, recruited from the campuses. It was these white middle-class members who would later get factory jobs.

The most startling SWP statistic, however, was the number of comrades on the full-time staff. In December 1978, 196 comrades were employed by the party, 12 percent of the total membership! When Nancy and I joined this minibureaucracy in November 1976, we immediately sensed an oppressive insularity. A significant section of the membership had been separated from the day-to-day life of ordinary working people and existed in a very artificial environment. Most important, it was this layer of full-timers that directed party affairs and largely determined party policy. Under conditions of the general isolation of the party in a very conservative period, this layer contributed to the SWP's political degeneration.

I had not known Jack Barnes particularly well when I was last in the SWP. Jack had joined the party in Minneapolis while a student at Carleton College. In those days, he was not prominent in the YSA. Later, he came to New York while I was still in the party, and eventually he became the New York organizer. From that point on he remained a full-time staff member. His next job was head of the YSA. Then he became National Organizational Secretary of the SWP under Farrell Dobbs. He worked well with Farrell, who groomed him as his successor. In 1975 Farrell felt the grooming process was completed and retired to the Bay Area to live with his daughters. Nancy and I joined the staff at the moment when Barnes was finally crafting the party to his own liking and personality.

Jack Barnes's style was quite different from Dobbs's. Jack was a thin fellow with little hair, and he had lost an arm at some point in his life, so he had a stump at the end of one of his arms, which he used effectively to gesture. He talked with a distinctive Midwestern twang, and while Dobbs was careful and parsimonious in speech, Jack was garrulous and a bit impressionistic. Jack could get excited about an idea or a project and his listeners could easily get caught up in his excitement.

We were certainly testimony to Jack's ability to convince people to do what he wanted them to. The only problem was that once you were convinced, Jack could drop you as quickly as he had taken you up. We found this out at West Street. After he formally welcomed us to the staff, we rarely saw the man. He certainly made no effort to take us into his confidence.

Jack was an inside man. He rarely spoke in public or to nonparty people. Mass-movement work, such as the forming of peace coalitions, was left to others like Fred Halstead or Harry Ring. Jack rarely even visited the party branches. He worked skillfully at the top through a group of totally loyal supporters won primarily out of the student movement in the 1960s.

This layer included Larry Seigle, a good-looking, sharp political operator who reminded me of an IBM salesman or a Harvard MBA; Mary Alice Waters, a very pleasant, bright comrade who was a talented party leader; Doug Jenness, also from Carleton College; and Barry Sheppard, a lone survivor from the early days of the YSA who became something of a hatchet man for Barnes, the way Mike Banda served Gerry Healy. There were also a small number of older comrades, holdovers from the party of Cannon and Dobbs, who still played important roles in the party in that period. These included Joe Hansen, who ran *Intercontinental Press* and relations with the USec, and who died in 1979; George Breitman, who did a brilliant job editing the Trotsky Writings series and played a role on the Political Committee; Frank Lovell, an old-time trade unionist, also on the PC, who directed trade union work; and George Novack, involved in writing and speaking for the party and constantly available for consultation and special projects.

I was assigned to the educational department and Nancy was assigned to circulation. My department consisted of Fred Feldman and me, and though there were only two of us, we were not overworked. Fred was a good comrade to work with and he knew a great deal about the history of the Fourth International, its various political disputes and numerous splits. The problem with our department was that education was not given a high priority in the SWP, which at that time was basically an activist organization of former students who no longer studied or even read that much.

In spite of Fred's company, I found my job most frustrating. I wrote some very good study outlines that were sent to the branches. I doubt if more than one or two branches out of thirty or forty used them. Then we made a list of speakers available to branches for educational weekends. I was put on the list, and I figured I would get a lot of requests just because I was new to most comrades in the party and a bit of a novelty. I made only one trip during my entire tenure on staff.

Nancy's job started out better at the beginning. The party launched a big subscription drive and Nancy went to a number of cities to work with comrades on selling subscriptions in the neighborhoods. For a month or so it was like the old days in the Workers League for Nancy. Once the drive was over, however, she found herself doing simple office work, such as keeping the subscription list up-to-date.

In 1973 the SWP initiated a lawsuit against the FBI, the CIA, and other government bodies for spying, harassment, and disruption. When I joined the SWP staff in 1976, Jack Barnes asked me to be one of the party members whose files would be requested as part of the disclosure process in preparing the case for trial. I readily accepted, and because of this many documents that have recently been released to me were stamped indicating that they were originally released as part of this suit.

On September 16, 1976, a telegram was sent to "All SACS Routine" and it was captioned "Socialist Workers Party (SWP): IS." It read:

"For the information of all offices the Attorney General, United States Department of Justice, has advised that the investigation of captioned groups should be terminated as it does not meet the standards set forth in domestic security guidelines or foreign intelligence or foreign counterintelligence. . . . Each office should therefore discontinue your investigations of the SWP; the Young Socialist Alliance (YSA); their chapters, leaders and members; and any individuals or group being investigated because of his or her affiliation with the SWP. Informants who report on the SWP/YSA should be advised to discontinue active information gathering on the SWP/YSA on behalf of the FBI."

The FBI left itself an out by stating that surveillance could be continued on an individual "who engaged in activities which indicate he is likely to use force or violence in violation of a federal law." I, at least, did not fall under this more rigorous criterion, as the FBI has not released to me any documents dated later than this cut-off.

The judge found in the SWP's favor and awarded it $264,000. In March 1988 the Department of Justice withdrew its appeal of the judge's ruling, making the decision final.[2]

The Central Intelligence Agency has released to me two documents from the same period, dated July 27, 1976, and August 2,

1976. The documents assert that the CIA did not carry out a surreptitious entry into my apartment at any time. However, the CIA denied to me a third document, a memorandum dated June 3, 1976.

This certainly suggests that there never was any legal basis for the more than twenty years of surveillance that I was subjected to. Furthermore, the files accumulated for those years remain in the cabinets of various governmental agencies.

It was the Political Committee meetings that really drove me up the wall. The contrast with the PC of the old SWP could not have been greater. The old body had included workers who were not on the full-time staff, so that PC met in the evenings and quit around 10 P.M. so that comrades could get some sleep before going to work in the morning. The new PC met in the morning, around nine or so, and the marathon sessions could last the *whole day*! There were usually about six or seven points on the agenda. With the exception of an international report of some kind, usually given by Joe Hansen, the agenda was devoted to organizational matters: the subscription drive or tactics in arenas we worked in such as the National Organization for Women (NOW). The discussions were on a low level, which unfortunately did not mean people kept their remarks brief! Jack was in the habit of speaking on all points at great length, rambling on and on with impressions and speculations of one sort or another. I began to miss closed-mouthed Farrell!

There was always unanimity on all motions, no differences were ever expressed, and certainly no amendments or countermotions were ever proposed. It was clear that each report given to the PC had first been cleared in discussions with Jack or passed through a secretariat that included Jack, Mary Alice, and Larry. I doubt if serious disagreements even took place on this level. The party leadership was, at least on the surface, the very model of the political homogeneity that Cannon and Dobbs had striven for in the old SWP.

Another disturbing aspect of life at West Street was that it was isolated from the life of the party locals. In the Workers League almost all the full-timers were also branch organizers. The rest were active branch members. This meant that the full-time staff was not only the national party leadership but intimately involved in the day-to-day work of the key branches in New York, and New York was where we had made the greatest headway in our important youth work. In the SWP, while comrades at West Street were assigned to local branches, they were not expected to be active in them. Most comrades rarely attended branch meetings, except for preconvention discussions. This norm deprived the branches of some of the most politically developed party comrades and in turn isolated these comrades themselves from the current life of the branches. West Street was a world unto itself.

Nancy and I did have some good moments, and we made some contribution to the movement in that period. We were helpful in bringing into the party a small group with a state capitalist analysis of the Soviet Union. This group was headed by Bruce Levine and Shelley Kramer and was called the Revolutionary Marxist Committee (RMC).[3] The RMC had recently gathered its scattered forces in Detroit to conduct an intensive study program. This program led it to adopt a very complex theory of state capitalism, but the theory did not give members much of an idea of what to do politically as a small group. Bruce and Shelley, no doubt in part affected by my own evolution, decided to explore the possibility of joining the SWP.

After a number of discussions the comrades agreed to join. The SWP leadership, ever fearful of factionalism, insisted on dispersing these comrades to different branches throughout the party. Nancy and I had worked hard for the admission of the group and we were hoping that their presence would add some life, some diversity, to the SWP. Otherwise, we were afraid, the SWP might die of autointoxication from the same set of ideas, tactics, and even moods.

The Big Lie

While I was making my rocky adjustment to a second life in the SWP, Gerry Healy reared his head and entered my world once again. It was critical to Healy that he react strongly to one of his followers going over to the "enemy camp," and react he did. Healy extended the accusation he had raised against Nancy and me to Joseph Hansen and the entire SWP leadership. Hansen was accused of being a GPU agent (Soviet secret police, now called the KGB) or an FBI agent or both. This was no minor matter. Healy devoted considerable resources to the project, sent reporters around the world, ran several extensive series of articles, held rallies and press conferences, centering the activities and resources of his organization for over a year on the matter.[4]

Hansen was not chosen as the central target of Healy's campaign accidentally or even because of his prominent role in defending Nancy and me. Hansen had devoted himself to international matters since 1960. He had developed the theoretical explanation of the Cuban Revolution, which conflicted sharply with that of the British SLL as well as with that of our tendency within the SWP. On the basis of his essentially positive, supportive assessment of Castro, Hansen had been instrumental in regrouping world Trotskyism. His reappraisal of the world situation led to the split between the SWP and its old collaborators, Healy's group in England and the group around Pierre Lambert in France, and to the subsequent unity with the European groups led by Ernest Mandel. Therefore, it is easy to see why Hansen would be very high on Healy's list of enemies within the world Trotskyist movement.

Hansen had one other characteristic that did not endear him to opponents of the SWP. He was a very skilled polemicist who clearly enjoyed that art to the fullest. Hansen would very carefully choose the ground he wished to defend, marshal his facts, and then with no small amount of humor, quite thoroughly take on his opponent. Hansen had written a sharp word here or there directed against Healy.[5] Healy was not a man to forget such things.

Gerry Healy's "case" was on the face of it contradictory and absurd. For instance, at one point in the 1930s Hansen was contacted by a person who seemed to be a Russian agent. Hansen informed Trotsky of this contact and Trotsky urged him to maintain the contact for a while so that he could learn something of the Soviet's activities in relation to the Fourth International. Then at the time of Trotsky's assassination, Hansen contacted the U.S. government, hoping to encourage the FBI to uncover the assassin's American connections. This activity was also reported to the appropriate party body. Healy used the first incident to accuse Hansen of GPU connection and the second to accuse him of an FBI connection. Not only was there nothing in the conduct of Hansen to suggest that he was either a GPU or an FBI agent, but it was ridiculous to suggest that he was both! But Healy was not interested in such subtleties. His technique was to repeat over and over as many accusations as he could, hoping that the sheer volume of the material would convince his audience that his target must be guilty of something.

Healy's slanders did not stop with Hansen. George Novack rushed to Hansen's defense. I remember George so well as a gentle man with silver-gray hair, wire-rimmed glasses, a Bostonian accent, and the demeanor of a college professor. In the 1930s George had given up a promising career in publishing to devote himself to the movement. It was George Novack who organized the Commission of Inquiry headed by John Dewey to hear Trotsky's response to Stalin's murderous slanders during the Moscow Trials. Healy immediately added George Novack to his list of GPU/FBI agents. George's "crime" was that during World War II he had spent considerable time helping Trotskyist refugees to escape from Hitler's terror in Europe and to settle in the United States. No one knew it then, but one of these refugees, Marc Zborowski, was later revealed to be the GPU agent who had arranged the murder in Paris of Trotsky's oldest son, Leon

Sedov.[6] Soon Healy added Jack Barnes and the entire leadership of the SWP to his list.

The voluminous material produced by Healy was interesting in one respect. It illustrated the considerable effort Stalin put into hounding this small movement of critics of Soviet society. The FBI, particularly in the 1950s and 1960s, also devoted resources to watching and penetrating the Trotskyist movement. It is to the great credit of the leader of the Fourth International and the SWP that they persevered under these conditions, avoided panicky witch-hunts of the ranks, and continued to function politically.

Here and there, certainly, a mistake was made. Healy made a plausible case that Sylvia Franklin (Caldwell), a woman who had been Jim Cannon's secretary in the 1940s, may have been a GPU agent.[7] Cannon did not believe she was an agent. Yet, if she had been an agent, it is difficult to see how Cannon could have discovered this at the time she was his secretary. Considering the resources of the Soviet Union and its worldwide network of millions of supporters, it would be surprising if a penetration on such a level did not occur.

The most sickening side of Healy's campaign was that he had gone over to slandering his political opponents in much the same way Stalin had done during the Moscow Trials. Healy's problem was that he did not have state power and therefore could not coerce his opponents into confessing to his outrageous charges; nor could he punish them with death. Yet his methods certainly suggest that if Healy had had state power, he might very well have acted as Stalin did.

A central characteristic of the totalitarian regime—be it Stalinist or Fascist—is the utilization of the oppressive apparatus of the state to carry out the whims of the personality of the ruler. In Hitler's case an anti-Semitic prejudice became a state-run Holocaust that killed six million people. In Stalin's case fear of potential political opponents was transformed into a police regime that hunted down, imprisoned, and killed millions of people, most of whom were completely loyal followers of the dictator. Both terror campaigns served the political purpose of securing the power of the ruler. Yet in neither case can the extent of the terror be explained simply in terms of political utility. An aspect of the personality of the ruler was imposed upon society as a whole through the institutions of state rule.

Healy's case was different only in degree. He succeeded in transforming his small organization into an instrument for smearing and slandering his political opponents within the world Trotskyist movement. Healy's "Big Lie" served the political purpose of sealing off his membership from the criticisms of competing groups. Further, it also gave members an explanation for the failure of Trotskyism to become a serious world force. But it also represented an expression of the distorted psychology of Healy himself. Certainly Healy, the wily politician, was aware of the political usefulness of his campaign. Yet I suspect he believed, at least in part, his own slanders.[8]

The SWP leadership decided to organize a meeting in London to answer Healy, with the aid of its allies the British International Marxist Group (IMG) and other figures in the Fourth International. Jack Barnes decided to send George Novack and me to represent the SWP at the rally. I was extremely excited about the trip. I could not wait to publicly answer Healy's slanders. I also wanted to meet with my friends with whom I shared a common history. Together we had tasted some of the triumphs of Healy's movement and together we had had the shattering experience of breaking with the movement we had devoted our lives to.

George and I stayed at the home of Connie and Alan Harris. Connie had been a member of Healy's organization in the 1950s, serving for a time as Healy's secretary. In 1960 Connie supported a minority led by Brian Behan, brother of writer Brendan Behan. In the course of the faction fight Healy had her picked up bodily and tossed down the stairs at 186A Clapham High Street. Those stairs are quite steep, and it is amazing she was not very seriously injured. Alan was a Canadian who had joined the group there led by Ross Dowson. The two were operating a bookstore that carried primarily material published by the American SWP. They were subsidized by the SWP and headed a small group within the IMG that supported uncritically all SWP political positions. They were very warm and gracious hosts.

The world Trotskyist movement, split in many directions for years, came together for a moment on January 14, 1977, at a meeting of over a thousand in London to defend Hansen and Novack and to reassert its common heritage.[9] Tariq Ali, representing the sixties generation, chaired the meeting. Others on the dias included Ernest Mandel, representing the Usec; Pierre Lambert, an old collaborator of both Healy and the SWP, representing the OCI; Betty Hamilton, the warm Swiss woman who had been with Healy since World War II; Tamara Deutscher, the wife of the deceased Isaac Deutscher, whose writings on Trotsky and on the USSR had made such an impact on thinking in the 1960s; George Novack of the SWP; and me. Michel Raptis (Pablo), the International Secretary of the Fourth International in the immediate postwar years, sent greetings, as he wàs unable to make the meeting due to his wife's illness. Among those who had, in the interim, rallied to the victims of the attack were six former guards and secretaries to Trotsky, including Raya Dunayevskaya and Jean Van Heijenoort; Trotsky's grandson Vsevolod Volkov; Marguerite Bonnet, the European executor of Trotsky's literary estate; the French writer Daniel Guerin; and the West Indian C. L. R. James.

We all made our way to the platform. Tamara sat on one side of me and George Novack on the other. There was a commotion at the door as the audience of one thousand was settling down. The door opened and Gerry Healy marched in surrounded by a contingent of his supporters. He made his way down an aisle on the side of the hall and seated himself relatively close to the speaker's platform. I could clearly see his round face, eyes narrowed, teeth clenched, and expression grim. He held a rolled-up copy of the program tightly in his right hand. The IMG shifted a number of its ushers to Healy's side of the hall. I hoped it would not come to a punch-up, for the IMGers looked about as capable at street fighting as the average attendees at a graduate seminar in the classics department. Healy's crew, however, while more likely to have been recruited from the theater than from factories in that period, certainly gave the appearance of being toughs.

While I am sure I appeared calm on the surface, deep inside I was seized by an almost uncontrollable fear. It was amazing how this man, accompanied by only a dozen supporters and surrounded by one thousand people sympathetic to what I was about to say, could still create such a reaction in me. No matter what else is said about Healy, no one, after that night, should question his courage or his flair for the dramatic. I had little time to regain my composure, for I was to be the first speaker to follow Tariq's brief introductory remarks. I made my way to the podium, taking care not to look at Healy and instead focusing on my close friends and comrades in the audience who had left Healy's movement around the same time as my break. In a voice that sounded at least to me just a touch too shrill, I started out:

> In my opinion, the only kind of inquiry that we need, really need, is an inquiry into how it can be that an organization which began and started out in the struggle against Stalinism, in the struggle for Trotskyism, has ended up going over to the methods of Stalinism. Healy, like Stalin, has now started on a path of slander and fabrication for which there is no end.

As the *London Observer* noted, Healy sat through the entire meeting "pink-faced, grim-jawed and expressionless." I concluded my emotional speech with the statement that "being on this platform, taking this stand with these comrades, yes, these comrades, is the proudest moment in my life."[10]

When the speeches were over, Healy rose from his seat, waving a handbill, while his supporters yelled that he be allowed to speak. The chair refused, explaining that the purpose of the meeting was a defense rally and not a debate. That was the last time I ever saw the man.

Robin Blick was in the audience with his wife, Karen, a schoolteacher who had also been in the Healy group. Mark Jenkins was also present, as was Kate Blakeney, Adam Westoby, and other former party members. It was a special occasion for us. These comrades came up to the stage after the meeting. Tears were in our eyes. The truth was now known. Healy's methods were no longer our own private nightmare. We will never forget that meeting.

MEETING OLD FRIENDS AND NEW GROUPS

In the days after the meeting, I visited with Robin Blick (Robert Black) in his modest home in a poor neighborhood in North London where Robin lived with Karen and their two children. Robin and Karen took me to a social sponsored by their local Labour Party. It was my first Labour Party affair. There was a raffle, of course, and the winning ticket was picked out of a bowl by a young man who proved to be Tony Benn's son.[11] Lo and behold, the fellow was calling out my number! I am not the kind of person who wins things. I went to the table to choose my prize. I could have either a complete set of the works of Kim Il Sung, North Korea's illustrious leader, or a set of beer glasses. I chose the beer glasses. Robin came over beaming. "Admit it, Tim. This is the first party that has ever given you something." He was right.

I also spent quite a bit of time with Adam Westoby. Adam was a very English-looking fellow, blond hair, slightly reddish cheeks, a long nose. He was partially handicapped by a spinal problem. He was married to a woman named Sabe, a Pakistani lawyer who was physically impaired from polio. Adam had been a member of the SLL and then, for a brief period, a member of the IMG. While in the IMG, Adam had gotten interested in my theory of Stalinism, and Gerry, who had contact with him, arranged for a meeting for me with him during one of my trips to England. After the Thornett group broke from Healy, Adam joined it, and there initiated a discussion about my theory. These comrades became interested enough to publish my document "The Theory of Structural Assimilation" along with a lengthy introduction/critique by Adam.[12]

Of course I was most pleased about all the attention my fifteen-year-old theory was now getting, and the episode led to a friendly collaboration with Adam that has continued to this day. Adam did not stay long in the Thornett group and soon broke theoretically with Leninism and Trotskyism. He became, along with Robin, a kind of new-class theorist who saw Stalinism as an expression of the rise to power of the intelligentsia.[13] Adam is typical of the many intellectuals who, breaking from Trotskyism, continue to be gripped by it. This is shown in their continued deep concern with the central questions that gave rise to Trotskyism: socialism, bureaucracy, and democracy.

Robin and Adam were more than political collaborators for me. Together we had been possessed by the intoxicating dream of communism. We had given our lives totally to this movement and then each in our own way suffered from its degeneration. We found our ways out of the movement individually yet came together through a common search to understand this experience. We did not come to the same political conclusions in the end but were bonded to each other nonetheless.

Perhaps my evening with Kate Blakeney will make this clear. I first saw Kate on a trip to England in 1973. Healy had invited me to attend a weekend cadre school held in Margate, one of the many British working-class seaside resorts. The town council had generously made facilities available to us for the school in order to drum up a bit of business off season.

It was a dreary day, cold, cloudy, but not actually raining. We met in the town hall, a richly paneled room, surrounded by paintings of past lord mayors in black gowns with silly red hats. This architectural anachronism seemed a strange place to plot Britain's revolutionary future.

It was a gathering of about thirty or so comrades, and it was a rather routine affair. There was the usual abstract discussion of philosophy but no moments of conflict or crisis, or even interesting new material being presented. Healy, I thought, must be disappointed. He liked fireworks, confrontation, conditions that permitted the exposure of a comrade's weakness, his alien class nature. Healy, however, felt the shindig went rather well. He was particularly impressed with the development of Kate Blakeney. She sat in the front of the class and was given special consideration and asked the most significant questions. She was the star for the weekend.

My eyes rarely left her that weekend. There was something more than her natural beauty that attracted me. She had a fire and enthusiasm that contrasted so sharply with the heavy paneling, the portraits, the dull light coming in the partly stained glass windows, and the arcane discussion of Hegelian dialectics.

I next met Kate on the platform after the big meeting against Healy's slander campaign, and we agreed to see each other later in the week. It was raining when Kate met me at the Harris's apartment where I was staying. We walked to a nearby pub and sat in a quiet corner. It was one of those middle-class pubs with comfortable plush chairs and a dark interior. We ordered pints of bitter and she prepared to tell me her story.

I mentioned that I remembered her from that strange cadre school in

Margate, where she had appeared to be Healy's special pet, the rising star in the party's leadership. She was, she told me, at that time a member of the Central Committee as well as the party leader in the Reading area.

"Let me tell you what was really going on," Kate began. I sat in the pub absorbing Kate and her story at the same time.

Her area, like all the areas, was stretched beyond endurance. Every penny they could collect and a sizable portion of comrades' pay packets were being shipped off to the center. Comrades were running around from dawn to dusk trying to sell their bundles of papers. They were getting exhausted.

"We didn't think. We were too busy, always busy, and could hope only to catch a few hours of sleep."

The more money they raised, the more was demanded by the insatiable center. The more papers they sold, the bigger was the bundle next week. The center charged the comrades for the papers even if they didn't sell them.

"My closet became full of papers, and I had to find extra money somewhere to pay for them. We signed bank drafts so that the party could take money directly out of our accounts each week."

Kate had four children. She was finding it increasingly difficult to scrape together the money to buy food for them; no one would lend her money any more; she was cut off from her family. Yet she believed and put the party first. She drove herself and those around her to greater and greater effort. They all believed the party would triumph soon. The crisis was getting deeper. Maybe a military coup was in preparation? They had to build the party, to prepare. How well I, also, knew the litany!

Healy called her to the center for consultation. She went hoping to get some consideration for the pressures on her area, some appreciation for what they'd accomplished. It was pretty late in the evening when she arrived at the office, as she had to cook something for her kids before driving to London. Her husband was out on his party paper route. The comrades said Healy was across the street at the rooms he kept there and was expecting her. I had often visited Healy's little apartment, with its garish, overstuffed, red imitation leather furniture, a desk in one corner covered with papers, a small kitchen alcove off the end of the room. In my mind I could see Kate entering, exhausted, looking for help.

"Healy opened the door for me. He had been drinking. Something was all wrong. I pushed by his large body, sat down in a chair, and started to make my report. Healy came toward me, was hovering over me. He was not listening to a word I was saying.

"He wanted only one thing from me: my sexual submission. For a moment I just stared at him: fat, ugly, red-faced. Was this the price I was supposed to pay for some respite for my area?

"Something snapped in me. I guess it was my faith, my belief. The dream that filled my head and drove me forward now seemed unreal, and reality entered, tawdry, petty, dirty, seamy reality. It wasn't a matter of morality or some special virtue on my part. It was as if everything I believed in was proved, in one revealing second, to be false, lies. I, my husband, my children, my comrades had sacrificed so much, had worked so hard for this—this animal."

At the next Central Committee meeting, Healy launched a bitter political attack on Kate. She was sure that this was how the struggle began that led to the expulsion of Alan Thornett and the entire western region in 1974. Over two hundred members were expelled, mostly workers. Healy lost his base in the automobile industry. There were major issues involved in the split, and it might have happened anyway. Yet the catalyst was Kate, and Healy's sexual appetites.

"Those of us who were out there in the working class got a daily bath in reality, in the lives of real human beings. It was becoming harder for us to relate experiences, the ordinary needs of working people, with the increasingly wild political ranting of Healy."

She fell silent. Neither of us spoke. We had returned to those days in our minds. It was a strange moment. I looked directly into her eyes and she into mine. We both smiled, saying nothing. We were close at that moment, as close as I ever remember being with anyone. We shared a feeling of deep bitterness.

There was something more—a feeling of loss. I sensed it in the wistful tone of her voice when she described the battles, the comrades, the paper sales. Those who had never passed through a movement would have had no difficulty understanding our bitterness. But could they have sensed our loss? It was that loss that tied us so close and set us apart from the well-dressed patrons of the pub who sat around us living in such a different world from that which we had experienced. No matter what happened or how well we prospered over the coming years, we would be different.

It was getting late. We both got up to leave. I helped her on with her raincoat, wrapped my scarf around my neck (I had foolishly left my heavy coat in the United States), and soon we exchanged the warm cozy pub for the wet chill of a London night. We walked slowly to the tube station with the rain coming down lightly. It was only two blocks. Kate slipped her hand around my arm and walked close by me. In the distance the lights from the tube station penetrated the rain.

We reached the entrance and she bought her ticket. Then, before going through the turnstile she paused, turned toward me, smiled, and gently gave me a light kiss on my forehead. Then she turned away, pushed through the stile, and ran to catch the last train to Reading that night.

That was the last time I saw Kate. I heard that soon after this meeting she and her family moved to Australia, where she became active in the Australian Labor Party.

After my stay in London visiting with former members of the Healy organization, I traveled to Oxford and met with Alan Thornett and his group. The group occupied a house in a nondescript residential neighborhood. When I walked into the place there were several people about, talking on the phone, typing, and talking to each other. I gathered it was a kind of headquarters as well as living quarters for some of them. I was taken to the top floor, a bare white room that was used primarily for staff meetings. There I talked with the three leaders of the group: Alan Thornett, John Lister, and Tony Richardson.

They were a likable group, though I sensed a formality, a desire to distance themselves from me even though their emotions drew them toward me. We had gone through the same experiences in the same time period and felt personally close. Yet Alan and the others had chosen to build a group with well-defined politics and lines of demarcation separating it from competing groups on the Trotskyist left. This gave them a certain rigidity, a tendency to carry on some of the approaches of the Healy group, though without its extremes.

I believe they could have gone further and made more of a contribution to the Left in England if they could have learned how to approach other groups with whom they did not have total agreement, work with them, and move toward a regroupment of the Trotskyist Left. However, this would have required them to define "truth" a little differently than they did. They needed to realize that they were not the sole possessors of this commodity, and that all others were not "revisionists." Alan, in particular, was a very nice fellow with solid experience in the working class and was completely dedicated to building his group. Yet he also possessed a self-righteousness that could blind him, a trait rooted in the British non-conformist religious tradition.

I spent the night at John Lister's apartment, and it was like stepping back into my own past. We got there around ten o'clock at night and chatted for a while. Then Lister's wife came in, full of excitement, from some union meeting or other. She gave us a report on the meeting while she reheated some food on the stove. Then off to bed we all went, John's wife having to get up early in the morning to go to work. Such is the life of the committed party member. I must say I missed it a little.[14]

I got a feel for the International Marxist Group (IMG). These comrades toured me around the country and I gave a little talk on Healy. There were Healy people at each meeting, so it was a bit of an ordeal, though it went rather well. It took a while to get used to the British approach to meetings.

These were usually held in a student center on a campus. Just outside the meeting room would be a pub. I found beer placed on the speaker's podium for me. When I emptied a pint, someone ran out and got me another one. I was not used to speaking while drinking beer, so I had to be careful. One meeting dragged on, as representatives of various small groups were doing their best to bait me during the discussion period (I discovered to my horror that there was a Spartacist group in England—poor country!), and the audience started to leave. At first I was worried that the meeting had not gone well, but comrades assured me that the real problem was that the pub was about to close!

I attended a couple of IMG National Committee meetings, visited a very good educational school in Brighton, and I met groups of comrades in places like Manchester and Leeds. I got to like the group, which definitely had its own political personality. It was, without question, the most democratic party I had ever observed. There were so many tendencies within it that they were assigned letters for identification rather than names. Proceedings at an NC meeting could be a bit messy, and too much time was spent on procedural points. Certainly some of the IMG comrades had adapted too well to the factional life and could be characterized as professional factionalists. Yet most of the membership was very bright, and many were capable of independent thinking. Most amazing of all, the IMG did actually succeed in *doing* things effectively from time to time. Just as remarkable, this rather fragile organization succeeded in holding itself together for over a decade and a half.[15]

I made a short trip to Greece in 1977 to meet with a group of former members of Healy's International Committee. It was headed by Dimitri Toubanis, whom I knew from his days in exile in London. Dimitri had a lovely wife, Cissy, who spoke perfect English. (Despite his decade in London, Dimitri's English was abominable.) Dimitri had attended an international school soon after my split with Healy. He had raised some questions about that split, which earned him Healy's ire. Then he had the audacity to take Healy up on matters of philosophy during a school session. He soon found a faction organized against himself in his own group, and a split took place.

Dimitri, sensitive to his isolation, then decided to take his group into one of the two Greek Communist parties, the Interior.[16] This one was Euro-Communist[17] in orientation and relatively open. I do not believe the entry proved particularly successful because even an "open" Communist Party is really not that open. Most workers remained in the very Stalinist Exterior Party. Papandreou was organizing a party (PASOK) around his personality, which would prove to be a kind of cross between a nationalist and a social democratic formation. PASOK won over the middle classes and those workers not attached to the Exterior Communists.

One evening the whole group took me outside Athens to a small town that had a row of restaurants along its main street. About twenty of us took over a large table and settled in for the evening. Wine was served, large pots of yogurt, which tasted rich like cream, and round loaves of fresh baked bread were put on the table, then a kind of barbecued intestines (the house specialty) was served. By this time the comrades were loudly singing Greek revolutionary songs. The restaurant was now full, and not all the patrons considered themselves revolutionaries. Soon other tables started singing Greek patriotic songs. To bring the restaurant together, the political task of the moment, our comrades started up an immensely popular song directed against the Junta, which had been toppled only a couple of years earlier. Everyone in the restaurant took up the song, which ended with some dramatic, bloody reference to the death of the Junta. As the song reached this crescendo, our comrades picked up their knives and stabbed the round breads in the center of the table. The Greeks are definitely expressive people.

By this time everyone was a bit drunk and our comrades took to the floor to dance traditional Greek dances, handkerchiefs and all, with the patriotic patrons from the other tables. I kept peering at the door expecting Zorba to walk in at any moment! The evening was getting on, the stomachs were getting full, and everyone was drinking too much wine. When it was time to leave, attention suddenly centered on a woman comrade who lived in the neighborhood. Her husband was a worker who had been in the group but had recently resigned to join the Exterior Communists. The husband had stayed home to baby-sit their children. Our task was now clear. We had to go up the hill and convince him to break from Stalinism!

Our mob ascended the hill, woke this poor fellow out of a sound sleep, and proceeded to have a long, intense discussion with him about Stalinism and the Greek trade union movement. The little children stared bleary-eyed at the mob of invaders and then went back to sleep. After a while it became clear we were not going to convince him, since his conversion was a practical matter. In his trade union the Stalinist Communists were also the most militant unionists and this fact, rather than abstract considerations of the nature of the Soviet Union, swayed him in the end. It was an example of the problems Trotskyists faced everywhere in Europe.

My Last Stand

By May of 1977 both Nancy and I had reached the end of our tether from the life at West Street. We freely admitted to ourselves that our frustrations were brought about by a combination of the stifling, isolated, and remarkably unpolitical life of the place and by the pull of our own personal needs. We had recently run out of money. We would never again be the

100 percent political people to whom nothing but politics mattered. We had seen too many such people transformed into zombies following the orders of petty dictators like Healy. We were, without fully being conscious of it, winding down politically.

All these factors convinced us to leave New York City, where I had been politically active for twenty-two years, and make a new start in San Francisco. We were assigned to the Oakland branch. Our branch office was on Fruitvale Avenue, in the middle of a poor Hispanic neighborhood that featured community services of various kinds offered by the La Raza organization. It might have been situated in a shiny downtown office building for all the attention the branch gave to its surroundings. It was, in fact, difficult to determine exactly what the branch *did* do. It engaged in very little public work, yet its members were busy all of the time. It turned out that everybody's time was absorbed almost entirely by a myriad of internal meetings: of the executive committee, the trade union fraction, the women's fraction, the educational committee, the finance committee, the local area committee, etc., etc., etc. It took a full-time organizer simply to organize all these committee meetings and patiently attend each one!

The branch meeting was one aspect of the SWP that had not changed one iota during the more than ten years that I was outside the party. The various committees made reports into an executive committee. This body then revised the reports for the branch meeting. The result was a deadeningly dull agenda given over entirely to organizational detail. Any attempt to bring some political discussion into the meeting or even to disagree on tactical matters was viewed by the branch leadership as factional conduct. The New York branches had not been any different, and discussions with comrades from other locales suggested that these routines and attitudes were prevalent in all the branches.

It became clear to Nancy and me that the SWP was turning inward, becoming increasingly preoccupied with self-perpetuation rather than with changing the external world. What we did not fully realize at the time was that the problems of the SWP were largely caused by the drying up of political opportunities. The SWP leadership might not have reacted perfectly to the conservativization of American political life, but no leftist group escaped this development unscathed.

The national leadership's solution to the party's malaise was to call for an all-out "colonization" drive to send all party members into industry. This began with an orientation toward the United Steel Workers (USWA). A militant opposition group in that union had formed in the Chicago area around Ed Sadlowski. It seemed at the time that the SWP would be able to work in Sadlowski's campaign much in the manner that it had worked in the peace coalitions. This way it could utilize its party apparatus and mobilization techniques to help affect the outcome of the struggle while it built a party base in the steel industry. But Sadlowski lost that election campaign and abandoned oppositional struggle, leaving the SWP high and dry. What's more, the Sadlowski challenge proved exceptional and did not open a new stage of radicalization in the unions.

On the heels of this disaster, the party leadership decided to extend its colonization efforts to *industrial* unions as a whole. The word was now coming directly from Jack Barnes, who believed he was interpreting party history in the spirit of Cannon and Dobbs. Basic industry, we were told (at a time when this sector was shrinking in size and importance in American life) was where the central power in the capitalist system lay. We needed a strong base in basic industry if we were serious about mobilizing the power of the working class to overthrow the capitalist system. How could one oppose that?

The SWP was a marvelous *campaign* party and did a bang-up job of systematically motivating comrades to enter industry, of aiding them in finding jobs, and of helping them to sustain themselves in the new situation. In a matter of a couple of years virtually the entire party membership was colonized. The only problem was that there was very little labor unrest at the time, and the party leadership did not know what to do with the small opportunities that were there. As a result, this new turn actually *deepened the party's isolation*.

At the same time as these changes in orientation on the national scene were taking place, the party leadership was shifting its position on international questions. A key issue, once again, was Cuba. I was really *not* looking for a fight with anyone over Cuba. When I came back into the party I sincerely believed that what differences remained on this issue were largely terminological. I believed that Cuba was a deformed workers' state, essentially the same as the East European countries and China. I had many informal discussions on the question in West Street, and all comrades I talked with were in general agreement with me. There were some who hesitated to advocate a political revolution in Cuba, but all realized that over the past fifteen years or so the system there had been institutionalized in a manner that entrenched the leadership and a bureaucratic layer around the leadership.

It was George Breitman who raised the question for discussion on the Political and National Committees. George was a very thin, frail man with a roundish head. He suffered from arthritis and moved about with considerable pain. I had known George slightly during my first spell in the SWP in the late 1950s. He was part of the Detroit branch then and was adored by the younger party members. He was somewhat dour and taciturn, speaking very infrequently at Political Committee meetings. He had a cot in the room where the meetings were held and had to lie down from time to time because of his physical condition. This made George's intervention on Cuba all the more dramatic. In a quiet voice he simply asked that the question be placed on the agenda. When nothing happened over a period of weeks, he repeated his request. Finally he simply stated his political position on the matter. Barnes delayed discussion for a few more weeks, but finally a discussion was held.

Breitman stated that he believed Cuba had changed since the party had last pronounced upon it in 1960 and that our position needed to be discussed again. He tended toward the view that it was now a deformed workers' state. Since the matter had been brought up in a very calm, objective, and diplomatic manner, I felt that it was incumbent upon me to say what I thought. A discussion was finally launched on a National Committee level. It was then revealed that Jack Barnes deeply believed that Cuba was a revolutionary country with a revolutionary leadership and that our assessment of it should remain exactly as it had been written in 1960.

As the national convention approached, I suddenly found himself in the middle of a discussion I did not want. The "consensus" in the party was immediately formed around Jack Barnes's belief, and I was almost totally isolated. George Breitman, for his own tactical reasons, chose to play his own game, commenting during the discussion but not supporting either position. It was a rather strange faction fight. I had no faction and was not particularly concerned about how much support I received. I felt a moral obligation to state the views that I had held since 1960 and that I believed had been borne out by the concrete facts of the evolution of Cuba. I felt it was harmful for our party to suggest to young revolutionaries in lesser-developed lands that they uncritically follow the model of Cuba. That meant, as far as I could see, urging them to support the Stalinist governments and to create regimes that were not democratically controlled by the working class.

One preconvention discussion meeting sticks in my mind. It was one of those marvelous sunny days Oakland has in June. Warm, but not hot, air crystal clear, a slight breeze. Yes, I thought, I was wise to come out here from New York. But the beauty of the day was not to be enjoyed.

The headquarters was a large storefront next to a welfare hotel and across from a Mexican grocery. It was a deep hall with a small partition that separated it from the bookstore and office section in the front. There was only a scattering of books in the bookstore, all published by the party. The desk in the corner was piled with unsold papers. The light did not fully penetrate the cavernous inside of the hall. It cut its way through the interior but was defused by the time it reached past the rows of straight-backed wooden folding chairs to the podium. The hall was painted a dreary gray, which did not help much. The only color was some red and blue twisted crepe paper strips along one wall, which the cleanup committee had missed after our last social.

Ruth, our organizer, was speaking as I entered. She was a short, heavyset woman dressed in jeans, a "Solidarity with Nicaragua" T-shirt, and running shoes. She was a no-nonsense organizer who always had everything under control by keeping little lists in her pocket-sized notebook, which she carried everywhere. She was good at what she did, very good, in fact, but she lacked imagination and originality. But that was the way the party had trained her to be.

"Today we are assessing the Cuban Revolution twenty years later. Its internationalist actions in Angola prove beyond a shadow of a doubt that Fidel Castro continues on a revolutionary course. It continues to be our task to support the Cuban Revolution here in the heartland of imperialism." She droned on and on.

I found my way to a seat in a corner in the back of the hall. From there I could watch the podium, the thirty or so comrades sprawled on the hard seats, and also glance out through the opening in the partition, through the bookstore area, to the outside. John, who was chairing the meeting, had spotted me when I came in and had glared at me. I was late and I was sitting in the back. That was not good. John was a large fellow in his late thirties, handsome in a way but a bit overweight. He lived with Ruth but had a reputation for womanizing. This did not prevent him from being the most ardent defender of feminism and all good causes endorsed by the party leadership. John was more facile than Ruth, but was a lousy organizer. Ruth ran things, but John liked to think that he ran Ruth.

I spotted the dissidents across the hall, sitting in a little knot near the front. There was Frank, a union activist with fourteen years in the party, a former antiwar GI, thin, intense, enthusiastic. Next to Frank sat his wife, Blanca, a thin Chilean woman with lovely, long, straight blond hair and a pretty, angular face. Blanca was less involved in party life than was Frank. Jack sat just behind the two with a couple of his friends. Jack was an outspoken union organizer and a veteran of innumerable petty battles with the local leadership. Jack had a sneer on his face, which became more marked the longer Ruth droned on. Frank, however, followed Ruth's speech closely and was taking notes furiously, while Blanca's lovely face was impassive, her eyes unfocused on anything, dazed.

The meeting was having a numbing effect on me. I was finding it more and more difficult to concentrate on the argumentation. The room was beginning to warm up and a comrade propped open the front door to let in fresh air. I found my attention drifting to the street.

A thin middle-aged black man with curly, close-cropped gray hair jogged by. He looked familiar. Then he returned and jogged in the door. It was Paul Boutelle. I had known him in New York twenty years ago. Paul's son had played with my boys in the early days of the YSA. He was once the party candidate for vice president, but he was no longer active. He seemed surprised that a meeting was going on.

He sat in the outside room and caught his breath, listening a bit to the discussion. Our eyes met for a moment and he smiled. If he had decided to stick around we would have taken opposite sides on the issues being discussed, but that did not matter. We were both disengaged, each in our own way. Paul got up and jogged out of the hall into the sunlight.

My attention was pulled back to the meeting. Jack jumped up from his seat, glaring at John: "Point of order! Ruth is way over her allotted time. The chair should be cutting her off."

"I am chairing this meeting, not you," John answered. "Ruth, could you sum up, please?"

Finally Ruth had finished and I took the floor for some extended remarks in rebuttal.

"I wish to raise some questions on our assessment of Cuba. I think we should not overlook Cuba's ties to the Soviet Union, and the one-party system there. Certainly Cuba is not without some bureaucratic and Stalinist characteristics. . . ."

"That's a slander! I won't sit here and allow the revolution to be attacked," interrupted a leadership supporter from the floor.

"Point of order, chairperson. Let the comrade speak!" It was Jack again. I retired to my seat in the back. It was not worth the effort to continue. One by one supporters of the leadership took the floor to repeat virtually word for word what the organizer had said. Blanca appeared to be coming out of her trance, looking around the room at the bitter faces as the factional atmosphere heated up. I just watched the scene from my perch in the back of the hall. In past years I would have been in the thick of it, but this day I found myself strangely untouched by the intense emotions.

My attention shifted as I caught a flash of color out of the corner of my eye. A lovely butterfly was making its way toward the middle of the hall. It had an intricate design of deep reds, blues, and blacks on its wings. It fluttered right down the shaft of light from outside toward the podium in the front of the hall. It lighted on the floor. I was not the only one to notice the butterfly. Comrades on both sides of the aisle had been watching the creature's progression to the podium. The tension of the meeting, for a moment, was broken.

I could see John stiffen. Suddenly Clifton DeBerry, who had been sitting in the front row to lend his support to the local leadership, stood up. Dee, as he was called, was a very light-skinned black man who had been recruited from the Stalinists in Chicago in the immediate postwar years. He had also been a party vice presidential candidate and was the son-in-law of former party leader Farrell Dobbs. He was not about to put up with this disruption. Action was required for the good of the party and to maintain proper decorum and respect for the importance of the debate going on. Dee rushed up the aisle and got ready to step on the butterfly.

Suddenly Blanca, face flushed with anger, leapt from her chair, knocking it over, and dashed toward Dee. She screamed:

"No, you don't! Don't touch that butterfly! That's Stalinism!"

The butterfly, sensing the motion around it, stretched its wings and slowly began its ascent from the floor and up, up into the beam of light. Flitting first to the left and then to the right, it made slow progress toward the opening in the partition. Soon it had found its way out the front door to sunlight and freedom.

Blanca was right, of course. It was Stalinism to crush the butterflies of the world, the beautiful but perhaps not always practical and, occasionally, very utopian thoughts and dreams of men and women in the interest of apparatuses.

I went to Oberlin that year for my last SWP convention. It was not a very pleasant affair for me. The Cuba discussion was scheduled for an entire day. Larry Seigle gave a one-and-a-quarter-hour presentation. I finally got my half-hour to argue for what I felt was a reasonable and objective assessment of Cuba. I didn't do it in order to win anyone to my position, however; I felt it was too late for that. I just said what I believed was true.

When I finished my presentation, several hundred people broke into hearty applause, which rather startled me. The applause came almost entirely from the foreign delegates and observers, almost all of whom were supporters of Ernest Mandel. The SWP had swung so far toward Cuba that the Mandel majority was now the more anti-Stalinist, "orthodox" Trotskyist wing of the USec![18]

The outburst from the Mandel supporters did not prevent the floor discussion from getting ugly, however. For two hours, I was stridently denounced by every speaker who came to the podium, just like old times. I then was given eight minutes to respond!

I had had it by then with banging my head against the wall in the SWP. It was Jack's party now and he could do with it whatever he chose. I did not even have to quit the party. I was headed for Mexico for a while and I put in for a transfer so I could function with the Trotskyist group there. The SWP did not recognize my right to transfer to another section of the Fourth International and dropped me from SWP membership.

The evolution of the SWP, clearly evident at the 1979 convention, deepened after I left. Jack Barnes's enthusiasm over both Cuba and Nicaragua, as well as his hollow perspectives on the trade unions, led to the formation of two opposition groups as well as to the loss of many comrades. One group was led by Frank Lovell and George Breitman and the other by Nat Weinstein and Jeff Mackler in the San Francisco Bay Area.[19] These groups have since been expelled, and just about all of the old party members have been lost. The party now belongs completely to Barnes and reflects his moods and politics. Membership has fallen to somewhere between five hundred and seven hundred. Most of my friends and acquaintances of the 1975–1979 period are now outside the SWP.

My break with the SWP lacked the bitterness of my break with Healy. I was treated, on the whole, reasonably decently. Of course, Jack Barnes saw to it that the factional cards were clearly stacked in favor of the "house." But I left more out of ennui and weariness. I am reminded of a line from a Kurt Weil/Bertolt Brecht song. "Is that all there is?"

Notes

1. The statistics in this section come from documents in the possession of the author that were compiled by the SWP national office and issued to National Committee members at the 1979 convention. The table based on these statistics is my own.
2. Nelson Blackstock, *Cointelpro* (New York: Pathfinder Press, 1988).
3. The International Socialists, as we have already noted, was created out of those followers of Shachtman who did not support the Democratic Party and who had left the Socialist Party. A little later, as part of the kind of crisis that affected the whole Trotskyist Left and broke up the Maoists, a leftist group called the Revolutionary Socialist League and headed by Ron Taber split from the IS. The RMC was a minority split of about thirty people from the RSL.
4. *Healy's Big Lie—The Slander Campaign against Joseph Hansen, George Novack, and the Fourth International* (New York: Education Department, SWP, 1977).
5. Joseph Hansen, *Marxism vs. Ultraleftism: The Record of Healy's Break with Trotskyism* (New York: Education Department, SWP, 1974).
6. Zborowski died in San Francisco in 1990. For facts about his disgraceful life, see Elisabeth K. Poretsky, *Our Own People: A Memoir of "Ignace Reiss" and His Friends* (Ann Arbor: University of Michigan Press, 1969).
7. Questions about Caldwell's GPU role were first raised by Max Shachtman, who, sometime in the late 1940s, alerted Cannon privately to certain rumors that were circulating. The ex-Communist Louis Budenz publicly denounced Caldwell as a GPU agent before the House Un-American Activities Committee in 1950. In testimony given in a 1958 grand jury probe into the espionage activities of Abraham Sobolevicius (Jack Soble), Caldwell admitted that she had been a spy, turning over to Soble everything that passed her desk while she worked for Cannon. Of course, Caldwell would not have been particularly useful to the GPU if, as Healy maintained, Hansen was also an agent.

8. For Healy's "case," see *Security and the Fourth International: An Inquiry into the Assassination of Leon Trotsky* (New York: Labor Publications, 1976).
9. *Intercontinental Press* (New York, February 7, 1977).
10. *Intercontinental Press* (New York, February 7, 1977), p. 94.
11. Tony Benn is a member of Parliament and the leading figure in the left wing of the British Labour Party.
12. Wohlforth and Westoby, *"Communists" against Revolution.*
13. See *Communism since World War II* (Brighton, England: Harvester Press, 1981), which was a kind of transitional book, written as his thinking was changing. See also his introduction to Bruno Rizzi, *The Bureaucratization of the World* (London: Tavistock, 1985). His latest book is *The Evolution of Communism* (New York: Free Press, 1989).
14. Recently Thornett appears to have changed his mind and come over to a position closer to what I had advocated ten years earlier. He has fused with a remnant of the IMG, which supports Ernest Mandel politically.
15. The IMG has since split up. A group associated with Brian Grogan and Alan Jones works with the American SWP, while the more Mandelite group, as previously mentioned, has fused with Thornett.
16. The names came from the period of Communist guerrilla activity when one section of the party leadership remained underground within the country and the other section went abroad, primarily to the Soviet Union.
17. At this time the major Communist parties in Europe were distancing themselves from the Soviet Union, criticizing it for its lack of democracy.
18. For those readers of this book who are keeping score of which group ended up where in relation to the Fourth International, it should be noted that Nahuel Moreno's supporters—and he had some significant groups in Argentina, Colombia, and a few other Latin American countries—broke with the SWP's Leninist-Trotskyist faction in this period. They became known as the Bolshevist Tendency. Moreno began purging his ranks of possible dissidents, running his groups in a fashion very similar to the way Healy ran his. Soon he dropped out of the United Secretariat as well. Moreno has recently died, but his international formation continues to exist.
19. The Breitman-Lovell group, known as the Fourth Internationalist Tendency, is located in New York, and is oriented toward influencing the SWP. George Breitman has since died. The Weinstein group is called Socialist Action and is centered in the Bay Area. A small group, Socialist Unity, left Weinstein and has since fused with the International Socialists and Workers Power, two groups from the Shachtman current, to form Solidarity. In addition to doing trade union work, Solidarity publishes a lively intellectual journal, *Against the Current.* Peter Camejo, a founder of the YSA and longtime party leader, has also left the SWP and built a group made up of former party members who have dropped out. It is called the Northstar Network and is oriented toward the Rainbow Coalition. Peter has established a stock brokerage called Progressive Asset Management for ecologically sound and socially responsible investment.

12

Winding Down

Another Woman

I will never forget that terrible night in November 1978. My head was pounding. It was past midnight and I knew I had to get up at 5:30 the next morning to go to work. Yet Shane gave no indication that she would be leaving anytime soon. She was not talking to me, anyway. She was only interested in Nancy. The two of them had been going at it all evening. It had started with poetry, drifted to party politics, and now had degenerated into gossip.

This was getting ridiculous. Here I was sitting in the living room, which also served as a bedroom, of our tiny apartment just off San Francisco's marina, trying to block out their discussion. I could hear and yet I could not hear. Just the occasional phrase, just enough to distract me from anything else but not enough to quite understand what they were talking about. I didn't care, anyway. I just wanted Shane to go. Damn it! I would go to bed, anyway! To hell with both of them! I ostentatiously got undressed, made as much noise as I could, threw a bathrobe over my naked body, and announced to the two of them that I was going to sleep.

"Fine, Tim. Good night." Nancy wore a silly grin.

"See you, Tim," said Shane. Then they whispered something to each other and snickered. I climbed into the bed and soon found myself straining to catch the words they were whispering to each other. I could not sleep. Now the pounding in my head was becoming unbearable. The three aspirins I had taken were having no effect.

I had had it. I jumped out of bed and stomped into the kitchen.

"For God's sake, Shane! Leave! Some of us work for a living, you know. I'm sorry but I'm a light sleeper. There's no way I can sleep with the two of you chattering away in here."

"Look Tim, we're whispering for Christ's sake! It's not our fault if you're a lousy sleeper. It's my apartment, too, you know. I pay half the rent. I'll talk with my friend in my half and you do what you want in your half." Nancy was getting set for a real row with Shane as a witness. I was being cast as the male chauvinist villain.

My eyes shifted to Shane. She had a slight smile on her face—I was clearly the subject of their whispers. Shane was thin and had closely cropped hair and an angular face, and she peered at me with intense, expressive eyes. I thought for a moment about how alike and unalike the two of them were. Nancy had shoulder length brown hair and wore a neat white shirt and blue jeans. The effect was softer, more conventional, and, at least to me, more sensual. Both women were exceptionally bright, and they shared a love of poetry, people, and long conversations about everything under the sun.

"Of course you have a right to do what you want in the apartment but please, *please* have some consideration. I just can't sleep and my head is pounding!" I was answering Nancy but staring at Shane. I felt a hatred of that woman welling up in me. Was I jealous? No, I couldn't be. I was just mad at her for taking advantage of Nancy. Nancy would talk all night if someone would listen to her.

"I'll go. I don't want to cause any problems between the two of you."

"If she goes, I go. I've had enough of you, Tim. You can't boss me around. I have my rights and I intend to live my own life. I'm going whether she goes or not!"

Nancy got up from her chair and started walking toward the door. She pushed me away roughly as she passed me, got to the door, and then turned around in a bit of a daze. She spotted her Levi's jacket, grabbed it, and continued out the door. Shane, no longer able to contain herself, was grinning by this time. She ran after Nancy and they left the apartment house.

I felt a marvelous sense of relief. The two of them were gone. The tension was over. Now I could go to bed and sleep. This feeling did not last for long. Shane's grin pushed it out of my mind. Damn it! That woman had won! She had set this all up. She had kept Nancy going. She had turned her against me. God, I hated that bitch. She was trying to break us up, I could see it now. And I stupidly helped her by leaving the conversation and turning Nancy over to her. Then my outburst. Sure, I had my right to sleep, but she had her rights too. Oh, it was a crazy situation. Nancy and I could have resolved it. We always had in the past. But we couldn't with Shane here poisoning everything.

My hatred and jealousy of Shane became a physical pain in my side and my stomach. I expected that I would have stomach pains all week. Between this crap and the pressure of my job I figured I might get an ulcer.

Then I thought of Nancy. My hatred of Shane had blocked her from my mind. Now she came back, not the Nancy with circles under her eyes and hostility in her voice, but the pretty Nancy, my companion for five years, the Nancy I shared political adventures with, the Nancy who suffered political persecution with me, the Nancy who lay beside me in a small tent on that beach at Cape Hatteras, the Nancy I made love to. I kept hoping to hear her at the door. But I knew she wouldn't come back. It was a power game now. She could not admit defeat. I was the one who had to be defeated.

I fell into the bed, alone. Now I really couldn't sleep! Real smart, Tim! You've accomplished a lot! Nancy did not return that night. That's when their relationship started.

The affair had gone on for six months before I decided that I could no longer live with the situation. For her part, Nancy would not even admit that Shane was anything more than a friend. Finally I told her that she would have to choose between continuing to see Shane and living with me. So I moved out.

A month later, in March of 1979, Nancy and I arranged to meet again for the first time since our separation. We sat together for some minutes in the camper parked in the lot at our old Bank of America branch. We had canceled our joint savings account, and I had our account book, stuffed with eight one-hundred-dollar bills, in my lap. Five years together, both of us working, and this was all we had to show for it. Ours had been a relationship of debt!

"Living with Isabel, Tim?" Nancy broke our silence, referring to a mutual friend we had at the time.

"No, as a matter of fact I have my own place over in the Mission. But that's my own business now, Nancy. Just like you and Shane. There's no sense in getting into all that."

I picked up the bankbook, took the crisp bills, and counted four out for her. Her hand was shaking as she took the money.

"I guess this is it. I'll drive you home now, Nancy."

I headed out of the lot and up Brannon, then DuBois to Broadway. I turned left and we slowly went up the broad windy street toward our last apartment, recently rented in the Twin Peaks area of San Francisco. In no time we became completely engulfed in fog. I had to turn on the windshield wipers. I pulled into the garage under the apartment building. It was her apartment now and the camper, worth less than what was still owed on it, was mine.

I couldn't just drop her off. I got out of the camper and walked with her to the door. Nancy turned toward me and there were tears in both our eyes. We grabbed each other, pressing so tight. I could feel her fingers dig into my flesh. She was shivering. Luckily the fog swallowed us, protected us from everything, blanking out past and future. For the moment there were only the two of us. She reached for her key in her jeans pocket. She opened the door while we still clung to each other.

"Don't mind me!" It was Shane! We nearly fell on top of her as the door opened. I turned away and soon Nancy, Shane, and the apartment were lost from my view in the fog. I entered the camper, alone.

Nancy had been right to suspect that Isabel, who was from Mexico, was becoming more than a friend. Isabel was petite, with a pretty face, black hair and brown eyes, and a lovely brown mestizo coloration. Isabel had a small son, around nine in 1979, very handsome, bright, and unbelievably spoiled. Most important, she was sympathetic and supportive in a time when my personal life was falling apart.

I can remember one night very well. I was convinced that the affair between Nancy and Shane had been going on for months. Nancy calmly announced that she was going to spend the weekend with "women friends" in Oakland. This was a common occurrence. I decided I would not spend another Saturday night alone, so I invited Isabel over for dinner. She would bring her son, Carlos, and after dinner the three of us would go to Chinatown to watch the fireworks, as it was Chinese New Year.

The three of us had a nice dinner together and then Carlos retreated into another room to watch TV for a while. Isabel and I settled on the couch to talk, and soon Carlos fell sound asleep. Before I knew it I was telling Isabel the whole sad tale of my relationship with Nancy. It was not news to her, of course, as she had been close enough to both of us to sense what was happening.

"I don't believe in love without contradiction, without resentment, without conflict, Isabel. I just don't! It starts out all right, or so it seems, but later the conflict grows. Maybe it's the way human beings are shaped by our society. They can't ever fully connect with another person without also hurting the person. This is the way it has always been in my life. I'm sure I may be part of the cause. But I just think it is idealistic to believe that any two people can avoid such antagonisms. I guess we have to accept something less perfect, something flawed."

Isabel looked up at me with her large brown eyes and spoke with the deepest conviction: "No! No, Tim. That's not true. There can be real love, beautiful love without conflict, love which builds each other instead of hurting each other, love that grows each day. You cannot give up hope. You must strive for real love because you deserve to experience it."

What could I say? I did not fully believe her, but God, I wanted to. I felt the love coming from her as she spoke. It grasped me almost physically. Soon she was in my arms. Carlos did not wake up. Later that night I picked up the sleeping boy, as I would on so many future occasions over the next five years, and carried him downstairs to Isabel's car. I spent the rest of the night at her place near Berkeley.

OFF TO MEXICO

Isabel started talking about going back to Mexico in June. She had been living in California for several years, and I had not really thought much about her Mexican roots. She was dead serious. She had had a government job for eighteen years and had been on leave in order to study. Now she had to return or lose her accrued pension and benefits.

She asked me to come with her. I really never planned to live in Mexico. I loved California, had begun to develop some friends, and had a pretty good beginning of a new career in printing production. In addition I knew I was just terrible at languages and had no confidence whatsoever that I could ever learn Spanish. But she certainly was lovely looking and so romantic, and I was head over heels in love with her. I had lost my job and had no place to live. Nothing was really holding me in the Bay Area. "Well," I thought, "why not? I might as well give it a try!"

We packed our possessions in Isabel's very old Volkswagen Squareback and spent a wonderful week driving to Mexico City. Then we moved into Isabel's house, which was situated in a pleasant suburb just north of the Federal District. It was a nicely designed middle-class home with three bedrooms, a courtyard, and a maid's room off the courtyard. The entire "colonia" was made up of similar houses. Yet all you had to do was walk a couple of blocks to the main boulevard, down this street a few more blocks, cross a bridge over a sewage-filled river, and you entered a "colonia popular." Here poor people lived in shacks without running water. Children, goats, turkeys, and chickens were everywhere in the dirt streets.

I spent my mornings studying Spanish with other foreigners at the National University (L'Universidad Nacional de Mexico—UNAM) in the southern part of the city. I returned around noon and spent the afternoon writing. Then I went back to UNAM in the evening to teach a seminar on postcapitalist societies in the graduate school of political science. This meant that most of my day was spent traveling back and forth across the city in terrible traffic.

I got to know the PRT, Partido Revolutionario Trajabadora (Revolutionary Workers Party) pretty well while I was in Mexico. I became a member of a cell made up exclusively of university professors from UNAM. The cell met once a week in different comrades' homes, usually in the southern part of the city. The meeting would start around 8 P.M. and would usually go on to at least 1 A.M.! This was a bit much for me.

Comrades would straggle into the meeting at all hours, sometimes as late as 11 P.M. This situation was not simply an expression of middle-class lack of discipline; these were extremely busy people holding down several jobs, supporting families, writing in the daily press, working on books, and doing some party work. Many times they did not finish teaching until ten or so at night.

Our cell had two major responsibilities. It edited a theoretical journal, *Criticas de la Economia Politica*, a rather thick publication that came out three or four times a year. Hard as it was for an American radical to believe, the journal required no subsidy. It usually sold out and its publisher made a little money from it. It printed material by European intellectuals around the Trotskyist movement as well as by Mexicans. The publication was not a strictly "party" organ, and a relatively broad spectrum of leftists wrote for it. Interestingly, there was another group of PRT intellectuals around the Argentine Adolfo Gilly that published the journal *Coyoacan*. That journal was similar to *Criticas*, though it tended to publish slightly more topical material. The existence of two separate journals can be traced to differing political histories. The *Coyoacan* people had been supporters of Juan Posados[1] in the past; the *Criticas* people were from the Ernest Mandel intellectual tradition. The PRT had no problem with managing two journals in friendly competition, and it did not try to impose a party line on either.

The other major task of our cell was political work at the university. While we had economists and sociologists as members, our core was a group of political scientists who at that time controlled the graduate department (which is how I got my teaching job). The main figure was an astute politician and political writer, Octavio Rodríguez Araujo. The Economics Department was controlled by the Communist Party. The Communists were called the *pescados* at our meetings, which at first confused me, since the word means "dead fish." Then I was told that the word for fish (*pesces*) sounds the same as the initials of the party in Spanish (PC).

The PRT presence in the department enabled the comrades to arrange a number of conferences at which Trotskyist intellectuals from around the world were heard. I do not believe the comrades took advantage of their position because they also invited intellectuals belonging to other tendencies to these conferences. But our position did permit us to give Trotskyism more of a hearing than would have been the case if the *pescados* had controlled the department.

The most exciting conference I attended was held around the same time as the congress of the Communist Party. Certain guests to that congress were able to participate. The topic was Eurocommunism, and the panel included Santiago Carrillo,[2] then General Secretary of the Communist

Party of Spain, and Ernest Mandel, representing the Fourth International. The hall was packed with well over one thousand people, as this was the first time a leader of the Fourth International shared the platform with a leading European Communist. Ernest spoke in precise Spanish (I could even understand most of it), demanding that Carillo openly repudiate the Moscow Trials, the Stalinist slanders that Trotskyists were Fascist agents, and the murder of Trotskyists and semi-Trotskyists like Andrés Nin[3] during the Spanish Civil War. Carrillo ducked no issues. He openly repudiated Stalinism and its past practices and stated that he viewed Trotskyists as a legitimate part of the Left. He then went on to spell out his political criticisms of the Trotskyist movement. I was impressed. It was definitely a historic occasion.

Of course during my stay in Mexico, the government party, Partido Revolutionario Institutionario (PRI), dominated Mexican life as it has done for over fifty years. It is both committed to capitalism and extremely corrupt. But the left-wing opposition to this party is more often Marxist than liberal. This opposition is supported by a significant and highly articulate layer of the middle class, as well as by dissatisfied workers and peasants. And even PRI has within it a layer of trained Marxist intellectuals who seek to give its policies a leftist appearance to counter the influence of the leftist critics. The *pescados*[4] made up the major party on the left, but the PRT was also significant.

Adolfo Gilly wrote regularly for the moderately leftist daily paper *Uno Mas Uno*, which was widely read at the UNAM. My friend Francisco Gomezjara wrote for *Excelsior*, the major daily paper, which strongly supported PRI. Ricardo Pascoe, another PRT member, wrote for the conservative daily *El Universal*. What this meant was that a trained and respected group of Trotskyist intellectuals received a relatively broad hearing in Mexico. This gave Trotskyism at least a crack at *hegemony*, to use Gramsci's term. I might add that what these people wrote was not necessarily "party line." Gomezjara, for instance, wrote a series in *Excelsior* on Stalin that took the unorthodox view that the socialist countries represent a new form of class rule. The PRT somehow survived this theoretical indiscretion.

I liked the PRT. I believe Ernest Mandel did a very good job in encouraging its development, and a few key leaders, such as my good friend Manuel Aguilar Mora, were able to regroup a number of small Trotskyist groups and individuals and hold them together in a party that was effective in mass work yet that contained within it diversity, permitting intellectuals to contribute to the party in the best way they could, as intellectuals.[5]

Homage to the Old Man

The most moving political experience I had in Mexico was the Trotsky centennial celebration. This was organized by the Mexican government, a fact that says something about Mexico's different political climate. Can you imagine the American government commemorating Lenin or Trotsky? Leon Trotsky has a special place in Mexican history because the Cardenas government—which had nationalized the oil industry and which was the most radical regime since the Zapata days—gave Trotsky sanctuary when all other nations refused to do so. Trotsky died on Mexican soil in 1940, murdered by Stalin's agent Ramon Mercader.

The centennial drew Trotskyists from all over the world, brought at the Mexican government's expense. I attended one talk given by Adolfo Gilly; Tamara Deutscher sat on one side of me and Michel Raptis (Pablo) sat just behind me. The most moving talk was the one given by the American Trotskyist George Novack. George, with his white hair and glasses and speaking in his strong Bostonian accent, looked his most professorial. He recounted his experiences as organizer of the Commission of Inquiry headed by the American philosopher John Dewey, which traveled to Mexico to interview Trotsky as part of its independent investigation into the Moscow Trials.[6] As George remembered those days, and as the image of the Old Man came into his mind, tears filled his eyes. His voice began to break. He stumbled through the rest of the speech.

After the meeting two teenage girls ran up to the platform babbling away in Spanish. They were Trotsky's great-granddaughters, and soon they were joined by two men. One, Vlady, now a painter, was a middle-aged man with a beard and long hair. Vlady was the son of the novelist Victor Serge, former anarchist and Trotskyist who died in exile in Mexico in 1947.[7] The other man was the girls' father, Esteban "Sieva" Volkov. A thin, Russian-looking fellow, he had been living a private life in Mexico for many years as an engineer.

As a young boy, Sieva had left the Soviet Union in the 1930s with his mentally disturbed mother (Zina Volkov, Trotsky's daughter by his first marriage). Soon after arriving in Europe his mother committed suicide and Sieva went to stay with his uncle, Leon Sedov, Trotsky's son and a leader of the International Left Opposition. Soon thereafter Leon Sedov was murdered by Stalinist agents and the little Sieva was shipped off to Mexico to be brought up by his grandfather and grandmother. One evening he was awakened from his sleep by the sound of someone in his room. Then gunfire burst out in the dark, and the little boy was slightly wounded. This was the attack upon the Trotsky compound led by the Mexican painter David Siqueiros. A few months later there was a commotion in the house. Sieva ran into his grandfather's study to see what was happening. There he saw Trotsky on the floor with an ice axe in his head. Trotsky saw him and in almost his last breath he asked people to remove the little boy from the room.[8]

Leon Trotsky certainly had his weaknesses, and his theories are subject to vigorous critique. Yet he helped lead a revolution that transformed a nation and much of human history. But he did more than this. His was a tragic history, for he lost power and died a hounded man. This permitted him to speak with a voice of moral authority that the possessors of power generally lack.

I visited Trotsky's home in Coyoacan that year. It is a walled-in house in the old Spanish style with the living quarters facing inward onto a garden area. Coyoacan is now a municipality just to the south of Mexico City's center and quite close to the university. Where a muddy river once flowed near the home, a four-lane highway now brings commuters and pollution in and out of the downtown area of the city. Despite its pretty gardens, the house struck me as depressingly drab. The house itself was starkly furnished with little color or life. Nearby was the home of Frida Kahlo—a painter and leftist married to Diego Rivera—where Trotsky and his wife, Natalia, first stayed when they arrived in Mexico. There could have been no greater contrast! Kahlo's home was warm, colorful, filled with striking Mexican artifacts such as grotesque papier-mâché puppets from Day of the Dead celebrations.

The signs of old battles still mark Trotsky's home, now owned by the Mexican government. At the corners the old walls have been reinforced and small guard towers constructed. In Trotsky's bedroom you can still see the bullet holes made by the machine-gun attack on the home, the one in which Sieva was slightly wounded. What a pitifully vulnerable spot to defend an aging revolutionary from a man who held state power and had almost limitless material resources, as well as the fanatically loyal support of literally millions throughout the world. Stalin wanted Trotsky dead and did not rest until he accomplished that grisly deed. It is amazing that a small band of Trotskyists were able to defend the "Old Man" as long as they did.

I Visit Cuba

In the summer of 1983 Isabel arranged for us to travel together to Cuba as part of a university tour group. By this time I was living by myself in the Bay Area, though the two of us remained quite close. I flew to Mexico City, where Isabel and I boarded a plane for Havana. I had written about this island for twenty years, revolutionary Cuba, and now I finally had an opportunity to make a visit. Isabel had insisted upon the trip.

"You write documents, theses, and articles and yet you don't go there. Why not take a look? It might not be as bad as you say it is or it may be worse. But at least you will have been there. Anyway the beaches are lovely and I can get a cheap trip through the university."

Her last argument was the most convincing. I was not a strong believer in gaining objective knowledge of a country on the basis of a week's vacation. Yet I had to admit I was curious to take a look at Cuba. It was actually a short flight and in a little over two hours we were making our descent. As we made a wide circle over Havana, Isabel and I began to see the beautiful island laid out before us. Green and lush, Cuba was covered with palm trees and was such a contrast from the smoggy browns and grays of Mexico City.

Havana Airport was quite disappointing. It was like an airport in a small American city such as Springfield, Massachusetts, or Fresno, California. It had not changed since Batista's day, and it had not been Batista's great triumph. After a delay of an hour or so we were processed through customs and we assembled beside a waiting bus that had been assigned to our tour group. Isabel and I were part of a tour of Mexican teachers and students, most of very modest means, interested in an inexpensive vacation. Fidel was not to earn much foreign exchange from the likes of us.

Our bus arrived in Havana just at dusk. We passed through a suburban area with luxurious homes. They all appeared to be occupied; cars were parked in the driveways. Some people in socialist Cuba, I thought, were prospering. Soon we were in the center of Havana with its still majestic Spanish architecture, wide boulevards and, here and there, modern high-rises. It was a hot evening, damp, with barely a breath of air. It was so peaceful and romantic. Everywhere I looked there were couples: holding hands and walking, holding each other tightly, leaning against the walls of the ancient edifices, kissing, whispering in each other's ears. Three pretty teenage girls walked down a street in brightly colored clothes, and two teenage boys in designer jeans drove slowly next to them on a motor scooter, trying to pick them up. No one paid attention to the large billboard sporting a painting of a red flag, a Cuban flag, the initials "PCC" and a slogan urging greater production under the leadership of the party.

We arrived in front of the Hotel National. It had a red-tiled roof and stately palms lining the entranceway. It was an impressive hotel in the old Spanish style, Cuba's best until the Havana Hilton was built in the late fifties. Our room was clean, though it could have used some paint, and there was no seat on the toilet. The air-conditioning did not work, but we were given a fan. The Cubans are doing their best to repair an infrastructure that is decaying due to our trade embargo, my political mind told me. We gazed out over the Caribbean and we could see the lighthouse and the colonial fortress at the entrance to Old Havana Harbor with a string of lights coming from the decaying tenements along the crescent beach front. We became just one more couple in love.

Isabel had Leon Ortiz's address in her wallet, stuffed between her Banamex and Bancomer credit cards. She did not want immigration officials to see it. Isabel explained that Leon and his father were old-time Trotskyists and that they were part of the group that Castro had imprisoned. His address was given her by Adolfo Gilly, the Argentine journalist then living in exile in Mexico City. Gilly had spent some time in Cuba in its early revolutionary days.[9] The next morning Isabel tried to reach Leon on the phone. There was no answer. We had to assume he was at work. We decided we would try to find Leon on our own that evening.

It was dusk when Isabel and I forced our way onto a crowded bus and headed toward Old Havana near the harbor. Once we had gotten to the district where Leon lived, we got off the bus and started to walk. The streets were narrow in this part of the city and the buildings were very old and in disrepair. Few had windows; instead they had large shutter doors that went almost from the ceiling to the floor. The second- and third-story apartments had little balconies with wrought iron railings. It was a hot night, so most of these shutters were wide open, allowing us to see the human activity inside: the glow of black-and-white TVs, the smell of cooking, children at play, the incessant hum of Spanish conversations. I knew so few words that for me it was a kind of background drone wherever I went, making me feel more distant, separated from my surroundings.

The streets were packed with people, as sidewalks were nonexistent and there were few cars or taxis. As we passed down one particularly narrow street, we had to force ourselves around a large 1959 Buick in the process of being repaired by its proud owner. Somehow parts would be found and the pre-Castro vehicle kept on the road to take the family to the country on weekends. On the right side was the famous restaurant La Bogeguita del Medio, where Ernest Hemingway used to hang out sipping *mojitos* (made with fresh mint, lime, and rum).

We stumbled into a large crowd of young girls dressed in their school uniforms: bright red skirts held up by red straps, white blouses, and red bandannas. They were pouring out of a school building that must have run two shifts, as schools so often do in Mexico. Isabel asked for directions, and soon we were completely surrounded by smiling, chattering children, a sea of red and white. "Mexicana," "Mexicana." I picked up a word or two of their Spanish. The girls spontaneously broke out into a chant: "Viva Mexico!" The crowd was growing. We shouted back "Viva Cuba!" and then we all chanted "Viva Cuba y Mexico!"

It was a wonderful moment; the spirit of the revolution had not totally faded. However, we were creating a minor sensation in the middle of

Havana when we wished to make a very private journey. We made our good-byes, Isabel had to hug some dozen different girls, and finally we were able to slip away down the street deeper into the old city.

Soon we were in a strictly residential neighborhood. Here and there were little piles of brick and sand with a red sign announcing that a microbrigade was at work. An effort was being made to patch the decaying city center after decades of giving priority to building the high-rise apartment complexes that ringed Havana. No one was at work on repairs, probably because of a shortage in cement to make the needed mortar. A bright light shone from a wide-open storefront in the middle of the block. It was the headquarters of the local Committee for the Defense of the Revolution. A fat man in a white short-sleeved shirt sat behind a desk and a couple of cronies leaned against the wall, chatting.

Isabel suggested that we check in and ask for directions, for by this time we were completely lost in the labyrinth of narrow alleyways. Isabel asked the man at the desk, giving an address close to Leon's. You can never be too careful. As a small knot of people gathered, offering conflicting directions, the man started grilling Isabel.

"What are you doing in this part of town? How are you related to these people?" Isabel translated for me. "Why do you want to go to this address? How do you know this person you wish to visit?"

Luckily the animated discussion about the best route for us to follow distracted the white-shirted man. He was trying to keep order in his little office, which was unused to crowds, and we were able to ease out of the place and back into the street, heading as fast as we could out of his jurisdiction. Soon we were in a quiet old square just a couple of blocks from the waterfront. There, finally, we found Leon's place in a darkened area under an overhanging balcony. The street name had been misspelled.

We began banging on the metal shutters that served as a door, for the bell did not work (did any in Cuba?). We were creating such a ruckus that I was afraid the police would show up and we would be grilled again. Finally a small boy appeared at the door and asked our business.

"Does Leon Ortiz live here?" Isabel asked in Spanish. "We are friends from Mexico."

"He is my father. I will show you the way."

He opened the shutters wide, revealing a little courtyard with a pile of bricks and sand in one corner and the requisite microbrigade sign hanging over the unfinished project. We carefully walked up a decrepit inner stairway covered with plaster dust, and then along a dingy hallway past apartments filled with activity, children playing on the landings, and the smell of black beans cooking. The almost-deserted square was now closed behind us, and we had entered a teaming beehive of life.

The little boy opened the door to a small apartment on the third floor. There was a small bed on the right as we entered and a large black-and-white TV on the left. An old lady, a middle-aged, pretty woman, and a thin, bright-eyed girl of about ten were sitting on the bed. The two older women were watching the TV while the little girl was engrossed in her homework, occasionally glancing up at the set. This rather narrow room led right into a kitchen with an old-fashioned gas stove on the right and an old sink next to it. In the corner on the left was a small refrigerator and a little portable washing machine with Russian letters on it. It could not have held more than four pounds of clothes. The kitchen opened to the left onto a dining area, and two rooms used for sleeping could be seen beyond that with shutters opened wide to the street. It was clear that two generations were sharing the small apartment.

An old man in his seventies sat at the kitchen table talking with a heavyset, middle-aged man. They were ignoring the noise coming from the TV and from the street. The younger man arose.

"I am Leon Ortiz and this is my father, Fernando. My son tells me you are from Mexico. Are you friends of Gilly?" Isabel translated for me. She handed him a letter of introduction, which Leon passed to his father.

"I want you to meet Tim. He's from the United States. Used to be part of Cannon's group."

Fernando rose and came straight up to me, ignoring Isabel.

"Do you think he ever got my letter?"

"Who got what letter?" I asked through Isabel.

"Trotsky, of course. We sent him a full report on the political situation here and our strategy but we never received an answer."

It was clear Fernando was referring to some communication he had sent to the old Russian revolutionary in Mexico, probably in 1938 or 1939, just before he was killed by Stalin. I suggested that it was quite possible such a letter did exist in the Trotsky Archives at Harvard and that I knew someone who did research there and would check for him. The four of us sat around the chipped enameled kitchen table while Leon told us their story. The TV droned on in the background. The old lady, however, got up to make some Cuban coffee and joined us. She, too, was an old revolutionary. The younger woman, Leon's wife, was not political and remained glued to the tube while the little boy, I guessed his age as eight, joined his sister on the bed with his homework.

"When the revolution triumphed there were not many of us here. We had lost contact with comrades in other countries. Here in Havana we had my father, my mother, my mother's brother, and myself. Then there were around a dozen comrades in Guantánamo. We got out a leaflet or two but were unable to do much. Then Gilly arrived with some other Argentines.

Soon we had a monthly paper out and we began work setting the type for a new edition of Trotsky's book *The Permanent Revolution*. We were very excited. People began coming around us. It looked like the revolution of our dreams was unfolding before us. Of course, we didn't trust Fidel. He was petty bourgeois. He wasn't linked to the workers. We were afraid he would not go far enough. He would not follow the path of permanent revolution; he would compromise with Wall Street.

"But we were proven wrong on that account. Suddenly Fidel embraced Marxism-Leninism and began to nationalize everything. We supported all this. At the same time, though, Fidel supported the Soviet Union uncritically. Our old enemies, the Stalinists, found cushy jobs in the government. He began to clamp down on the unions. He took no steps to institute workers' democracy. We continued to support Fidel, to support the revolutionary process, but we had our criticisms."

Fernando broke in: "I kept thinking, what would the Old Man think of it all? Where are the soviets, the real workers' councils and control?"

"Suddenly they hit us." Leon took over the narrative. "The government sent the police to the print shop and broke up the type for Trotsky's book. Our little office was seized, the mimeo taken. The Argentines were picked up and expelled from the country. My father was arrested and then they came and picked me up."

"I was so worried." It was Maria, Fernando's wife and comrade. "I came home from work, to this place, and it was a wreck, it was in a shambles. My husband and son were gone. Luckily Leon's children hadn't been born yet. My brother was even picked up for a while. I was picked up when I went to my brother's apartment looking for him. But they let me go. The group was dispersed. We were cut off from the outside. No one cared. I guess we were an embarrassment to the Left abroad. They all loved Fidel so much in those days. Yet we supported him, too. We really did. It's just that we had some questions. We had an obligation to raise them."

Maria was sitting opposite me with her back to the kitchen area. No air was moving in the small stuffy apartment. It must have been after 9 P.M., yet Havana was not cooling off. I could see small beads of sweat trickling down Maria's forehead. My eyes wandered from her head to the stove. A small mouse was scurrying along the gas pipe that went from the stove to somewhere under the sink. It kept going back and forth. Every now and then it would stick its head out from between one of the burners. I forced myself now to look back at Leon, who had begun talking again. He was talking theory. About the permanent revolution: Castro, in his opinion, was "objectively" fulfilling Trotsky's revolutionary strategy as outlined in his *Permanent Revolution*.

"Why, then, did he smash up Trotsky's text?" I intervened and Isabel translated.

"It is a revolution not without its contradictions. But perhaps Fidel is learning. Things are better now."

"What happened after that?" I intervened again. "When did they let you out?"

"It was not so bad the first time. I was in for only six months but they kept my father for a full year. Mother was very worried."

"There was a second imprisonment?" Isabel asked.

"That came in 1970. There was a lot of unrest within the working class, which resented the lack of material gains and the pressure placed upon workers during the Ten Million Tons sugar-harvest drive. A dissident current arose within the Communist Party. So they jailed us once again. This time I got out in a year but they held my father in prison for six years.

"We made good use of the time. We had some very fruitful discussions with the dissident Communists. Then the prison authorities let us hold classes in Marxism for the *gusanos*, those that had opposed the revolution. We were able to explain the revolution, the class struggle to some of them, to get them to support the revolutionary process."

Now I was fully awake and was totally absorbed in these people: a frail old man who had corresponded with Trotsky in the 1930s, whom Castro imprisoned twice, and his son, named after the Russian leader, imprisoned also. Why did Castro fear this family? Why did he need to use the great power of the state against these humble individuals?

The two continued to support the revolution that imprisoned them, to aid it even when in jail. They lived in this poor, run-down tenement while others who had lived comfortably under Batista now enjoyed a pleasant life-style in Havana's suburbs. It was such a lonely heroism! The Left in the West did not know or care about them. I felt they were important, they were part of the story. They should be remembered. I was choked up and felt an almost uncontrollable desire to cry. It was helpful that the discussion was in Spanish. I could let it bathe me in its sounds while I composed myself.

"How are you doing now?" I broke in.

"Things are better. The government has made serious concessions to the workers in order to sustain their support. I work in the construction industry where I receive a wage of four hundred pesos a month. Some of my supervisors get only three hundred pesos a month! I am secretary of the union branch."

"Do the workers know your politics?" Isabel asked.

"Yes, they know. That's why they elected me. They feel they can trust me to stand up for them. My father works in the same trade, too, but the officials still watch him. He keeps quiet."

It was getting late and I could see that the two children were having trouble keeping awake. Leon's wife had dozed off in front of the TV. Of course! They couldn't go to bed until we left. This was the bedroom for some of them. Isabel and I stood up and got ready to leave. Isabel opened her large purse and brought out a few thin volumes of Trotsky's writings recently published in Mexico, which Fernando held reverently in his wrinkled, calloused hands.

Leon's eyes brightened as he introduced us to his two children on our way out. He was very proud of how well they were doing in school. How much hope he had for their future! He told us their names, but they made no sense to me. They sounded exotic, not Spanish at all. Leon noticed our reaction and smiled.

"The names are acronyms for famous quotes of Trotsky. Her name," Leon patted his daughter's head, "is based on 'Marxism without the dialectic is like a clock without a spring,' while his name is based on 'Forward to victory under the banner of the Fourth International.'"

The children smiled, as proud of their father and grandfather as they were of them. They would somehow survive the awkwardness of their names. They were achievers and the revolution would open the university to them. The politics would probably fade and their intelligence would find sustenance in science, in medicine. But someday, I suspected, they would tell their children the meaning of their names, the tradition of their family. That night I felt privileged to have been touched by a movement that produced human beings of the caliber of this family.

The next day the old lady came to visit us at the hotel. We insisted on a gift for the family. They had no relatives in Miami to bestow presents upon them. This family remained loyal to a regime that did not understand them, that persecuted them. We offered her a fan or a portable radio/cassette player. She chose the former. At least there would be some breeze in that crowded apartment.

"Don't forget to check on Fernando's letter," she whispered to me as we parted in the hotel lobby. "It's important to him. He doesn't have a copy any more. They seized everything during that first raid."

Soon we were back in Mexico. We drove through the poor neighborhood near the airport. The streets were darkened in midday by pollution, and our minds were still in Cuba. Then we were traveling down a main boulevard in the northeastern part of the city. We passed the railroad station and then on the left loomed a large public-housing complex—it looked much the same as projects in New York City—and Isabel started talking quietly to me.

"That's where it happened in 1968. The students gathered in front of those buildings to start a march through the city. The police, supported by the army, moved in, coming right down this boulevard. Soon there was tear gas everywhere and they started to fire live ammunition. The people in the project threw pots and pans out the windows at the police and troops and took the students who escaped into their homes. Then they arrested everybody, everybody on the left. That was how they prepared for the Olympics."

"And you, Isabel?"

"I was there but I had friends in the project who protected me. I was young then and not very involved. They arrested my brother. They also arrested Gilly, even though he was Argentine, and held him for five years. Maybe you understand why we support Cuba, why we can't be as critical as you. I know you are right. But it is not the same for us."

Soon we had passed through working-class Mexico City and entered the clean, pretty, middle-class world of the northern suburbs. Lovely homes, neatly trimmed little lawns, marble facades, two cars pulled up in front of each house.

The next day we headed for the huge UNAM campus, where friends had organized a meeting for me. The occasion was the publication of a book I had written three years earlier during my stay in the country.[10] We drove to the meeting with Manuel Aguilar Mora, one of the leaders of the PRT and its representative for many years at the Paris headquarters of the Fourth International, and his large blond Latvian wife, Mara. Manuel was one of the panelists. I felt I might as well utilize the occasion to present my impressions of Cuba, since about one quarter of the book was devoted to Cuba. I concluded with the admittedly impressionistic remark that "Cuba is undoubtedly the nicest of the Stalinist states." What I meant by this was that the country had the same *structure* as the other state socialist countries but retained a greater degree of popularity, particularly because its people united with the government in its efforts to sustain the country despite U.S. imperialist pressure.

Manuel then launched a rather bitter polemic against me, defending Cuba so vigorously that he left out entirely those criticisms that he actually believed in. Such is the way of polemic on the left. While I felt the attack was a bit out of place at a meeting devoted to promoting my book, I took it in good spirits. I knew Manuel did not take such polemics personally and was just getting a bit carried away, grandstanding for his supporters in the audience.

Isabel and I drove Manuel and Mara home in our car. Mara spent the entire trip giving Manuel a piece of her mind. She believed he was completely out of order, factional and ill-tempered. The next I heard of the two was that they had separated. This discussion had been the beginning of the end for the two of them. Manuel was a 100 percent party person, while

Mara had developed a hatred of the polemic, of the factional, intolerant, strident side of party life. I understood them both so well. Thirty years of training and living in party circles had made me, in many ways, like Manuel. Yet my emotions that day were with Mara. I had lost a tolerance for the intolerant. I was definitely winding down.

AILEEN JENNINGS'S STORY

One day in October 1985 the telephone rang, and I heard a distant voice with a British accent. I was taken aback; it was as if the past had returned. I even felt a moment of terror, a flashback to my last phone conversation with Healy in the fall of 1974, over ten years ago. This time it was a reporter from a British newspaper. He informed me that Healy had just been expelled from his own organization, and he asked for my thoughts on the matter. I was at the same time both shocked by this news and at too much of a distance from Healy to give the reporter much of an answer. Since that awkward phone call, however, I have had time to think about the events that led to and issued from the breakup of Healy's world.

Healy was indeed expelled that month by a majority of the Central Committee of the Workers Revolutionary Party, led by Mike Banda and Cliff Slaughter. He was charged with endangering the security of the group through his many liaisons with young women. On July 1, 1985, Aileen Jennings wrote a letter to the Political Committee of the Workers Revolutionary Party. It said, in part,

> I can no longer go on covering up a position at both the office and in the flats which . . . opens the party to police provocation; namely that whilst for 19 years I have been the close personal companion of Comrade Healy I have also covered up a problem which the Political Committee must now deal with because I cannot.
>
> This is that the flats in particular are used in a completely opportunist way for sexual liaisons with female members employed by the Party or News Line,[11] female members of the International Committee and others [twenty six individuals were then named]. . . .
>
> In 1964, after a Control Commission of Investigation, Comrade Healy gave an undertaking that he would cease these practices. This has not happened and I cannot sit on this volcano any longer.[12]

Jennings's letter leaked out and caused quite a sensation in Fleet Street, where the *Mirror* headlined the event "Red in the Bed."[13] The more I thought about the curious details of the scandal, however, the more I became convinced that behind all the sensationalism lay the real story, the important story, the human story. It was the story of a talented man who led a movement dedicated to the highest ideals. Yet this movement was transformed over time into an instrument for Healy's personal tyranny over the membership. Acting with inhumanity internally, the movement betrayed the ideals that were its sole reason for existence.

My first thoughts were of Aileen Jennings. She had been so close to Healy for so long. She appeared to me incapable of ever thinking differently from Healy, and she was always attending to his needs. When Healy came to our Canadian summer camps, Aileen was with him. We put the two up in a nearby motel, in separate rooms, of course. Once Healy came with Aileen to Montreal to meet with our Political Committee members. I remember going with Healy to the shopping district, as he wished to buy a gift for Aileen. If I hadn't been so sure their relationship had been simply platonic and "comradely," it would have appeared to me that the old fellow was actually in love with this young lady. I never suspected, nor did any of the American comrades, anything intimate in Healy's relations with Aileen until I broke with him in 1974. Then I learned a few things that made me look at this relationship in a different light. I suspect that intimacies never occurred to me mainly because Gerry was, quite frankly, a rather ugly man: He was overweight and had a face about as appealing as an English bulldog's. I underestimated his persuasive talents, however!

It is now quite clear that Healy maintained a liaison with Aileen for some nineteen years and *at the same time and with her full knowledge* had liaisons with at least twenty-six other women. While all this hanky-panky was going on Aileen was married to and lived with Paul Jennings, who remained a hardworking and loyal party member. While Paul grew to resent Healy because he took so much of Aileen's time, he claimed not to have known what was really occurring. The situation was certainly rather complex, and full of emotional tensions for all concerned. What, for example, was going on inside Aileen for all these years? What a puzzle she was. Always apparently in control of herself, self-assured, even a little cocky, proud of her good looks, and not the outwardly emotional type. Why, *after nineteen years*, did she decide to break with Healy and go to the Political Committee to report a situation that she admittedly had covered up for all those years?

Bizarre yet intriguing. Aileen is the only one who knows the answers to these questions, and perhaps we will never know. We can be sure that Aileen's break with Healy must have been all the deeper and more explosive given the length of time Aileen spent totally devoted to the man. The evening that Aileen wrote her letter she met with her husband and told him about it. She also told him that spinal injuries she had received two years earlier, which required hospital treatment and had led to her becoming slowly crippled, had been inflicted by Healy, who broke a chair across her back.[14] The next day Aileen was observed leaving her south London flat with two suitcases.[15]

She was taken in by her mother, the old-time Trotskyist Mickie Shaw. Aileen's father, Robert, had died in 1980. Gerry Healy had transformed Bob Shaw's death into a major political campaign. Memorial services and demonstrations were held across Great Britain. In 1983 Healy published a whole book, written by Mickie, on Bob's life.[16] Bob Shaw came from a very religious family in the Midlands. He became a Methodist lay preacher. At the same time, he was radicalized by the depression and joined the Independent Labour Party.[17] There he met Trotskyists including Mickie, who came from a working-class family. Soon he dropped his religious activity and beliefs and became a Marxist. He went to work in a factory and joined a Trotskyist group, the Workers International League. During World War II he moved to London to help with the Trotskyist center there. He needed a place to stay, and as luck would have it, Gerry Healy kindly put him up, recruiting him in the process to his faction. Bob remained Healy's loyal follower from that moment until his death in 1980.

Bob devoted himself to Healy's brand of Trotskyism with all the intensity and single-mindedness he had developed as a Methodist. I remember him well: dressed in a grayish-brown cardigan sweater, pipe stuck out of a corner of his mouth and gripped so tightly I was afraid the stem would break off, a glum expression on his face. Whenever I met Bob, something tragic had just occurred in the area of the country under his charge (usually Scotland), and Healy had just subjected him to a bitter political attack. He deeply believed that he had sinned and he was determined to try harder to avoid sinning in the future. Yet you knew he knew he would sin once again.

It is painful even now to realize that Bob may have known of his daughter's arrangement with Healy, and if he did, he did nothing!

HEALY'S FALL

The scandal had the effect of a pin that pricks a huge boil. Soon the puss was flowing out as comrade after comrade told deeply felt, personal stories of sexual and physical abuse. Healy was locked out of the headquarters, so the party files became available for all to see. I read the resulting internal bulletins and began to get a picture of the life of that party over the ten years since I had broken with Healy. Having lost most of his working-class base in the Thornett split, Healy had turned his attention to Vanessa Redgrave, her brother, Corin, and their theater circle. Considerable sums flowed in to help support the daily paper and the apparatus being built around the paper. Yet even Vanessa's considerable resources could not support a daily paper with such a small circulation. Healy had to find more money somewhere.

The ever-resourceful party leader soon found the needed funds. Healy discovered that supporting the cause of Arab nationalism could be translated into serious funding from such "leftist" regimes as those ruling Iran, Iraq, and Libya. Vanessa made a pro-PLO television documentary called "The Palestinians" and visited with Yasser Arafat and then Muammar Qaddafi. Soon Arab governments began granting lucrative printing contracts to Healy. The result was what appeared on the surface to be a success. By the time of his demise Healy had assembled an apparatus employing ninety-one people, a large web printing facility in the North, a mansion in Derbyshire used as a "Marxist college," six bookstores, flats opposite party headquarters at Clapham, and a £15,000 sports car for himself. All told, WRP resources were estimated to be worth in the neighborhood of £1,500,000.[18] Yet the membership at the time of Healy's expulsion was no more than one thousand.

The picture emerges of a cult life with Healy increasingly turned inward and supported by a coterie drawn from the middle class, including the Redgraves and *News Line* editor Alex Mitchell. Quite amazingly, the party's intellectuals—Jack Gale, Cliff Slaughter, Geoff Pillings, Tom Kemp—hung on, but they played only a small role in the internal life of the party. The Young Socialists, according to Maureen Bambrick, simply disintegrated. A small bureaucracy maintained a weekly youth paper, and from time to time, youth were rounded up like cattle from the range to populate the latest Healy demonstration or meeting.[19]

Healy maintained absolute personal control over this apparatus and the relatively small membership that, with the help of theatrical stars and Arab governments, sustained and staffed it. General Secretary Mike Banda was formally in charge of the WRP, but he took his orders from Healy. Mike was not above a punch-up to maintain his and Healy's regimes, as ex–Central Committee member Stuart Carter has testified.[20] Sheila Torrance was in charge of driving the members to produce the Potemkin village demonstrations and seeing to it that they were milked of every available pence.

I must say I felt great satisfaction in the belated recognition of Healy's crimes by his closest collaborators. Mike Banda wrote:

> The crisis with Wohlforth was artificially exacerbated by Healy with his paranoid ravings about security and his total failure to deal with the Workers League's problems of perspective and policy. The issue of Nancy Fields was exaggerated and distorted beyond all proportion. In

> my opinion Wohlforth's weaknesses were maliciously exploited by Healy to drive him out. . . . The case of Nancy Fields must be reexamined in the same way as Thornett, Blick, and other victims of Healy's malice and bureaucratic sadism.

He then went on to comment on Healy's "security" campaign directed against Joe Hansen, George Novack, and the SWP, which he characterized as "a manic witch-hunt" whose aim was "to satisfy Healy's paranoid schizophrenia. . . . No one who honours Trotsky's impeccable and scrupulous regard for absolutely verifiable facts will have anything more to do with his monstrous frame-up based entirely on circumstantial evidence and political innuendo."[21]

A short time after learning of the expulsion of Healy, I received this note from Cliff Slaughter:

> I want to say to you that we are very anxious to put the record straight on the whole series of incidents in which you were driven out of the movement and subsequently slandered. I will not try to say we will make amends, because that is not possible. I do want to say, personally, that my own complicity in helping perpetuate Healy's abominations was thoroughly discreditable and that I do not wish to claim any credibility except on the basis that I was eventually instrumental in expelling him, and fighting for a reorientation.[22]

The letter moved me deeply. I had always felt a certain closeness, a bond that was never verbalized, with Cliff. I respected his talent, his commitment to the movement, and I secretly sympathized with him as a fellow victim of Healy's temper tantrums. Cliff meant something to me even before I found myself in a factional alliance with the Healy group. He symbolized in my mind that whole group of Communist Party intellectuals who broke from Stalinism over Hungary and chose what I still believe is the higher moral ground of Trotskyism. Cliff had come through again, and wherever he may end up politically, I respect him for that.

Two images of Cliff came to my mind as I read that letter. The first was the all-night session in that cabin in the Canadian mountains when Nancy and I were going through the hell of our demotion and slander at that Central Committee meeting. I believe Cliff was reaching out to us with sympathy while he repeated all the "correct" party phrases to us. Then there was a meeting in Leeds in 1977. It was one of several organized for me by the International Marxist Group (IMG)[23] following the big London meeting. The meeting was held at the Trades Council, a rather pleasant place run by the unions that had a nice pub and many meeting rooms. Cliff turned up with other Healyites. He looked so haggard, like a broken man. His intervention was spiritless. Somehow, even though he was clearly part of this fantastic campaign of lies, it saddened me to see him.

Healy, with his followers reduced to a small band, did not, I am afraid, totally retire from politics.[24] *Nation* columnist Alexander Cockburn spotted him in Moscow, of all places, at the time of the Bolshevik Revolution celebration in 1987:

> Moscow presents ironies at levels both petty and majestic. Strolling through the National Hotel on Red Square, I am astounded to see Vanessa Redgrave loping along beside the squat, toad-like form of Gerry Healy, one of the most rabid Trotskyist sectarians in Britain. I meet a bemused writer the next day who reports that Redgrave has given a speech to his union, concluding with the cry, "All power to the soviets!"[25]

On December 14, 1989, Gerry Healy died of a heart attack at the age of seventy-six. There were many obituaries in the British press, largely written by old enemies settling old scores. Why should my reaction have been any different from theirs? I had become an old enemy and I certainly had old scores to settle. Yet in a curious way I was saddened by his death. When he was alive I had no difficulty hating him, but now that he was dead an ancient feeling, deeply buried in my subconscious, of respect, even affection, arose within me. I suppose I could no longer view life and people in the Manichaean manner in which Healy himself originally trained me to do.

As I thought back over my experiences with Healy, I felt strongly that he deserved some credit as well as blame. Healy made his first impression on me when I was a member of the American SWP in the late 1950s. I followed closely *Peter Fryer's Newsletter* and *Labour Review*, the two journals Healy sponsored. They were written by those intellectuals from the British Communist Party whom Healy had recruited. He encouraged them to produce what became important theoretical contributions to our understanding of Stalinism. These writings made me feel that our ideas could affect others and that the truth could not be denied with impunity forever. Healy had a similar effect on me in the 1960s when I met the cultural figures he began to recruit, witnessed the intellectual level of the classes they participated in, and saw how they were able to utilize their dramatic talents as part of a living movement of young workers. Then Healy introduced me to the Cowley trade unionists, including Alan Thornett, who for a period led those in the working class who were training themselves in Marxism as party members.

Healy could *touch* you. He could make you feel almost *physically* the socialist dream. The only other left-wing politician I met who had that effect was Jim Cannon. Those of us who were Healy's followers for so many years did his bidding not because he terrorized us—certainly not at the beginning—but because he *inspired* us.

Healy's ability to commit great crimes sprang from the strength of his personality. He took advantage of his gift of vision and his ability to affect others to control them for his own petty purposes. The goal of human liberation was forgotten and replaced by the building of a petty political machine serving only its increasingly unstable leader. The blame for this state of affairs goes beyond Healy to the traditions and institutions that permitted it to happen. There have been far too many Healys[26] in the Trotskyist movement, not to mention humanity's bitter experience with Stalinism.

Perhaps I reacted differently to Healy's death because, unlike my friends in England for whom Trotskyism was Healy, I had spent at least as much time in Shachtman's and Cannon's organizations. This broader experience with Trotskyism has left me with a respect for the movement's positive traditions and its many idealistic and self-sacrificing members, a respect that overshadows the horrors of a Healy.

Whither Trotskyism?

What in the Trotskyist political tradition should be abandoned and what is worth preserving? Certainly my own experiences suggest one very fundamental aspect of Trotskyism that should be looked at more closely: its *Leninism*.[27] Trotsky saw himself as a defender of the Leninist tradition against a usurper—Stalin—who had corrupted its practice and betrayed its politics. After joining Lenin in 1917, Trotsky never again explored his earlier criticisms of Bolshevism. His supporters have uncritically followed Trotsky on this question.

This has created within Trotskyism a conflict between its strong commitment to workers' democracy and the authoritarian policies actually practiced by Lenin and Trotsky while in power. Stalin did not invent the one-party state; rather, he institutionalized it and used it to consolidate the bureaucratic state.[28] In the 1930s this was not a major problem for Trotskyism, as the Left as a whole was in the grip of the October Revolution. However, in the 1960s Marxist dissidents from within the Soviet bloc and New Left students began to question the *substitutionist* side of Leninism in power and, therefore, Trotskyism. The notion that a vanguard party could represent the *real* interests of the masses even when these masses had no way to check the conduct of these self-appointed leaders was rejected.

The collapse of the Communist countries, predicted for so long by Trotskyists, has not led to a growth of Leninism in the former Soviet bloc countries primarily for this reason. Ferenc Fehér, a former Hungarian

Marxist dissident and student of George Lukács, sums it up well when he states that "for the average intelligent citizen of Soviet-type societies, the slogan 'return to Leninism' stands for courting [Tiananmen-like] disaster."[29]

The vanguardism of the Leninist tradition has been central to the life of virtually all Trotskyist groups. It has had an extremely contradictory effect on the history of the tendency. It has contributed to the élan and the dedication of members and the effectiveness of Trotskyist groups. Belief in the ultimate importance of the group and its positions has inspired the members, as it once did me, and extracted from them a much higher degree of dedication and energy than is typically found in politics. The Leninist democratic centralist organizational structure permitted even relatively small Trotskyist groups to exert influence within mass organizations far beyond what other organizational structures would provide.

However, it was precisely this belief system and structure that encouraged the factionalism and splits that have plagued the Trotskyist movement since its origin. While petty personal considerations may be involved, all factionalism and every split is justified on the basis that the revolutionary process depends upon the vanguard adhering to correct theory and practice. Some Trotskyist groups have achieved reasonable size and a high degree of internal cohesion, which has permitted them to be effective. However, they have restricted internal democratic practice. In time, the result has been personal cults and political degeneration. Other groups have done a commendable job in promoting an internal democratic life, only to become ineffectual when promoting their policies to the working class.

If one is to remove the Leninist shell that encrusts the political kernel of Trotskyism, what, then, is left? An orthodox Trotskyist could argue that nothing at all would remain. Trotskyism, he or she would maintain, is the defense of Leninism against its betrayal by Stalin. I would agree and take the argument further. What we can call the *personality* of Trotskyist groups is rooted precisely in this Leninist heritage. The vanguard notion justifies the group's existence, its separation from other groups (much like religious doctrine in churches), the sacrifices its members make in the interests of the group, and much of the personal satisfaction that the membership derives from a sense of being an important player in the historical process.

I concede that Trotskyism without Leninism may not be Trotskyism. Let me, therefore, ask my question in a different way: What is there in the Trotskyist political and theoretical tradition that could be of use to a post-Trotskyist socialist movement? We need to return to the original objective of the New Left, which its leaders abandoned in a frenzy of Maoist vanguard sect-building at the end of the sixties. The New Left started out to create a radical democratic socialist movement that would go beyond the Russian experience, beyond Trotskyism, communism, and Leninism. We can strengthen the radical democratic socialist idea both through the consciously rejecting vanguardism and through assimilating the positive content of past revolutionary experience and thought.

I will only sketch here some elements of Trotskyist thought that could be useful in such a movement:

1. *The notion that democracy and socialism are inseparable.* Trotskyism was born in a rebellion against bureaucratic dictatorial rule in the Soviet Union. While, as we have noted, its record is far from perfect, it has championed democracy as essential to socialism in the course of its history and has suffered deeply at the hands of Stalin's agents because of this view. The imprisonment and murder of left oppositionists within the USSR, the systematic murder of Trotsky's family, his supporters in Spain, and finally the Old Man himself has given Trotsky's movement a deservedly heroic cast. Contemporary socialists can best pay tribute to this past through their own democratic practice.

2. *The Marxist analysis of "Marxist" society.* Trotsky brilliantly applied the Marxist method to an understanding of the Soviet Union under Stalin's rule. While his theory of Stalinism is certainly subject to criticism and revision, it remains a powerful analytical tool to help us understand why so many contemporary state socialist societies have collapsed, as well as the crises the post-Stalinist regimes are passing through.

3. *A socialist alternative to the centrally planned command economy.* The free-market model is proving to be a failure, particularly in the nations that once made up the Soviet Union. Socialism can have a new relevancy to the extent that it is able to project a *feasible* alternative to bureaucratic Stalinism and capitalism. Trotsky's ideas (as well as those of Bukharin) on developing a planned economy containing market mechanisms can be useful.

4. *Socialism as a radical alternative to capitalism.* Trotskyism is one expression of the revolutionary socialist tradition, which includes non-Leninists like Rosa Luxemburg and which stands for socialism as an *alternative* to capitalism, not just as an "add on" to capitalism. Much can be learned from its critique of the reformism of social democracy as well as that of the official Communists. At the same time, it is necessary to reject the movement's sectarianism, which again is rooted in its adherence to Leninism.

5. *The transitional method.* Trotsky believed that the workers could not be won over to socialist ideas simply by passing out leaflets or lecturing them. He felt that far more powerful than the best written piece of propaganda is an actual movement of millions of people who collide with

capitalist interests as they assert their own will. In this fashion workers feel their own strength as well as come to understand the need to change the nature of the social system in order to fulfill their needs. Two examples of American Trotskyists effectively applying this method are the Minneapolis Teamsters Union struggles in the 1930s and the anti–Vietnam War movement in the 1960s.

When Perry Anderson wrote his seminal *Considerations on Western Marxism* in 1974, he discerned a shift in the development of Marxist thought from Eastern Europe to Western Europe. However, the minds of these Western Marxists—for example, Lukács, Korsch, Gramsci, Marcuse, Sartre, Althusser, Colletti—continued to be gripped by the Russian Revolution and its aftermath. Anderson even went so far as to speak of the "objective possibility of the reappearance of the political ideas associated with Trotsky in the central arenas of working class debate and activity."[30]

The fall of the Berlin Wall and the creation of democratic regimes throughout Eastern Europe suggest that the time may very well be at hand when Western Marxists will be able to break free of the Leninist grip.[31] At the same time, a Marxism could flourish that is no longer divided into West and East.

Perhaps we are finally entering a postvanguardist era. I make predictions on this score with considerable trepidation. I realize that there is a natural human tendency for a person breaking with a deeply held view of the world to assume that the rest of the world has passed through the same emancipatory experience. Those who have broken from religious cults find it difficult to understand why others remain in them. The Leninists will be the last to realize that Leninism is dead. Groups influenced to one degree or another by Leninism continue to play an influential role in America's small leftist community.

Still, I believe there is a sea change occurring. The Leninists will not disappear, but they may find themselves overwhelmed by a new American Left that *begins* its thinking process with the fall of the Berlin Wall rather than with the storming of the Winter Palace.

By now the reader should have a pretty complete understanding of how I spent my thirty or so years as a political activist on the left. During that time the FBI spied on me using informants, still cameras, motion picture cameras, and other surveillance techniques, assembling over 8,000 pages of documents. They were assisted by the State Department Passport Office, consular offices, the Central

Intelligence Agency, foreign intelligence services, Army Intelligence, the Secret Service, the Customs Service, and the Red Squads of various local police departments. My garbage was pawed through, equipment was stolen from our office, and my wife was bothered with many phone calls using a "suitable pretext."

All this close scrutiny has not produced a shred of evidence that I ever violated any law. I have never been prosecuted for anything. Quite the contrary, when the SWP initiated a suit over the surveillance of its members, including me, the SWP won and the government lost!

For many years American political life has been poisoned by this concept of the existence of "disloyal," "subversive," and "unpatriotic" political views. The revolutionary views discussed above were held by a minute section of the population, yet the Left in its broadest definition (at times encompassing the majority sentiment of the nation) has been affected, and political life in America has been distorted.

It is becoming increasingly difficult to sustain this concept, since the Soviet Union is no longer our enemy. Yet it would be a grave mistake to think that the "red herring" is no longer used. Just remember all the flag waving whipped up by the press and utilized by Bush and the Right during the Gulf War. The clear implication was that those who did not fervently wave the flag were somehow suspect, less patriotic, perhaps tainted with subversive thoughts.

As the recent exposure of FBI COINTELPRO operations against CISPES illustrates, the political police remain in place and at work. But it is my contention that it is not enough to oppose the unlawful activity of government agencies who break into offices. It is important to challenge the basis for all this activity, including what can be called passive surveillance.

I maintain that the very existence of this thirty years of surveillance and a dossier on me is a violation of my First Amendment rights as well as my right to privacy. It is not the proper function of government to keep files on people because of their political views, no matter how unpopular those views may be. The existence of such files inhibits political life.

The citizen has a right to privacy, to not be photographed, to not be followed, to not have his garbage picked through, to not be called up under a "suitable pretext," to not be reported on by unidentified informants. There must be a reasonable limit to an investigation for possible violation of dubious statutes that have not been enforced against anyone for decades. Certainly a thirty-year investigation is not reasonable!

The Soviet Union permitted the people to tear down the Berlin Wall. Does the U.S. government have the capacity to take the far more limited step of giving up its political dossiers?

Notes

1. See chapter 5, "The Cuban Revolution."
2. See his book *"Eurocommunism" and the State* (London: Lawrence and Wishart, 1977).
3. Nin, who had been a supporter of Trotsky, was a leader of the Party of Marxist Unification (POUM), which had serious influence in Catalonia. George Orwell described his experience with this group in his book *Homage to Catalonia.*
4. It is now known as the Unified Socialist Party of Mexico (PSUM).
5. There have been important changes in Mexico since 1980. Most significant was the split of Cardenas from the PRI and the organization of a leftist populist political party, which competed with the PRI in the recent presidential elections. A minority emerged within the PRT, led by Adolfo Gilly, which supported Cadenas. The majority ran its own presidential campaign.
6. *The Case of Leon Trotsky* (New York: Merit Publishers, 1968).
7. Victor Serge, *Memoirs of a Revolutionary* (London: Writers and Readers, 1984).
8. I heard Volkov tell this story in Berkeley in the spring of 1990 while on a tour of the United States drumming up support for the rehabilitation of Trotsky in the Soviet Union. His speech appears in *Gorbachev's USSR: Is Stalinism Dead*? ed. Carl Finamore (San Francisco: Walnut Publishing, 1989). See also Jean Van Heijenoort, *With Trotsky in Exile* (Cambridge: Harvard University Press, 1978), pp. 7, 24, 25, 35–37, 143, 144; Albert Glotzer, *Trotsky; Memoir and Critique* (Buffalo: Prometheus Books, 1989), pp. 35, 36, 49–50, 77–78, 182–83, 293.
9. Adolfo Gilly, *Inside the Cuban Revolution* (New York, 1964).
10. Tim Wohlforth, *Teories Del Socialismo En El Siglo XX* (Mexico City: Ediciones Nueva Sociologia, 1983).
11. Years after I broke with Healy, he changed the name of his paper to *News Line* and moved his printing to the north of England in a move to lower his labor costs.
12. Ibid.
13. *Mirror* (London, October 31, 1985).
14. *Star* (London, November 4, 1985).
15. *Daily Express* (London, November 3, 1985).

16. Mickie Shaw, *Robert Shaw: Fighter for Trotskyism 1917–1980* (New Park, London, 1983).
17. This left-wing break away from the Labour Party was led by Fenner Brockway, a pacifist and a sympathizer of colonial causes.
18. *Telegraph* (London, November 4, 1985).
19. Maureen Bambrick, "Contribution to the Roots of the Party Crisis," *Internal Bulletin* no. 5 (Workers Revolutionary Party, February 6, 1986). Maureen Bambrick headed the Young Socialists during the last years of my association with Healy.
20. Stuart Carter, "What Went Wrong with the WRP" *Internal Bulletin* no. 7 (Workers Revolutionary Party, March 14, 1986).
21. "Michael Banda's '27 Reasons'" *Intercontinental Press* (New York, March 24, 1986), pp. 187–199.
22. Letter dated March 6, 1986, in the author's possession.
23. The British affiliate of Ernest Mandel's united secretariat. Its most prominent member was Tariq Ali.
24. The expulsion of Healy from the WRP led to a breakup of the old organization and the creation of a number of new groups. At the beginning there was a WRP (*Workers Press*), the majority group led by Banda and Slaughter, and a WRP (*News Line*), the minority headed by Healy, Torrance, and the Redgraves. A small group that supported Dave North and the American Workers League soon split away from the WRP. Mike Banda's break soon followed, and then some additional small groups also broke away. In Healy's camp Torrance broke away, taking the *News Line* with her; Healy and the Redgraves renamed their group the Marxist Party.
25. *The Nation* (New York, November 28, 1987), p. 618.
26. Those who come first to my mind are Juan Posados, Nahuel Moreno, and James Robertson. Others who have shared at least some of Healy's characteristics as a personalist leader rather intolerant of minorities and who dominated a small group include Pierre Lambert, Ted Grant, Tony Cliff, Michel Raptis (Pablo), and James P. Cannon.
27. My assessment of Leninism is developed more thoroughly in "The Two Souls of Leninism," *Against the Current* (Detroit, September/October 1986).
28. See my "Leninism's Grip," *Against the Current* (Detroit, January/February 1992) and "Revolutionary as Conservative," *Against the Current* (Detroit, May/June 1992).
29. Ferenc Fehér, "Soviet-Type Societies: The Need for New Theory," *Problems of Communism* (May/June 1990).
30. Perry Anderson, *Considerations of Western Marxism* (London: Verso, 1987), p. 101.
31. See my article "What Role for Socialism in a New Eastern Europe?" *In These Times* (Chicago, February 6–12, 1991).

Addendum

Under Surveillance

A COLLECTION OF DOCUMENTS FROM THE FILES OF THE FBI AND OTHER FEDERAL SECURITY AGENCIES RELEASED UNDER THE FREEDOM OF INFORMATION ACT

The FBI routinely conducted photofisurs in front of the headquarters of political organizations, of demonstrations, and occasionally even of homes. These photos are from 1956. *Above*: I am picketing the Soviet Embassy in New York to protest the suppression of the Hungarian Revolution. *Next page*: I am *A* in the photo, shown leaving the headquarters of the Young Socialist League/Independent Socialist League at 114 West 14th Street, New York City, after a meeting.

JEWELRY
CAMERA

NY 100-4013

The following rolls of film were taken on 5/31/57 and 6/1/57 and the negatives and master prints are located in NY 100-4013-1A2208.

Number	Agents	Location
C1,C2,C3	SAS [redacted] b7C	Position in front of 16th Street entrance to Werderman's Hall
B3, B4, AB 5-2 through 18	SAS [redacted] b7C	Position across from four entrances to Werderman's Hall on 3rd Avenue
AB 5-21 through 32	SAS [redacted] b7C	Position on northeast corner of 3rd Avenue and East 16th Street with view of entrances on both sides of Werderman's Hall

The following rolls of film were taken on 6/1/57 and are located in NY 100-4013-1A2209.

A1, A5, A7, A8, A9, A12 L-1	SAS [redacted] b7C	Position on northeast corner of 3rd Avenue and East 16th Street

- 5 -

The documents on this page and the following page are part of a twenty-seven-page report furnished by the FBI describing their photofisur of the 1957 SWP Convention. Eighteen of these twenty-seven pages were withheld in their entirety while agents' ("SAS") names, as well as names of those identified at the convention, were blacked out. The report described an elaborate process whereby the photos were passed from field office to field office in an attempt to identify all those who attended the event. A separate document revealed that, as a backup, a motion picture was also shot.

NY 100-4013

The following rolls of film were taken on 6/1/57 and are located in NY 100-4013-1A-2012.

Number	Agents	Location
D1, D3 through D8	SAS [redacted] b7C	Position directly opposite 16th Street entrance to Werderman's Hall

The following rolls of film were taken on 6/2/57 and are located in NY 100-4013-1A2010.

A6, A10, A11, A13 through A16; L-2	SAS [redacted] b7C	Position on northeast corner of 3rd Avenue and East 16th Street
D-2	SAS [redacted] b7C	Position directly opposite East 16th Street entrance to Werderman's Hall

In the identifications made at the NYO it is noted in several instances that the same individual may appear in a great many different photographs. When this occurs, the NYO in the interest of economy will prepare extra prints for dissemination only of the better photographs.

There follows a listing of photographs taken during the SWP National Convention 5/31-6/2/57, which contain what appear to be recognizable photographs of individuals in attendance.

- 6 -

NY 100-131940

The announcement added that a panel of members of the National Committee of the AFSE would be on hand to answer audience questions. The panel was to include among others, the following:

ALBERT BLUMBERG
BERT COCHRAN
DAVID DELLINGER
FARRELL DOBBS
CLIFFORD T. MC AVOY
JOHN T. MC MANUS
JOSEPH STAROBIN
GEORGE STRYKER
DOXEY A. WILKERSON b7c

SA [redacted] attended the above described meeting. The information set forth in this letter is the result of the personal observations of the SA. He estimated about 500 people attended this meeting.

Contributions of $1 were solicited at the door for admis[redacted]en by [redacted] also took a turn at collecting the admission contributions. b7c

A. J. MUSTE called the meeting to order at about 8:30 p.m. He was the first speaker and continued as Moderator through the meeting. MUSTE stated that the purpose of the AFSE meeting was to have Socialists of various tendencies get together for an exchange of views in a free and untrammeled discussion. It was his hope that Socialists could get together on specific issues, such as Civil Rights, Negro Rights, Abolition of Nuclear Weapons and the like.

MUSTE said that opposition to the AFSE comes from two-quarters: from Senator EASTLAND and J. EDGAR HOOVER. MUSTE stated that he has refused and would

- 5 -

The documents on this and the following two pages are excerpted from a thirteen-page report on a meeting called by the American Forum for Socialist Education, which was held on the evening of June 12, 1957, at Community Church in New York City. Note the FBI agent's interest in the remarks directed by Reverend A. J. Muste to J. Edgar Hoover. The AFSE played a role in encouraging discussion of the Hungarian Revolution within Communist Party circles. Hoover viewed the AFSE as the Communist Party's effort to create a new front organization. References in my files to "Attempts of the CP, USA to form a broad socialist organization" reflect this viewpoint.

NY 100-131940

continue to refuse the information demanded by the Eastland Committee. He told the audience that the American Civil Liberties Union had informed him that they would be happy to give him any aid needed as the result of his stand taken before the Eastland Committee.

MUSTE asked any employees of the FBI present to take the message contained in his next remarks to Mr. HOOVER: He charged that Mr. HOOVER was prostituting his office when on one hand he claimed that the files of the FBI were super secret, while on the other hand on his own initiative, HOOVER made public statements smearing certain people, including MUSTE and ELEANOR ROOSEVELT, as allegedly Communists because they signed the "Amnesty Appeal." MUSTE charged again that Mr. HOOVER was prostituting his office when he alleged that MUSTE and other impartial observers at the CP National Convention of February, 1957, were Communists or Communist sympathizers.

b7c

[redacted]

Dr. STRINGFELLOW BARR was the second speaker. MUSTE said that he would discuss "discussions." BARR said he was attracted to the AFSE because he was concerned about curtailment of the freedom to discuss. He charged that people were afraid to discuss issues because of possible repercussions or being labeled subversive.

DOROTHY DAY was the third speaker. She pointed out that the "Catholic Worker" was not an official publication of the Catholic Church. She said they were members of the Catholic Press Association which meant that the "Catholic Worker" had not been disapproved of by the Catholic Church. She gave a brief history of the "Catholic Worker" movement. Miss DAY said that she, as a Catholic, was working for

- 6 -

NY 100-131940

When DOBBS concluded, BLUMBERG requested permission to make some comment on the same question. He agreed with DOBBS that there were many very basic differences between the CP and other Socialist groups generally and with the SWP in particular. However, BLUMBERG felt that these differences should be discussed in an effort to get together. He promised the greatest possible Communist cooperation with the AFSE.

TIM WOHLFORTH was asked to comment on his impressions concerning the role of youth in the AFSE, particularly in view of the fact that he had just completed a tour of the US during which he conferred with various youth groups. WOHLFORTH stated that the youth throughout the nation is being attracted to the radical movement and he feels that the AFSE will aid considerably in the eventual unification of the youth in the radical movement.

MILTON ZASLOW was asked to comment on a question concerning civil rights in the Soviet Union. ZASLOW stated that no one on the platform was an apologist for the dictatorship in the Soviet Union. He said there was much to be done in the field of civil rights both in the US and in Russia. According to him, one of the purposes of the AFSE was to discuss these questions.

MUSTE, throughout the program, while introducing the speakers, made several comments of his own. He stated that the AFSE was operating on the principal of "non exclusion." That is, any Socialist tendency was welcome to cooperate with and join with the National Committee of the AFSE. There was one exception, however. In order to avoid the charge of Communist domination and to encourage the die-hard foes of Communism to participate in the AFSE, it was decided to limit the number of Communist members of the National Committee of the AFSE to two.

- 30 -

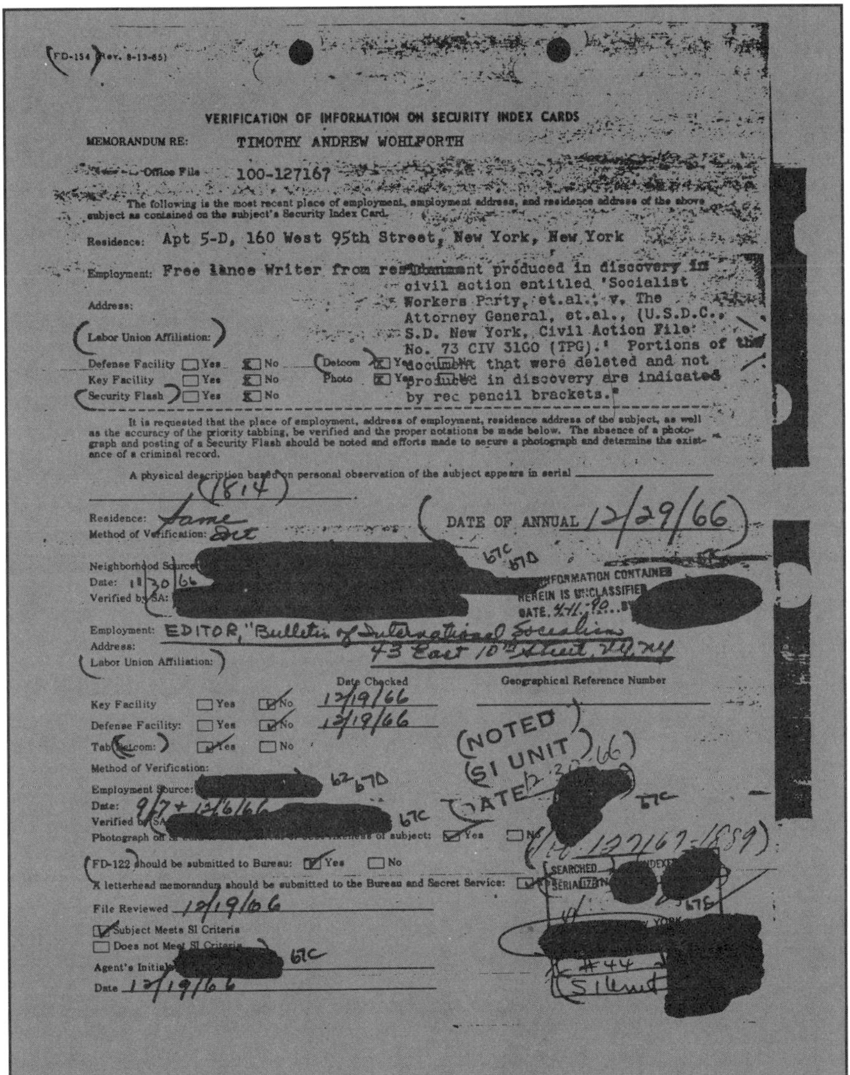

FD-154 (Rev. 8-13-65)

VERIFICATION OF INFORMATION ON SECURITY INDEX CARDS

MEMORANDUM RE: TIMOTHY ANDREW WOHLFORTH

Office File 100-127167

The following is the most recent place of employment, employment address, and residence address of the above subject as contained on the subject's Security Index Card.

Residence: Apt 5-D, 160 West 95th Street, New York, New York

Employment: Free lance Writer from reproduction of document produced in discovery in civil action entitled 'Socialist Workers Party, et.al., v. The Attorney General, et.al., (U.S.D.C., S.D. New York, Civil Action File No. 73 CIV 3160 (TPG).' Portions of the document that were deleted and not produced in discovery are indicated by red pencil brackets."

Address:

Labor Union Affiliation:

Defense Facility ☐ Yes ☒ No — Detcom ☒ Yes ☐ No

Key Facility ☐ Yes ☒ No — Photo ☒ Yes ☐ No

Security Flash ☐ Yes ☒ No

It is requested that the place of employment, residence address of employment, residence address of the subject, as well as the accuracy of the priority tabbing, be verified and the proper notations be made below. The absence of a photograph and posting of a Security Flash should be noted and efforts made to secure a photograph and determine the existance of a criminal record.

A physical description based on personal observation of the subject appears in serial (1814)

Residence: Same

DATE OF ANNUAL 12/29/66

Method of Verification: Pret

Neighborhood Source: [redacted] b7C b7D

Date: 11/30/66

Verified by SA: [redacted]

INFORMATION CONTAINED HEREIN IS UNCLASSIFIED DATE 4/11/90 BY [redacted]

Employment: EDITOR, "Bulletin of International Socialism"

Address: 43 East 10th Street, NY, NY

Labor Union Affiliation:

			Date Checked	Geographical Reference Number
Key Facility	☐ Yes	☒ No	12/19/66	
Defense Facility:	☐ Yes	☒ No	12/19/66	
Tab Detcom:	☒ Yes	☐ No		

(NOTED SI UNIT DATE 12-20-66)

Method of Verification:

Employment Source: [redacted] b2 b7D

Date: 9/7 + 12/6/66

Verified by SA: [redacted] b7C

Photograph of subject: ☒ Yes ☐ No

(100-127167-1859)

FD-122 should be submitted to Bureau: ☒ Yes ☐ No

A letterhead memorandum should be submitted to the Bureau and Secret Service: ☐

SEARCHED INDEXED SERIALIZED FILED [redacted] b7C

File Reviewed 12/19/66

☒ Subject Meets SI Criteria

☐ Does not Meet SI Criteria

Agent's Initials [redacted] b7C

Date 12/19/66

#44 SI Unit

A typical Security Index form from the many in my files. This one was an annual review, even though place of employment and residence were checked every ninety days. Note that my file is marked DETCOM (Detain Communist). In case of a national emergency I was to be picked up and placed in detention. This particular document was released to the SWP in response to its suit against the FBI.

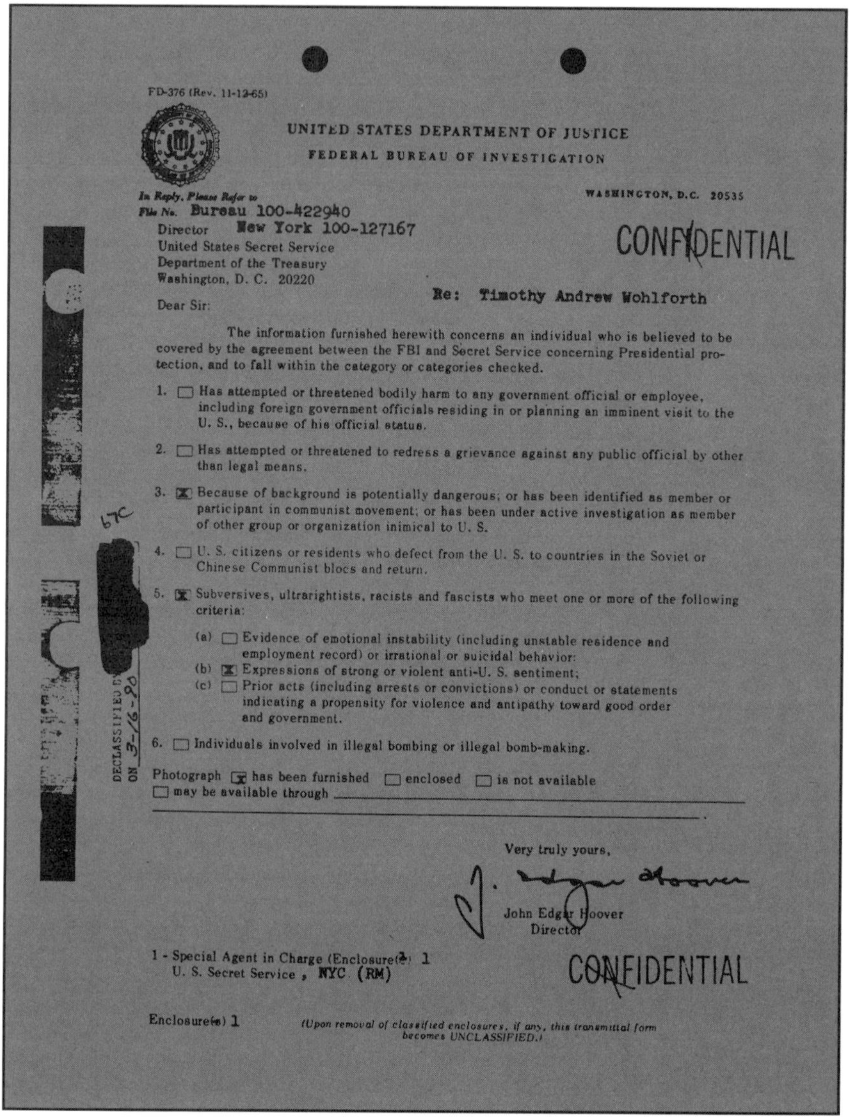

FD-376 (Rev. 11-13-65)

UNITED STATES DEPARTMENT OF JUSTICE
FEDERAL BUREAU OF INVESTIGATION

In Reply, Please Refer to
File No. Bureau 100-422940
New York 100-127167

WASHINGTON, D.C. 20535

CONFIDENTIAL

Director
United States Secret Service
Department of the Treasury
Washington, D. C. 20220

Re: Timothy Andrew Wohlforth

Dear Sir:

The information furnished herewith concerns an individual who is believed to be covered by the agreement between the FBI and Secret Service concerning Presidential protection, and to fall within the category or categories checked.

1. ☐ Has attempted or threatened bodily harm to any government official or employee, including foreign government officials residing in or planning an imminent visit to the U. S., because of his official status.

2. ☐ Has attempted or threatened to redress a grievance against any public official by other than legal means.

3. ☒ Because of background is potentially dangerous; or has been identified as member or participant in communist movement; or has been under active investigation as member of other group or organization inimical to U. S.

4. ☐ U. S. citizens or residents who defect from the U. S. to countries in the Soviet or Chinese Communist blocs and return.

5. ☒ Subversives, ultrarightists, racists and fascists who meet one or more of the following criteria:

(a) ☐ Evidence of emotional instability (including unstable residence and employment record) or irrational or suicidal behavior;
(b) ☒ Expressions of strong or violent anti-U. S. sentiment;
(c) ☐ Prior acts (including arrests or convictions) or conduct or statements indicating a propensity for violence and antipathy toward good order and government.

6. ☐ Individuals involved in illegal bombing or illegal bomb-making.

Photograph ☒ has been furnished ☐ enclosed ☐ is not available
☐ may be available through

b7C [redacted]

DECLASSIFIED BY [redacted] ON 3-16-90

Very truly yours,

J. Edgar Hoover

John Edgar Hoover
Director

1 - Special Agent in Charge (Enclosure(s)) 1
U. S. Secret Service, NYC (RM)

CONFIDENTIAL

Enclosure(s) 1

(Upon removal of classified enclosures, if any, this transmittal form becomes UNCLASSIFIED.)

As part of the Security Index process, the Secret Service was alerted that I might represent some sort of threat to the life of the President.

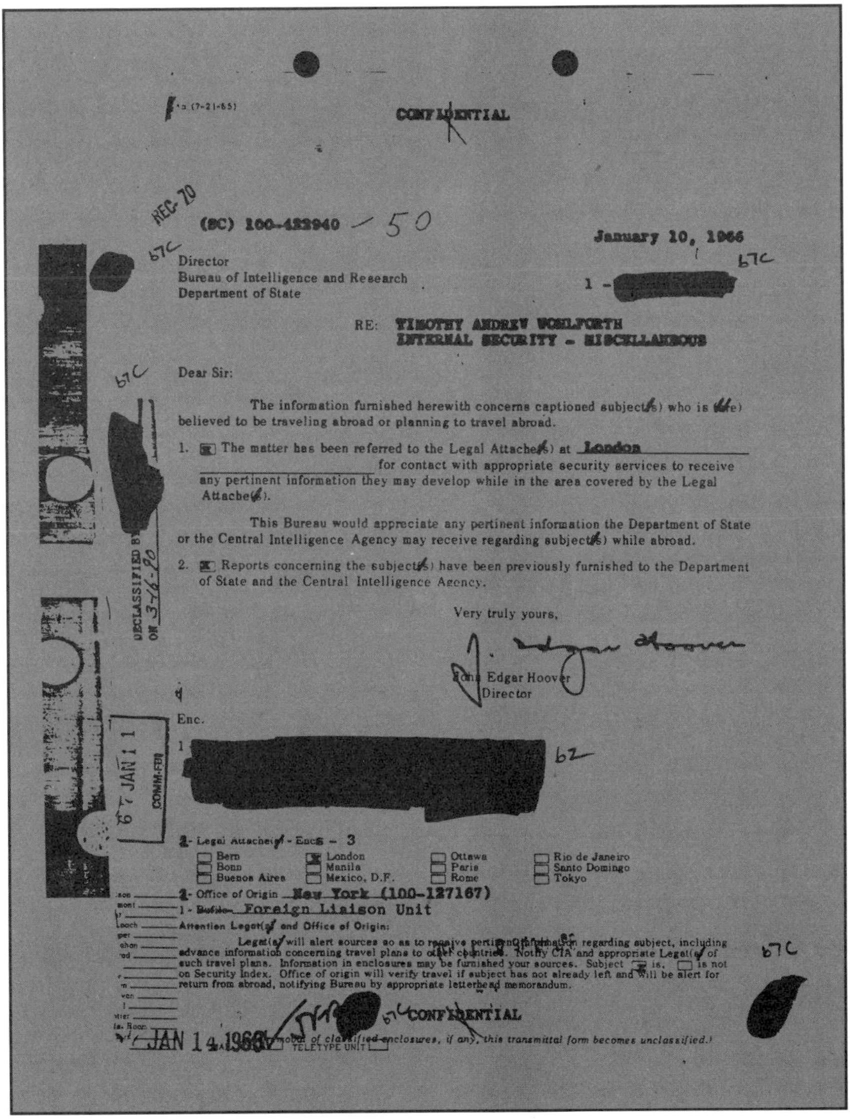

FD-(7-21-65)

CONFIDENTIAL

REC-70

(SC) 100-422940 — 50

January 10, 1966

Director
Bureau of Intelligence and Research
Department of State

1 - [redacted]

RE: TIMOTHY ANDREW WOHLFORTH
INTERNAL SECURITY - MISCELLANEOUS

Dear Sir:

The information furnished herewith concerns captioned subject(s) who is (are) believed to be traveling abroad or planning to travel abroad.

1. [X] The matter has been referred to the Legal Attache(s) at London for contact with appropriate security services to receive any pertinent information they may develop while in the area covered by the Legal Attache(s).

This Bureau would appreciate any pertinent information the Department of State or the Central Intelligence Agency may receive regarding subject(s) while abroad.

2. [X] Reports concerning the subject(s) have been previously furnished to the Department of State and the Central Intelligence Agency.

Very truly yours,

John Edgar Hoover
Director

Enc.

DECLASSIFIED BY ... ON 3-16-90

1 [redacted]

67 JAN 11 COMM-FBI

2 - Legal Attache(s) - Encs - 3

[ ] Bern	[X] London	[ ] Ottawa	[ ] Rio de Janeiro
[ ] Bonn	[ ] Manila	[ ] Paris	[ ] Santo Domingo
[ ] Buenos Aires	[ ] Mexico, D.F.	[ ] Rome	[ ] Tokyo

2 - Office of Origin New York (100-127167)
1 - Foreign Liaison Unit
Attention Legat(s) and Office of Origin:

Legat(s) will alert sources so as to receive pertinent information regarding subject, including advance information concerning travel plans to other countries. Notify CIA and appropriate Legat(s) of such travel plans. Information in enclosures may be furnished your sources. Subject [X] is, [ ] is not on Security Index. Office of origin will verify travel if subject has not already left and will be alert for return from abroad, notifying Bureau by appropriate letterhead memorandum.

CONFIDENTIAL

JAN 14 1966 TELETYPE UNIT

(Upon removal of classified enclosures, if any, this transmittal form becomes unclassified.)

The documents on this page and the following three pages reveal the complex web of security agency collaboration between the United States and Great Britain that was set up to monitor my political conduct abroad. This document exposes the cooperation between the FBI, the State Department's Bureau of Intelligence and Research, the Legal Attaché assigned to the London Embassy, and the CIA.

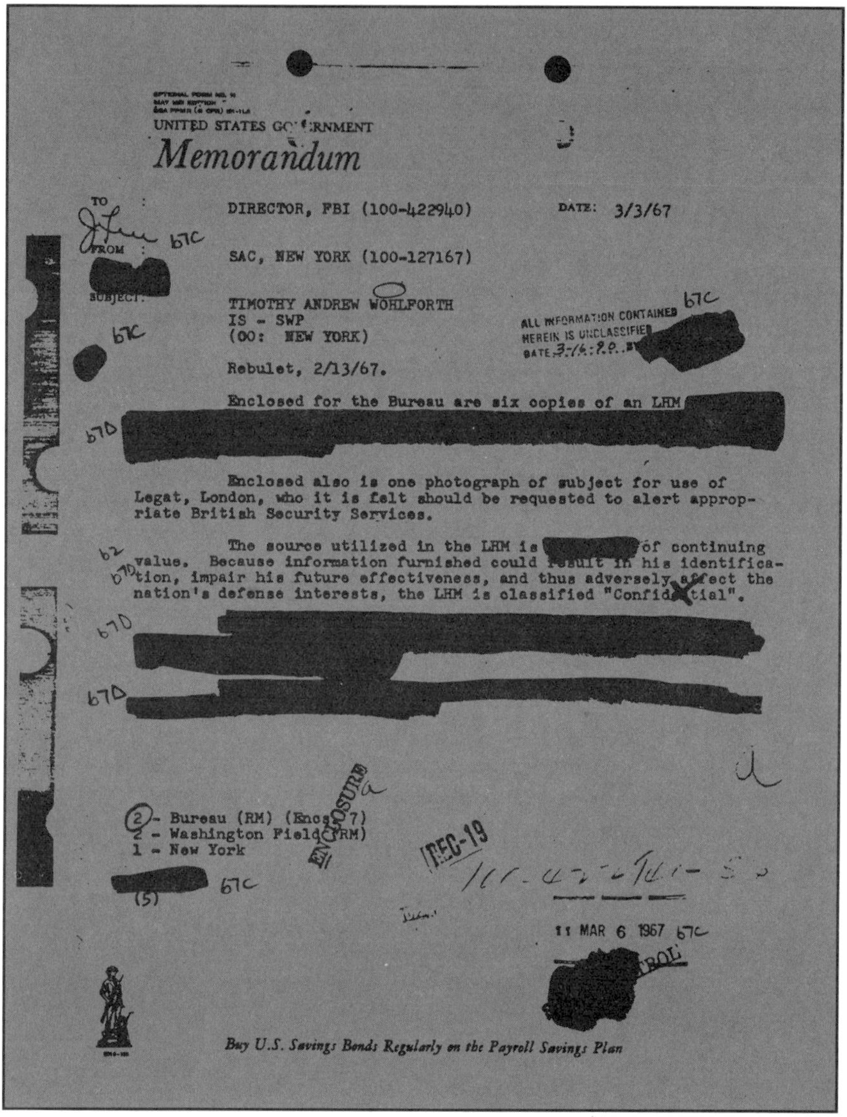

UNITED STATES GOVERNMENT

Memorandum

TO : DIRECTOR, FBI (100-422940) DATE: 3/3/67

FROM : SAC, NEW YORK (100-127167)

SUBJECT: TIMOTHY ANDREW WOHLFORTH
IS - SWP
(OO: NEW YORK)

ALL INFORMATION CONTAINED HEREIN IS UNCLASSIFIED DATE 3-14-80 BY [redacted]

Rebulet, 2/13/67.

Enclosed for the Bureau are six copies of an LHM [redacted]

Enclosed also is one photograph of subject for use of Legat, London, who it is felt should be requested to alert appropriate British Security Services.

The source utilized in the LHM is [redacted] of continuing value. Because information furnished could [redacted] his identification, impair his future effectiveness, and thus adversely affect the nation's defense interests, the LHM is classified "Confidential".

[redacted]

2 - Bureau (RM) (Encs. 7)
2 - Washington Field (RM)
1 - New York

[redacted]
(5)

ENCLOSURE

REC-19

MAR 6 1967

Buy U.S. Savings Bonds Regularly on the Payroll Savings Plan

In this document the FBI requests that the British Intelligence Services be contacted.

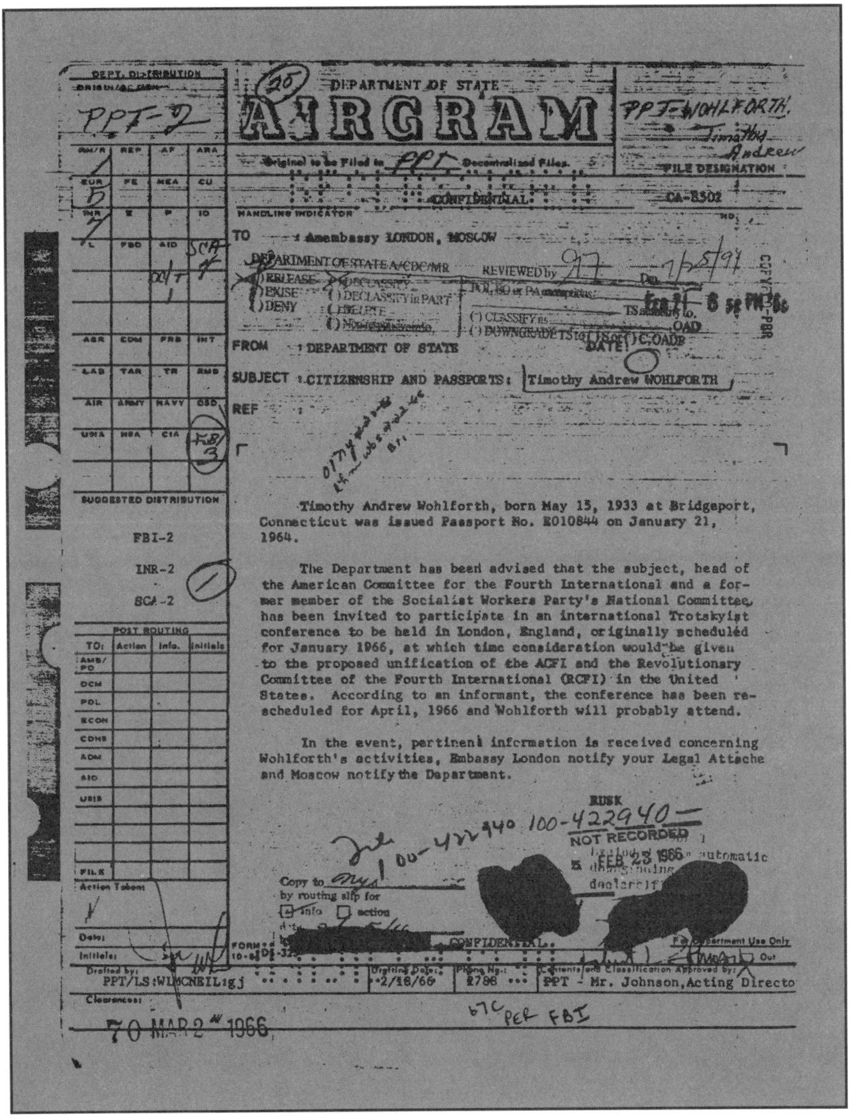

DEPARTMENT OF STATE

AIRGRAM

PPT-WOHLFORTH, Timothy Andrew

FILE DESIGNATION

CONFIDENTIAL

CA-8502

TO : Amembassy LONDON, MOSCOW

FROM : DEPARTMENT OF STATE

SUBJECT : CITIZENSHIP AND PASSPORTS: Timothy Andrew WOHLFORTH

REF :

SUGGESTED DISTRIBUTION

FBI-2

INR-2

SCA-2

Timothy Andrew Wohlforth, born May 15, 1933 at Bridgeport, Connecticut was issued Passport No. E010844 on January 21, 1964.

The Department has been advised that the subject, head of the American Committee for the Fourth International and a former member of the Socialist Workers Party's National Committee, has been invited to participate in an international Trotskyist conference to be held in London, England, originally scheduled for January 1966, at which time consideration would be given to the proposed unification of the ACFI and the Revolutionary Committee of the Fourth International (RCFI) in the United States. According to an informant, the conference has been rescheduled for April, 1966 and Wohlforth will probably attend.

In the event, pertinent information is received concerning Wohlforth's activities, Embassy London notify your Legal Attache and Moscow notify the Department.

RUSK

100-422940

NOT RECORDED

FEB 23 1966

[redacted]

CONFIDENTIAL

Drafted by: PPT/LS:WLMCNEIL:gj

Drafting Date: 2/16/66

Phone No.: 2788

Contents and Classification Approved by: PPT - Mr. Johnson, Acting Directo

b7C PER FBI

70 MAR 2 1966

This AIRGRAM was sent by the Passport Office to the London and Moscow embassies to inform them of my possible trip to attend an international Trotskyist meeting. Note "per FBI" at bottom, which reveals the source of information in the letter. The Passport Office maintains extensive files on United States citizens. An improper search of passport files—conducted during the 1992 presidential campaign in the hopes of finding damaging information on then Governor Clinton and his mother—became the subject of an investigation by an independent counsel.

Index